When I saw the first draft lay-out, I asked the designer what kind of logic she used to place the images in that particular order.
"None" she said "It was purely emotional."
"Then it's okay" I said.

Nedko Solakov
Emotions

Kunstmuseum Bonn
Kunstmuseum St.Gallen
Mathildenhöhe Darmstadt

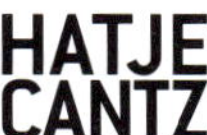

Acknowledgments / Dank

To Vessi, Dimmi, Slava, and my parents with gratitude and love

Thank you to all the people who made the exhibition **Emotions** possible:

Harry Arabian
Matthias Arndt
Aneta Atanasova
Veronika Azarova
Ralf Beil
Stephan Berg
Konrad Bitterli
Mario Cristiani
Georgi Dimitrov
Tinko Dimov
Charles Esche
Lorenzo Fiaschi
Valentin Georgiev
Nikolina Georgieva
Georgi Gospodinov
Svetla Gradanska
Veselin Ignev
Ivan Iliychev
Peter Kogler
Borislav Konstantinov
Silvia Krusteva
Christy Lange
Filip Luyckx
Yana Mechkarova
Daniella Minini
Massimo Minini
Dimitar Mitovski
Slava Nakovska
Nikolai Nikolov
Vessela Nozharova
Georgi Pashov
Johnny Penkov
Evgenia Petkova
Verusca Piazzesi
Kristin Rieber
Enea Righi
Maurizio Rigillo
Dragomir Sarachev
Liubomir Savov
Kalin Serapionov
Dimitar Solakov
Vesselina Solakova
Georgi Sotirov
Miroslav Sotirov
Kalina Stanoeva
Dimitar Stefanov
Violeta Tanova
Angel Tsvetanov
Tsvetomir Tsvetanov
Aleksey Turlakov
Vladimir Valchev
Iliya Vassov

Contents / Inhalt

Foreword

Nedko Solakov's work is far-reaching, continually escalating, and formally difficult to contain. Its contents comprise one big attack on the demand for perfection, finality, and clarity. Born in 1957, the Bulgarian artist began as a student of mural painting at the art academy in Sofia, but has spent the last twenty-five years developing an oeuvre as humorous as it is playful, as trenchant as it is melancholy—a body of work that fundamentally questions the validity of every sort of representational system there is. Ever since his participation in the 2007 Venice Biennale and Documenta 12, Solakov has assumed a central position in contemporary European art.

Hardly any other work expresses the artist's basic skepticism toward our desire for clarity and lucidity more than **A Life (Black & White)** (1998–present) does. In it, a painter paints an exhibition space white, while a second painter paints the white paint black, which in turn is painted white by the first artist, and so forth, without this absurd "round dance" ever reaching an and.

Looking at the many forms his work takes, it can be seen that Solakov aims to create an encyclopedia of the absurd, the remote: a history of deviations, differences, embarrassments, and aborted utopias. The collapse of the Communist system in the late nineteen-eighties significantly influenced his work and, at the same time, it spurred him on to search for a new language of his own (**Encyclopaedia Utopia,** 1989–90) that would adequately capture the complexity and fragility of reality.

His drawings, texts, videos, photographs, performances, installations, sculptures, and murals question what are apparently collective truths and the conditions of the art system and the art market (**Leftovers,** 2005); they use his own publicly exposed fears to reflect upon failure as a metaphor for human existence (**Fear,** 2002–03) and discover paradox as a dominant structure in the political ways of the world (**Discussion [Property]**, 2007). Solakov has the ability to take all of these different themes and put them into narratives that maintain an exact balance between a poetic, rhapsodic joy in narrative and constant, ironic breaks; and it is this ability that makes his body of work not only wholly inimitable, but also highly entertaining and humorous.

The Kunstmuseum in Bonn, the Kunstmuseum in St. Gallen, and the Mathildenhöhe in Darmstadt are now producing the first large retrospective in Germany and Switzerland of Solakov's important oeuvre. The show includes pieces from the late nineteen-eighties to 2007, as well as **Some Nice Things to Enjoy While You Are Not Making a Living** (2007–08), a new, multipart installation that the artist has created specifically for our exhibition.

We would first like to thank Nedko Solakov himself: from the start, he has worked on this project with a great deal of commitment and extreme precision. Acknowledgments also go to the Arndt & Partner gallery—especially to Matthias Arndt and Kristin Rieber for their support in obtaining catalogue materials and loans; to Annett Frey for the felicitous catalogue design; and to Georgi Gospodinov for his illuminating literary essay on the artist's work. We would also like to thank our colleagues at our various institutions for the perfect realization of the show's concept.

Stephan Berg, Kunstmuseum Bonn
Roland Wäspe, Kunstmuseum St.Gallen
Ralf Beil, Mathildenhöhe Darmstadt

Vorwort

Nedko Solakovs weitgespanntes, ausuferndes und formal kaum zu bändigendes Werk ist inhaltlich ein einziger großer Angriff auf das Verlangen nach Perfektion, Endgültigkeit und Eindeutigkeit. Ausgehend von einem Studium der Wandmalerei an der Kunstakademie in Sofia hat der 1957 geborene Bulgare in den letzten fünfundzwanzig Jahren ein ebenso humorvolles wie verspieltes, ein ebenso bissiges wie melancholisches Œuvre entwickelt, das die Gültigkeit jedweden Repräsentationssystems grundsätzlich infrage stellt. Spätestens seit der Teilnahme an der Biennale di Venezia (2007) und der documenta 12 (2007) nimmt Solakov innerhalb der aktuellen europäischen Kunst eine zentrale Position ein.

In kaum einer Arbeit kommt dabei die grundlegende Skepsis des Künstlers gegenüber unserer Sehnsucht nach Klarheit und Übersichtlichkeit so deutlich zum Ausdruck wie in **A Life (Black & White)** (seit 1998), bei dem ein Maler einen Ausstellungsraum weiß streicht, während ein zweiter Maler den weißen Anstrich schwarz übermalt, der wiederum vom ersten weiß überstrichen wird, ohne dass dieser absurde Reigen je ein Ende findet.

Solakovs Anspruch zielt, quer durch die vielfältigen Ausformungen seines Werks, auf eine Enzyklopädie des Absurden, Abseitigen, auf eine Geschichte der Abweichungen, Differenzen, Peinlichkeiten und gescheiterten Utopien. Dabei erweist sich der Zusammenbruch des kommunistischen Systems Ende der 1980er-Jahre als prägende Erfahrung und gleichzeitig als Auftakt für die Suche nach einer neuen, eigenen Sprache (**Encyclopaedia Utopia**, 1989/90), mit der die Komplexität und Fragilität der Wirklichkeit adäquat eingefangen werden kann.

Seine Zeichnungen, Texte, Videos, Fotografien, Performances, Installationen, Skulpturen und Wandarbeiten hinterfragen scheinbare kollektive Wahrheiten, die Bedingungen des Kunstsystems und Kunstmarktes (**Leftovers**, 2005), reflektieren anhand öffentlich gemachter eigener Ängste das Scheitern als Metapher menschlicher Existenz (**Fear**, 2002/03) und entdecken in den politischen Weltläufen die Paradoxie als herrschende Struktur (**Discussion [Property]**, 2007). Solakovs Fähigkeit, all diese unterschiedlichen Themenfelder in Form von Geschichten zu erzählen, die eine präzise Balance zwischen poetisch-rhapsodischer Lust an der Narration und kontinuierlichen ironischen Brüchen halten, macht dieses Werk nicht nur vollkommen unverwechselbar, sondern auch in hohem Maße unterhaltsam und humorvoll.

Das Kunstmuseum Bonn, das Kunstmuseum St. Gallen und die Mathildenhöhe Darmstadt widmen diesem wichtigen Werk nun die erste große institutionelle Überblicksausstellung in

Deutschland und der Schweiz. Die Schau umfasst künstlerische Beispiele vom Ende der 1980er-Jahre bis 2007 sowie mit **Some Nice Things to Enjoy While You Are Not Making a Living** (2007/08) eine neue, vielteilige Rauminstallation, die der Künstler eigens für unsere Ausstellungen hergestellt hat.

Unser erster Dank gilt Nedko Solakov selbst, der dieses Projekt von Anfang an mit großem Einsatz und hoher Präzision begleitet hat. Ein weiteres Dankeschön geht an die Galerie Arndt & Partner, namentlich an Matthias Arndt und Kristin Rieber, für die vielseitige Unterstützung bei der Beschaffung des Katalogmaterials und der Leihgaben, an Annett Frey für die gelungene Gestaltung des Katalogs, und an Georgi Gospodinov für seinen erhellenden literarischen Essay zum Werk des Künstlers. Bei den Mitarbeitern unserer Häuser bedanken wir uns für die perfekte Umsetzung des Ausstellungskonzeptes.

Stephan Berg, Kunstmuseum Bonn
Roland Wäspe, Kunstmuseum St.Gallen
Ralf Beil, Mathildenhöhe Darmstadt

Stories from the Periphery against the Phantasm of the Absolute

Stephan Berg

Anyone who wants to understand Nedko Solakov's artistic work has to go to Sofia, the home of this Bulgarian artist. There one will not only experience a city whose communist past collides wildly with the spirit of capitalist enterprise. In Sofia, one can experience a life characterized by a fundamental paradox: that each and every thing has its exact opposite. One gains insight into a social and urban context whose economic dynamo is powered by ambivalence and pervasive instability. Questioning what is true and what is false, what is façade and what is reality, is not here a matter of philosophical contemplation. Rather, it is simply and plainly an ordinary, everyday, practical experience of life. Managing this experience is absolutely necessary for survival. Solakov's art is based in these types of experiences, which are closely connected to the ordeal of witnessing the demise of the Communist system and the resulting distortions.

In a sense, this touches upon Ilya Kabakov's strategies; to this day, Kabakov continues to examine the collapse of the Soviet Union, looking for material for his melancholy installations. In this context, too, we recall how the young Christo came up with the basic idea for his world-famous wrappings during a train trip through Bulgaria, when he realized that the threshers and agricultural buildings carefully lined up along the railway tracks were nothing but plywood façades—Potemkin villages designed to simulate a glorious workers' and farmers' state. Christo's wrapping of buildings and interventions in rural areas made it possible to re-experience reality and, at the same time, to illustrate the glittering intangibility of reality by taking what was actually visible and removing it from the line of sight. However, compared to Christo, who clings to his trademark, and to Kabakov, who is focused on the Soviet context, Solakov's work is much broader in terms of the themes and the variety of media he employs. Though his work is grounded in his own history, he is constantly aiming for the universal, for nothing less than a history of the human condition, including its predictable, certain failure.

To do this, the artist, who originally studied mural painting at the art academy in Sofia, uses all of the different variety of media available. From drawing to painting, video, sculpture, object assemblage, performance, and large installations, he creates a universe of narrative that is full of fairy-tale-like, surreal allusions and, at its core, tries to avoid constructing any sort of definitude. One of the works that aptly illustrates Solakov's philosophical, artistic credo is his now-famous installation/performance, A Life (Black & White) (1998–present), which was first performed in 2000. In this work, over the course of each exhibition, one painter paints the entire exhibition space white, while another paints it black. Indeed, there is hardly a simpler or more forceful way to show how absurd it is to try and divide our reality into black and white. Yet, at the same time, this long performance, which Rosa Martinez aptly described as "Malevich in motion," is also a grand, ironic about-face, a turn away from the absolutism and assumed autonomy of the early twentieth-century avant garde and the rigorous discourse of Minimal Art.[1] To oppose their claims to objectivity and the complete purification of the work of art, Solakov sets up a Sisyphean ritual, where the act of constantly orbiting around oneself permanently refutes the possibility of absolute purity.

Serialism, one of the most important characteristics of Minimal Art, is turned into a type of motion here, citing the return of something that is always the same, while simultaneously continuing it ad absurdum: the constant attempt to create a purely black or a purely white room produces an endless series of minimally different white-black moments, an alphabet of differentiations whose only constant is its deviation from the norm. Last, but not least, the space created in A Life (Black & White) also represents a reference to the two dominant modes used almost exclusively to present art since the beginning of the twentieth century: the white cube and (ever since the rise of video art in the nineteen-sixties) the black box. In particular, the white cube—as well as its hidden ideological claim that it is able to separate art entirely from the world and turn it into a pure manifestation of itself—has repeatedly been the starting point for Solakov's interventions. A (not so) White Cube (2001–present) is the most succinct expression of this attempt. Under this title is gathered a series of tiny, handwritten notes, pictograms, and inscriptions, all affixed somehow to the walls of very different exhibition spaces. These items have become characteristic of the artist's approach. Solakov's work is always based on a calculated paradox, according to which the nothing that is first seen is transformed, on closer inspection, into a dendritic cosmos of stories, notes, and digressions. We enter what seems to be a completely empty, white exhibition space and are about to leave, disappointed, when we discover a small note on the wall, written in pencil. As a rule, this note turns out to be an ironic, poetic description referring directly to the place where it is located. Solakov is stimulated by all of the little "disturbances" in and on the apparently virgin white walls: the hollows and recesses in the walls, the spots that have been repaired, the drilled holes left over from earlier exhibitions, et cetera. Here, as in many of his other works, Solakov wants the material world to speak for itself. For instance, a brief dialogue is written across the floor painted in slightly different tones of gray: *"'You are a very depressing color!' this very light grey said to the dark grey. 'No, I'm just mature,' answered the dark grey."*

Right away, this first finding leads to further sightings of phrases, comments, and little drawings. Thus begins an intensely exciting, enjoyable journey of discovery, during the course of which the visitor turns into a hunter of secreted written treasures. The effect of this inconspicuous intervention is inversely proportional to its almost invisible pragmatism. The longer we move around in these "not very white" spaces, the more they are transformed into places full of whispered murmurs and private emotions, where the blatantly unquestioning nature of the white cube crumbles to pieces. In ways that are as charming as they are sly, Solakov strips away the cool aura of white absolutism with his marginal, passing remarks. The apparently humble attitude of the white cube is revealed for what it is: a gesture of control. With his tiny inscriptions, the artist not only sullies the emotional impact of the pure and the absolute, which is inherent in the structure of the white cube, but he also appropriates these spaces with his marks, turning them into places that are affected by his personal commentary. Apropos, his work On the Wing (1999–present) functions in a similar way—that is, as an act of gentle annexation, as a kind of "territorialization" of the context described. Motivated by his fear of flying, Solakov affixed quirky stories about big and little clouds or mysterious silver coins on the wings of six Luxembourgian airplanes as his contribution to a group show at the Casino Luxembourg. Both A (not so) White Cube and On the Wing demonstrate the author's conviction that art does not live in abstract generalities, but in specific subjectivity.

Solakov expands on his primary, essential objection to Minimal Art's credo of objectivity and self-referentiality by emphatically acknowledging the narrative dimension of the work of art. An almost erotic desire for narrative permeates the Bulgarian artist's entire oeuvre, from Encyclopaedia Utopia (1989–90), The Story of Saint Pipo (1998), the installation Good News, Bad News (1998–present), or the wonderful, black-and-white pen-and-ink drawings from the series Well-Known Stories (1992–95), Once upon a Time (1995–96), and Fears (2006–07), to the Romantic Landscapes with Missing Parts (2002) and his much-discussed work for the Venice Biennale, Discussion (Property) (2007). Solakov is a storyteller par excellence, with an apparently inexhaustible storehouse of minor and major subjects, all of them worth the telling. However, his rhapsodies no longer try to provide a complete, grand saga of the world—as has been the usual aim since time immemorial. Instead, his oeuvre is an incomplete, fragmentary network of idiosyncratic comments and putative anecdotes, even though the work is neither the type of textual strategy employed in Conceptual Art, nor is it a kind of concrete poetry.

Basically, Solakov takes the fundamental, conceptualist conviction—according to which the idea (usually summed up in text) is actually the work of art—and uses it to create absurd, personal stories. These narratives are constantly getting out of control and are therefore always taking digs at Conceptual Art, while in the meantime, they gain an uncanny, intractable life of their own.[2] Yet another element of this context is the fact that Solakov's stories of the material world always assume intrinsic or human characteristics, and are therefore in accordance with mythical ideas. The authorial, narrative self that is expressed here employs familiar narrative patterns, not only from fairy tales and sagas, but also from news reports, verbal jokes, or journal entries. At the same time, this narrative self is also undermined, since it is identified as a formal pattern which can no longer be satisfactorily padded with content. Behind his humorous irony and his often fabulous tone, there is hidden an occasionally bitter acerbity marked by a profound pessimism and the loss of any sort of narrative definitude. Marginal observations, ironic foils, paradoxical straits, finely woven psychological phenomena, and aporetic conclusions create a convolute of deviations, byways, and wrong tracks, where each and every desire for a meaningful context breaks down completely. Every piece of track Solakov lays either obliterates itself or leads to yet another byway. The network of smattering narratives, which proliferates in his work like a rhizome, does not produce a pattern that can be clearly interpreted. There is no consistent text. Instead, there is a deliberate, polyphonic babel of voices surrounding a core consisting of the marginal and the contradictory.

Good News, Bad News is an example of the type of contradiction inherent in the system the artist has developed for his work—a contradiction which, for the most part, references the banal and the incidental. Various toys (such as a plastic crocodile and a pig), an artificial flower, and a glass of water are placed directly on the ground and lit by spotlights. Also on the ground, next to these items, are comments about the objects written in felt pen. For instance, the comment on the artificial flower says: *"The bad news: he was dead. The good news: the flower on his grave will last forever."* Shining a spotlight on the cheap plastic flower emphasizes its pathos and produces the exact, aesthetic, dramatic downfall of the heroic that Solakov aims to achieve in all of his works. His blatantly obvious emphasis on the marginal always serves a double purpose: for one, it makes it possible to see what has been concealed—the invisible part of the structure, so to speak. At the same time, the staging of the piece demonstrates the inadequacy of this visibility. This double encoding—which simultaneously ennobles what is seen and yet makes it appear even more ridiculous—is also pursued by the text, which systematically and perfidiously compares the finitude of human existence to the infinite lifetime of the artificial flower. A double irony arises out of this paradox: first, the fact that a cheap plastic product far outlasts the complex human beings to whom it owes its very existence; and second, this simple product serves as a decoration for a grave, as well as a memorial gesture. Here, as in many of the Bulgarian artist's other works, the ridiculous is always simply the hidden reverse of the tragic.

In his works, Solakov always attempts to comprehend reality by questioning both it and himself. El Bulgaro: The Sensational Discovery (2000) is one of his crucial works concerning the impossibility of ever gaining reliable knowledge about the consistency of reality and the individual. In this work, we are confronted with the imaginary alter ego of El Greco, which was provoked by the pressure put on El Greco to always produce his long, mannerist figures. As El Bulgaro, this figure is like someone sleepwalking by moonlight; he begins to produce an alternative, lunatic kind of painting. In this major work, Solakov deals with the theme of "the self as another" on several levels at once. First, El Bulgaro is, of course, an allusion to Solakov, the Bulgarian, and hence also describes an oeuvre that is so multifaceted and encompasses so many different types of media and content that the viewer occasionally has the impression that he is looking at the work of several artists, or at least, the work of an artist with several different selves—a fact that the artist takes into account in his other works, such as This is me, too.... (1996). Moreover, El Bulgaro can also be seen as a play on the name El Greco, which is, in turn, also a pseudonym, as we know. Primarily, however—and here is where the work takes on a political meaning outside of the individual dimension—El Bulgaro is also an ironic, but nonetheless keen reflection upon the invisibility of Bulgarian art and culture in the Western world. Even Solakov's work at the 1999 Venice Biennale was simply a postcard featuring the Bulgarian flag and some text that announced Bulgaria's pleasure at being able to officially participate in the next Biennale in 2001, after a thirty-year absence.[3] As is the case with almost all of his works, the artist here uses the paradox as an argument, pairing a sense of humor and tractability with biting acuity and accusation. In this game, Bulgaria becomes a metaphor for all of the West's hegemonic, marginalizing attempts to exclude from the discourse all cultures and countries that do not think the way it does about the Western system. Solakov recommends a counter-strategy: basically, subversion, whose efficiency is derived from its disguise as a humble, harmless, little joke. "It was just a joke," many of the artist's works seem to say, and this type of camouflage permits the work to do an even more durable job of undermining and infiltrating.

In the context of this strategy, Top Secret (1989–90) can be considered a masterpiece, and it occupies a central position in Solakov's oeuvre. It reflects not only upon the schizophrenic element of the structure of the artistic self, but also on the impossibility of objective truth. Simultaneously, it is also a politically charged confrontation with Bulgaria's Communist era. Top Secret consists of a filing cabinet full of filing cards which are supposed to prove that the young artist collaborated with the Bulgarian secret police. Exhibited for the first time in early 1990—just at the apex of political change in Eastern Europe—the work created a great deal of controversy. This work, which drew a great deal of attention at the last Documenta in 2007, is extreme in the degree to which the artist exposes and criticizes himself while, at the same time, revealing nothing real. It is not possible for the viewer to find out if the files really contain documents that would prove Solakov had had any connections to the Bulgarian secret police or if he had ever actually worked for them. The artist's text accompanying the documents reads: *"The Action is on (for the time being)."* Owing to the text's air of mystery, it is impossible for the reader to decide if the statement is fact or fiction. In this bewildering game, the best trick is that the only authority that could actually verify the truth—the Bulgarian secret police—cannot do so without exposing itself. Thus the title of the work is also an ironic description of the hermetic structure of the secret police: even the most open of confessions remains, at the same time, "top secret." This highly personal information has been a dicey topic for the artist for years because it has led to a certain amount of condemnation—but, at the same time, it might also possibly be part of a conceptual set-up.

Solakov's strategy was clearly exposed in Top Secret. This strategy—of relating general philosophical and political questions and problems to his own life, and thus of charging abstract themes with subjectivity—can be seen in a number of his other works. His approach of personalizing the works becomes most obvious in the pieces that deal with the artist's fears. A group of small clay sculptures and boarding pass stubs comprise Fears, a work that can, in a certain way, be understood as an act of self-therapy, a way for Solakov to battle his real fear of flying. Each of the sculptures is a direct expression of the tension Solakov felt as he kneaded the clay in his hands during the flight. In other words: the "in-formation" in the sculptures expresses both his fear as well as the instrument used to fight it and is, therefore, an expression of the artist's aplomb. Ultimately, this work is always a presentation of the artist's own weakness, as well as an exorcism of it. Solakov also works with fears in the captivating, precisely ninety-nine page series of drawings, Fears. However, in this case, he does it in a more metaphorical form, containing a number of fairy-tale-like characteristics.

The title of this exhibition, Emotions, reflects the program behind Solakov's work. He makes it very clear that these strategies of subjectifying and emotionalizing are highly effective when it comes to the task of dislodging the fantasies of absolutism and objectivity in both art and reality. As has already been explained, he is not simply employing self-expression as a naïve gesture of authenticity. Rather, Solakov uses references to himself to thwart his own plausibility. After the emotional build-up that dominates this cosmos—with all of its touching, handwritten notes on walls and images, its marginalia, its sometimes embarrassing, personal confessions, and its legends and digressions—there is always an equally great slump, a moment of unavailability. Solakov has mastered the art of including himself in each of his works so perfectly that he himself has become an artificial figure that is both present and absent in everything that he does, says, and writes. The personal, often intimate dimension of Solakov's works creates a sense of emotional chafing, which gives the viewer the feeling that he is somehow very close to the artist—that he somehow knows him—but that he is unable to track him down completely. **I Love Them** (2007), Solakov's first large video installation, plays with just this ambivalence. A total of seven prcjections are shown on different-size surfaces, monitors, and flat screens. These projections translate Solakov's seven favorite films into a beguilingly beautiful selection of monochromatic colors and various commentaries. The work is a synesthetic approach to translating into corresponding colors what one feels while watching such different films as **City Lights, The Big Lebowski,** or **The Seven Samurai.** At the same time, it is in two respects also a clever play on proximity and distance, visibility and invisibility. Just as Solakov seems to appear on the screens in completely unprotected, emotional proximity and, at the same time, is entirely absent, the films he refers to are equally present and yet invisible in actuality. In this way, **I Love Them** demonstrates the power of imagination that is so significant for his entire oeuvre. Even the withdrawal of the visible creates the ability to project, and this, in turn, allows the possible to arise from out of the actual.

As in other places in the work, the appellative dimension is also important here. None of Solakov's work—calm, immersed in meditation—is intended to exist for its own sake alone. Rather, a need for contact, as well as for a dialectic, occasionally interactive structure is literally inscribed in them. This is also clear in the large, multi-part installation, **Some Nice Things to Enjoy While You Are Not Making a Living** (2007–08), which was created for this touring exhibition. Almost half of the works collected here attempt to elicit a direct reaction from the viewer. A fluffy shag rug, about 7 x 7 meters, invites visitors (without their shoes) to touch or stroke it. Piles of cardboard boxes next to the rug can be torn up by visitors, so that they can work off some aggression. In a completely soundproofed booth, anybody can yell as loud as he wants to, while visitors can also write down all of their brief observations, desires, and frustrations on a large roll of paper. However, anybody who believes this is an interactive game is mistaken. Instead, it is part of Solakov's large-scale, universal contemplation of the strange contradiction inherent in the human condition: the eternal paradox people find themselves in when they are caught on the treadmill of daily routine and work, and thus increasingly neglect their own fundamental needs; here, they have a chance to have an emotional catharsis. Of course, at the same time, Solakov is aware of the limits of playing with this emotional course. Still, he uses it as the foundation for his strategy. Seen in this way, the installation tools that he spreads out before us only offer a sort of model of the elementary, emotional unconditionality, which, in reality, either does not occur anymore, or else is always failing.

In this respect, all of Solakov's works are fundamentally lessons about a "paradise lost." The viewer can rest on a large leather sofa and, from a certain position, he becomes aware of three miniature landscapes set in the backrest of the sofa, including a lovingly carved wooden forest and a three-dimensional model "printed" from a computer drawing. The accuracy of the models triggers a desire to dive straight into them, which in turn makes us aware of how impossible it is to fulfill this type of wish. This is the dialectic of Solakov's work: using the mode of actual impossibility, he gives us the pleasure of experiencing the possibility of fulfillment, so to speak. This is also true of the way he deals with the beautiful: one of a pair of paintings shows a dawn, the other depicts a sunset—two of the greatest visual metaphors for desire and, at the same time, two of the most clichéd motifs in our cultural iconography. Solakov solves the problem that each and every depiction of a sunrise is simply a cliché that has been reproduced to death by adding comments to the painting in which he discusses the bad parts of the painting, or the ones that did not turn out well. These paintings demonstrate how one can only succeed in citing the beautiful when one points out the failure of beauty and retains at least the memory of its original dimension.

The artist performs a particularly clever trick involving representation and presentation in a work consisting of a monitor that shows Solakov pricking with a needle into a Lucio Fontana pen-and-ink drawing from 1949, destroying the actual work, but supposedly raising its price. This is an ironic reference to the master of the *concetto spaziale,* which resembles, in a way, what Robert Rauschenberg did long ago with his Erased De Kooning Drawing (1953). Solakov's iconoclastic act is part of a series of works critical of the art market—a series he has been working on since the early nineteen-nineties. These pieces question the strategies used by the art market with regard to the way it evaluates and selects art. The works that must be mentioned here are The Collector of Art (1992–2000) and Mr. Curator, please... (1995). A high point for this group of works was the exhibition at the Kunsthaus Zürich, Leftovers (2005), which featured a selection of the existing works that Solakov's galleries had not been able to sell. As is so often the case with Solakov's work, the marginal became the actual experience, and through the act of being exhibited—through presentation—the purportedly worthless became potentially valuable. At the same time, this gave a touch of irony not only to the importance of the works themselves, but also to the notion that the system of appraisal is objective.

Everything in this work is moving both up and down at the same time: the animated video in The Bankrupt Businessman (2008), which is also part of the large installation Some Nice Things to Enjoy..., consists of a loop featuring a figure wearing a suit and falling through a reddish, abstract, colored space. The falling figure never hits the ground, but instead, time after time, more astonished and surprised than afraid, he goes into a tailspin in his reddish state of limbo. This image is an apt illustration for the Bulgarian artist's entire oeuvre: knowing that, ultimately, not everything will turn out well, and that none of his fairy tales try to achieve a "happy ending," the sad, normative reality does not shatter on the ground, but instead maintains the balance of a sleepwalker—more astonished and surprised than afraid, and full of insatiable curiosity about the wonderful stories life has in store.

1 Rosa Martinez, "Time Lost and Space Retrieved (Or Vice Versa)," in Nedko Solakov: Paisajes románticos con elementos ausentes, exh. cat., Museo Nacional Centro de Arte Reina Sofía (Madrid, 2003), pp. 44–46, here p. 44.

2 For more on this, see Kim Levin, "Marginalia," in Nedko Solakov: Stories 1, exh. cat., Center for Contemporary Art, Ujazdowski Castle (Warsaw, 2000), pp. 2–3, here p. 3.

3 The exact text on this postcard with the Bulgarian national colors, which was printed in an edition of 15,000, reads: *"Very Important Announcement: 'After nearly 30 years of absence from the officially participating countries at the Venice Biennale, The Republic of Bulgaria is proud to announce that it is prepared to properly participate in the next Venice Biennale in the year 2001.'"*

Randgeschichten gegen das Phantasma des Absoluten

Stephan Berg

Wer Nedko Solakovs künstlerisches Werk verstehen will, muss nach Sofia, in die Heimatstadt des bulgarischen Künstlers reisen. Dort ist nicht nur eine Stadt zu erleben, in der die kommunistische Vergangenheit ungebremst auf kapitalistisches Unternehmertum prallt. In Sofia begegnet man insgesamt einer Lebensrealität, die von der grundlegenden Paradoxie geprägt ist, dass es zu allem und jedem immer auch das genaue Gegenteil gibt. Es ist der Blick in einen gesellschaftlichen und urbanen Kontext, der seine wirtschaftliche Dynamik aus seiner Ambivalenz, aber auch aus seiner tiefgreifenden Instabilität bezieht. Die Frage, was wahr und was falsch, was Fassade und was Realität ist, gibt hier keinen Anlass zu philosophischer Reflexion, sondern ist schlicht und einfach tägliche, alltägliche lebenspraktische Erfahrung. Und die Bewältigung dieser Erfahrung ist pure Überlebensnotwendigkeit. Eben in solchen Erfahrungen, die zutiefst mit dem Erlebnis eines sich auflösenden kommunistischen Systems und den daraus resultierenden Verwerfungen verbunden sind, findet Nedko Solakovs künstlerische Arbeit ihr Fundament.

In bestimmter Hinsicht berührt sie sich hier mit den Strategien Ilja Kabakovs, der aus dem Zusammenbruch des Sowjetimperiums bis heute den Stoff für seine melancholischen Installationen schöpft. Ebenso kann in diesem Zusammenhang an den jungen Christo erinnert werden, der die Grundidee für seine weltberühmten Verhüllungen während seiner Zugfahrten durch Bulgarien hatte, als er erkennen musste, dass die akkurat an der Bahnlinie aufgereihten Mähdrescher und Landwirtschaftsbetriebe nichts anderes als Sperrholzfassaden waren, Potemkinsche Dörfer also, um einen glorreichen Arbeiter- und Bauernstaat vorzutäuschen. So werden das Verpacken von Gebäuden und die Eingriffe in landschaftliche Situationen zur Methode, Realität neu erlebbar zu machen und gleichzeitig die schillernde Ungreifbarkeit der Wirklichkeit zu verdeutlichen, indem das eigentlich Sichtbare der Sichtbarkeit entzogen wird. Allerdings arbeitet Solakov im Verhältnis zum auf sein Markenzeichen festgelegten Christo und dem auf den sowjetischen Kontext fokussierten Kabakov sowohl thematisch als auch im Hinblick auf seine medialen Ausdrucksformen sehr viel breiter. Sein aus der eigenen Geschichte gespeister Anspruch ist stets universal und zielt auf nichts weniger als eine Geschichte der Conditio humana, unter den Bedingungen ihres von vornherein feststehenden Scheiterns.

Dabei nutzt der an der Kunstakademie in Sofia ursprünglich in Wandmalerei ausgebildete Künstler die volle Breite aller zur Verfügung stehenden medialen Ausdrucksformen. Von der Zeichnung über Malerei und Video bis hin zu Skulptur, Objektassemblagen, Performances und groß angelegten, installativen Rauminszenierungen entsteht ein erzählerisches Universum, das voller märchenhaft surrealer Anspielungen steckt und in seinem Zentrum auf die strukturelle Vermeidung jedweder Eindeutigkeit zielt. Eine der Arbeiten, die das philosophisch-künstlerische Credo Solakovs treffend illustriert, ist die mittlerweile berühmt gewordene installative Performance **A Life (Black & White)** (seit 1998). Jeweils für die volle Dauer einer Ausstellung wird für diese Arbeit ein Ausstellungsraum von zwei Anstreichern gleichzeitig komplett weiß beziehungsweise schwarz gestrichen. Viel einfacher und gleichzeitig eindringlicher lässt sich in der Tat kaum zeigen, wie absurd der Versuch einer Einteilung unserer Wirklichkeit in Schwarz und Weiß ist. Aber zugleich ist diese Dauerperformance, die Rosa Martinez treffend als »Malewitsch in Bewegung« bezeichnet hat, auch eine große ironische Volte gegen den Absolutheits- und Autonomieanspruch der frühen Avantgarden des 20. Jahrhunderts und den rigorosen Diskurs der Minimal Art.[1] Gegen deren Anspruch auf Objektivierbarkeit und vollständige Purifizierung des Kunstwerks stellt Solakov ein sisyphoshaftes Wiederholungsritual, das im Akt der ewigen Selbstumkreisung die Möglichkeit von absoluter Reinheit permanent selbst widerlegt.

Serialität, eines der wichtigsten Markenzeichen des Minimalismus, wird hier zu einer Bewegung, welche die Wiederkehr des Immergleichen zitiert und zugleich ad absurdum führt: Der dauernde Versuch, einen rein schwarzen beziehungsweise rein weißen Raum herzustellen, produziert eine endlose Serie sich minimal unterscheidender weiß-schwarzer momentaner Zustände, ein Alphabet der Differenzierungen, welches als einzige Konstanz die Abweichung von der Norm kennt. Und nicht zuletzt ist der Raum, den **A Life (Black & White)** herstellt, auch als Referenz an die zwei beherrschenden Präsentationsmodi zu verstehen, in denen die Kunst seit dem Beginn des 20. Jahrhunderts fast ausschließlich gezeigt wird: der White Cube und – seit Aufkommen der Videokunst in den 1960er-Jahren – die Black Box. Gerade der White Cube und der in ihm verborgene ideologischer Anspruch, die Kunst vollkommen von der Welt zu separieren und zu ihrer reinen, ureigenen Erscheinungsform zu verhelfen, ist verschiedentlich zum Ausgangspunkt für Nekdo Solakovs Interventionen geworden. Am prägnantesten geschieht dies in **A (not so) White Cube** (seit 2001). Unter diesem Titel lässt sich eine in verschiedensten Ausstellungsräumen realisierte Folge von winzigen auf die Wände aufgebrachten handschriftlichen Notaten, Piktogrammen und Einschreibungen zusammenfassen, die zu einem Markenzeichen für das Vorgehen des Künstlers geworden sind. Stets basiert diese Arbeit auf dem kalkulierten Paradox, wonach das Nichts, das es auf den ersten Blick zu sehen gibt, sich bei näherer Betrachtung in einen weit verästelten Kosmos voller Geschichten, Anmerkungen und Abschweifungen verwandelt. Wir betreten einen augenscheinlich komplett leeren, weißen Ausstellungsraum und wollen uns schon enttäuscht abwenden, als wir an der Wand einen kleinen, mit Bleistift geschriebenen Kommentar entdecken. In der Regel handelt es sich dabei um eine ironisch-poetische Beschreibung, die sich direkt auf die Stelle bezieht, an der sie sich befindet. Dabei reizen Solakov vor allem all die kleinen »Störungen« an und auf den vermeintlich jungfräulichen weißen Wänden: die Mulden und Vertiefungen in den Wänden, die ausgebesserten Stellen, die von früheren Ausstellungen zurückgebliebenen Bohrlöcher et cetera. Wie in vielen seiner Arbeiten, lässt Solakov auch hier gerne die Dingwelt selbst zu Wort kommen. Über eine leicht unterschiedlich grau gestrichene Bodenstelle heißt es beispielsweise: *»›You are a very depressing color!‹ This very light grey said to the dark grey. ›No, I'm just mature‹, answered the dark grey.«*

Diese erste Entdeckung führt unmittelbar zu weiteren Funden von Sätzen, Kommentaren und kleinen Zeichnungen. So beginnt eine hochgradig spannende und vergnügliche Entdeckungsreise, in deren Verlauf der Besucher zu einem Jäger verborgener schriftlicher Schätze wird. Die Wirkung dieser so unscheinbaren Intervention ist umgekehrt proportional zu ihrer knapp an der Unsichtbarkeit angesiedelten Pragmatik. Je länger wir uns in diesen »nicht so weißen Räumen« bewegen, umso mehr verwandeln sie sich in von wisperndem Raunen und persönlichen Gefühlen erfüllte Orte, in denen sich die radikale Bedingungslosigkeit des White Cube vollständig auflöst. Auf ebenso charmante wie hinterlistige Weise demontiert Solakov die kalte Aura der weißen Absolutheit durch den Einsatz von marginalen Randbemerkungen. Dabei entpuppt sich die scheinbare Demutshaltung als eigentliche Herrschaftsgeste. Mit seinen winzigen Einschreibungen verunreinigt der Künstler nicht nur das Pathos des Reinen und Absoluten, das strukturell im White Cube steckt, er eignet sich vielmehr diese Räume durch seine Markierungen an und macht sie zu Orten, die von seinen persönlichen Kommentaren bestimmt sind. In ähnlichem Sinn, nämlich als Akt einer sanften Einverleibung, sozusagen als »Territorialisierung« des beschriebenen Kontextes funktioniert übrigens auch die Arbeit **On the Wing** (seit 1999). Damals brachte Solakov – motiviert durch seine eigenen Flugangst – als Beitrag für eine Gruppenausstellung im Casino Luxembourg skurrile Textgeschichten über große und kleine Wolken oder geheimnisvolle Silbermünzen auf den Tragflächen von sechs luxemburgischen Flugzeugen an. **A (not so) White Cube** wie auch **On the Wing** zeigen so auch die Überzeugung seines Autors, nach der Kunst eben nicht von abstrakter Allgemeinheit lebt, sondern von spezifischer Subjektivität.

Diesen ersten wesentlichen Einspruch gegen das auf Objektivität und Selbstbezüglichkeit setzende Credo der Minimal Art erweitert Solakov durch sein emphatisches Bekenntnis zur narrativen Dimension des Kunstwerks. Von **Encyclopaedia Utopia** (1989/90) über **The Story of Saint Pipo** (1998), der Bodeninstallation **Good News, Bad News** (seit 1998) und den wunderbaren schwarz-weißen Tuschezeichnungen der Serien **Well-Known Stories** (1992–1995), **Once upon a Time** (1995/96) oder **Fears** (2006/07) bis hin zu **Romantic Landscapes with Missing Parts** (2002) und seiner breit diskutierten Arbeit für die Biennale di Venezia **Discussion (Property)** (2007) durchzieht ein geradezu erotisches Begehren nach Erzählung das gesamte Werk des bulgarischen Künstlers. Nedko Solakov ist ein Geschichtenerzähler par excellence, mit einem scheinbar unerschöpflichen Fundus an mitteilenswerten Neben- und Hauptsächlichkeiten. Aber sein Rhapsodentum zielt – anders als vor grauer Vorzeit – eben nicht mehr auf die vollständige große Welterzählung, sondern auf ein lückenhaftes, fragmentarisches Geflecht aus ideosynkratischen Anmerkungen und vermeintlichen Nebensächlichkeiten, ohne sich dabei in die Textstrategien der Konzeptkunst oder der konkreten Poesie einzuordnen.

Im Grunde nimmt Solakov die grundlegende konzeptualistische Überzeugung, wonach die (meist als Text gefasste) Idee im eigentlichen Sinne das Kunstwerk ist, als Grundlage, um daraus skurril-persönliche Geschichten zu machen, die – als weitere Spitze gegen die Konzeptkunst – ständig außer Kontrolle geraten und ein bisweilen unheimliches, nicht mehr steuerbares Eigenleben gewinnen.[2] Auch die Tatsache, dass in Solakovs Geschichten die Dingwelt immer wieder wesenhafte beziehungsweise menschliche Züge annimmt und damit mythischen Denkmustern folgt, gehört in diesen Zusammenhang. Das auktoriale Erzähler-Ich, das sich hier zu Wort meldet, bedient sich vertrauter Erzählmuster von Märchen und Sage über den Bericht bis hin zum erzählten Witz oder dem Tagebucheintrag und höhlt sie gleichzeitig aus, indem es sie als formale Muster kennzeichnet, die inhaltlich nicht mehr befriedigend gefüllt werden können. Hinter seiner humorvollen Ironie und seinem oft märchenhaften Ton verbirgt sich nicht nur eine mitunter bittere, von tiefem Pessimismus geprägte Schärfe, sondern auch der Verlust jeglicher narrativer Eindeutigkeit. Aus marginalen Beobachtungen, ironischen Konterkarierungen, paradoxalen Engführungen, feingesponnenen Psychologismen und aporetischen Schlussfolgerungen entsteht ein Dickicht aus Abweichungen, Neben- und Holzwegen, an dem jede Sehnsucht nach finalem Sinnzusammenhang vollständig zerbricht. Jede Fährte, die Solakov legt, dient dazu, diese selbst zu verwischen oder führt auf eine weitere Nebenfährte. Das Geflecht an narrativen Einsprengseln, das sein Werk rhizomartig durchwuchert, ergibt kein eindeutig lesbares Muster, keinen konsistenten Text, sondern ein bewusst polyphones Stimmengewirr, in dessen Zentrum das Marginale und das Widersprüchliche stehen.

Als Beispiel für die diesem Werk systemimmanente Widersprüchlichkeit, die sich zumeist auf das Banale und Nebensächliche bezieht, darf **Good News, Bad News** dienen. Die Arbeit besteht aus verschiedenem Kinderspielzeug wie einem Plastikkrokodil und einem Schwein, einer künstlichen Blume, einem Glas Wasser, die direkt auf den Boden platziert und mit Spotscheinwerfern angestrahlt werden. Neben den Objekten befinden sich, ebenfalls auf dem Boden, mit Filzstift geschriebene Texte, welche die Objekte kommentieren. Zu der künstlichen Blume heißt es dort beispielsweise: »*The bad news: he was dead. The good news: the flower on his grave will last forever.*« Die pathetische Hervorhebung der billigen Plastikblume durch den Scheinwerferspot produziert genau die ästhetische Fallhöhe, die Nedko Solakov für seine gesamte Arbeit anstrebt. Die überdeutliche Betonung des Marginalen dient dabei immer einem doppelten Zweck: Sie macht das Verborgene, sozusagen das strukturell Unsichtbare sichtbar und zeigt gleichzeitig die Unangemessenheit dieser Sichtbarkeit durch die Inszenierung. Dieser Doppelkodierung, in der das Vorgeführte zugleich nobilitiert und ein Stück weit lächerlich gemacht wird, folgt auch der Text, der ebenso systematisch wie perfide die Endlichkeit der menschlichen Existenz gegen die unendliche Lebensdauer der Kunststoffblume ausspielt. Es ist eine doppelte Ironie, die aus dieser Paradoxie entsteht: nicht nur, dass ein billiges Kunststoffprodukt den komplexen Menschen, dem es seine Herstellung doch erst verdankte, bei Weitem überlebt. Nein, dieses simple Produkt dient auch noch als Grabschmuck und Erinnerungsgeste. Das Lächerliche ist hier, wie in vielen anderen Arbeiten des bulgarischen Künstlers, immer nur die verborgene Kehrseite des Tragischen.

Immer versucht Sclakov in seinen Arbeiten die Realität zu ergründen, indem er sie und damit gleich sich selbst mit infrage stellt. Eine der zentralen Arbeiten über die Unmöglichkeit, stabile Erkenntnisse über die Konsistenz der Wirklichkeit und des Individuums zu gewinnen, ist **El Bulgaro. The Sensational Discovery** (2000). Diese Arbeit konfrontiert uns mit dem erfundenen Alter Ego von El Greco, der, ausgelöst durch den Druck, ständig seine manieristisch in die Länge gezogenen Figuren erschaffen zu müssen, nachts bei Mondlicht schlafwandlerisch als El Bulgaro eine alternative lunatische Malproduktion beginnt. Gleich auf mehreren Ebenen verhandelt Solakov in dieser zentralen Arbeit die Thematik des »Ich ist ein Anderer«. Zum einen ist El Bulgaro natürlich als Anspielung auf Solakov, den Bulgaren, zu verstehen und damit als Selbstbeschreibung eines Werkes, das so breit gefächert, medial und inhaltlich unterschiedlich angelegt ist, dass der Betrachter bisweilen den Eindruck gewinnen kann, er hätte es mit mehreren Künstlern, mindestens aber mit einem multiplen Künstler-Ich zu tun. Ein Umstand, dem der Künstler unter anderem mit der Arbeit **This is me, too....** (1996) Rechnung getragen hat. Zudem ist El Bulgaro natürlich als Spiel mit dem Namen El Grecos zu lesen, der bekanntlich selbst ein Pseudonym darstellt. Vor allem aber, und damit gewinnt die Arbeit über die individuelle Dimension hinaus auch eine politische Bedeutung, ist **El Bulgaro** eine ironische, deshalb aber nicht minder scharfe Reflexion über die Unsichtbarkeit der bulgarischen Kunst und Kultur in der westlichen Welt. Schon auf der Biennale di Venezia 1999 bestand Solakovs Beitrag allein aus einer Postkarte, welche die bulgarische Flagge zeigte, und einem Text. Dieser kündigte an, dass sich Bulgarien darauf freue, sich nach dreißigjähriger Abwesenheit von der Biennale di Venezia bei der nächsten Biennale im Jahre 2001 offiziell vorstellen zu können.[3] Wie in nahezu all seinen Arbeiten argumentiert der Künstler auch hier mit dem Stilmittel der Paradoxie, die humorvollen Witz und Versöhnlichkeit mit beißender Schärfe und Anklage paart. In diesem Spiel wird Bulgarien zu einer Metapher für all die Marginalisierungsversuche, mit denen der westlich-hegemoniale Diskurs all die Kulturen und Länder ausschließt, die nicht in sein Systemdenken passen. Die Gegenstrategie, die Solakov empfiehlt, ist im Grunde die der Subversion. Einer Subversion, welche ihre Effizienz daraus bezieht, dass sie sich als kleiner, demütiger, harmloser Witz tarnt. War doch nur Spaß, scheinen viele Arbeiten des Künstlers zu sagen, um unter dieser Tarnung ihr Werk der Unterlaufung und Infiltration nur umso nachhaltiger entfalten zu können.

Top Secret (1989/90) darf im Rahmen dieser Strategie als frühes Meisterwerk gelten und beansprucht einen zentralen Platz in Solakovs Œuvre. Es ist zugleich Nachdenken über die strukturelle Schizophrenie des künstlerischen Ichs, Reflexion über die Unmöglichkeit objektiver Wahrheit und eine mutige und immer noch brisante Auseinandersetzung mit der kommunistischen Ära Bulgariens. **Top Secret** besteht aus einem Aktenfach mit Karteikarten, welche die frühere Zusammenarbeit des jungen Künstlers mit dem bulgarischen Geheimdienst belegen sollen. Zum ersten Mal im Frühjahr 1990 ausgestellt, also auf dem Höhepunkt der politischen Wende, sorgte die Arbeit für heftige Kontroversen. Radikal ist dieses Werk, das auf der letzten documenta im Jahr 2007 großes Aufsehen erregte, durch den Grad seiner künstlerischen Selbstentblößung und Selbstkritik, die jedoch nichts wirklich preisgibt. Ob sich in dem Karteikasten Dokumente befinden, die Solakovs Verbindungen und Tätigkeiten für den bulgarischen Geheimdienst beweisen könnten, ist für den Betrachter nicht überprüfbar, und der Text *»Die Aktion läuft (bis auf weiteres)«*, den der Künstler dazu liefert, macht es dem Leser durch seine im Stil eines Märchens gehaltene Form unmöglich zu entscheiden, ob es sich bei dem Gesagten um Fakten oder Fiktion handelt. Die schönste Volte in diesem Verunsicherungsspiel besteht darin, dass die einzige Instanz, die tatsächlich den Wahrheitsgehalt der Arbeit klären könnte, nämlich der bulgarische Geheimdienst, eben dies nicht kann, ohne sich selbst bloßzustellen. So wird der Titel der Arbeit auch zur ironischen Beschreibung ihrer strukturellen Hermetik: Das offenste Bekenntnis bleibt gleichzeitig »streng geheim«. Die so persönliche und für den Künstler über Jahre hinweg tatsächlich brisante, weil zur partiellen Ächtung führende Selbstauskunft, könnte möglicherweise auch eine konzeptuelle Inszenierung sein.

Solakovs in **Top Secret** deutlich werdende Strategie, allgemeine philosophische und politische Fragen und Probleme auf die eigene Biografie zu beziehen und damit abstrakte Themen subjektiv aufzuladen, lässt sich in einer Vielzahl seiner Arbeiten nachweisen. Am prägnantesten wird diese Haltung der Personalisierung in den Arbeiten deutlich, die sich mit den Ängsten des Künstlers beschäftigen. **Fears,** eine Gruppe von kleinen Tonskulpturen und Bordkartenabschnitten, ließe sich in gewisser Weise als selbsttherapeutischer Akt begreifen, mit dem Solakov seine tatsächliche Flugangst bekämpft. Die Skulpturen sind dabei jeweils der direkte Ausdruck der Anspannung, mit der Solakov während des Fluges den Ton zwischen seinen Händen geknetet hatte. Anders gesagt: Die »In-Formation«, die in den Skulpturen steckt, drückt zugleich die Angst wie auch ein Instrument zu ihrer Bekämpfung aus, ist also ein Ausdruck der Souveränität. Im Ergebnis ist diese Arbeit also immer gleichzeitig eine Darstellung und der Exorzismus der eigenen Schwäche. Ängste beschäftigen Solakov auch in der gleichnamigen, hinreißenden, genau 99 (!) Blätter umfassenden Zeichnungsserie **Fears**, hier in einer eher metaphorischen, oft märchenhafte Züge tragenden Form.

Emotions, der Titel dieser Ausstellung, hat programmatische Bedeutung für das Werk Solakovs. Er verdeutlicht, wie sehr dieser Subjektivierung und Emotionalisierung als wirksame Strategien begreift, um Absolutheits- und Objektivitätsfantasmen innerhalb der Kunst wie auch der Wirklichkeit auszuhebeln. Wie bereits ausgeführt, geht es dabei gerade nicht um Selbstausdruck als naive Authentizitätsgeste. Solakov benutzt die Bezüge zur eigenen Person vielmehr dazu, auch die eigene Glaubwürdigkeit zu hintertreiben. Der emotionalen Erhitzung, die in diesem Kosmos mit all seinen rührenden handschriftlichen Wand- und Bildnotizen, seinen Marginalien und zum Teil peinlich-persönlichen Bekenntnissen, seinen Legenden und Abschweifungen herrscht, folgt stets eine ebenso große Abkühlung, ein Moment der Unverfügbarkeit. Solakov ist das Kunststück gelungen, sich so perfekt in jede seiner Arbeiten einzubringen, dass er darüber selbst zu einer Kunstfigur geworden ist, die in allem, was sie tut, sagt und schreibt, anwesend und abwesend zugleich ist. Die persönliche, oft intime Dimension der Arbeiten Solakovs sorgt dabei für eine emotionale Reibehitze, durch die der Betrachter das Gefühl erhält, dem Künstler in gewisser Weise ganz nahe zu sein und ihn zu kennen, ohne dass man ihm restlos auf die Spur kommen kann. **I Love Them** (2007), die erste große Videoinstallation, die Solakov realisiert hat, spielt mit genau dieser Ambivalenz. Auf unterschiedlich groß dimensionierten Projektionsflächen, Monitoren und Flatscreens sehen wir insgesamt sieben Projektionen, welche sieben Lieblingsfilme Solakovs in einen betörend schönen Reigen aus monochromen Farben und verschiedenen Kommentaren übersetzen. Es ist der synästhetische Versuch, die eigenen Emotionen beim Betrachten so unterschiedlicher Kinofilme wie **Lichter der Großstadt, The Big Lebowski** oder **Die sieben Samurai** in die entsprechenden Farben zu übersetzen. Und es ist gleich in doppelter Hinsicht ein raffiniertes Spiel mit Nähe und Ferne, mit Sichtbarkeit und Unsichtbarkeit. So wie Solakov auf den Projektionsflächen in ganz ungeschützter emotionaler Nähe erscheint und sich dabei doch zugleich absolut entzieht, sind auch die Filme, auf die er Bezug nimmt, ebenso präsent wie real unsichtbar. Damit weist **I Love Them** auf die für sein gesamtes Œuvre bedeutende Kraft der Vorstellung hin. Gerade der Entzug des Sichtbaren sorgt für die projektive Fähigkeit, die aus dem Tatsächlichen das Mögliche macht.

Wichtig ist hier wie an anderer Stelle des Werkes seine appellative Dimension. Keine der Arbeiten Solakovs will – still und meditativ versunken – nur für sich selbst existieren. Ihnen ist vielmehr das Bedürfnis nach Kontaktaufnahme und einer dialogischen, bisweilen interaktiven Struktur buchstäblich eingeschrieben. Dies wird auch in der großen, neu für diese Ausstellungstour entstandenen vielteiligen Rauminstallation **Some Nice Things to Enjoy While You Are Not Making a Living** (2007/08) deutlich. Fast die Hälfte der hier versammelten Arbeiten zielt auf eine direkte Reaktion des Betrachters. Ein etwa 7 x 7 Meter großer Flokati lädt die Besucher dazu ein, ihn (ohne Schuhe) zu begehen oder zu streicheln. Daneben aufgebaute Pappkartonhaufen können von den Besuchern zerfetzt werden, um so Aggressionen abzubauen. In einer komplett schallisolierten Kabine darf jeder schreien, so laut er will, und auf einer großen Papierrolle können Besucher all ihre kleinen Beobachtungen, Sehnsüchte und Frustrationen notieren. Wer dies als naiven »Mitmachparcours« versteht, liegt falsch. Es ist vielmehr Teil des großangelegten, universalen Nachdenkens Solakovs über die merkwürdige Widersprüchlichkeit der Conditio humana: die ewige Paradoxie des Menschen, der, eingespannt in die Tretmühle von täglicher Routine und Arbeit, seine eigentlichen Grundbedürfnisse zunehmend vergisst und hier die Möglichkeit zu emotionaler Katharsis erhält. Natürlich ist sich Solakov gleichzeitig der spielerischen Begrenztheit dieses Parcours der Gefühle bewusst. Mehr noch: Er macht ihn zur Grundlage seiner Strategie. Die installativen Werkzeuge, die er vor uns ausbreitet, offerieren so gesehen immer nur modellhaft die elementare, emotionale Unbedingtheit, die real eigentlich nicht mehr stattfindet, beziehungsweise permanent scheitert.

Insofern sind alle Arbeiten Solakovs im Grunde auch Lektionen über ein »Paradise Lost«. Auf einem großen, lederbespannten Sofa kann sich der Betrachter ausruhen und gewahrt sodann aus einer bestimmten Position heraus drei in die Sofalehnen eingelassene Miniaturlandschaften, darunter eine liebevoll aus Holz geschnitzte Baumlandschaft und ein aus einer Computerzeichnung entstandenes 3-D-Modell. Die Akkuratesse der Modelle löst die Sehnsucht aus, in sie einzutauchen, und macht damit die Unerfüllbarkeit eines solchen Wunsches erst recht deutlich. Dies ist die Dialektik des Werkes von Nedko Solakov: Es zeigt das Glück, die Möglichkeit der Erfüllung sozusagen immer im Modus seiner realen Unmöglichkeit zu erfahren. Dies betrifft auch den Umgang mit dem Schönen: Zwei Gemälde zeigen einmal einen Sonnenauf-, einmal einen Sonnenuntergang, also zwei der größten bildlichen Sehnsuchtsmetaphern und zugleich zwei der am massivsten kitschbelasteten Motive aus unserer kulturellen Ikonografie. Nedko Solakov löst das Problem, wonach jede Darstellung eines Sonnenaufgangs eigentlich nur ein zu Tode reproduziertes Klischee bedient, indem er es in seine Darstellung einbaut und mit verschiedenen Kommentaren im Bild auf die schlecht gemalten oder nicht geglückten Partien hinweist. So zeigen diese Bilder, wie das Schöne nur als Zitat gelingt, nämlich indem es auf sein eigenes Scheitern hinweist und zumindest die Erinnerung an seine ursprüngliche Dimension wachhält.

Eine besonders raffinierte Volte zwischen Repräsentation und Präsentation gelingt dem Künstler mit einer Monitorarbeit, die Solakov dabei zeigt, wie er einen Schnitt in eine von ihm erworbene Tuschezeichnung von Lucio Fontana aus dem Jahr 1949 macht. Damit zerstört er die konkrete Arbeit, steigert aber vermutlich auch ihren Preis. Damit erweist er dem Meister des »concetto spaziale« eine ironische Referenz, nicht unähnlich wie dies lange vor ihm Robert Rauschenberg mit seinem **Erased De Kooning Drawing** (1953) getan hatte. Der ikonoklastische Akt ordnet sich zudem in eine Reihe kunstmarktkritischer Arbeiten ein, mit denen Solakov seit den frühen 1990er-Jahren die Strategien des Kunstbetriebs im Hinblick auf die Bewertung und Selektion von Kunst hinterfragt. Zumindest genannt werden müssen hier **The Collector of Art** (1992–2000) und **Mr. Curator, please....** (1995). Einen Höhepunkt findet diese Werkgruppe in der im Kunsthaus Zürich gezeigten Ausstellung **Leftovers** (2005), die eine Auswahl der Arbeiten präsentierte, die bislang von Solakovs Galerien nicht verkauft werden konnten. Wie so oft bei Solakov wird auch hier das Marginale zum eigentlichen Ereignis, das vermeintlich Unwerte verkehrt sich im Akt des Ausstellens, der Präsentation zum potenziell Wertvollen und ironisiert so zugleich nicht nur die eigene Wichtigkeit, sondern die Objektivitätsanmaßung von Bewertungssystemen überhaupt.

Alles in diesem Werk ist zugleich in einer Abwärts- und einer Aufwärtsbewegung: Die Videoanimation **The Bankrupt Businessman** (2008), ebenfalls Teil der Großinstallation **Some Nice Things to Enjoy...**, zeigt eine Endlosschleife eines durch einen rötlich abstrakten Farbraum fallenden Anzugträgers, der nie auf dem Boden aufschlägt, sondern ein ums andere Mal, mehr staunend und überrascht als ängstlich, durch seine rötliche Vorhölle trudelt. Es ist ein Bild, welches das Werk des bulgarischen Künstlers insgesamt treffend illustriert: Im Wissen, dass sich am Ende nicht alles zum Guten wenden wird und keines seiner Märchen einem »Happy End« zustrebt, zerschellt es dennoch nicht am Boden der tristen normativen Realität, sondern hält eine traumwandlerische Balance: eher staunend und überrascht als ängstlich und voller unstillbarer Neugier auf die wundersamen Geschichten, die das Leben bereithält.

1 Rosa Martinez, »Time Lost and Space Retrieved (Or Vice Versa)«, in: **Nedko Solakov. Paijsajes románticos con elementos ausentes**, Ausst.-Kat. Museo Nacional Centro de Arte Reina Sofia, Madrid, Madrid 2003, S. 44–46, hier S. 44.

2 Vgl. dazu: Kim Levin, »Marginalia«, in: **Nedko Solakov. Stories 1**, Ausst.-Kat. Center for Contemporary Art, Ujazdowski Castle, Warschau, Warschau 2000, S. 2–3, hier S. 3.

3 Der genaue Text auf dieser mit einer Auflage von 15 000 Stück gedruckten, die bulgarischen Landesfarben tragenden Postkarte lautet: *»Very Important Announcement: ›After nearly 30 years of absence from the officially participating countries at the Venice Biennale, The Republic of Bulgaria is proud to announce that it is prepared to properly participate in the next Venice Biennale in the year 2001.‹«*

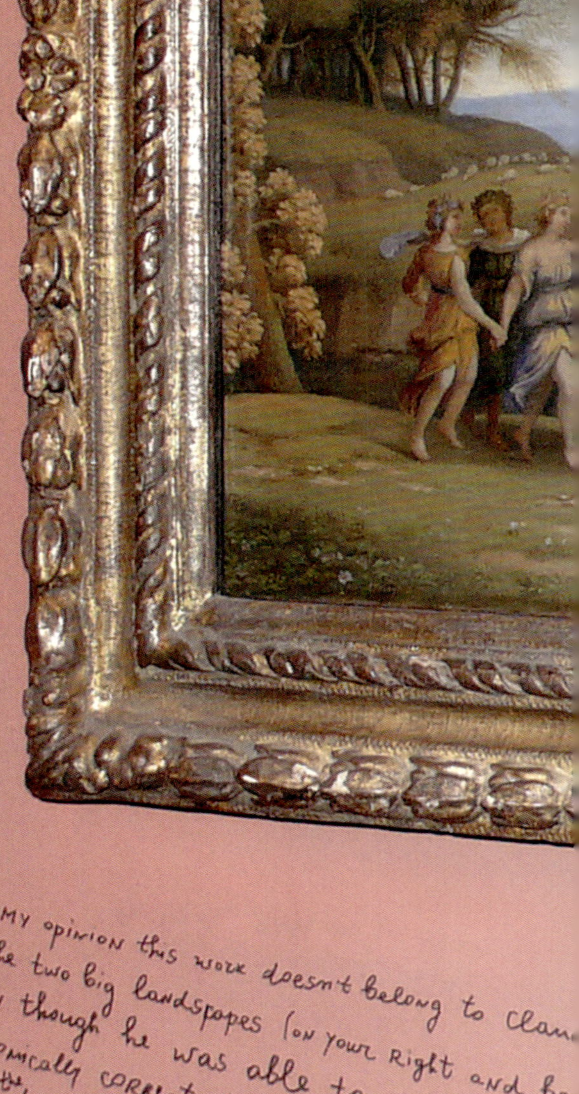

A Claude Lorrain painting (maybe) from Kunsthaus Zürich permanent collection, felt-tip pen, handwritten text; dimensions variable

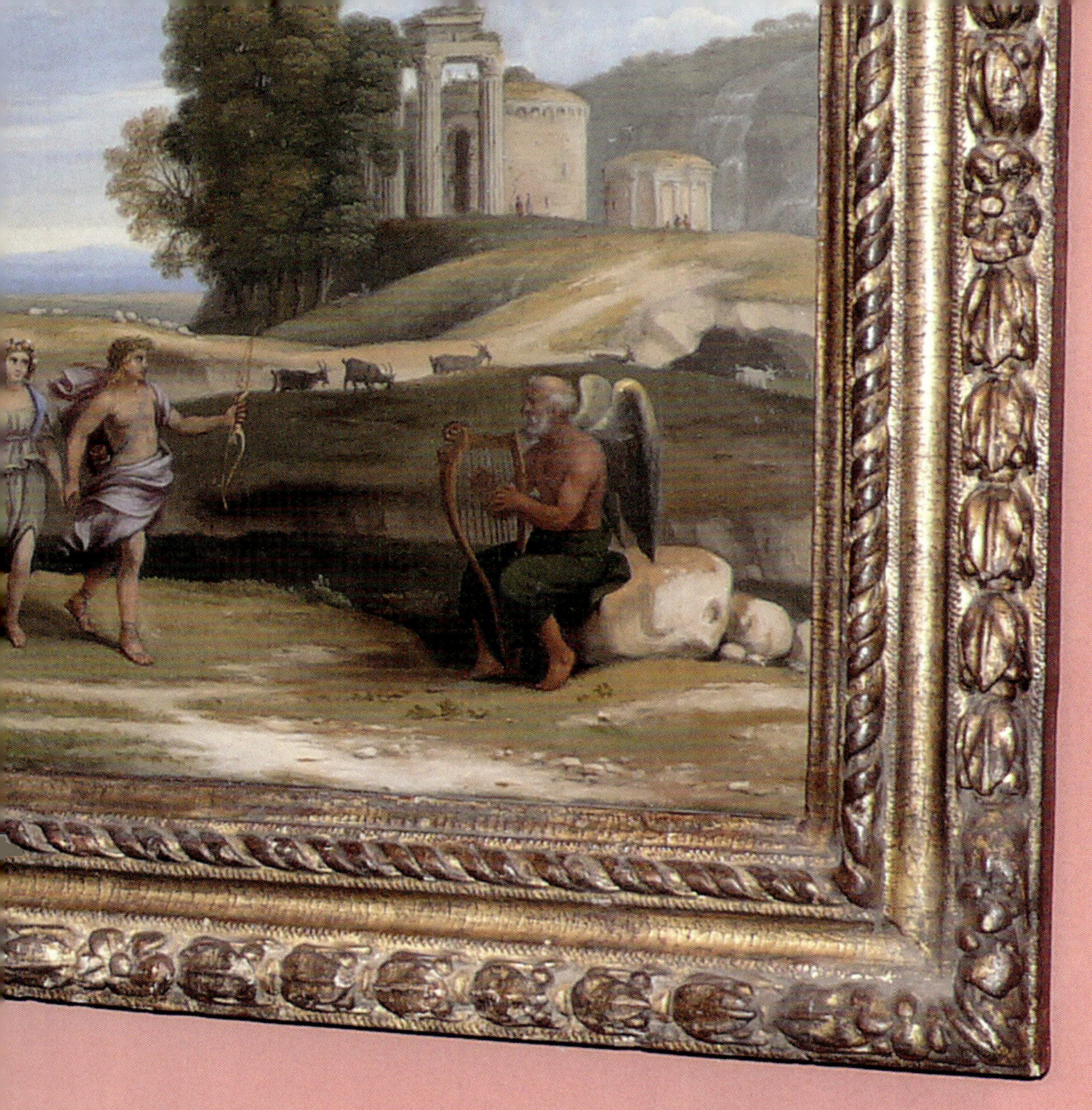

rain. Just have a look
our back) By this genious called Claude L-
tmosphere, his abilities to draw/paint
were not so good. Look at the figures
ad to do the mythological personages
nd the goats too). They are pretty skillfully
this painting (which is not a landscape

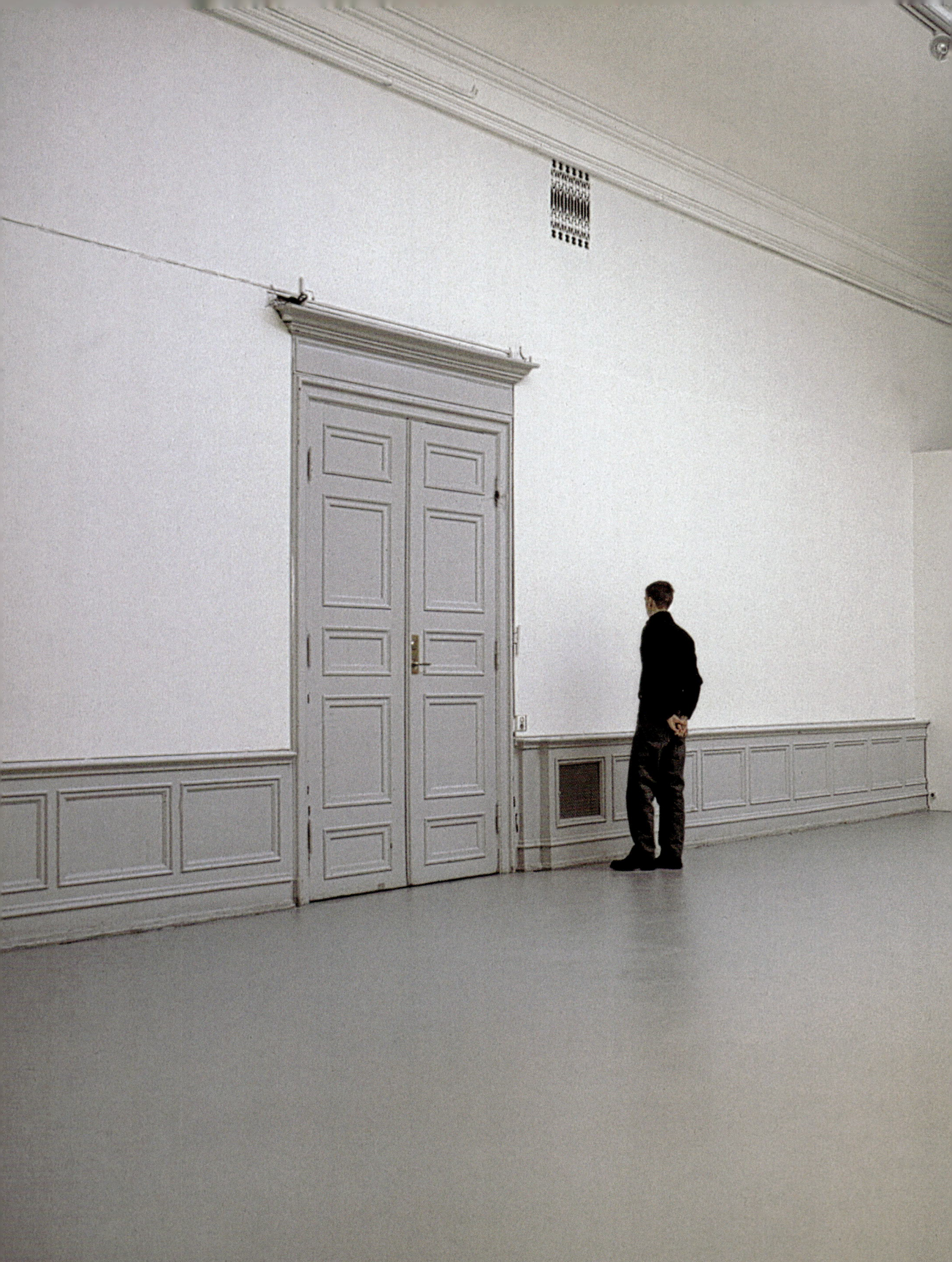

 Mixed (almost invisible) media; dimensions variable

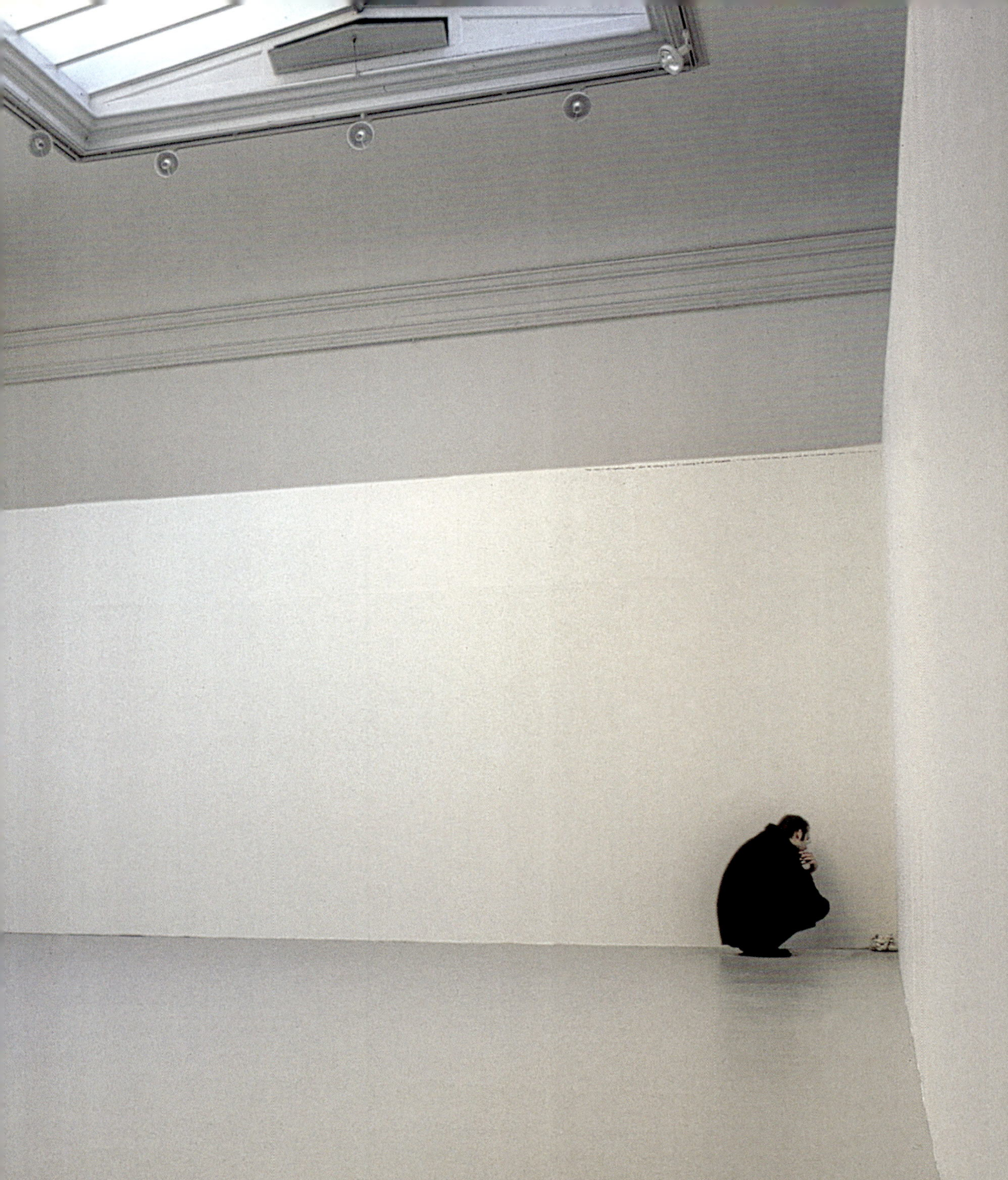

A (not so) White Cube, 2001–present

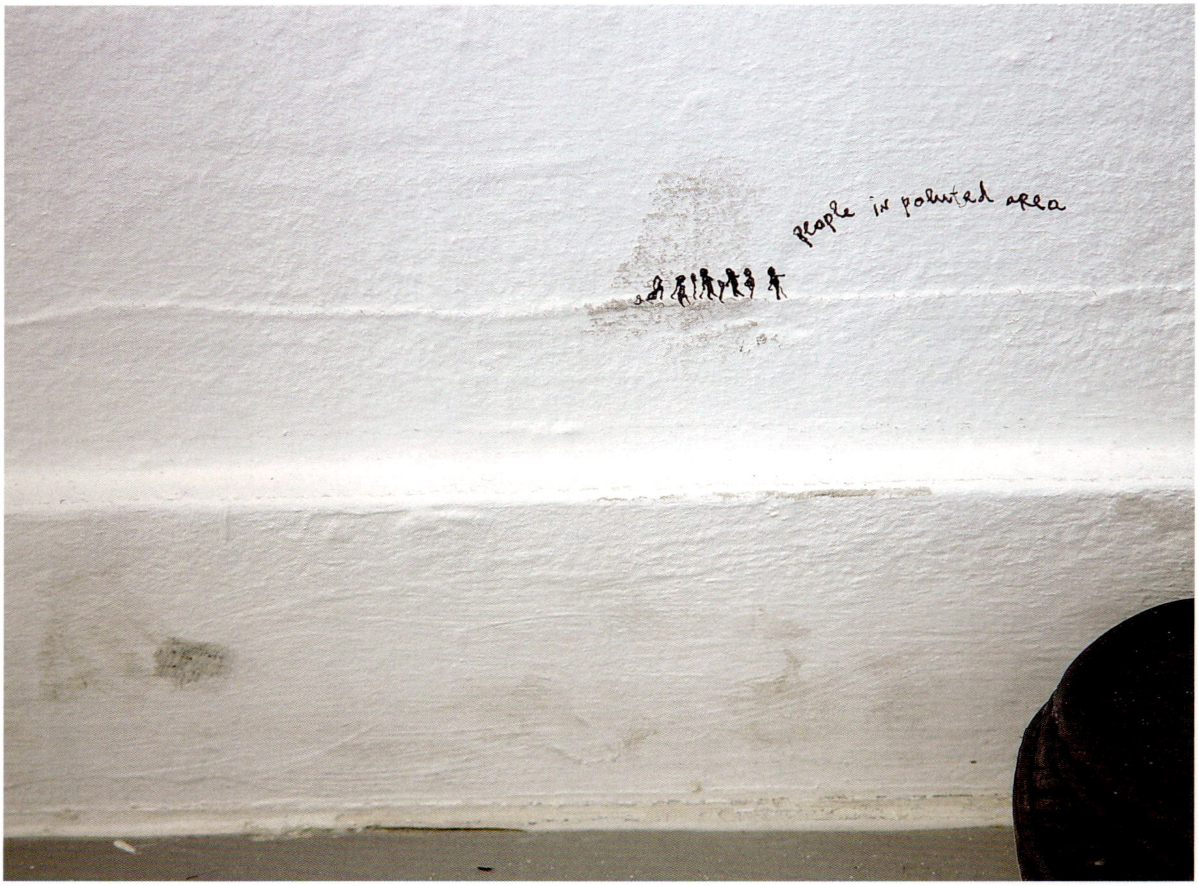

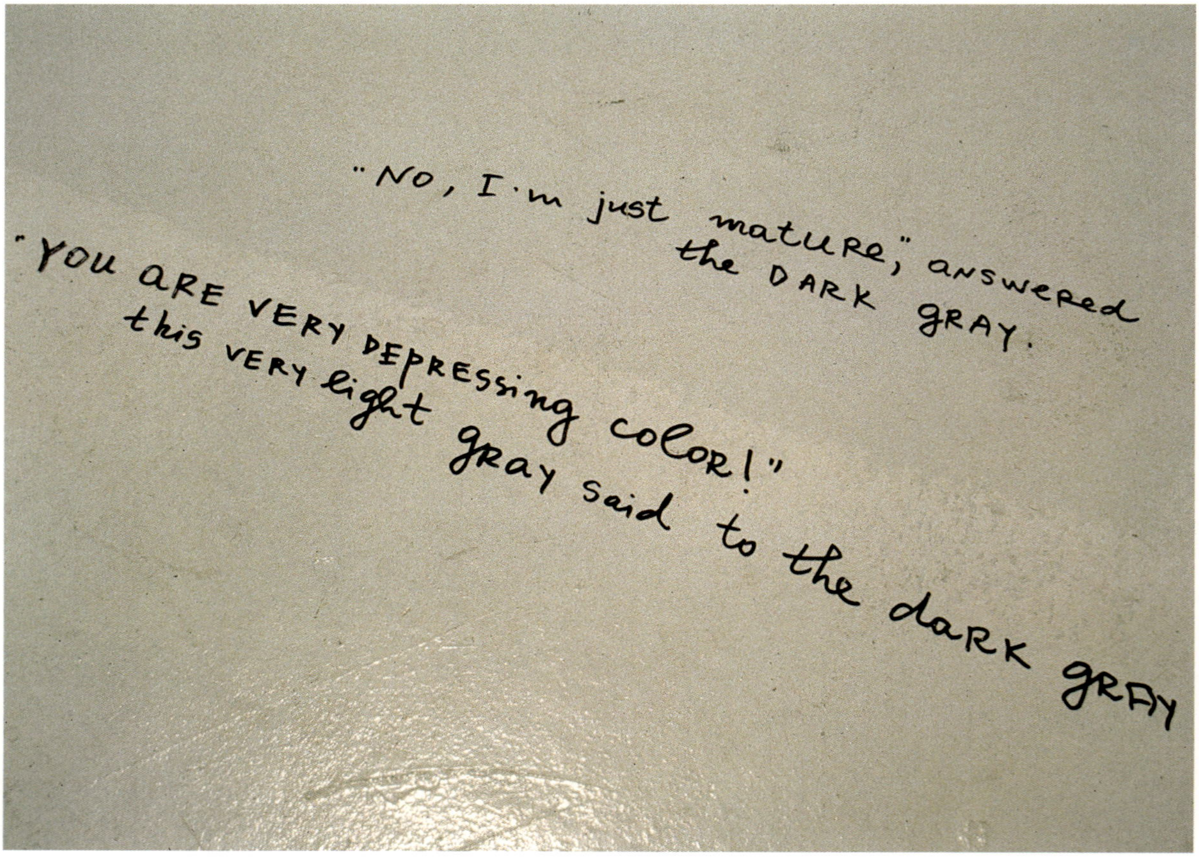

Felt-tip pen, handwritten texts on various surfaces; dimensions variable

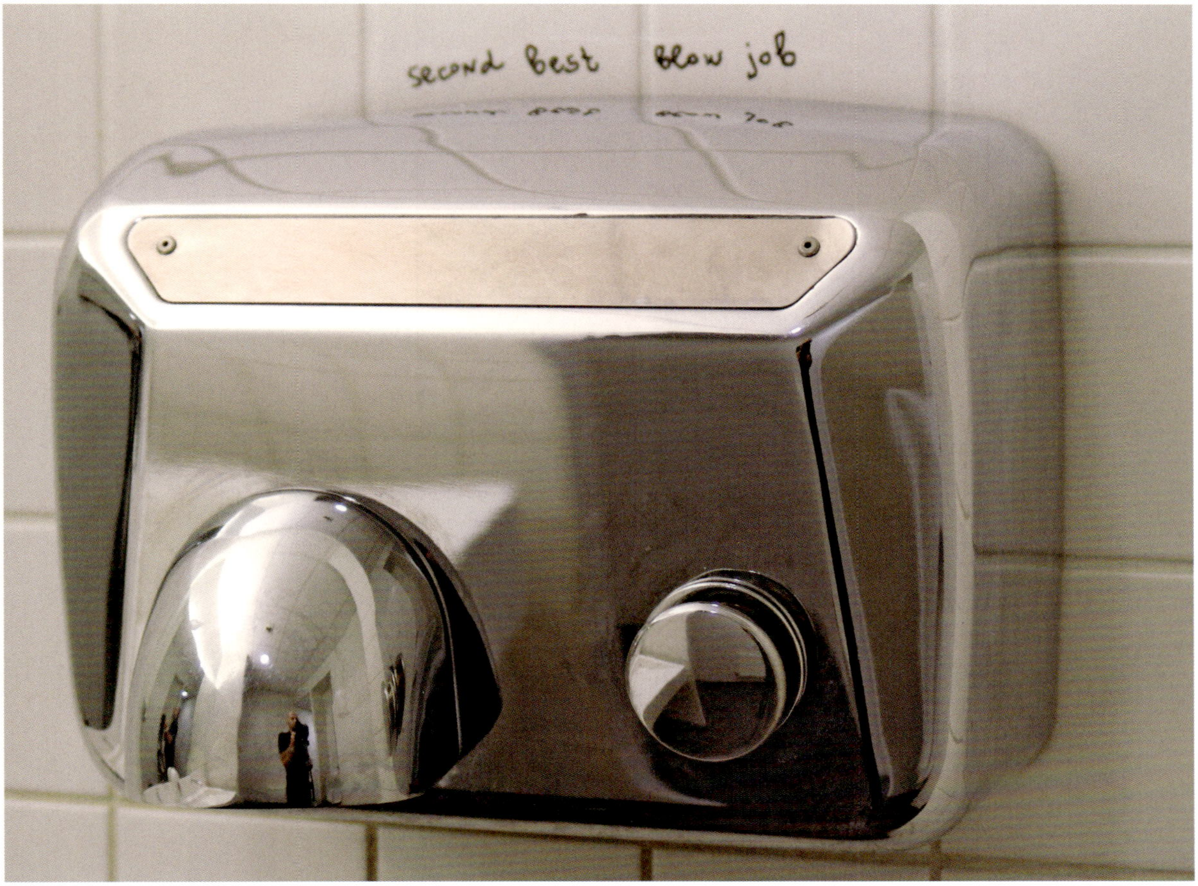

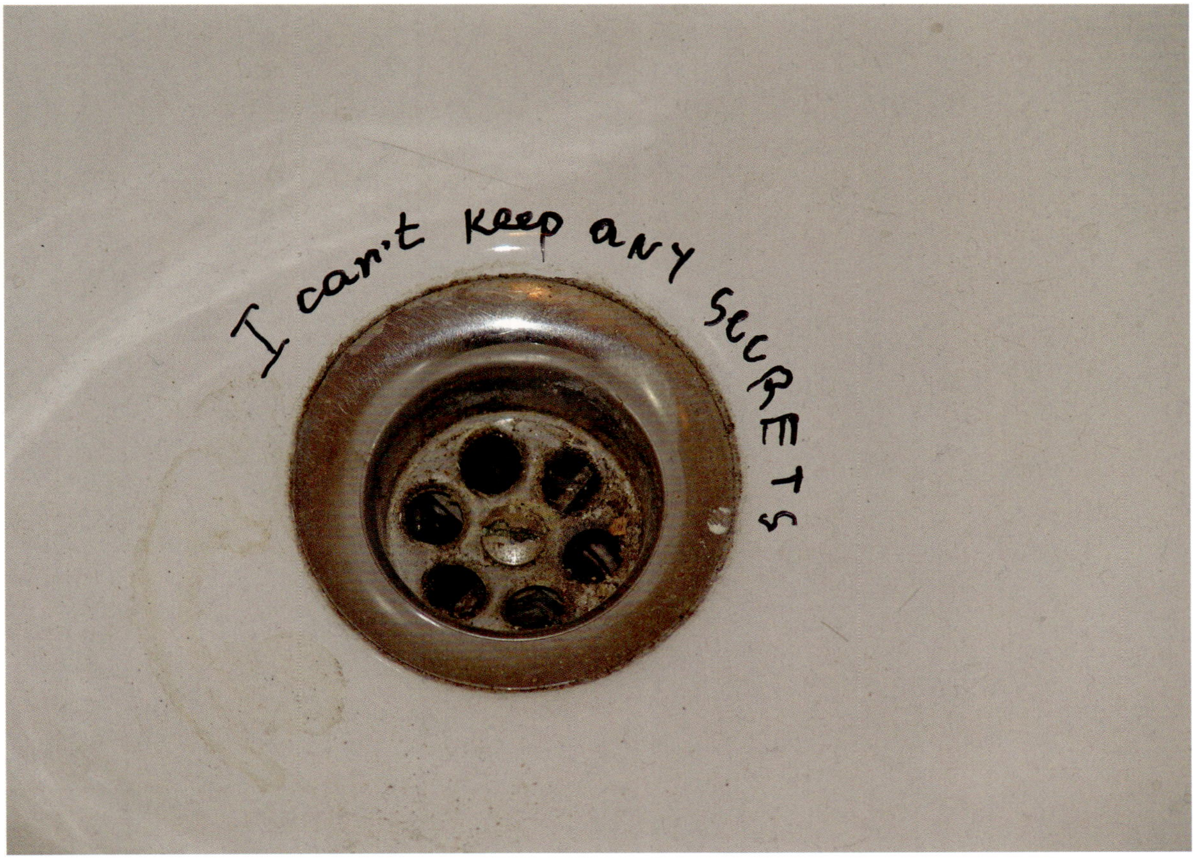

A (not so) White Cube // **Bad** (detail), 2006 / **Toilettes** (detail), 2006

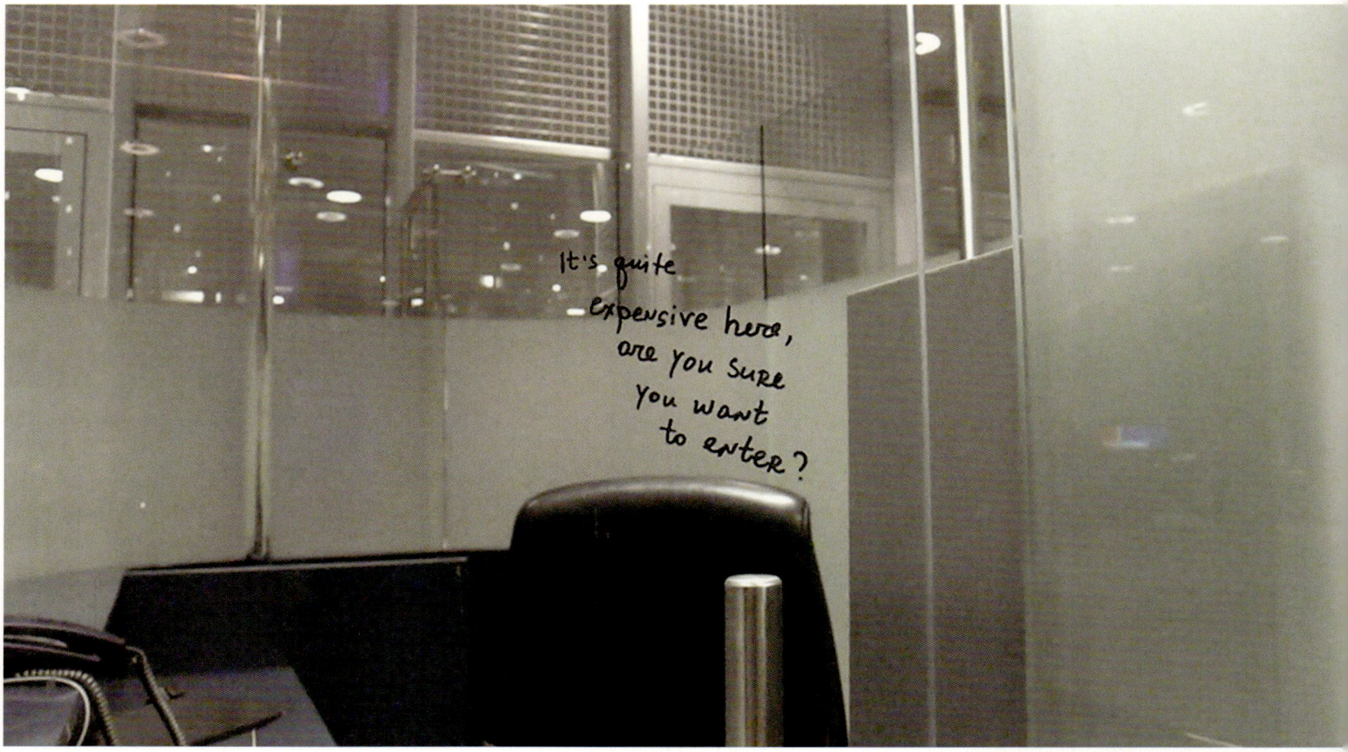

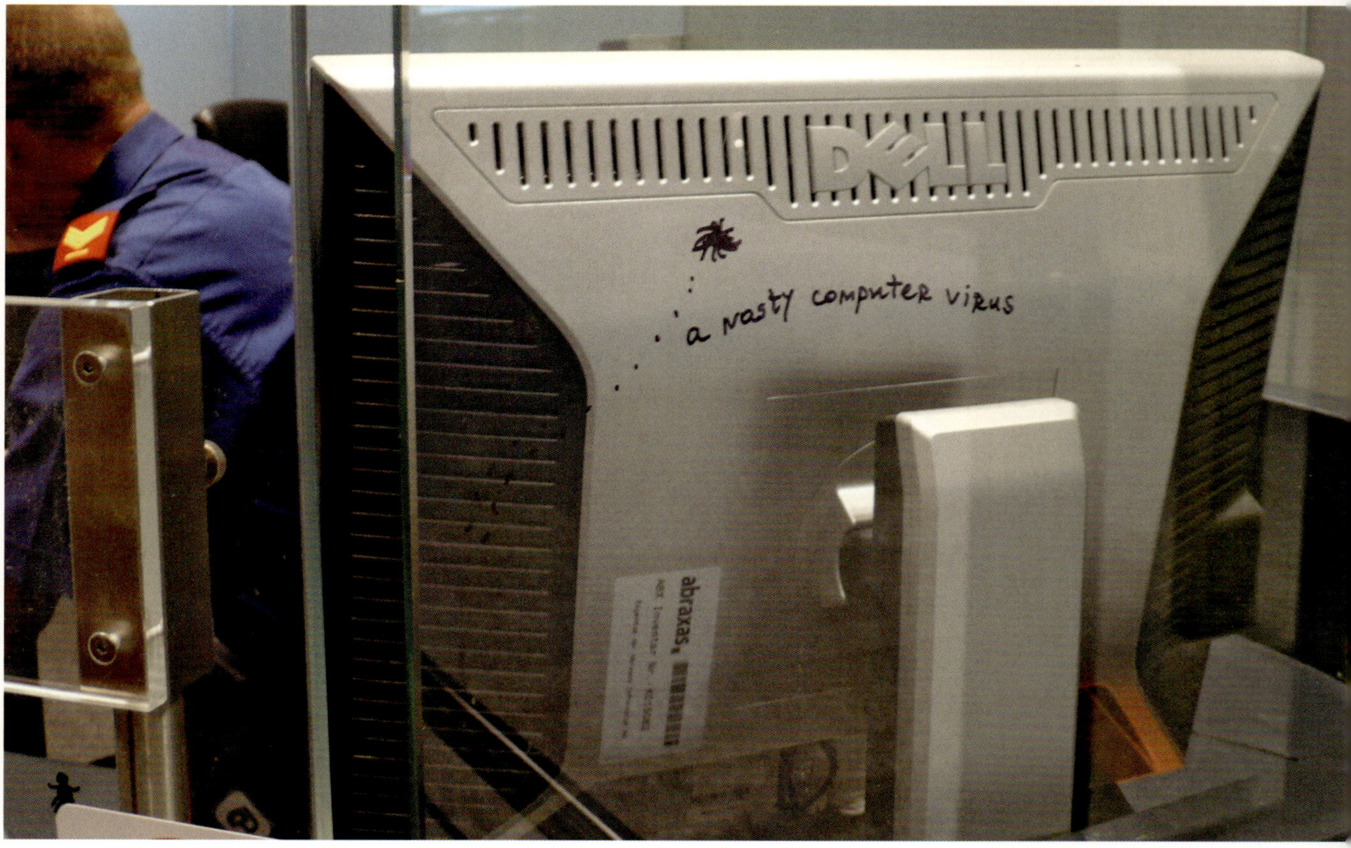

Felt-tip pen, discreet texts and drawings on all passport control counters at the Zurich airport (the following day all removed by the authorities); dimensions variable

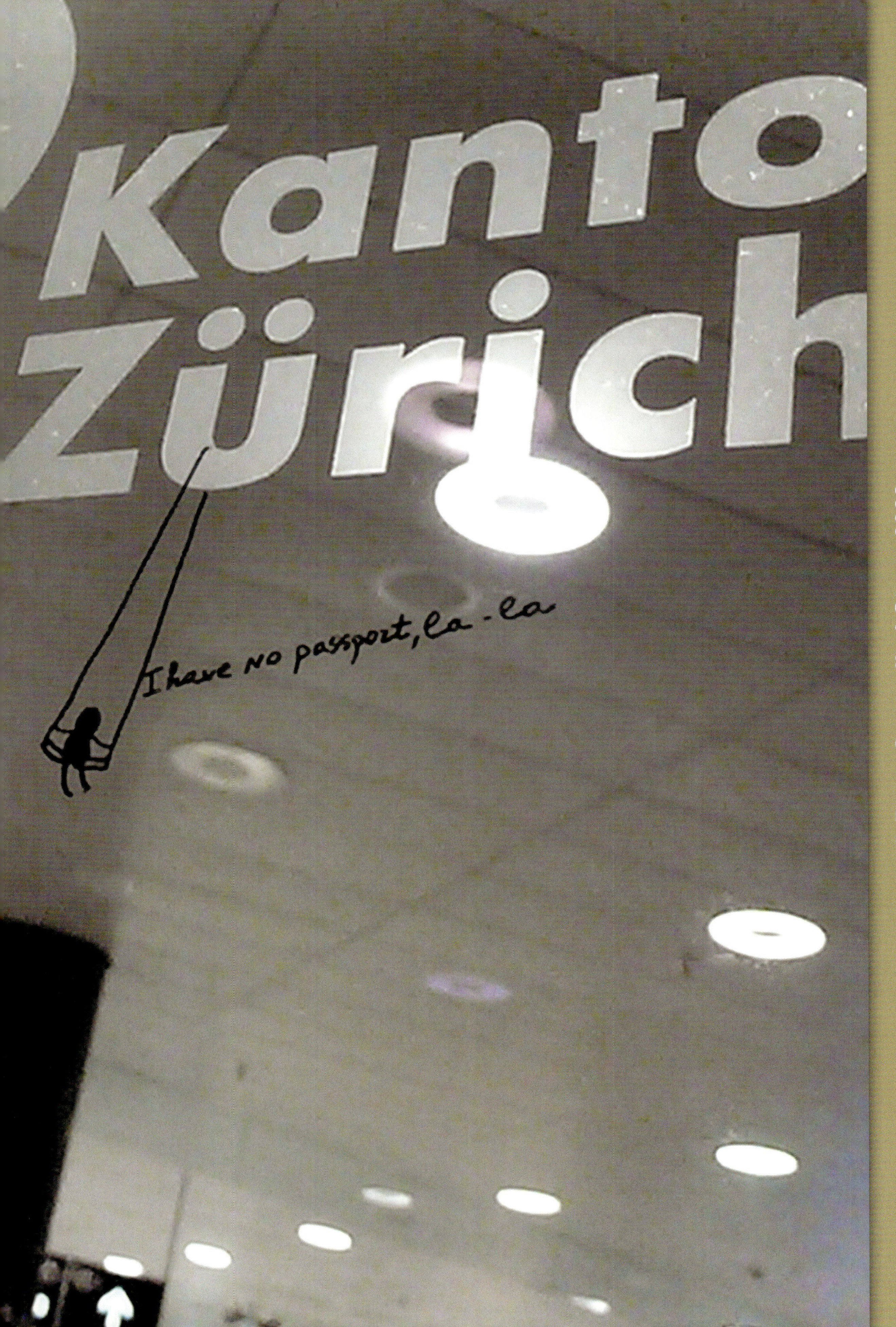

A Pass-Controlled Story, 2008

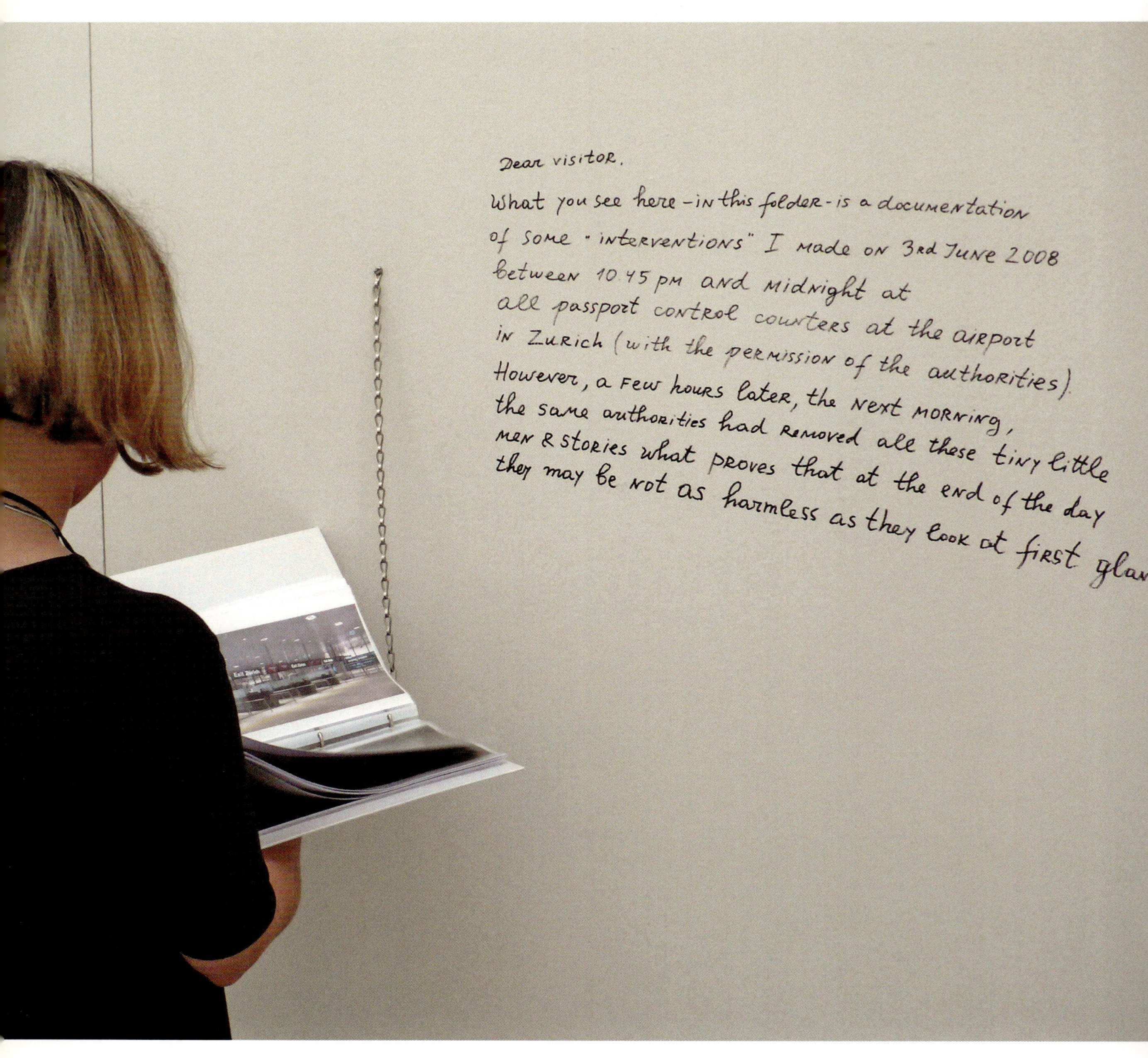

A folder chained on the wall of Kunsthaus Zürich containing photo documentation from all interventions, handwritten text; dimensions variable

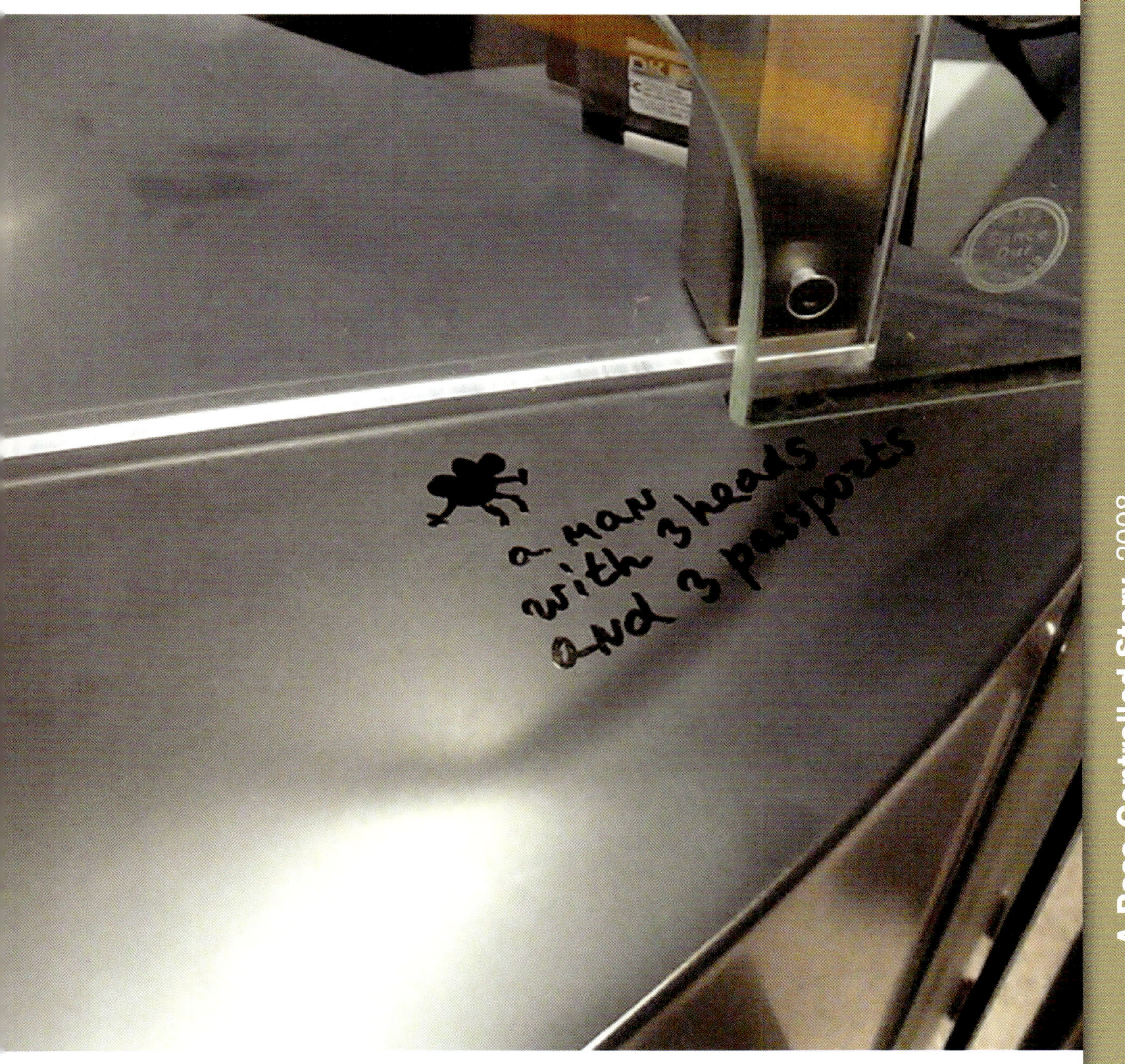
a man
with 3 heads
and 3 passports

 Yellow paint, handwritten text on wall; dimensions variable

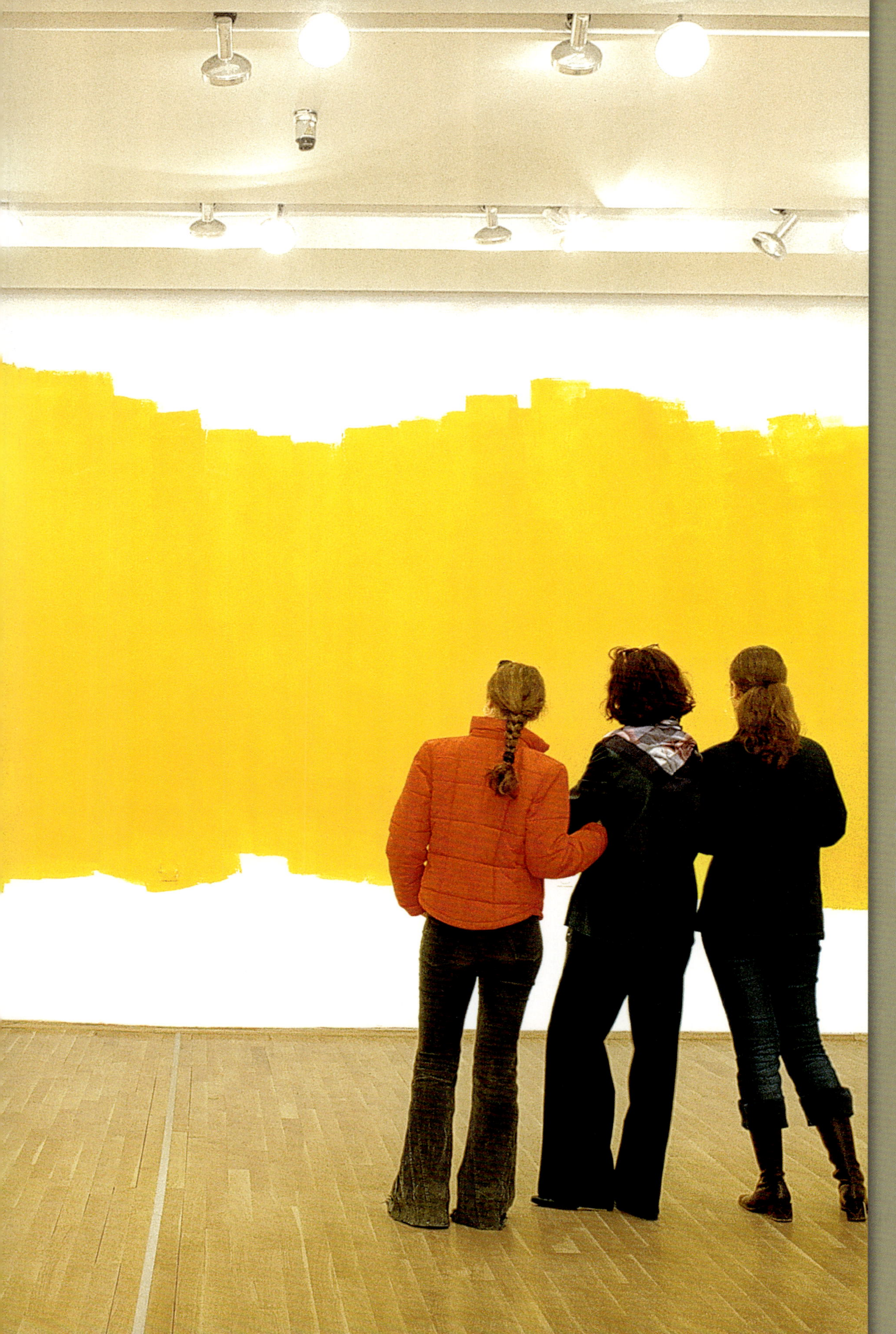

The Yellow Blob Story, 1997–present

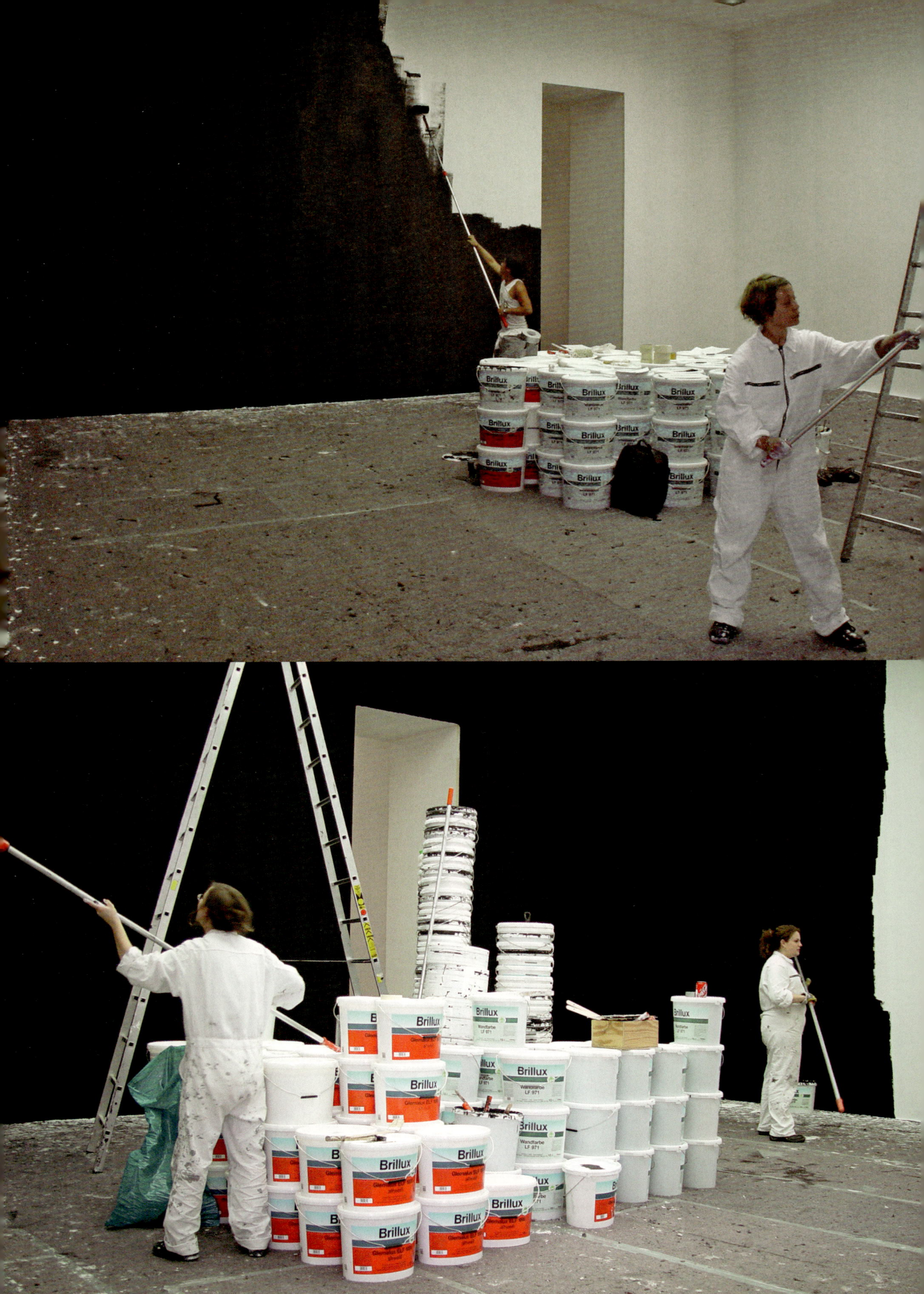
Brillux
Wandfarbe
LF 971

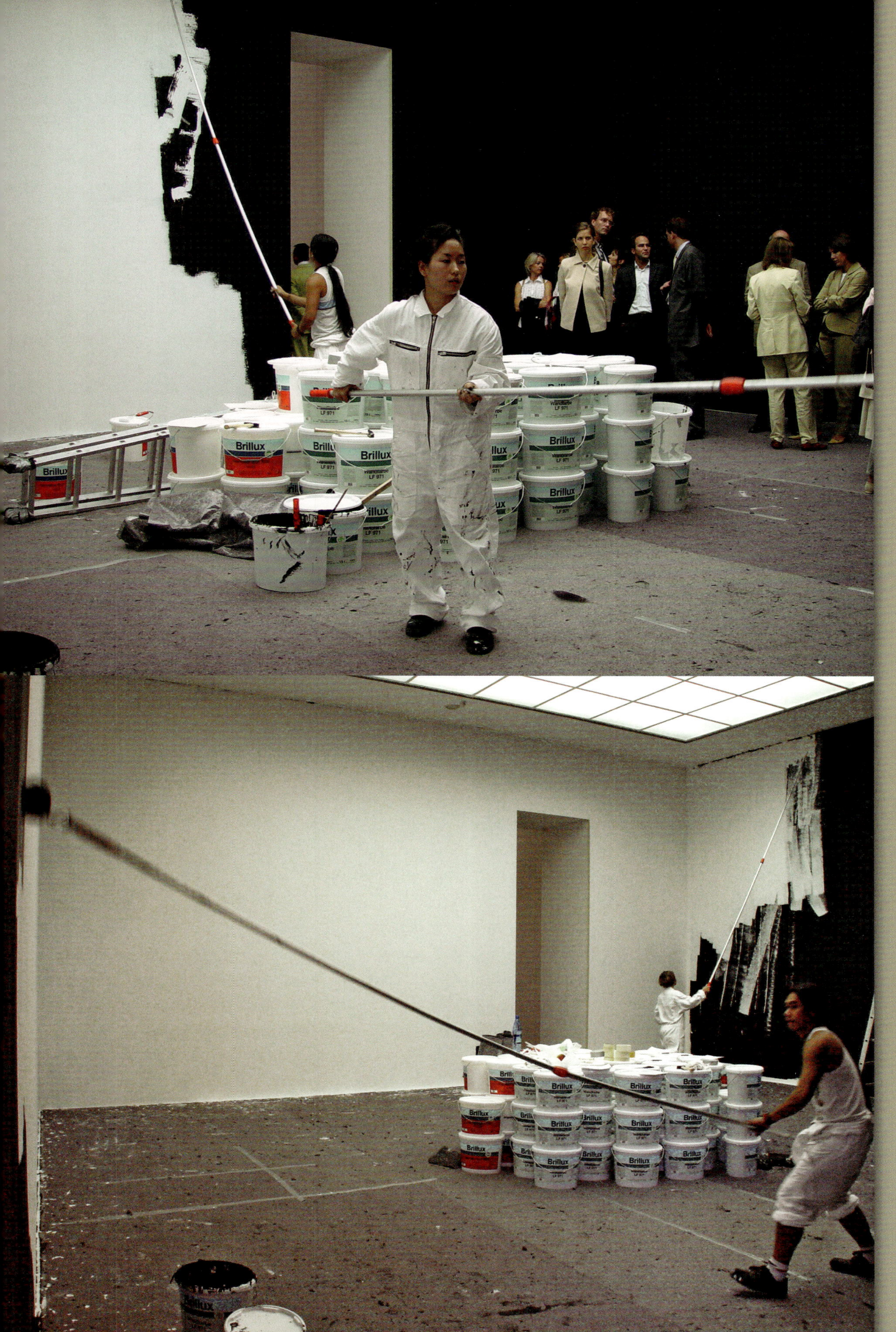
Brillux
LF 971

Black and white paint;
two workers/painters constantly repainting the walls of the exhibition space in black and white for the entire duration of the exhibition, day after day (following each other);
dimensions variable

Deutsche Übersetzung siehe Seite 196

The complete work requires:

—A team of two adult painters, with no special regard to their gender, race, geographical origin, social status, etc. It is not necessary that they be professional painters, as the use of professional painters could limit the work's social appearance because professionals usually do not communicate in a free, easygoing way with the audience passing by. Also, by its very nature, the constant repainting of the wall space in two opposite colors with thick, undiluted paint without adequate drying time or periodic removal of built-up layers of paint is absolutely against professional painting standards. The selected amateur painters should be paid of course. The painters should wear either coveralls or overalls with their own shirts, which should not be brightly colored. No special shoes are required. Additional shifts of painters are allowed, but the painters should never change places during the working process, nor should they exchange their overalls/coveralls (for example, it would not be appropriate for the painter using black paint to start painting in white in the middle of the session).

—Sufficient quantities of the best possible quality water-based paint in black and white (preferably exterior paint, which gives superior coverage). It is recommended that the paint be tested in advance for sufficient coverage, etc. It is also recommended that the estimated supply of the paint for the entire project be stored in the middle of the exhibition space along with all the empty buckets/barrels of used paint and that they remain in the space until the end of the exhibition.

—The necessary tools/equipment for painting: rollers, brushes (for corners and zones where rollers are inappropriate), rags, abundant supply of paper towels, moveable scaffolding and ladders (appropriate to the wall height), 2 buckets of water for storing the rollers and paint brushes at the end of the working day, 2 sets of signs (each set is comprised of 2 white cardboard signs (A4 size). One reads "10 Minutes Break" and the other, "Lunch Break."). Each painter receives one set of signs. The signs should be prepared in advance. The text is to be in black letters, 2 cm in height, and centered on the horizontal length of the sign. If the work is performed in a non-English speaking country, the text should be translated into the local language. All of this equipment should be placed/stored within the exhibition space, preferably in the center.

—A suitable space: preferably this should be a passage-type of space, with two entries, so the public has to walk through the room and therefore becomes more engaged with the piece. It is possible that the work could be executed on a single wall or on two walls cornering each other. In these cases, the painters should follow the same basic principles for the action described herein—to follow each other and all the time the sum of the part/s painted in black should be equal to the part/s painted in white. Because of the necessary drying time for the walls, it is not recommended that the space be smaller than 50 sq. meters. The walls must be properly isolated with a primer (adequate for water-based paint) before applying the first layer of paint. Preferably, the plywood support should be thick enough (minimum 16 millimeters) to withstand the requirements of extended repainting. Do not use cartogesso-covered walls. The ceiling and the floor are not areas to be painted/repainted. All "borders" of the field to be

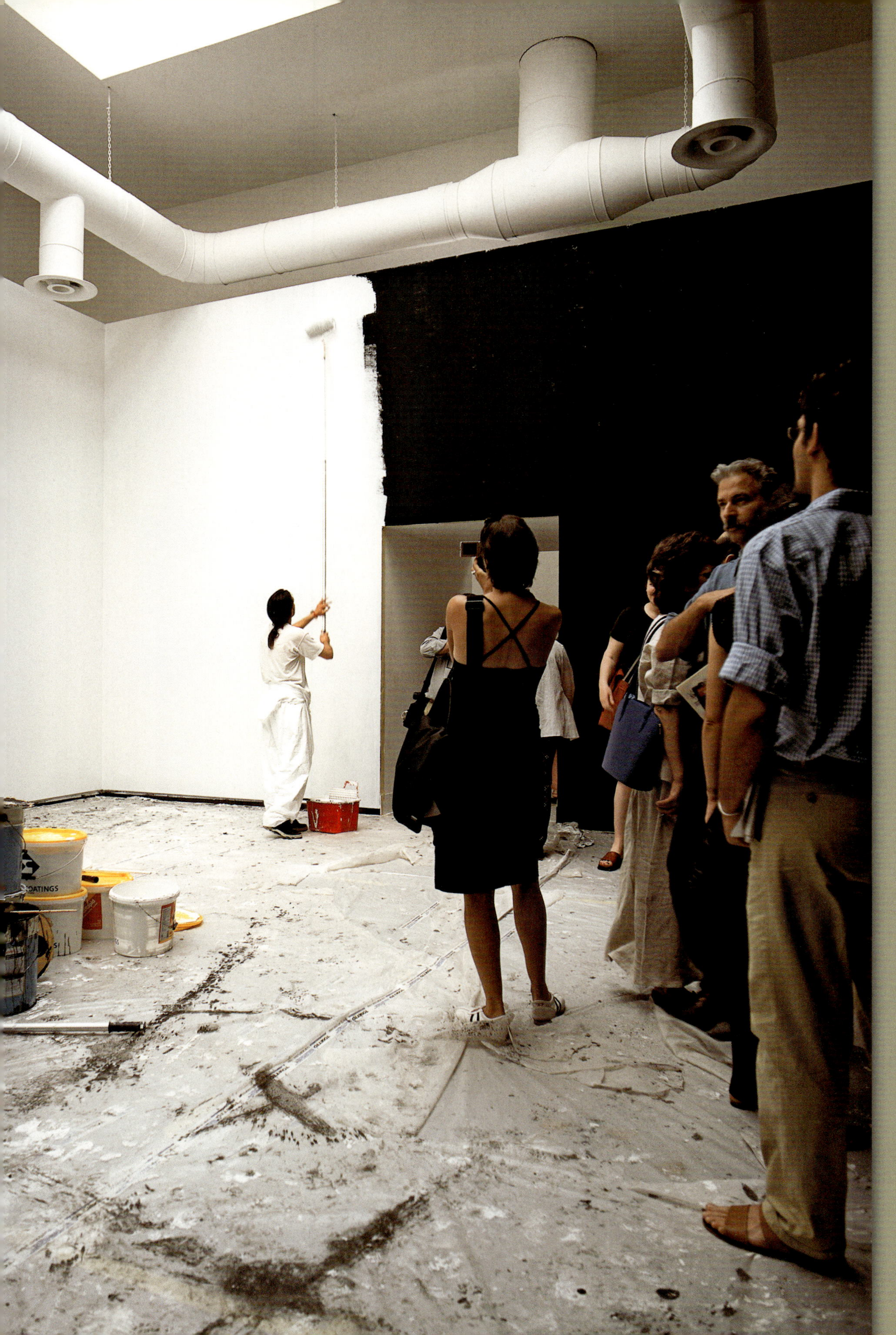

A Life (Black & White), 1998–present

repainted must be taped properly as done in standard household painting. If additional areas within the walls need to be isolated from the paint, they should be taped and protected as well (for example, emergency exit sign). It is recommended that a professional examine the walls before starting the work and that his/her instructions be followed for preparing the supporting walls. The floor should be covered with protective plastic and if necessary new layers should be applied.

—A working process: before the exhibition opens, it is necessary to prepare the space, the supplies, and tools and to organize the shifts of painters. The space must be half-black and half-white when the exhibition opens. The pre-primed exhibition walls should be painted with one layer of black paint and, over this layer, a white layer should be painted that covers half of the total length of the walls. Then the space (half-black, half-white) is ready for work.

At the opening hour of the exhibition, the two painters should start to work (it doesn't matter if visitors are present yet or not). In general, the direction of painting should be clockwise, but it is possible to be performed counter-clockwise. Once a direction is established, it must be followed for the entire duration of the action. The painters should not rush, but should cover the walls in the best possible way. They can speak with the visitors while working. All the time, they must keep in mind that half of the space must be white and half must be black—that is a basic condition. The painters should receive a 10-minute break each hour and they should break separately. Before each break, the painter should place the "10 Minutes Break" sign against his/her bucket of paint and leave the room or remain there if he/she prefers. The lunch break is once per day, and it lasts 30 minutes (again not to be taken at the same time). At the beginning of the lunch break, the painter places the "Lunch Break" sign against his/her bucket of paint and leaves the room or remains there if he/she prefers. It is best that the painter who remains working in the space slows down the tempo of working. The painters should work even when there are no visitors in the room. Five minutes before the daily closing of the exhibition, the painters should prepare to leave—all brushes and rollers should be placed in their respective buckets of water, the paint containers should be covered. These repainting activities must go on for the entire duration of the show—it doesn't matter if this is for several days or for several months. The painters must paint constantly every working day. At the end of the show, the "memorabilia"—the empty paint buckets, the paint brushes and rollers, the plastic, and parts of the multi-layered walls—can be kept by the actual owner of the work and used as a kind of visual/physical archive of that very installment of the piece.

Please follow the above instructions when executing the practical details of this action rather than referring to the original handwritten A4-size project description, which differs from the above.

Artist Nedko Solakov has the right to use the photo and video documentation of the different installments of this work to create new, independent works of art.

Nedko Solakov, 2001

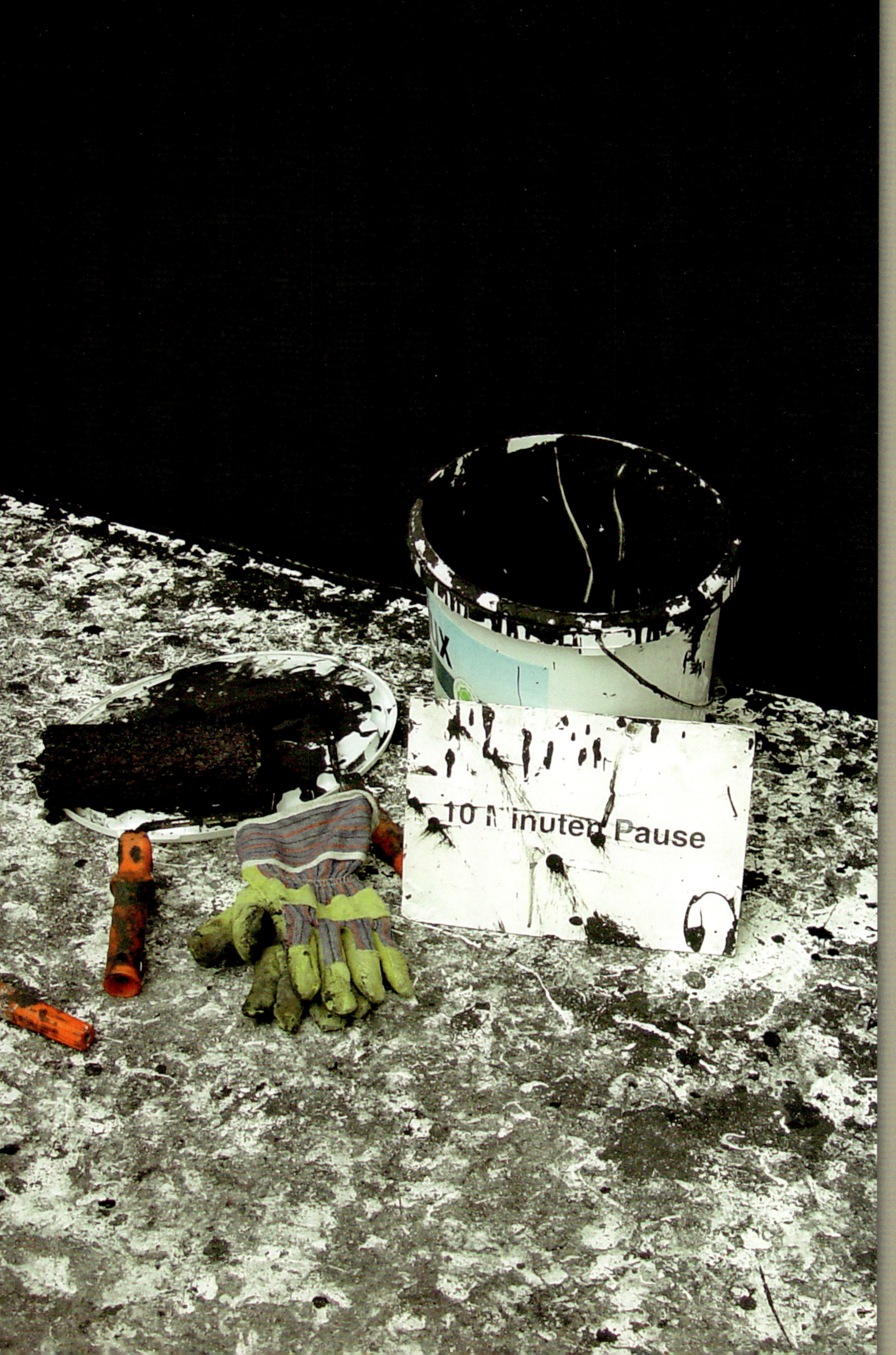

A Life (Black & White), 1998–present

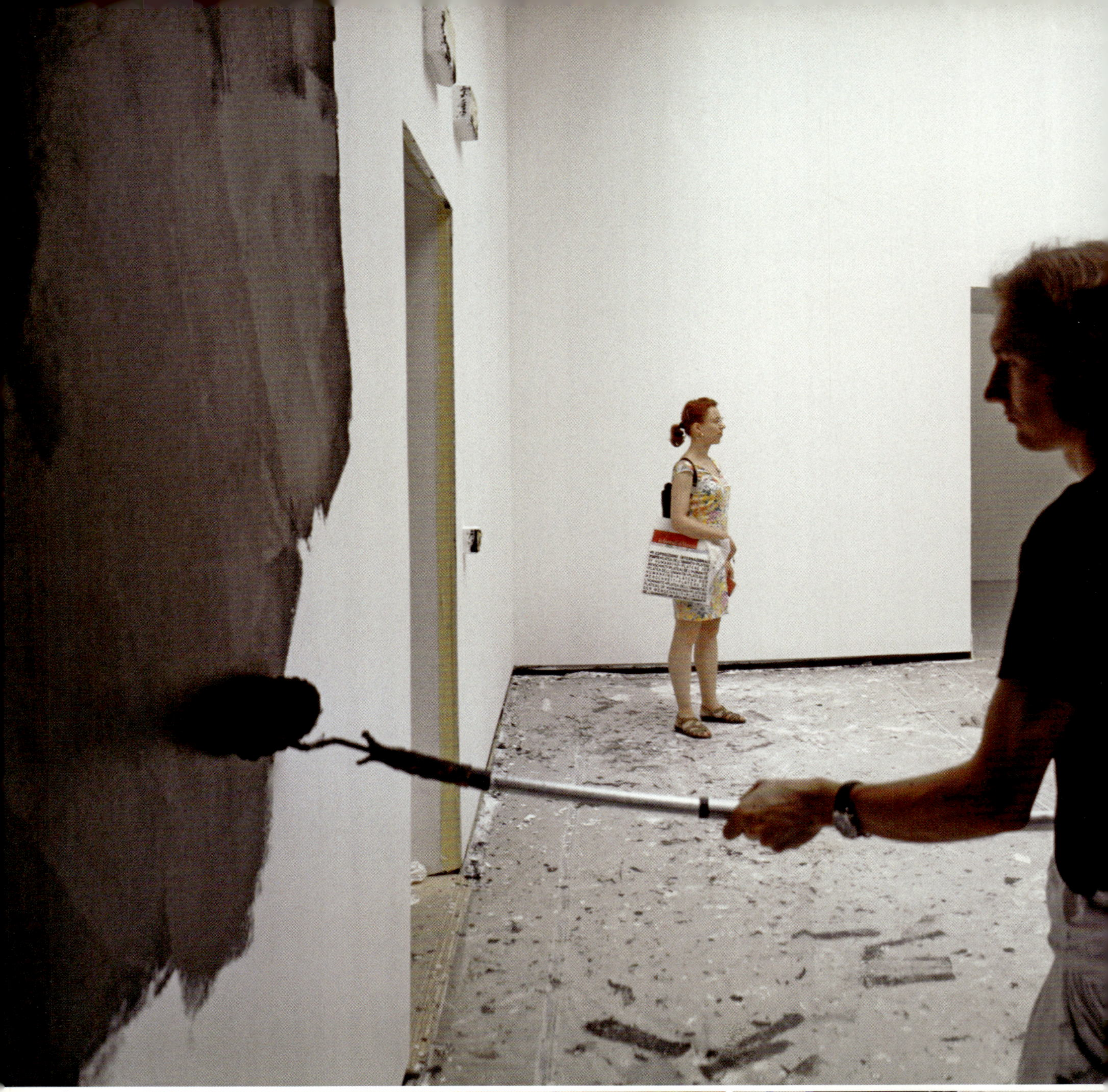

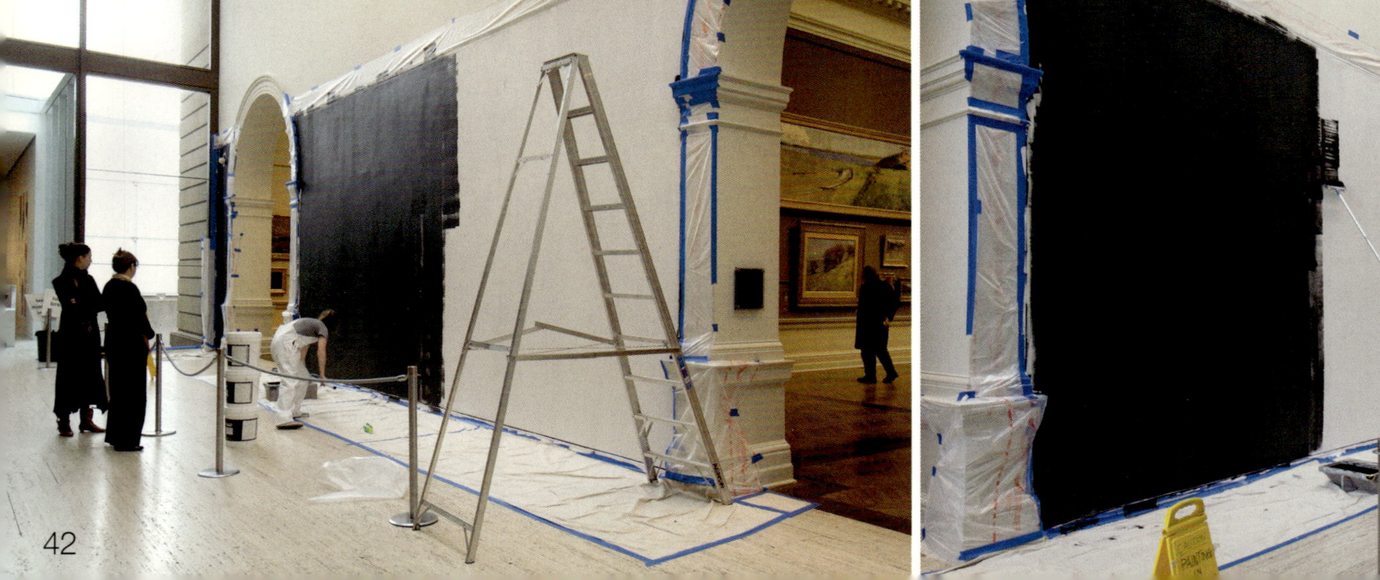

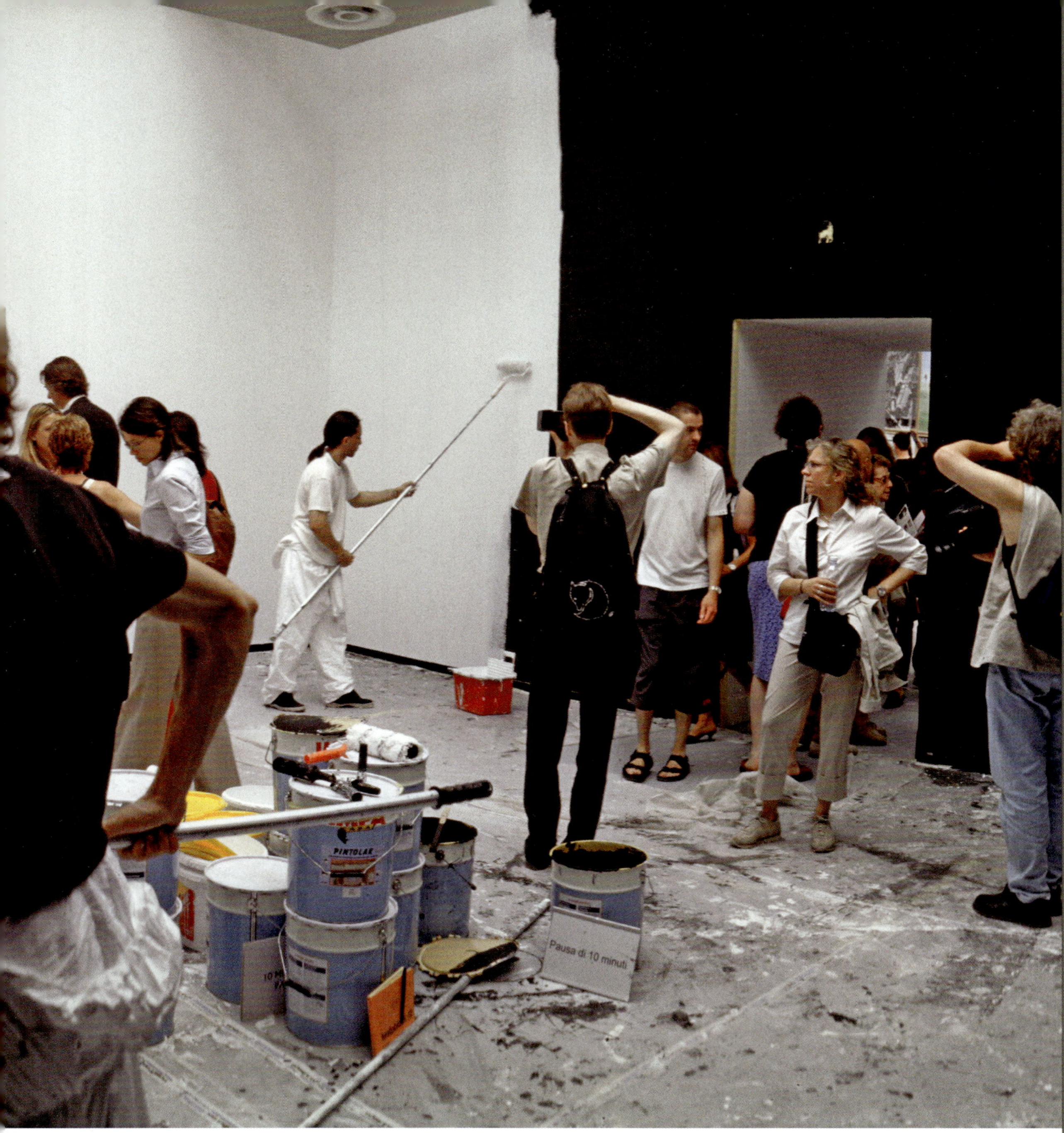

A Life (Black & White), 1998–present

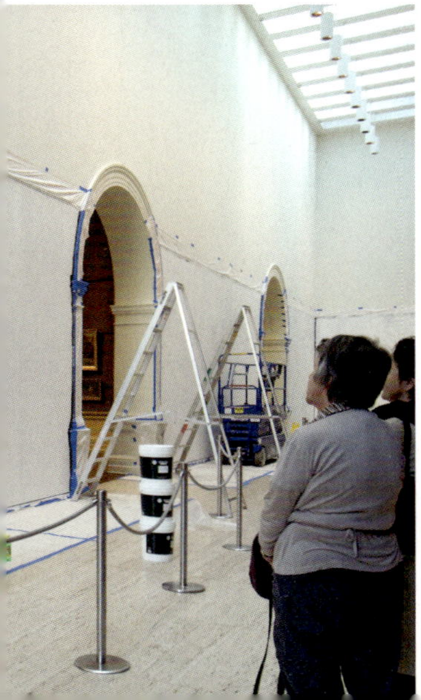

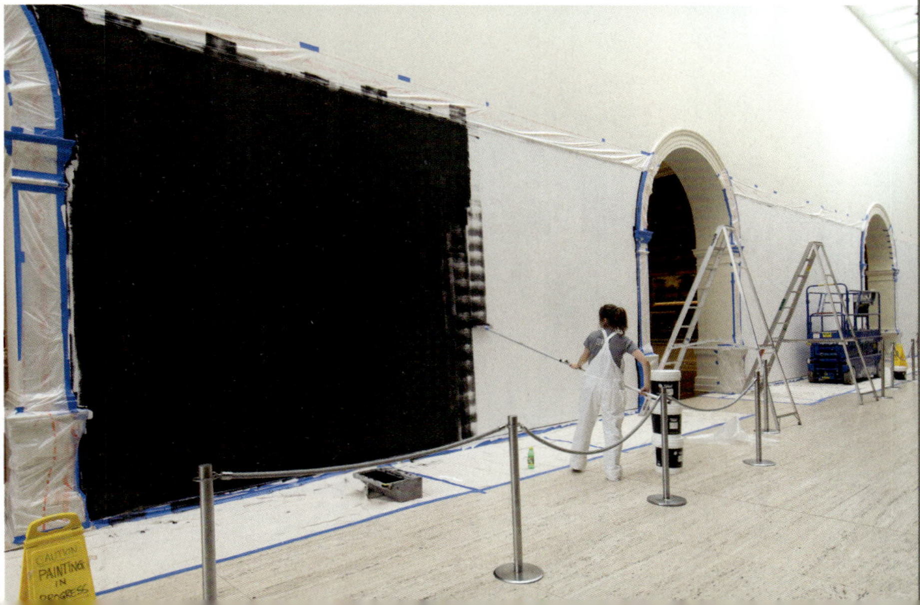

Things In Between
On the (Precarious) Relationship between Image and Text

Konrad Bitterli

"It's like talking to people. This kind of drawing is the next best thing to talking to people."

Nedko Solakov

At the Royal Academy in Stockholm, the IASPIS exhibition space looks clean, completely empty—but still it is open to curious visitors. The space recalls Le Vide by Yves Klein, who in 1958 presented an empty gallery as an installation. One of the most radical statements of modernism continues to be effective: only a small ball of seemingly crumpled paper lies neglected in a corner. Does it represent a subtle artistic gesture, or was it just thoughtlessly left behind when the last show was dismantled? The latter is probably not the case, since the ball of masking tape seems to have been tidily pressed into a spherical shape, while its two ends are neatly laid right up against the edges of the wall, running along the floor, so that they meet in a corner of the room. Right above is a scrawled comment: *"'I'm sick of being constantly used to define others' fields of interest. I'm sick of it. I will remain till the rest of my life in this corner, grieving...'—the adhesive tape said to the white wall and the grey floor."*

It is as if the masking tape is speaking to the public, spontaneously expressing its frustration over its awkward situation between the floor and the wall. After being properly used, this ordinary, everyday item was carelessly left behind, but it has been given a human voice, a personality, just like the floor and the wall, even though these remain mute. Personalizing objects is a narrative method used in fables and fairy tales, where animals talk to each other, as do trees and bushes, or the sky and the moon. In an exhibition of contemporary art, however, this odd, naïve directness might be jarring. Yet, upon closer reading, the monologue spoken by the frustrated masking tape is indeed precisely related to an art exhibition. Basically, the topic is the invisible infrastructure—invisible because it is fastidiously cleared away. This infrastructure makes it possible to realize an exhibition. In this particular case, the infrastructure is represented by the masking tape. It was originally placed there to ensure that the wall would be meticulously painted white (or the floor gray): it prevented the two shades of paint from running into each other.

In the (Untidy) Cell

The masking tape's brief monologue could be (mis)interpreted as an annoyed artist's acidic comment on the carelessness of the museum staff that oversaw the clean-up. But Nedko

Solakov was probably happy about the Scandinavian untidiness: the ball of crumpled tape seems to have been left there. And in fact, the museum assistants wanted to throw away the tape.

It is, however, precisely these moments of imperfection, of the profoundly human, that the Bulgarian artist likes to seize upon as the starting point for his work, which can consist of surprising commentary, anecdotal narrative, or mental expansions. Furthermore, it functions as a motor, driving his artistic imagination. Solakov invents anecdotes in which ordinary neglectfulness can turn into contemplations about human wellbeing. The visual process transforms into an actual act of reading: the familiar inspires witty narratives and, at the same time, a fundamental reflection upon art. For, in referring to the things left lying around in between two exhibitions, Solakov draws the viewer into a discourse concerning the exhibition of art or the circumstances under which it is presented. Unlike other contemporary artists, he does not do this by analyzing the conventions of the museum and giving priority to the topic of "art about art." Rather, he disguises his astute, hidden analysis in a parenthetical story, an anecdote involving three protagonists: the wall, the floor, and the masking tape—a precarious triangle that resembles the three-cornered, complicated relationship between art, artist, and curator. However, Solakov's barely visible intervention is not all. In actuality, the apparently empty gallery is thickly populated by fragments of text (and the occasional sketch), which he puts on walls, over corners, or next to switches or drill holes left in the wall that have yet to be spackled. A casual remark about one hole reads, *"a major hole (one of the biggest in this very room),"* while a blobby-looking, miniature man volunteers a surprising bit of knowledge about himself: *"I'm stupid and I kind of like it."*

Chat (2001) was Solakov's title for this exhibition of text and miniature drawings, which was empty of material, yet full of ideas. Others followed, and the artist summarized the works in A 12 1/3 (and even more) Year Survey (2003–05)[1] into a block of works, A (not so) White Cube (2001–present), as in the title of his show at New York's P.S.1. The term "white cube" itself specifically refers to Brian O'Doherty's essay, Inside the White Cube: The Ideology of the Gallery Space, which deals with the circumstances under which art is exhibited: "The development of the pristine, placeless white cube is one of modernism's triumphs—a development commercial, esthetic, and technological… The white cube kept philistinism at the door and allowed modernism to bring to an endpoint its relentless habit of self-definition."[2] Solakov drily counters with "the notion of the 'White Cube' is that of a perfect background for exhibiting two- or three-dimensional artworks, which in reality does not exist."[3]

Traditions in between Image and Text

In referring to the white cube, Solakov combines what is ostensibly narrative work with a decidedly conceptualist approach—something categorized in contemporary art as "post-conceptual." He juggles with modernist notions of purity and self-referentiality in the visual arts, for instance, by using language as a means of communication with a clear reference to reality. If his usage of texts in his work is questioned, then there has to be an inquiry into the possible resulting connections between word and image—whereby "image" always means a variety of very different visual media. As part of his hybrid artistic strategy, Solakov uses language as an intellectual catalyst within the image, about the image, and on the image.

There are precedents for this kind of process in early twentieth-century avant-garde works as the boundaries between traditional genres dissolved, the use of language in art gained unexpected significance. Cubist collages contain fragments of text, representing references to reality. By the time Marcel Duchamp had shifted from the optical to the intellectual concept of art, language had already become an integral element of visual art. These developments culminated in the language-oriented communications of the nineteen-sixties, in which the work of art as an object disappeared entirely. Ever since, artists have continued to test new varieties of linguistic strategies.

Critic Wolfgang Max Faust described the phenomenon as "lingualization."[4] He differentiates between the use of language in the work of art itself, its use as a medium in the visual arts, and its use as an accompaniment to the work. Solakov is outstanding among contemporary artists in playing with the entire spectrum of potential ways to use language in the context of the visual arts. Even though the following will discuss the exemplary functions of texts in selected works, they still remain fragmented when faced with the fact that his oeuvre overflows with his abundant desire to tell stories; it confidently makes use of all the possibilities that contemporary art offers in the spaces between objects, in between media, and in between word and image—from the commentary mentioned above to (not so) pure textual works, to narrative structures and complex combinations of word and image.

(Not So) Pure Textual Works

"The beginning of ... It smells a bit in a doggy way, isn't it? These stones down here. And you wonder how did the dogs make it up here. I'll tell you—I just took the stones from the garden behind you." Thus begins the intervention at Malmö Konsthall. As if the museum had been turned inside out, Solakov takes his textual works outdoors. Along the edge of the roof, there are playful comments, brief sketches, and witty interventions—although the public is given less to see than to imagine. A catalogue with Swedish translations of the English texts serves as a guide to be taken along on a journey of discovery "through" the exhibition: A High Level Public Art Project with a Catalogue (2004) is the deep title for the work that is way overhead.[5] Here, too, the artist comments on things found by accident, or on subtle, miniature scenarios. However, the things themselves do not speak to the visitor; rather, the artist gives himself his own voice and takes an authoritative perspective. In other works, he even gives himself—the "little man"—an alter ego: he refers to the work process, comments upon and invents wonderful anecdotes about displaced roof tiles, loose screws, and wind-blown feathers. Even though the work is attached to a museum, its theme is not actually the function of the building. Instead, it is about ordinary things, which certainly opens up the museum to the rest of the world.

The artist succeeds at doing the same thing, not just four meters above the ground, but a few thousand meters, i.e., 10,000 meters, overhead: *"Actually the aileron closest to you would very much like to say 'Hello!' and to greet you by waving up and down three times. But his mother, the cockpit, has rules. He will greet you later while landing."* This can be read on the wing of a Luxair airplane. Fortunately, the cockpit of the Boeing 737 does not acquiesce to the wishes of its wing. For the Faiseurs d'histoires show at the Casino Luxembourg, Solakov created airy works of text that were placed on six airplanes and are distinguished by their surprisingly formal austerity. They are purely textual works, resembling works of classic Conceptual Art. Texts evoke images; they analyze and reflect upon the categorical possibilities of art. Solakov, however, overcomes the self-referential framework of "art about art." He finds the content for his works outside of the closed system of art, in human existence, in his emotions and fears. In turn, the material world communicates in a slightly mischievous way with the viewer. That means a lack of protective exhibition space, which is why the texts are not primarily interpreted as art. This results in a completely "detached" reading by members of the public, who probably also suffer from a fear of flying, just like the artist. On the Wing (1999–present) has its own disturbing potential, which allows those of us above the clouds to ponder the highs and lows of everyday life.

Drawing (Art) Histories

As a rule, fairy tales start with "once upon a time..." This introduction evokes epochs past, in which a story has taken place not as a fictional tale, but as a factual report—at least in the imagination of a child. Another type of reality is conjured up, a parallel world, which relates to its own experience of reality, but also expands it to the extreme by eliminating rational laws. Tales, therefore, often contain something that is both profoundly disturbing and, at the same time, liberating. The same is true of Solakov's stories, which are created by combining images and texts into multi-part cycles. Their consecutive numbering makes them seem like a narrative sequence that is occasionally and deliberately counteracted. Once upon a Time (1995–96), ...and they lived happily ever after (1999), Good & Bad (2003), and Fears (2006–07) are products of the classic medium of sepia and ink on paper and, in an almost exemplary way, they make it possible to see Solakov's drawing strategy between the image and the text. "For me, text and image are absolutely inseparable; they create a unit. When I do a drawing... I always have the stories underneath the image that has been drawn. When I draw an image, I only have a vague idea of how the story will develop."[6]

Once Upon a Time deals in fifty stories with present issues but takes us back to a period haunted by knights or, even further into the past, to the Vikings or prehistoric times. The series is not set up as a linear narrative but, instead, each individual drawing relates one anecdote—such as the one about the woman who always went back to her house to see if the iron was turned off—ironically set in medieval surroundings. By narrating this ordinary experience at arm's length, it is turned into a recurring worry about the inevitability of human existence. Step by step, Solakov develops his stories: "I start writing them down on the lower edge of the page. ...I generally don't know how these stories are going to turn out, and so it is very engrossing to take them to a logical (and nevertheless highly absurd) ending—and to do this on the few millimeters of paper left over. But the text does not explain the image, nor does the image illustrate the text. They can't do anything else except interact."[7]

The artist carefully fills the sheet of paper by drawing and washing with sepia and black and white ink. As in a children's book, the text accompanies the image on the lower edge of the paper. Image and text form an inseparable unit, even when there are surprising turns in the in-between space and paradoxical interpretations appear. Solakov plays with the conventions of illustration by adding cryptic drawings to ordinary events, or by diverting standard visual references in the text into the realm of the fantastic. In short, he creates in-between things: witty, occasionally mean, always absurd visual narratives from a world in which delicate wit opens up space for contemplating human deficiencies, where it is possible to think profoundly about human existence and the state of things in the world—even things in the world of art.

Hence, a drawing from Once Upon a Time will employ an apparently naïve anecdote to explore the theme of artistic creativity. In honor of his noble patron's lover, the court artist creates the ultimate work of art: *"Finally he ... got it—he just left the white canvas as it was—empty. The count really liked the stuff..."* The paper remains succinctly blank—except for the hand-written text on the edge. Consistently derived from the narrative, it avoids each and every convention, sounding a conceptual approach that amuses itself with artistic traditions and their phantasms of the pure work of art, which reaches perfection, of course, in the blank painting. Or, to put it another way, Solakov develops an alternative interpretation of the modernist search for the absolute in art and translates it into a wonderful visual narrative. Still, most of his drawings overflow with an irrepressible desire to invent stories, as well as a kind of visual imagination that utilizes all sorts of available sources, from the Bible, histories, and fairy tales, to present-day low and high culture.

Linguistic Translations

Despite the fact that they are skillfully executed in gentle washes and white highlights, each drawing always has its own fleeting quality. This links it to language: specifically, spoken language. Yet even though he employs narrative conventions, Solakov's use of language is not literary, but ordinary instead. This might have to do with the fact that most of the drawings since the nineteen-nineties have been accompanied by English-language texts, meaning that the artist writes them in a language that is foreign to him. Even though he has them corrected, he does not try to use language elegantly. Instead, he uses English as a lingua franca—he tries to make his language as widely comprehensible as possible.

This is why the artist avoids lofty, rhetorical turns of phrase, as well as expressions that lean too much in the direction of slang. Since communication in his texts often takes place in the form of dialogue, Solakov uses a kind of easy-to-understand, spoken English. As is generally known, spoken language is part of the oral tradition—the language of myths before they were ever written down. That means it is also a provisional language: it disappears as soon as it has been uttered. In this respect, it is related to the nature of drawing, especially the kind of drawing Solakov employs for his temporary interventions in exhibition spaces. Drawing and placing signs and symbols: in order to create his narratives, Solakov apparently derives a complex combination of drawing and symbol from ancient etymological sources.

"Complicated Works"

"Dear visitor, you have a choice to make." In 2001, at the Kunsthalle Zurich, Solakov used a method that has long been widely used by contemporary artists: verbal instructions, i.e., instructing the viewer. The direction mentioned above can be read at the entrance to his installation The Choice. After taking a moment to consider, the visitor chooses to enter either the room on the left or the room on the right, but he cannot go into both. He is then confronted with either a sealed golden chest sinking partially into the wall or, on the other side of the same wall, the inner part of the chest presented in a mirrored way, into which one can slip a hand, only to find nothing inside. The visitor, however, can only guess at the "contents" of the other room. Instructions—which, in this case, demand that visitors make a decision—are however only one of the many acts of speech Solakov employs in his large installations.

Far more layers are involved in his installations containing detailed texts that contribute considerably to the development of an entire complex of themes and combine with other visual media to create an actual *Gesamtkunstwerk.* The various media open up layer after layer of sometimes contradictory readings, fragmenting the work into a multifaceted cabinet of curiosities rich with content. Solakov himself simply describes these types of works as "complicated works."[8] Among this group are large installations such as The Truth (The Earth is Plane, the World is Flat) (1992–95), El Bulgaro. The Sensational Discovery (2000), and Discussion (Property) (2007).

The latter was created for the 2007 Venice Biennale. It consists of video works produced in the style of news reports, an AK-47 assault rifle, life-size technical-looking drawings of twelve different rifles manufactured in Bulgaria that, of course, all resemble the AK-47, Cyrillic letters in vinyl lettering, a drawing on the wall depicting *Lactobacillus bulgaricus,* and a handwritten text densely covering the entire surface of the wall. This forms the foundation for a disturbing, ambiguous, total multimedia installation. A first-person narrator—the artist—recounts the "dispute" between Russia and Bulgaria over the sale of Russian machine guns, i.e., the assault rifles produced in Bulgaria based on the license given free by the Russians in socialist times. He describes unsuccessful attempts to get manufacturers and diplomats to provide opinions on the licensing dispute. Despite the obvious narrative perspective, the mode of language remains factual, neutral. It cites dates and people; along with the videos, it is a sort of documentary-style language. Although he bases the work on journalistic methods, he remains open thanks to the process of writing things down by hand, and this forces the question of how far the narrator can be trusted, or of how closely the story sticks to the facts. Appropriately enough, the text ends by turning to the absurd—something that is typical of Solakov—and closing with the sarcastic remark: *"I don't know what arguments the two sides had offered to clear all the hurdles. If I can make an educated guess, they were probably more serious than: 'Did the Russians ever obtain a license for using our Cyrillic alphabet over the centuries, which, as everybody knows, was invented by the Bulgarian brothers Cyril and Methodius back in the ninth century, or for eating* Lactobacillus bulgaricus, *the tiny bacteria that makes the best yoghurt?' So, after all those years of wrangling over property rights, I feel personally satisfied that, at least in the assault rifle sector of the international arms trade, there will finally be relative peace."*

In Discussion (Property), the artist succeeds in translating with incomparable ease a politically controversial theme into a complicated narrative told through a variety of media—and despite an obvious tendency to favor the absurd, he applies analytical, keen commentary, full of acerbic irony, to contemporary events.

The End: Things In Between

Throughout his oeuvre, Solakov plays in a virtuosic manner with an endless variety of possible ways to use language in art. Besides classic visual media, language also serves the development of his absurd stories—and ultimately, the creation of a narrative work in which the world in its sheer complexity is permanently manifested.

From the succinct, brief text to the large installation overflowing with narratives, he presents histories and stories as highly unique phenomena, located in between word and image, between art and reality. In the process, he proves to be a gifted narrator, as well as an extraordinarily unorthodox conceptual artist, who encounters the world—including the art world—with burlesque humor, an ironic sense of distance, and even sometimes with blatant sarcasm. In his wonderful, absurd image and text stories, this alert observer of human deficiencies tells of a world that long ago squandered its ideals—but does not seem to have lost its sense of (black) humor in the process.

1 Nedko Solakov: A 12 1/3 (and even more) Year Survey, exh. cat. Casino Luxembourg: Forum d'art contemporain, Luxembourg; Rooseum Center for Contemporary Art, Malmö; O.K Centrum für Gegenwartskunst, Linz (Vienna and Bolzano, 2003).

2 Brian O'Doherty, "Inside the White Cube: The Ideology of the Gallery Space" first appeared in 1976 as a series of three essays in Artforum and was later published in book form as Inside the White Cube: The Ideology of the Gallery Space (San Francisco, 1986), pp. 79–80.

3 Dan Perjovschi and Nedko Solakov. Walls and Floors (Without the Ceiling), exh. cat. BA-CA Kunstforum, Vienna (Nuremberg, 2008), p. 74; in A Life (Black & White) he had two painters painting the exhibition space simultaneously for the duration of the 2001 Venice Biennale: one painting the room white, the other black.

4 Wolfgang Max Faust. Bilder werden Worte: Zum Verhältnis von bildender Kunst und Literatur (Cologne, 1987).

5 Nedko Solakov: A High Level Public Art Project with a Catalogue, exh. cat., Malmö Konsthall (Malmö, 2004).

6 Dan Perjovschi and Nedko Solakov 2008 (see note 3), p. 78.

7 Ibid.

8 See www.nedkosolakov.net.

Zwischendinge
Zum (prekären) Verhältnis von Bild und Text

Konrad Bitterli

»Es ist wie mit Leuten zu reden. Das, was dem Reden mit Menschen am Nächsten kommt, ist diese Art zu zeichnen.« *Nedko Solakov*

Aufgeräumt und vollständig leer wirkt der Oberlichtsaal der Königlichen Akademie, der Ausstellungsraum IASPIS, in Stockholm – und dennoch steht er neugierigen Besuchern offen. Er erinnert an Le Vide von Yves Klein, der 1958 eine entleerte Galerie zur Ausstellung erklärte. Eine der radikalsten Formulierungen der Moderne wirkt nach, nur ein kleiner Papierknäuel – in der Tat handelt es sich um Abdeckband – liegt verloren in einer Ecke: eine subtile künstlerische Geste oder doch ein achtlos liegengelassenes Überbleibsel vom Abbau der vorangegangenen Ausstellung? Letzteres eher nicht, denn der Knäuel scheint (zu) ordentlich zur Kugel gepresst, während die beiden Enden des Abdeckbandes auf Bodenniveau sorgsam mit der Wand verbunden und in der Raumecke zusammengeführt sind. Gleich darüber ist in krakeliger Handschrift zu lesen: *»›I'm sick of being constantly used to define others' fields of interest. I'm sick of it. I will remain till the rest of my life in this corner, grieving…‹ – the adhesive tape said to the white wall and the grey floor.«*

Es ist, als würde das Kreppband zum Publikum sprechen und seine Frustration angesichts der misslichen Lage zwischen Boden und Wand spontan zum Ausdruck bringen. Dem alltäglichen Gebrauchsgegenstand, nach ordentlicher Verwendung offenbar unordentlich liegengelassen, wird eine menschliche Stimme verliehen, es wird ihm eine Persönlichkeit zugestanden, genauso wie Boden und Wand, selbst wenn diese stumm bleiben. Die Personifizierung der Dingwelt ist eine erzählerische Methode, der man in der Tradition von Fabeln und Märchen begegnet, wo Tiere genauso miteinander sprechen wie Bäume und Sträucher oder Himmel und Mond. In einer Ausstellung zeitgenössischer Kunst hingegen mag die eigentümlich naive Direktheit irritieren. Allerdings hat bei genauer Lektüre der Monolog des frustrierten Abdeckbands sehr wohl mit einer Kunstpräsentation zu tun: Im Grunde handelt er nämlich von den unsichtbaren, weil sorgältig weggeräumten Infrastrukturen, die es ermöglichen, Ausstellungen zu realisieren, im gegebenen Fall eben das Abdeckband, das dazu gedient haben wird, die Wand sauber weiß zu streichen beziehungsweise den Boden grau, ohne dass die Farben ineinander verlaufen.

In der (unaufgeräumten) Zelle

Den kurzen Monolog könnte man als bissigen Kommentar eines genervten Künstlers zum nachlässig aufräumenden Museumspersonal (miss)verstehen. Doch Nedko Solakov dürfte sich ob der skandinavischen Nachlässigkeit gefreut haben: Der Knäuel scheint liegengelassen, obwohl ihn die Museumsmitarbeiter in Tat und Wahrheit wegwerfen wollten. Doch genau solche Momente des Unperfekten, des zutiefst Menschlichen greift der bulgarische Künstler mit Vorliebe auf und nutzt sie als Ausgangspunkt für sein Schaffen, das gleichzeitig überraschender Kommentar, anekdotische Erzählung oder gedankliche Weiterführung sein kann. Mehr noch: Sie funktionieren als Motor, der seine künstlerische Phantasie antreibt. Solakov erfindet Anekdoten, in denen sich alltägliche Nachlässigkeiten in Überlegungen zum menschlichen Wohlbefinden verwandeln können. Der Sehvorgang wird dabei zum eigentlichen Leseakt: Das Vertraute gerät zur Anregung für witzige Narrationen wie für eine grundlegende Reflexion über Kunst. Denn Solakov zieht den Betrachter mit seinem Verweis auf das zwischen zwei Ausstellungen Liegengebliebene hinein in einen Diskurs über das Ausstellen von Kunst beziehungsweise über die Bedingungen von deren Präsentation. Im Gegensatz zu anderen Vertretern der Gegenwartskunst tut er dies nicht, indem er die musealen Konventionen analysiert und vordringlich als »Kunst über Kunst« thematisiert. Vielmehr verkleidet er seine listig-versteckte Analyse in eine beiläufige Geschichte, eine Anekdote mit drei Protagonisten: Wand, Boden und Abdeckband, eine prekäre Dreiecksbeziehung wie jene von Kunst, Künstler und Kurator mit den dazugehörigen Beziehungskomplikationen. Doch nicht genug mit der einen, kaum sichtbaren Intervention. Die scheinbar leere Galerie ist dicht bevölkert mit Textfetzen, die er, zuweilen durch flüchtige Zeichnungen ergänzt, an Wänden, über Kanten, neben Schaltern oder unverputzten Bohrlöchern anbringt. Zu letzterem heißt es lakonisch *»a major hole (one of the biggest in this very room)«,* während ein blobartiges Minimännchen überraschende Selbsterkenntnisse zum besten gibt: *»I'm stupid and I kind of like it«.*

Chat (2001) betitelt Solakov die materiell entleerte, gedanklich übervolle Ausstellung mit Text- und Zeichnungsminiaturen. Weitere folgen, und der Künstler fasst sie in A 12 1/3 (and even more) Year Survey (2003–2005)[1] zum Werkblock A (not so) White Cube (seit 2001) zusammen, so wie der Titel der entsprechenden Ausstellung im New Yorker P.S.1. Der Begriff »White Cube« selbst bezieht sich auf Brian O'Dohertys Essay Inside the White Cube. The Ideology of the Gallery Space über die Bedingungen des Ausstellens von Kunst: »Die Entwicklung der freischwebenden weißen Zelle gehört zu den Triumphen der Moderne, eine Entwicklung, die ihre ästhetischen, ökonomischen und technischen Aspekte hat. [...] Die weiße Zelle hielt Philistertum draußen und erlaubte es der Moderne, ihre unablässigen Versuche, sich selbst zu definieren, zu einem Ende zu bringen.«[2] Dem erwidert Solakov nüchtern: »der Begriff des White Cube ist ja der eines perfekten Hintergrunds, um zwei- oder dreidimensionale Kunst auszustellen, den es ja in Wirklichkeit nicht gibt«.[3]

Traditionen zwischen Bild und Text

Mit dem Hinweis auf den White Cube verbindet Solakov sein vordergründig erzählerisches Schaffen mit einer dezidiert konzeptuellen Haltung, wie sie die Gegenwartskunst unter dem Begriff »postkonzeptuell« kategorisiert. Er jongliert mit modernistischen Vorstellungen von der Reinheit und Selbstbezüglichkeit bildender Kunst, indem er sich beispielsweise der Sprache als Kommunikationsmittel mit offensichtlichem Wirklichkeitsbezug bedient. Fragt man nach der Verwendung von Texten in seinem Werk, wird man danach fragen müssen, welche möglichen Verbindungen sich zwischen Wort und Bild ergeben – wobei Bild stets unterschiedlichste Bildmedien meint. In seiner hybriden künstlerischen Strategie nutzt Solakov Sprache als gedanklichen Katalysator, und zwar im Bild, ums Bild und übers Bild.

Ein solches Vorgehen findet Vorläufer in der Avantgarde des 20. Jahrhunderts: Mit der Auflösung überlieferter Gattungsgrenzen kommt der Benutzung der Sprache in der Kunst unerwartete Bedeutung zu. Bereits in kubistischen Collagen finden sich eingefügte Textfragmente als Wirklichkeitsverweise, spätestens aber mit Marcel Duchamps Verschiebung vom retinalen zum mentalen Kunstbegriff wird Sprache integraler Bestand bildkünstlerischer Werke. Diese Entwicklungen kulminieren in den 1960er-Jahren in sprachlichen Mitteilungen, in denen der Objektcharakter des Kunstwerks vollends aufgehoben wird. Seither erproben Kunstschaffende linguistische Strategien in immer neuen Variationen. Der Kritiker Wolfgang Max Faust hat das Phänomen als »Lingualisierung« bezeichnet.[4] Dabei unterscheidet er erstens den Einbezug der Sprache ins Kunstwerk, zweitens die Verwendung der Sprache als Medium der bildenden Kunst und drittens ihre Benutzung neben dem Werk. Wie kein anderer zeitgenössischer Künstler spielt Solakov das gesamte Spektrum potenzieller Sprachverwendungen im bildkünstlerischen Kontext durch. Wenn im Folgenden exemplarische Funktionen von Texten in ausgewählten Werken diskutiert werden, so bleiben sie fragmentarisch angesichts eines vor Fabulierlust überquellenden Schaffens, das sich aller Möglichkeiten zeitgenössischer Kunst zwischen den Dingen, zwischen Medien, aber auch zwischen Wort und Bild souverän bedient – von den erwähnten Ausstellungskommentaren über (nicht so) reine Textarbeiten bis zu narrativen Strukturen und komplexen Wort-Bild-Kombinationen.

(Nicht so) reine Textarbeiten

»The beginning of… It smells a bit in a doggy way, isn't it? These stones down here. And you wonder how did the dogs make it up here. I'll tell you – I just took the stones from the garden behind you.« Das steht zu Beginn der Intervention an der Kunsthalle Malmö. Als ob das Museum umgestülpt worden wäre, überführt Solakov seine Textarbeiten in den Außenraum. Entlang der Dachkante finden sich verspielte Kommentare, verkürzte Zeichnungen und witzige Eingriffe – vom Publikum allerdings mehr zu erahnen als zu sehen. Ein Katalog mit den schwedischen Übersetzungen der englischen Texte dient als Führer, mit dem man sich auf Entdeckungsreise »durch« die Ausstellung begibt: A High Level Public Art Project with a Catalogue (2004) lautet der tiefgründige Titel der hoch liegenden Arbeit.[5] Auch hier versieht der Künstler zufällig Vorgefundenes oder subtile Miniaturinszenierungen mit Kommentaren. Allerdings sprechen nicht die Dinge selbst zum Besucher, sondern der Künstler gibt sich eine eigene Stimme und nimmt eine auktoriale Perspektive ein – in anderen Arbeiten gibt er sich als »little man« gar ein Alter Ego: Er weist auf den Werkprozess hin, kommentiert und erfindet wundervolle Anekdoten zu versetzten Dachplatten, lockeren Schrauben, vom Winde verwehten Federn. An einem Museum angebracht, thematisiert das Werk weniger die Funktion des Gebäudes, sondern wendet sich alltäglichen Dingen zu und öffnet das Museum entschieden zur Welt.

Gleiches gelingt dem Künstler nicht nur vier, sondern auch ein paar tausend Meter, das heißt bis zu 10 000 Meter über dem Boden: *»Actually the aileron closest to you would very much like* *to say ›Hello!‹ and to greet you by waving up and down three times. But his mother, the cockpit, has rules. He will greet you later while landing.«* Dies steht auf einem Flügel eines Luxair-Flugzeugs zu lesen. Zum Glück befolgt das Cockpit der Boeing 737 die Wünsche seines Flügels nicht. Zur Ausstellung **Faiseurs d'histoires** im Casino Luxembourg entwickelt Solakov luftige Textarbeiten, die an sechs Flugzeugen angebracht werden und sich durch überraschende formale Nüchternheit auszeichnen. Es handelt sich um reine Textarbeiten, wie sie die klassische Konzeptkunst entwickelt hat. Texte evozieren Bilder, sie analysieren und reflektieren die kategoriellen Möglichkeiten von Kunst. Solakov jedoch überwindet den selbstbezüglichen Rahmen von »Kunst über Kunst« und findet seine Inhalte außerhalb des geschlossenen Kunstsystems im menschlichen Dasein, in seinen Emotionen und Ängsten. Wiederum kommuniziert die Dingwelt in leicht heimtückischer Art mit dem Betrachter. Es fehlt indes der schützende Ausstellungsrahmen, weshalb die Texte nicht primär als Kunst gelesen werden. Das führt zu einer vollständig »losgelösten« Lektüre durch ein Publikum, das wie der Künstler selbst möglicherweise ebenfalls an Flugangst leidet. **On the Wing** (seit 1999) ist ein Irritationspotenzial eigen, das über den Wolken über die Höhen und Tiefen des alltäglichen Daseins sinnieren lässt.

Gezeichnete (Kunst-)Geschichten

In der Regel beginnen Märchen mit »Es war einmal…«. Diese Einleitung evoziert zurückliegende Epochen, in der eine Erzählung stattgefunden hat – nicht als Fiktion, sondern, zumindest in der kindlichen Phantasie, als Tatsachenbericht. Es wird eine andere Realität beschworen, eine Parallelwelt, die in Bezug steht zur eigenen Wirklichkeitserfahrung, diese aber durch das Aufheben rationaler Gesetzmäßigkeiten radikal erweitert. Geschichten haben daher zugleich etwas zutiefst Beunruhigendes und Befreiendes. Gleiches gilt für Solakovs Geschichten, die als Bild-Text-Kombinationen in mehrteiligen Zyklen entstehen. Deren durchgehende Nummerierung gibt einen narrativen Ablauf vor, der zuweilen gezielt konterkariert wird. **Once upon a Time** (1995/96), **…and they lived happily ever after** (1999), **Good & Bad** (2003), **Fears** (2006/07), geschaffen im klassischen Medium Tusche auf Papier, lassen Solakovs zeichnerische Strategie zwischen Bild und Text in geradezu exemplarischer Weise sichtbar werden: »Für mich sind Text und Bild absolut untrennbar; sie formen eine Einheit. Wenn ich eine Zeichnung mache […], habe ich immer die Geschichten unter dem gezeichneten Bild. Wenn ich ein Bild zeichne, weiß ich nur sehr vage, wie sich die Geschichte entwickeln wird.«[6]

Once Upon a Time führt in fünfzig Episoden aus der Gegenwart zurück in eine Epoche, in der Ritter ihr Unwesen trieben, und noch weiter zu den Wikingern oder in prähistorische Zeiten. Die Serie ist nicht als lineare Geschichte angelegt, sondern jedes einzelne Blatt erzählt eine Anekdote, wie diejenige der Frau, die immer wieder ins Haus zurückkehrt, um zu überprüfen, ob das Bügeleisen abgeschaltet ist – ironischerweise vor dem Hintergrund einer mittelalterlichen Szenerie. Eine alltägliche Erfahrung, die in der distanzierten Erzählweise zur wiederkehrenden Sorge wird, in der sich im Grunde das Unentrinnbare menschlicher Existenz spiegelt. Stufenweise entwickelt Solakov seine Geschichten: »Ich fange an, sie am unteren Rand des Blattes aufzuschreiben. […] Im Allgemeinen weiss ich nicht, wie die Geschichte ausgehen wird, und darum ist es sehr fesselnd, sie auf logische (und trotzdem reichlich absurde) Weise zu Ende zu führen, und das auf den verbleibenden Millimetern Papier. Aber weder ist der Text Erläuterung des Bildes, noch ist das Bild die Illustration des Textes. Sie können gar nicht anders als zusammenzuwirken.«[7]

Sorgfältig lavierend, füllt der Künstler das Blattgeviert mit Zeichnungen in Sepia, schwarzer oder weißer Tusche. Wie in Kinderbüchern ergänzt am unteren Blattrand der Text das Dargestellte. Bild und Text bilden eine untrennbare Einheit, selbst wenn sich gerade im Dazwischen überraschende Wendungen ergeben, sich paradoxe Lesarten einstellen. Solakov spielt mit den Gepflogenheiten des Illustrierens, indem er alltäglichen Geschehnissen kryptische Zeichnungen hinzufügt oder visuelle Vorgaben im Text ins Fantastische umlenkt. Kurz: Er schafft Zwischendinge, witzige, gelegentlich bösartige, stets absurde Bild-Erzählungen aus einer Welt, deren leichtfüßiger Witz über menschliche Unzulänglichkeiten Denkräume öffnet und eine grundlegende Reflexion über die menschliche Existenz und den Stand der Dinge in der Welt ermöglicht – auch jener in der Welt der Kunst.

So thematisiert ein Blatt aus Once Upon a Time mittels einer naiv anmutenden Anekdote das künstlerische Schaffen. Ein Hofkünstler soll zu Ehren der Geliebten seines fürstlichen Auftraggebers das ultimative Kunstwerk erschaffen: *»Finally he ... got it – he just left the white canvas as it was – empty. The count really liked the stuff...«* Das Blatt bleibt lapidar leer – mit Ausnahme des handgeschriebenen Textes am Rand. Konsequent aus der Erzählung hergeleitet, unterläuft es jegliche Konventionen und lässt eine konzeptuelle Haltung anklingen, die sich belustigt an den künstlerischen Traditionen mit ihren Fantasmen des reinen Kunstwerks, wie es seine Vollendung im »entleerten« Bild findet. Oder anders formuliert: Solakov entwickelt eine alternative Lektüre zur modernistischen Suche nach dem Absoluten in der Kunst und übersetzt sie in eine wundervolle Bildgeschichte. Meist jedoch quellen seine Zeichnungen vor unbändiger Fabulierlust und bildnerischer Fantasie über, die sich von der Bibel über Historien oder Märchen bis zur heutigen Alltags- und Hochkultur hemmungslos aller greifbarer Quellen bedient.

Sprachliche Übersetzungen

Bei aller Raffinesse der Ausführung in zarten Lavierungen und weißen Höhungen ist der Zeichnung stets etwas Flüchtiges eigen. Das verbindet sie mit der Sprache, namentlich der gesprochenen. Solakovs Sprachgebrauch ist denn auch kein literarischer, auch wenn er sich narrativer Konventionen bedient, sondern ein alltäglicher. Das mag damit zusammenhängen, dass die Zeichnungen seit den 1990er-Jahren in der Regel von englischen Texten begleitet werden, also vom Künstler in einer Fremdsprache verfasst sind. Zwar lässt er sie korrigieren, er zielt indes weniger auf kunstvollen Sprachgebrauch als auf größtmögliche Verständlichkeit, die das Englische als Lingua franca erlaubt.

Deswegen verzichtet der Künstler sowohl auf hochtrabende rhetorische Figuren als auch auf allzu umgangssprachliche Ausdrücke. Da in seinen Texten oft in Dialogform kommuniziert wird, verwendet Solakov ein leicht verständliches gesprochenes Englisch. Gesprochene Sprache ist bekanntlich die Sprache mündlicher Überlieferung, von Mythen vor ihrer Festschreibung. Sie ist damit vergängliche Sprache; kaum geäußert, hat sie sich bereits verflüchtigt. Darin ist sie der Zeichnung wesensverwandt, speziell den temporären Interventionen in Ausstellungsräumen. Zeichnen und Setzen von Zeichen: Aus dem etymologischen Urgrund scheint Solakov seine Erzählungen als komplexe Verbindung von Zeichnen und Zeichen zu schöpfen.

»Complicated Works«

»Dear visitor, you have a choice to make.« Solakov bedient sich 2001 in der Kunsthalle Zürich einer längst zur weitverbreiteten künstlerischen Vorgehensweise gewordenen Methode, der

Handlungsanweisung. Am Eingang zur Installation **The Choice** ist diese Aufforderung zu lesen. Nach individuellem Ermessen betritt der Besucher den linken oder rechten Raum, während ihm der andere verwehrt bleibt. Und so sieht er sich mit einer halb in die Wand eingelassenen goldenen Schatulle konfrontiert beziehungsweise ihrem gespiegelten Gegenüber auf der andern Seite der Wand. In diese darf der Besucher zumindest hineingreifen, findet jedoch nichts vor, während er zugleich nur Mutmassungen über den »Inhalt« des anderen Raumes anstellen kann. Handlungsanweisungen, die in diesem Fall eine Entscheidung des Publikums fordern, sind indes nur einer der zahlreichen Sprechakte, die Solakov in raumgreifenden Installationen verwendet.

Vielschichtiger sind jene Installationen, in denen ausführliche Texte maßgeblich zur Entwicklung eines ganzen Themenkomplexes dienen und sich mit anderen bildkünstlerischen Medien zu eigentlichen »Gesamtkunstwerken« verbinden. Die Darstellungsmittel eröffnen sich überlagernde, zuweilen gar widersprüchliche Lektüremöglichkeiten und splittern die Arbeit in ein inhaltlich reich facettiertes Panoptikum auf. Solakov selbst hat diesen Typus einfach als »complicated works« bezeichnet.[8] Darunter finden sich raumgreifende Installationen wie beispielsweise **The Truth (The Earth is Plane, the World is Flat)** (1992–1995), **El Bulgaro. The Sensational Discovery** (2000) oder **Discussion (Property)** (2007).

Letztere, für die Biennale di Venezia 2007 entwickelt, umfasst Videoarbeiten im Stile von Nachrichtensendungen, ein Maschinengewehr vom Typ AK-47, technisch anmutende Zeichnungen im Format 1:1 all der Gewehrmodelle, die basierend auf der AK-47 in Bulgarien hergestellt worden waren, kyrillische Buchstaben in Folienschrift, eine Wandzeichnung des Lactobacillus Bulgaricus sowie einen von Hand geschriebenen Text, der sich über die gesamte Wandfläche verdichtet. Er bildet den Einstieg in die multimediale, irritierend-mehrdeutige Gesamtinstallation. Ein Icherzähler – der Künstler – berichtet vom »Disput« zwischen Russland und Bulgarien wegen des Verkaufs des russischen Maschinengewehrs, das aufgrund einer russischen Lizenz im vormaligen Ostblockstaat produziert worden war. Er schildert die erfolglosen Versuche, Hersteller und Diplomaten zu bewegen, sich zum Lizenzstreit zu äußern. Trotz offensichtlicher Erzählperspektive bleibt der Sprachduktus faktisch-neutral, führt Daten und Personen auf und wirkt zusammen mit den Videos im Grunde dokumentarisch. Obwohl er sich an journalistischen Methoden orientiert, bleibt er dank der manuellen Niederschrift offen, sodass sich die Frage aufdrängt, wie weit dem Erzähler zu vertrauen ist beziehungsweise inwiefern die Geschichte den Tatsachen entspricht. Sinnigerweise endet der Text in einer für Solakov typischen Wendung ins Absurde mit der sarkastischen Bemerkung: *»I don't know what arguments the two sides had offered to clear all the hurdles. If I can make an educated guess, they were probably more serious than: ›Did the Russians ever obtain a license for using our Cyrillic alphabet over the centuries, which as everybody knows, was invented by the Bulgarian brothers Cyril and Methodius back in the ninth century, or for eating* Lactobacillus Bulgaricus, *the tiny bacteria that makes the best yoghurt?‹ So, after all those years of wrangling over property rights, I feel personally satisfied that, at least in the assault rifle sector of the international arms trade, there will finally be relative peace.«*

Dem Künstler gelingt es mit **Discussion (Property)**, ein politisch brisantes Thema mit unvergleichlicher Leichtigkeit in eine komplexe, multimedial ausformulierte Erzählung zu übersetzen – und trotz offensichtlicher Tendenz zum Absurden einen analytisch-scharfen Kommentar zum Zeitgeschehen anzubringen – voll bissiger Ironie!

Ende: Zwischendinge

Virtuos spielt Solakov in seinem gesamten künstlerischen Œuvre in unendlichen Variationen mit den Möglichkeiten der Verwendung von Sprache in der Kunst. Neben den klassischen Bildmedien dient ihm die Sprache zur Entwicklung seiner irrwitzigen Geschichten – und letztlich zur Herstellung permanenter Welthaltigkeit.

Vom prägnanten Kurztext bis zur raumgreifenden Installation mit ausufernden Narrationen inszeniert er Geschichte und Geschichten als höchst eigenwillige Zwischendinge zwischen Wort und Bild, zwischen Kunst und Realität. Dabei erweist er sich als begnadeter Erzähler, zugleich auch als höchst unorthodoxer Konzeptkünstler, welcher der Welt – auch der Kunstwelt – mit burleskem Humor und ironischer Distanz, gelegentlich gar mit unverhohlenem Sarkasmus begegnet. In seinen wundervoll-absurden Bild-Text-Geschichten erzählt der wachsame Beobachter menschlicher Unzulänglichkeiten von einer Welt, die ihre Ideale längst verspielt hat – scheint dabei aber seinen (schwarzen) Humor kaum je zu verlieren.

1 Nedko Solakov. A 12 1/3 (and even more) Year Survey, Ausst.-Kat. Casino Luxembourg. Forum d'art contemporain, Luxemburg; Rooseum Center for Contemporary Art, Malmö; O.K Centrum für Gegenwartskunst, Linz, Wien und Bozen 2003.

2 Brian O'Doherty, Inside the White Cube. The Ideology of the Gallery Space (1976) erschien als eine Serie von drei Essays in der Zeitschrift Artforum und wurde später als Buch veröffentlicht: Inside the White Cube. The Ideology of the Gallery Space. San Francisco 1986. 1996 erschien es auf Deutsch: Brian O'Doherty, In der weißen Zelle. Inside the White Cube, hrsg. v. Wolfgang Kemp, Berlin 1996, hier S. 88–89.

3 Dan Perjovschi, Nedko Solakov. Walls and Floors (Without the Ceiling), Ausst.-Kat. BA-CA Kunstforum, Wien, Nürnberg 2008, S. 74; in A Life (Black & White) lässt er 2001 an der Biennale von Venedig seinen Ausstellungsraum während der gesamten Dauer gleichzeitig schwarz und weiß streichen.

4 Wolfgang Max Faust. Bilder werden Worte. Zum Verhältnis von bildender Kunst und Literatur, Köln 1987.

5 Nedko Solakov. A High Level Public Art Project with a Catalogue, Ausst.-Kat. Malmö Konsthall, Malmö 2004.

6 Dan Perjovschi, Nedko Solakov 2008 (wie Anm. 3), S. 78.

7 Ebd.

8 Siehe www.nedkosolakov.net.

Deutsche Übersetzung siehe Seite 198

(Left wing)

1. Dear passenger, somewhere down over there, behind the second mountain, on the left bank of a tiny river, is a little hill. In that little hill there is a little hole and in that hole lives a little mole. Frankly, she would love to be in your place right now—almost 10,000 meters above the ground....

2. Don't worry. Everything will be fine. You will make it. You will find the money....

3. This very wing has two edges—a leading edge and a trailing edge. They are brothers (or something). Sometimes the trailing edge gets paranoid. "I could never be a leading one!" he worries. Luckily, his brother is capable of calming him down: "My dear, I would never exist if I didn't have your support. Have you ever known a leading edge to fly alone?"

4. Under this very wing there is a very small raindrop hanging on to the silver metal.... somewhere close to the wheel.... She is very happy. Why? Because later on she intends to drop down on that (sometimes snowy) mountain where her beloved cousins live. They are some of the best snowflakes in the World.

5. The same text appears on the right wing too.... but you better check.

6. Dear passenger, would you try to look at the sky above you—yes, exactly above you.... at that place where the not so deep blue becomes a very deep blue and where the very deep blue transits into the Universe's deepest colour.... If you can make it, you will be able to see a beautiful scene—a sleeping extraterrestrial postman (maybe they use another word for the postman—who knows?). He is waiting for the nearest cable TV satellite to pass by. He missed the last episode of his soap and is waiting to get the story first hand....

(Right wing)

1. My dear passenger, did you see the silver dollar hidden at the very bottom of the compartment above your head? That's correct—it happens to be under your hand luggage. Take it later! It's yours.

2. Dear passenger, can you see that little cloud on the right.... so young and relatively small. He wants so much to be like the Big Mighty Guys (close to the horizon).... but, for the time being, he can't and that is why he is a bit sad.... but not so sad because his responsibility for the Atmosphere's image is not so big either....

3. Actually the aileron closest to you would very much like to say "Hello!" and to greet you by waving up and down three times. But his mother, the cockpit, has rules. He will greet you later while landing.

4. Hi! Yes, it's me who just said "Hi!"

4. (closer) If you keep staring at these very letters, be sure, you will fall asleep very, very soon.... just look at them. Look at us.... read us again and again.... again and again.... and your eyes are closing.... the friendly sound of the engine is caressing your body.... you are already sleeping although your eyes might be still open.... sleeping.... and the beautiful dream which disappeared so mysteriously this morning will visit you again....

5. The same text appears on the left wing too.... but you better check.

6. Lucky you! The most beautiful crew is in your plane.

6. (closer) If a housefly (Musca domestica) could be an astronaut, do you think she could, using appropriate housefly astronaut equipment, reach our altitude?

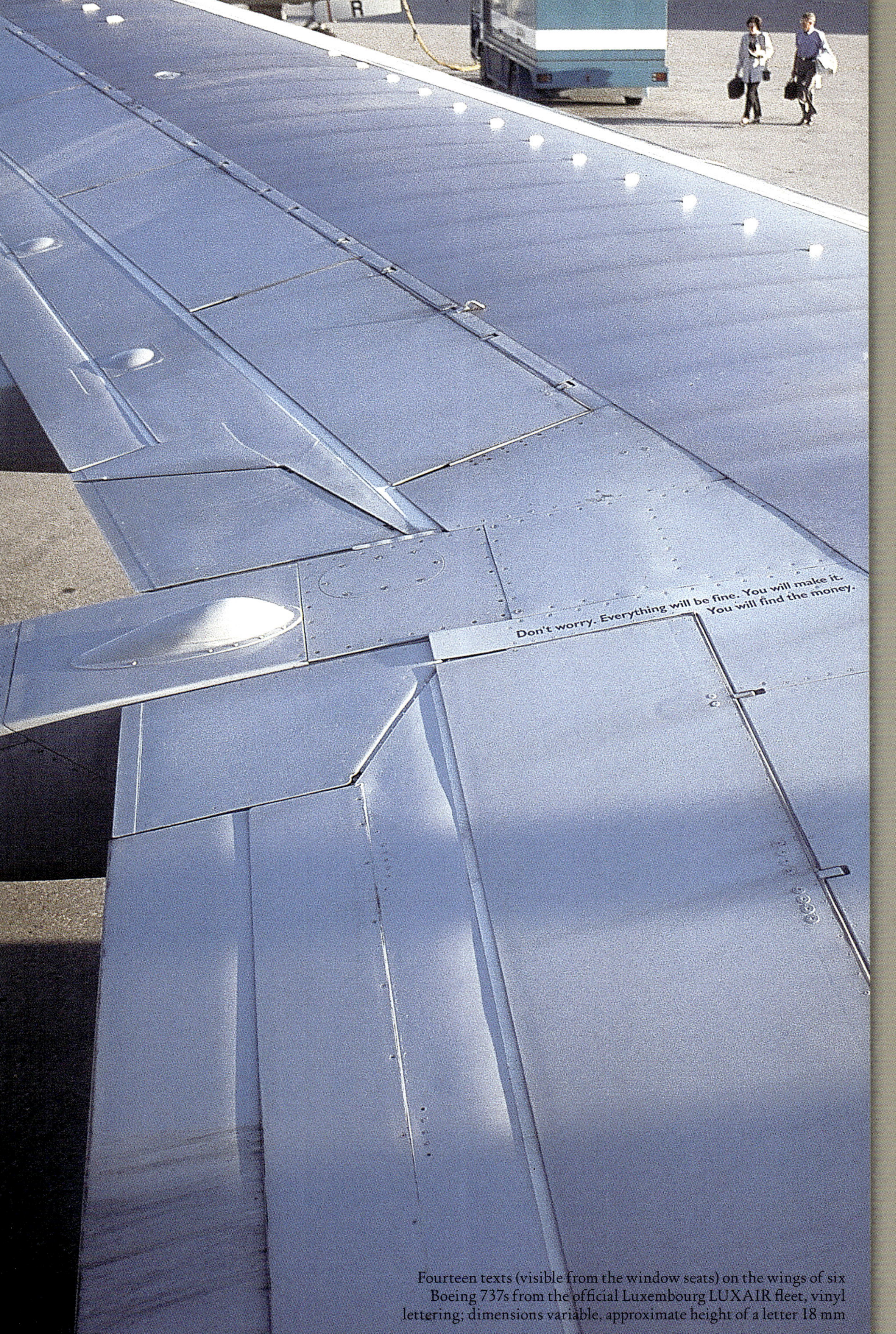

Fourteen texts (visible from the window seats) on the wings of six Boeing 737s from the official Luxembourg LUXAIR fleet, vinyl lettering; dimensions variable, approximate height of a letter 18 mm

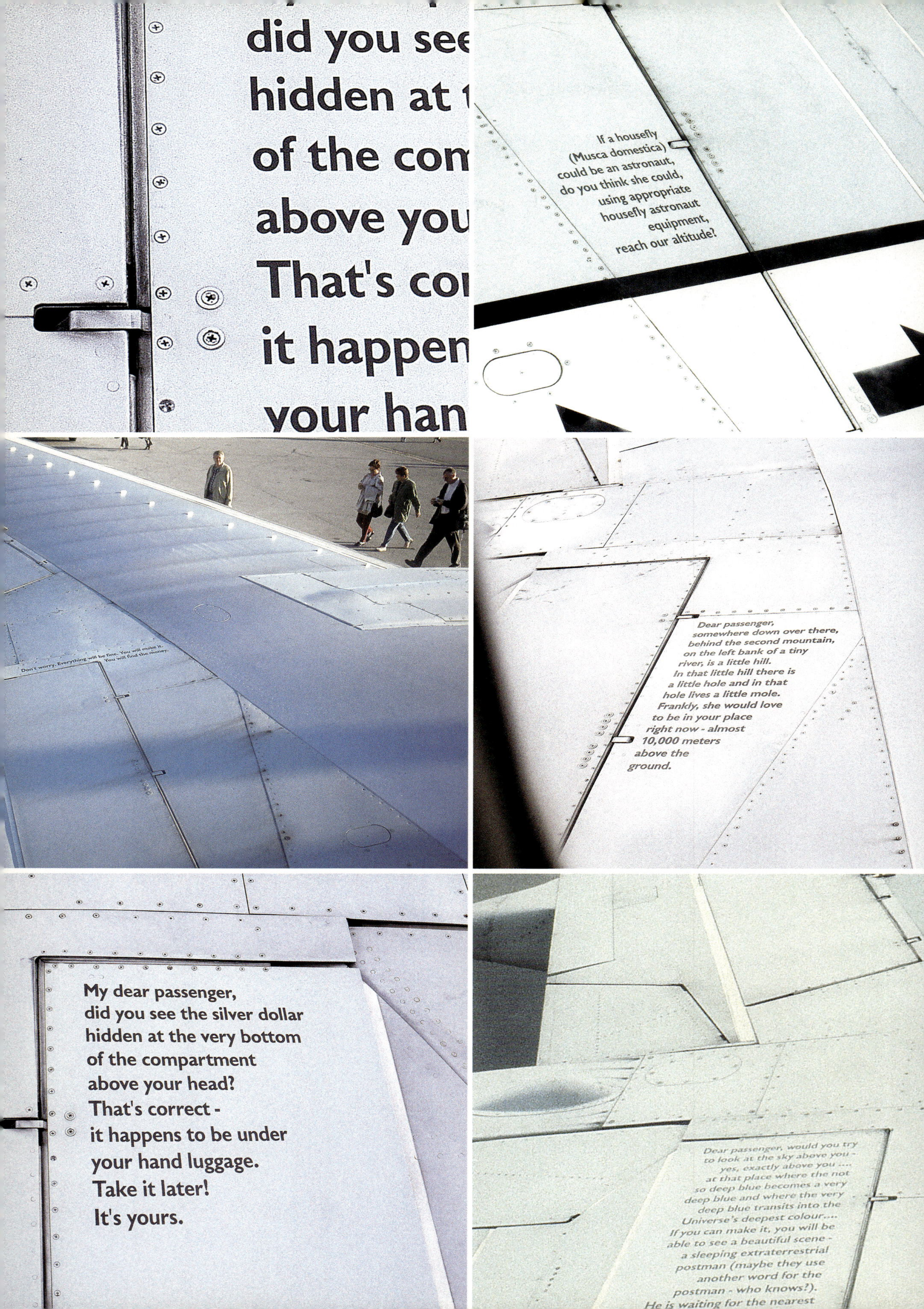
did you see
hidden at t
of the com
above you
That's cor
it happen
your han
If a housefly
(Musca domestica)
could be an astronaut,
do you think she could,
using appropriate
housefly astronaut
equipment,
reach our altitude?
Don't worry. Everything will be fine. You will make it.
You will find the money.
Dear passenger,
somewhere down over there,
behind the second mountain,
on the left bank of a tiny
river, is a little hill.
In that little hill there is
a little hole and in that
hole lives a little mole.
Frankly, she would love
to be in your place
right now - almost
10,000 meters
above the
ground.
My dear passenger,
did you see the silver dollar
hidden at the very bottom
of the compartment
above your head?
That's correct -
it happens to be under
your hand luggage.
Take it later!
It's yours.
Dear passenger, would you try
to look at the sky above you -
yes, exactly above you ....
at that place where the not
so deep blue becomes a very
deep blue and where the very
deep blue transits into the
Universe's deepest colour....
If you can make it, you will be
able to see a beautiful scene -
a sleeping extraterrestrial
postman (maybe they use
another word for the
postman - who knows?).
He is waiting for the nearest

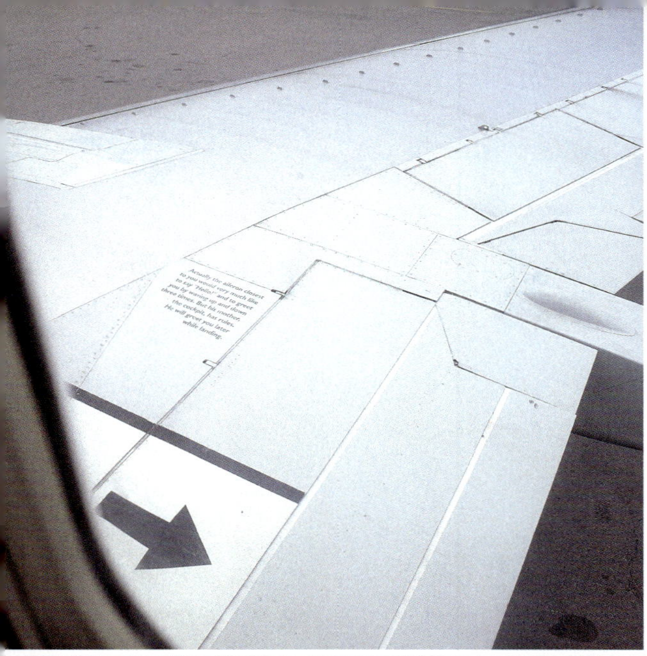

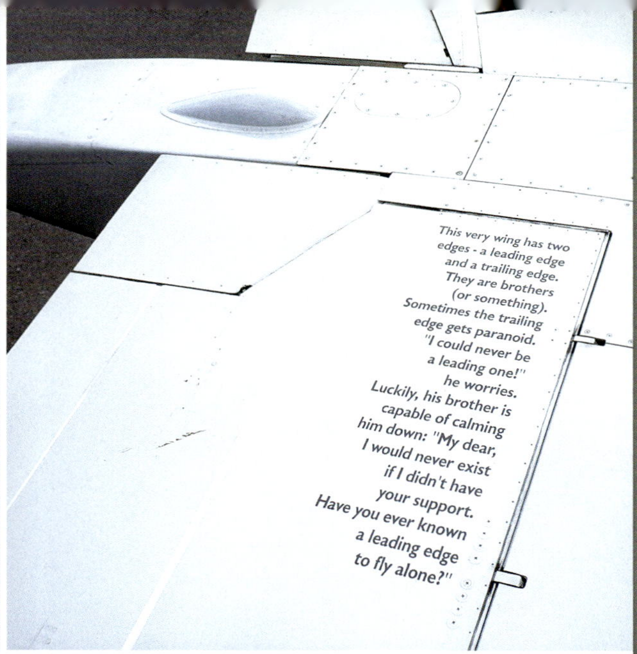

Actually the aileron closest to you would very much like to say "Hello!" and to greet you by waving up and down three times. But his mother, the cockpit, has rules. He will greet you later while landing.

This very wing has two edges - a leading edge and a trailing edge. They are brothers (or something). Sometimes the trailing edge gets paranoid. "I could never be a leading one!" he worries. Luckily, his brother is capable of calming him down: "My dear, I would never exist if I didn't have your support. Have you ever known a leading edge to fly alone?"

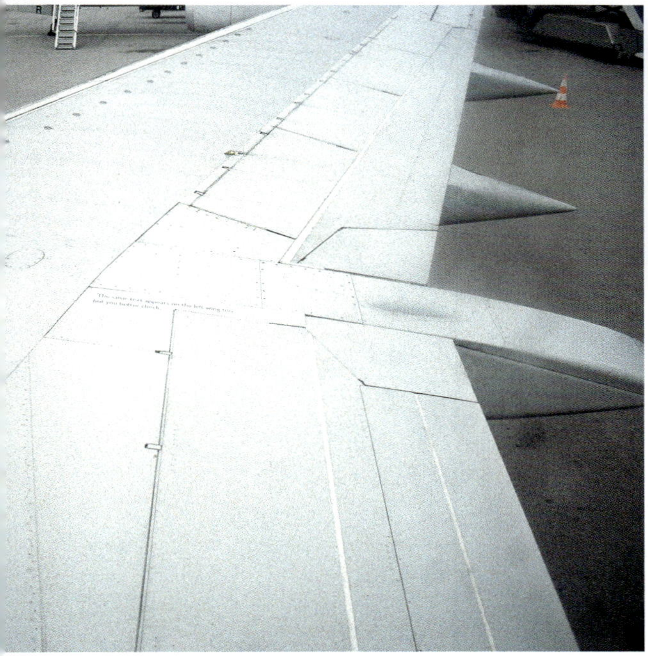

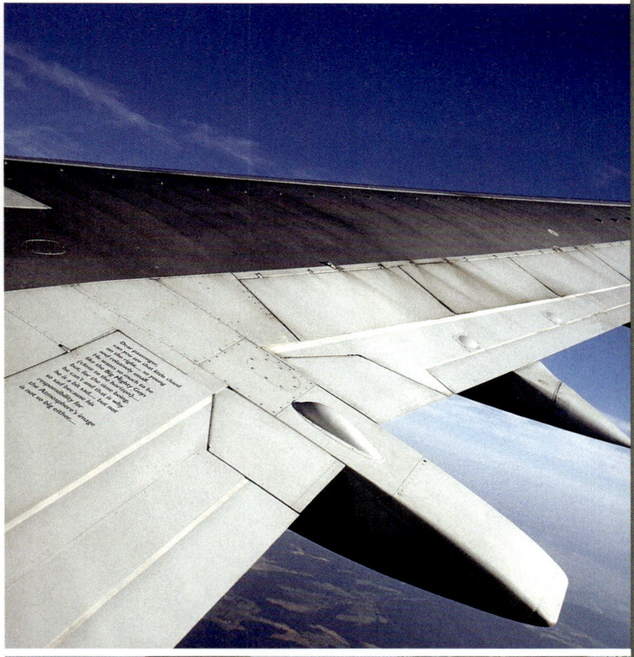

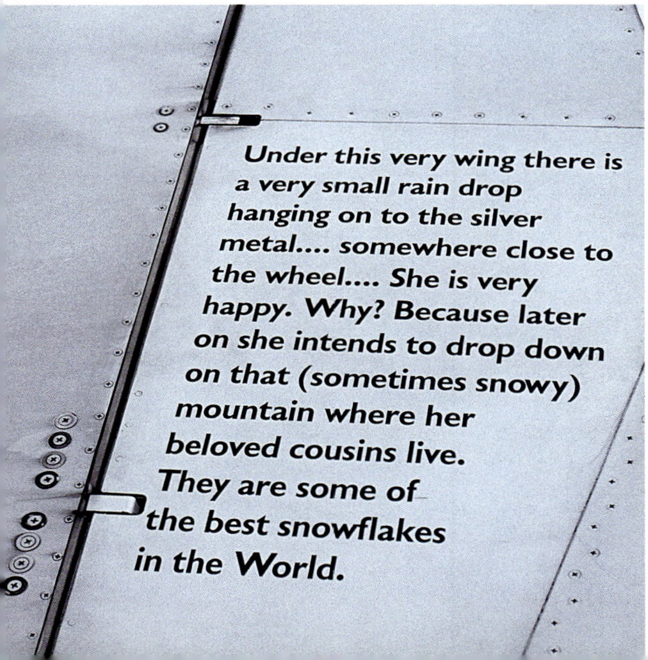

Dear passenger, can you see that little cloud on the right.... so young and relatively small. He wants so much to be like the Big Mighty Guys (close to the horizon).... but, for the time being, he can't and that is why he is a bit sad.... but not so sad because his responsibility for the Atmosphere's image is not so big either....

Under this very wing there is a very small rain drop hanging on to the silver metal.... somewhere close to the wheel.... She is very happy. Why? Because later on she intends to drop down on that (sometimes snowy) mountain where her beloved cousins live. They are some of the best snowflakes in the World.

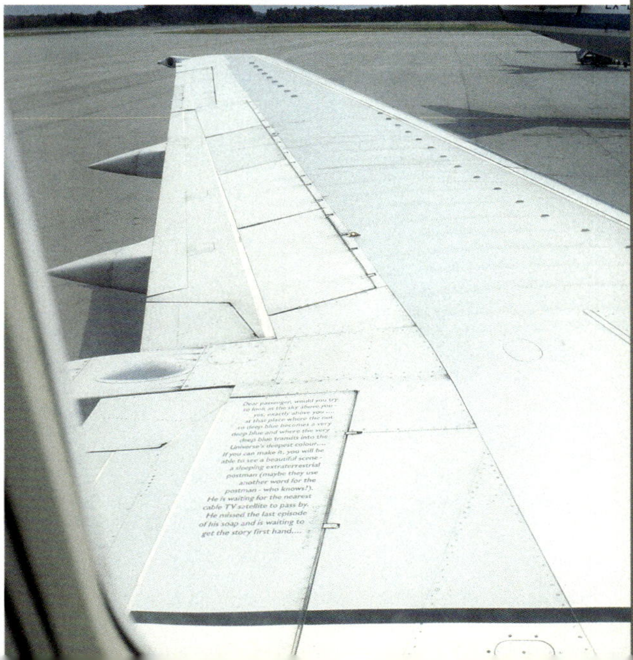

Dear passenger, would you try to look at the sky above you – yes, exactly above you .... at that place where the not so deep blue becomes a very deep blue and where the very deep blue transits into the Universe's deepest colour.... If you can make it, you will be able to see a beautiful scene – a sleeping extraterrestrial postman (maybe they use another word for the postman – who knows!). He is waiting for the nearest cable TV satellite to pass by. He missed the last episode of his soap and is waiting to get the story first hand....

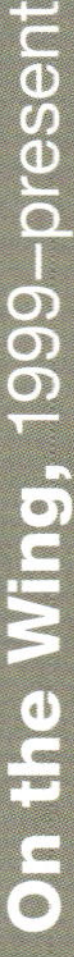

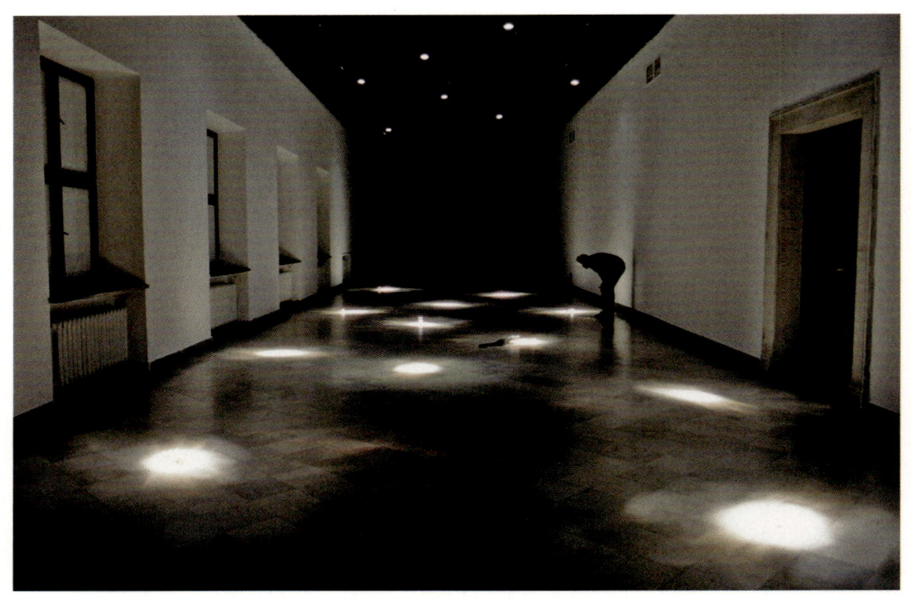

Children's toys, local sex advertisement, glass, water, dice,
artificial flower, felt-tip pen, handwritten texts on paper and stone,
twelve spotlights; dimensions variable

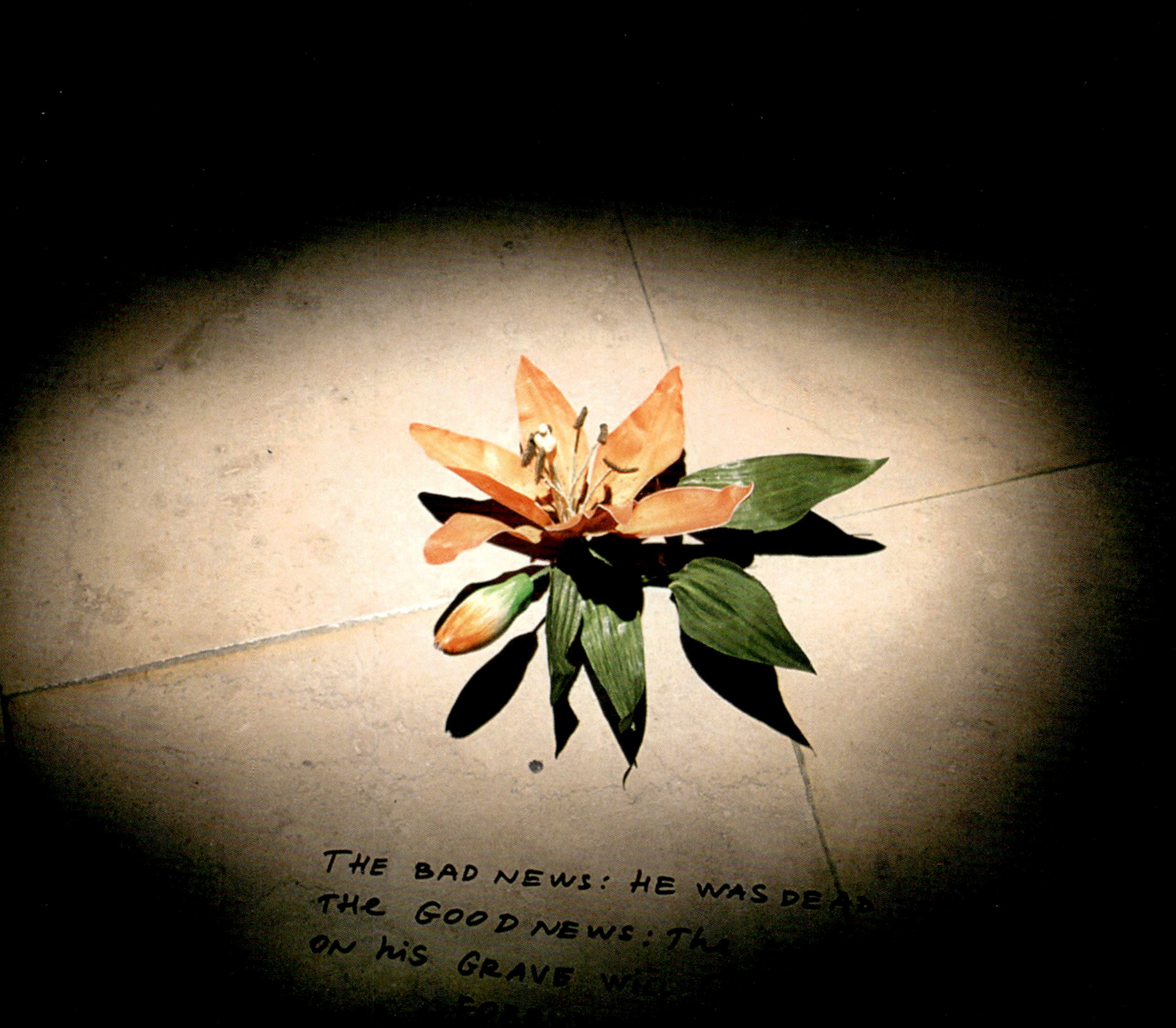

Good News, Bad News, 1998–present

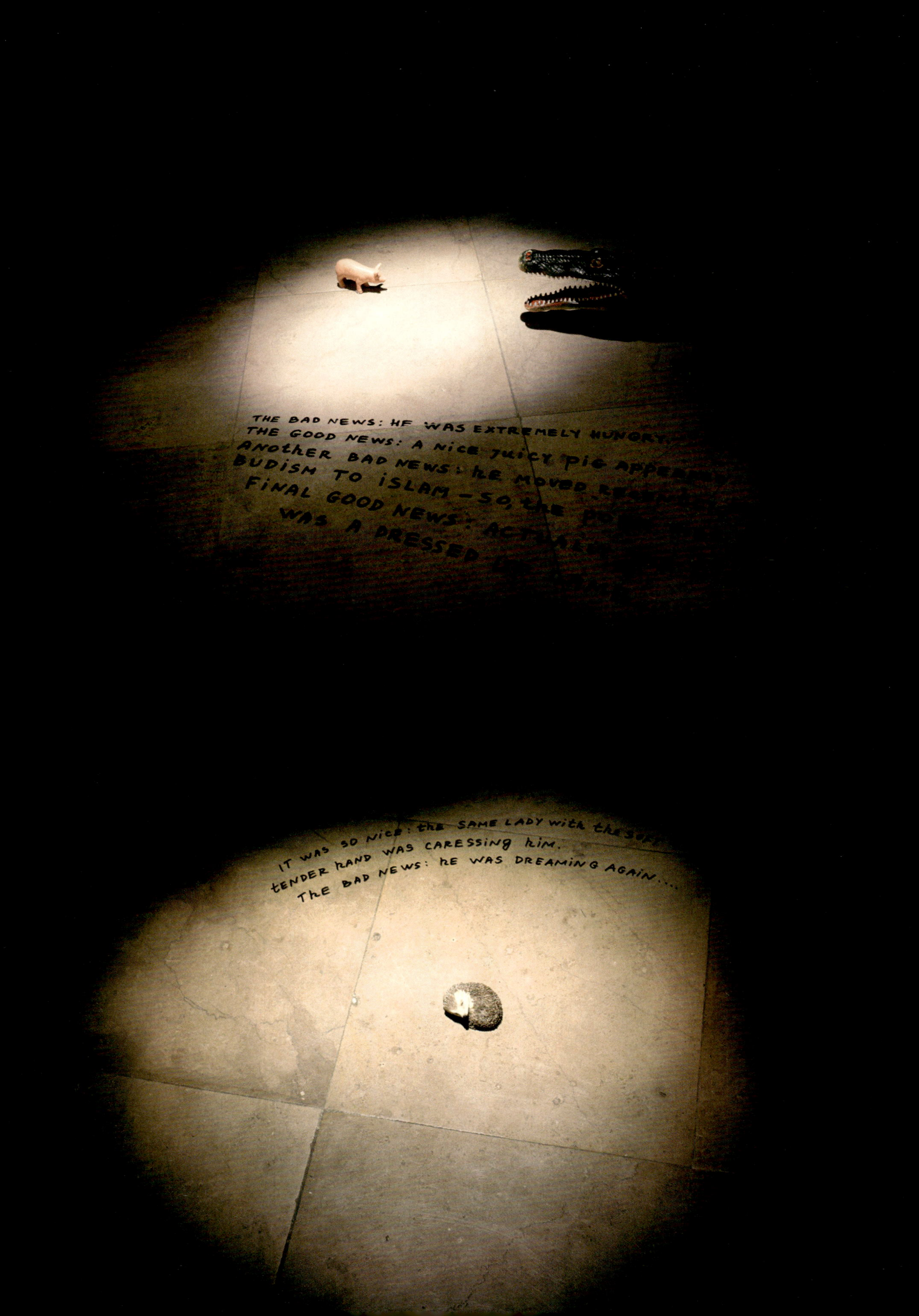

THE BAD NEWS: HE WAS EXTREMELY HUNGRY.
THE GOOD NEWS: A NICE JUICY PIG
ANOTHER BAD NEWS: HE MOVED
BUDISM TO ISLAM – SO, THE
FINAL GOOD NEWS:
WAS A DRESSED

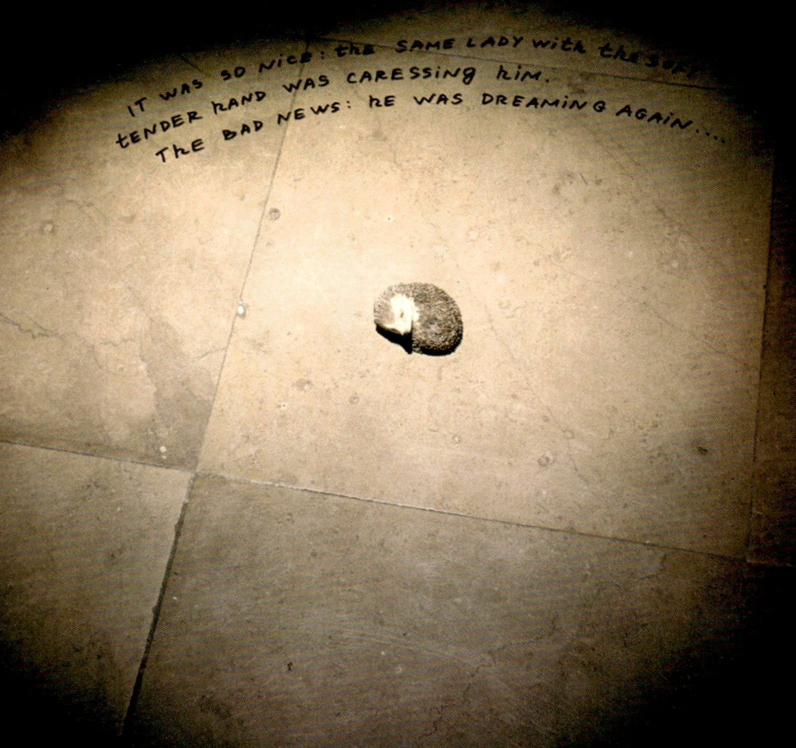
IT WAS SO NICE: THE SAME LADY WITH THE
TENDER HAND WAS CARESSING HIM.
THE BAD NEWS: HE WAS DREAMING AGAIN....

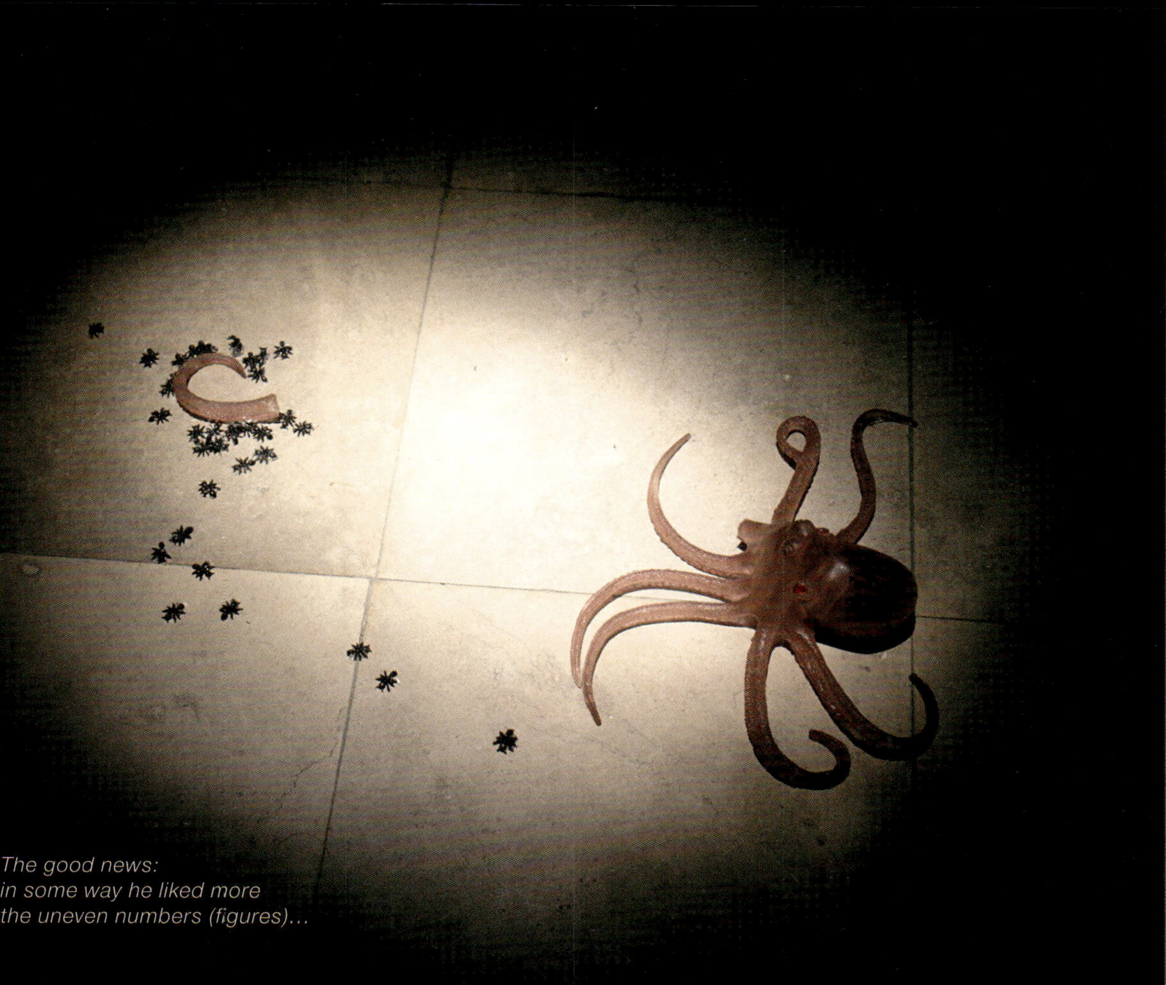

The good news:
in some way he liked more
the uneven numbers (figures)...

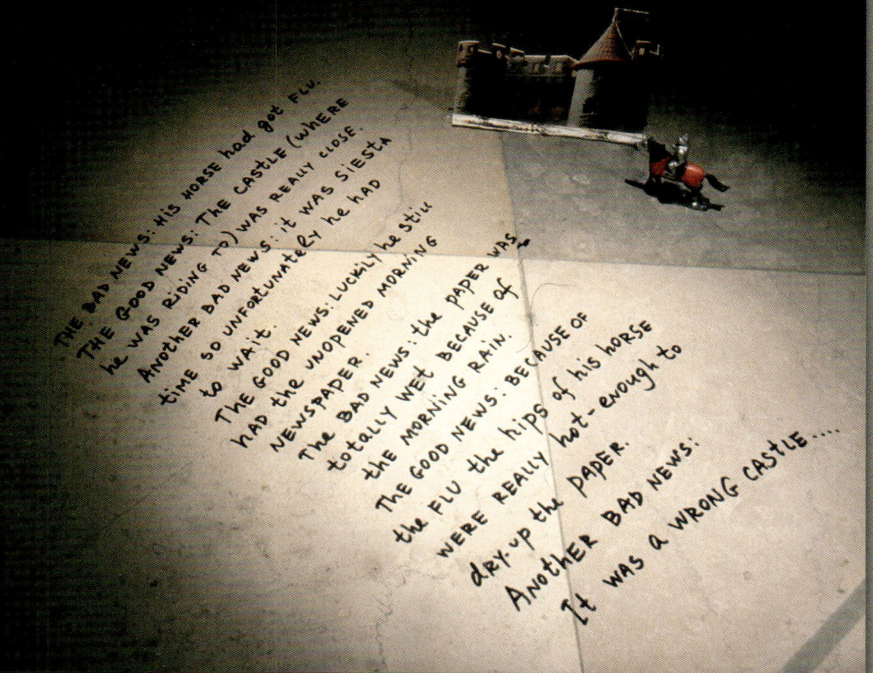

Deutsche Übersetzung siehe Seite 200

Top Secret *(created between December 1989 and February 1990) consists of an index box, filled with a series of cards detailing the artist's youthful collaboration with the Bulgarian secret police, which he stopped in 1983. In Bulgaria, nineteen years after the changeover, the official files remain closed, and there are no publicly known documents on the artist's collaboration. The work caused great controversy when it was first exhibited in the spring of 1990, at the height of the political changes to the long-standing Communist rule. The self-disclosing gesture in this artistic project is still unique in the context of post-Communist Europe, and since its appearance* **Top Secret** *has become an icon of its time.*

The forty-minute long video, which shows the artist rereading the index box's contents, was shot in his studio in Sofia in 2007.

The Action is on (for the time being)...

Once upon a time there was a boy.

They say he was a smart and obedient one. He got the highest grades in school, he read books at home and he drew. He drew rabbits, hunters, houses with chimneys, and airplanes with five-pointed stars on them destroying other airplanes with swastikas on them. He drew and read... He particularly liked the books with the adventure stories where the "good" guys won over the "bad" guys. He also liked spy stories. The brave Soviet *chekisti* and their Bulgarian colleagues Avakum Zakhov and Emil Boev were really attractive to him. They were making him confident that the enemies about whom it was spoken and written everywhere were not going to intrude upon his socialist fatherland.

The boy was growing up. He graduated with honors (gold medal) from the prestigious high school for mathematics in his native town and was accepted right away as a student in the Academy of Fine Arts (he was not drafted into the army then because of an ailment which he had suffered in his early youth). His usual diligence and obedience went on here as well.

In the autumn of 1976 (when he was in his second year at the academy) the boy went on a trip to Paris (his loving parents, whom he also loved, paid for the trip). Everything was wonderful—the Louvre, the Rodin (museum), the Dufy retrospective, a few porno movies. In the middle of the eight-day trip the tour leader of the group of Bulgarian tourists told him there were packages left by somebody for him and for B. (a kind older man, brother of a well-known professor) at the reception desk. To the boy's surprise his package contained "enemy" propaganda materials. The boy read this and that and handed the materials over to the tour leader with the words: "They are 'spitting' on Bulgaria!" The tour leader got worried and summoned right away a man from the embassy to whom the boy gave the package, happy to have carried out his patriotic duty.

A few weeks later though (already back in Sofia) the boy was summoned by the head of the "personnel" department at the academy, who told him with a secretive voice that there was this "comrade" here who wanted to talk to him. The "comrade" (a nice young man) asked for

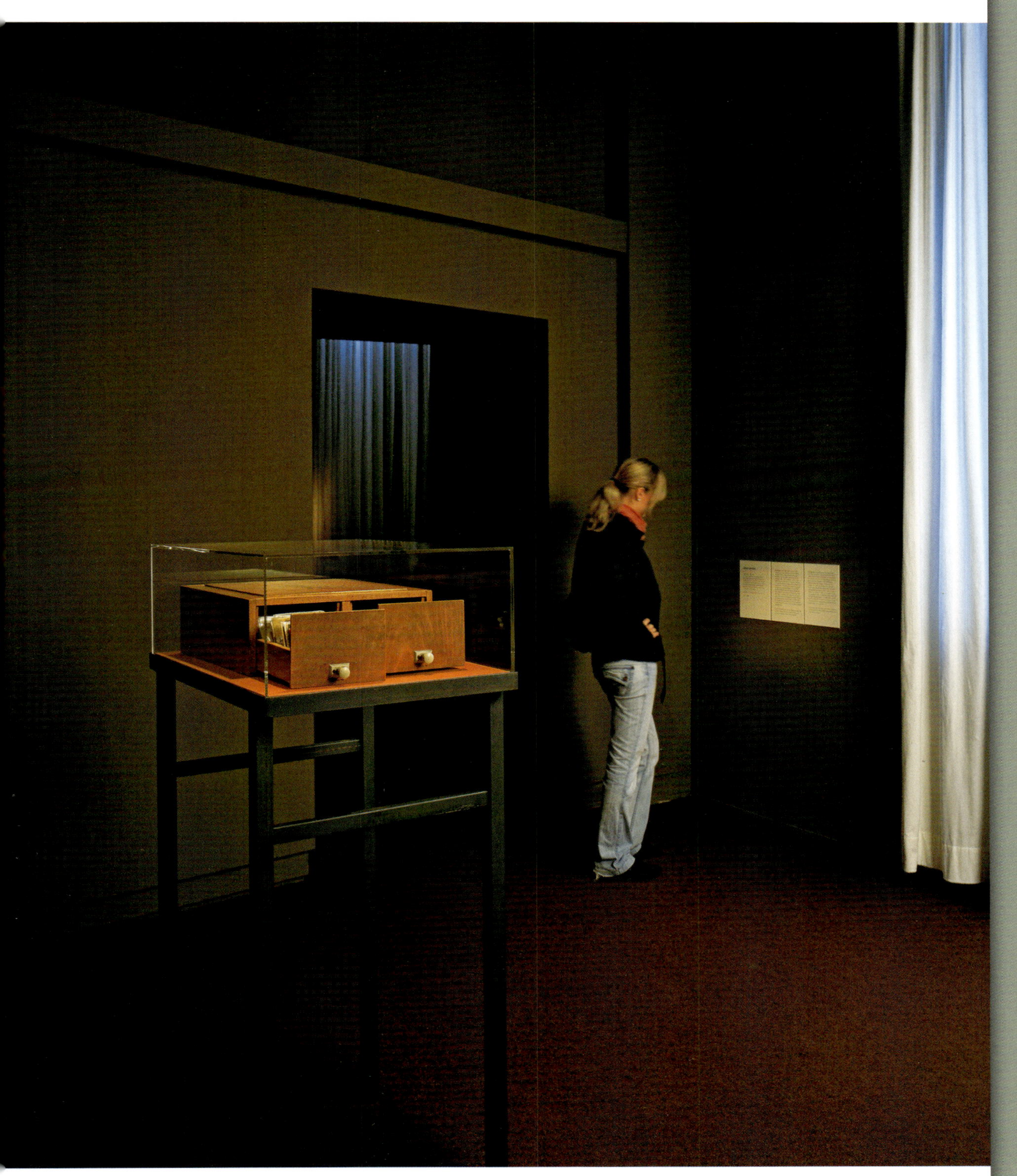

Top Secret, 1989–90

Acrylic, drawing ink, oil, photographs, graphite, bronze, aluminum, wood; shameful secret; 179 slips in original index box; 14 x 46 x 39 cm; video on DVD, sound (English), 40'07", looped, 2007

the "case" in Paris to be described in one or two pages. The boy did so. The "comrade" was satisfied and then asked an unexpected question: "Well, we are actually interested in..." and mentioned the name of a boy's colleague, one quiet and humble guy. "What's he like, is there something about him that strikes you as unusual, etc.?" The boy (diligent and obedient) answered that since it was necessary he would tell. Afterwards, filled with some peculiar pride, the boy shared that event with a friend and a girlfriend.

The nice young "comrade" appeared again (only this time in secrecy—eye-to-eye). And thus, little by little, the boy had entered a meadow from where the flowers were gradually disappearing, the thorns were getting thicker, the grass and the bush grew up to his eyes. To tell you the truth, the boy wasn't too active. But nevertheless when asked he answered (and always afterwards he wrote on a white sheet of paper leaving on purpose a blank white space at the top of the sheet) which exhibition was popular and which one was not, who had contacts with religious sects and who didn't, etc. Did the boy actually realize what he was doing? I would say yes and no. The boy had just trusted the institutions, had believed he was contributing to the realization of that great future society where everything would be great for everyone. Naturally he wasn't getting anything for all this (except maybe he was getting some strange feeling of security). While in the army, he was transferred to another young man (with epaulets). Here, at the beginning, he also believed he was carrying out his soldier's duty. But this belief was getting shakier and shakier.

Thus came the summer of 1983. Once discharged from the army, the boy gathered all his courage together (is this the usual expression?) and firmly refused to be used anymore. The "comrade" (with epaulets) had been trying hard to talk him into transferring him to another "comrade" in charge of the intelligentsia. But the boy "stuck to his guns."

That was the beginning of a long and painful awakening. The boy's diligence and obedience were getting displaced little by little by other, a lot more manly, things. But the boy (the man) was still afraid. The fear must have shown itself in his paintings.

That went on until his first child was born (in the summer of 1986). And then the man realized that his path must be chosen categorically if he was to look straight in the eyes of this child who had been carried around the blooming roses and daisies in its mother's womb during that sadly memorable May 1 of 1986.* And it seems the path he chose did not lead to the "bright future."

The audience trusted him. It trusted his drawings from the **Enlightened by the Decisions** and **The Endurance of a Nation** series from his one-man show in January 1988. It trusted as well his card index in the chest from the exhibition **The City?,** his telescope with the title sign **View to the West** pointing from the roof of the 6 Shipka Street Gallery toward the red pentacle on top of the Bulgarian Communist Party headquarters (the telescope though had been mysteriously dismantled by the state security, which had long ago lost its confidence in the man). And his studio was filled with just such honest paintings and objects lying around in expectation for better times.

Could he have stopped with his frankness here?

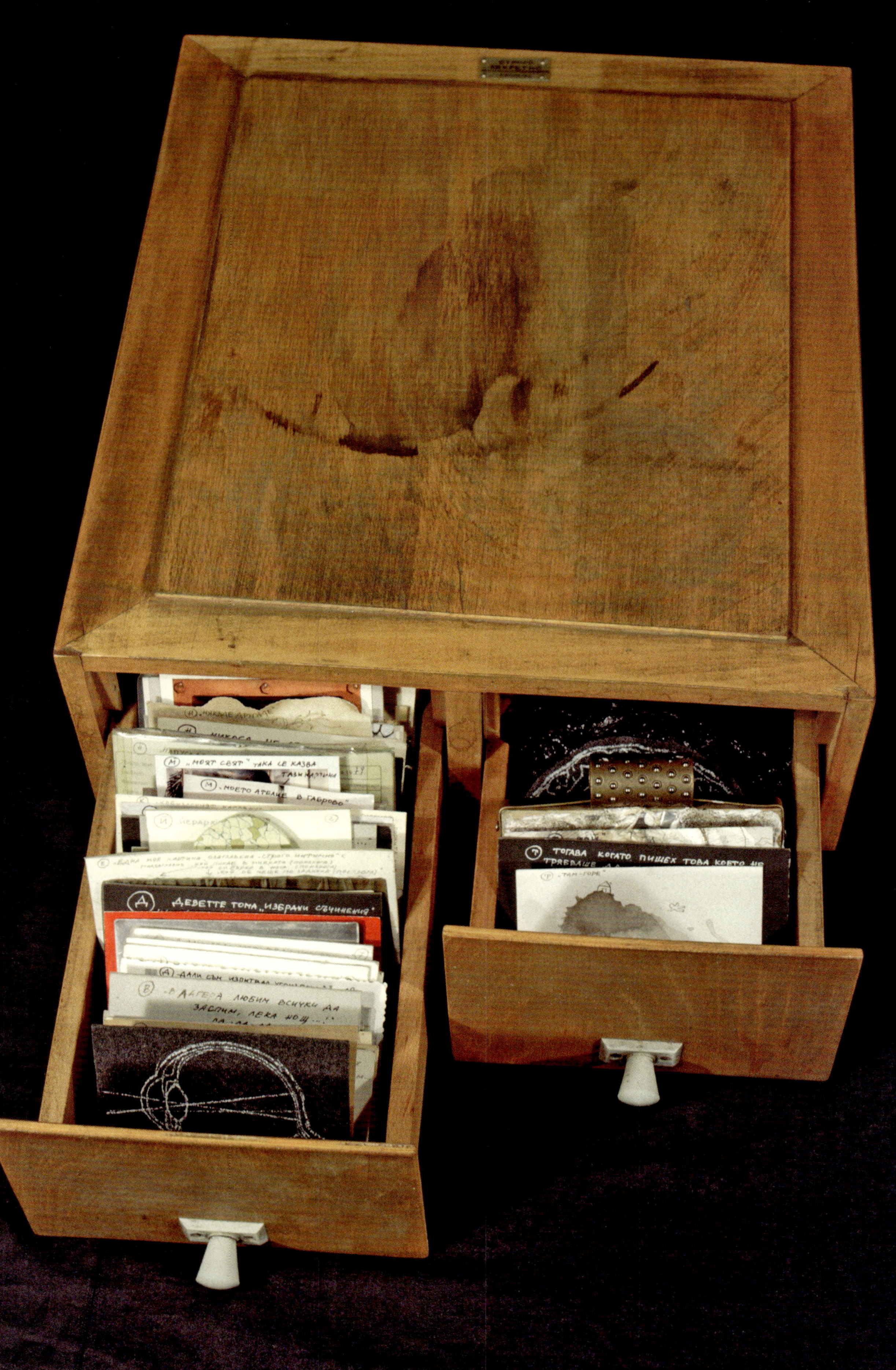

Top Secret, 1989–90

He could have. It is very unlikely his contacts with the nice "comrades" from seven years ago would have come out in the open. It is not in the best interests of any political party or movement to bring out in public the full lists of just such names (you know why, don't you?).

But the man had made up his mind that this revelation should see the light of day as well. So he made a new card index in a chest. There he drew and described, using Pop Art means, everything shameful and depressing which was still creeping around his ever more hurting heart. He described the case in question as well.

The man exhibited in public this card-index chest (called **Top Secret**) at the Club of Young Artists' exhibition entitled **End of Quotation** (April 20–May 26, 1990), and accepted internally once and for all that only he or she who can overcome his or her fears can be a true artist. It doesn't matter what kind of fear this may be—the fear of changing the direction of one's work in spite of the success it is gathering, or the fear of revealing oneself to the full at any cost and thus accomplish an artistic act.

Many of his younger colleagues (and some older ones as well) understood and shook his hand. About a month after the opening of the exhibition, the Congress of the Union of Bulgarian Artists was held. The man thought somebody would bring up the "question" (his) in front of everybody, but nobody did. Obviously (along the laws of safe existence) he should have kept quiet. But seeing that the conservatism in the union was once again taking the upper hand, he withdrew his initial decision not to run for Chairman of the Union and again put forward his candidacy. He felt morally obliged to help destroy this horrifying machine for oppression of artists called "Creative Union." He wanted his colleagues at last to feel free and confident in themselves (not in the union), to start trusting the audience which had been waiting for them for a long, long time. He was elected Vice-Chairman.

But the story doesn't end here. The rumor which was started after the **End of Quotation** exhibition that he was the man of the state security apparatuses in the union was getting threateningly widespread. Many of his colleagues (obviously not into going to art exhibitions) had not even realized that the man himself had publicly disclosed his own past one month before the congress. And that this "past" was very different indeed from the concept of the man of the state security in the union. Thus a not altogether artistic campaign was under way. The man was forced to exhibit once again his **Top Secret** chest in the former office room of the Communist party at the union. But since he knew not everyone would get to see it and the talk in the hallways and the cafés was going strong, he asked a newspaper, much respected by him, to publish the above words.

And at the end, stating that the boy, the man, and myself are one and the same person, let me give you one more reason for my showing the **Top Secret** piece. I wanted it to be a warning to all young people who might be misled to fall into the meticulously woven webs of the Institution. Because if in two or three years' time (or even sooner) some of these young people are asked by the future "appropriate services" whether some Communists, anarchists, etc., are having meetings together, these same young people may not hesitate to tell and this act would be perfectly normal and moral for them. I don't know if I, as an artist, should feel flattered

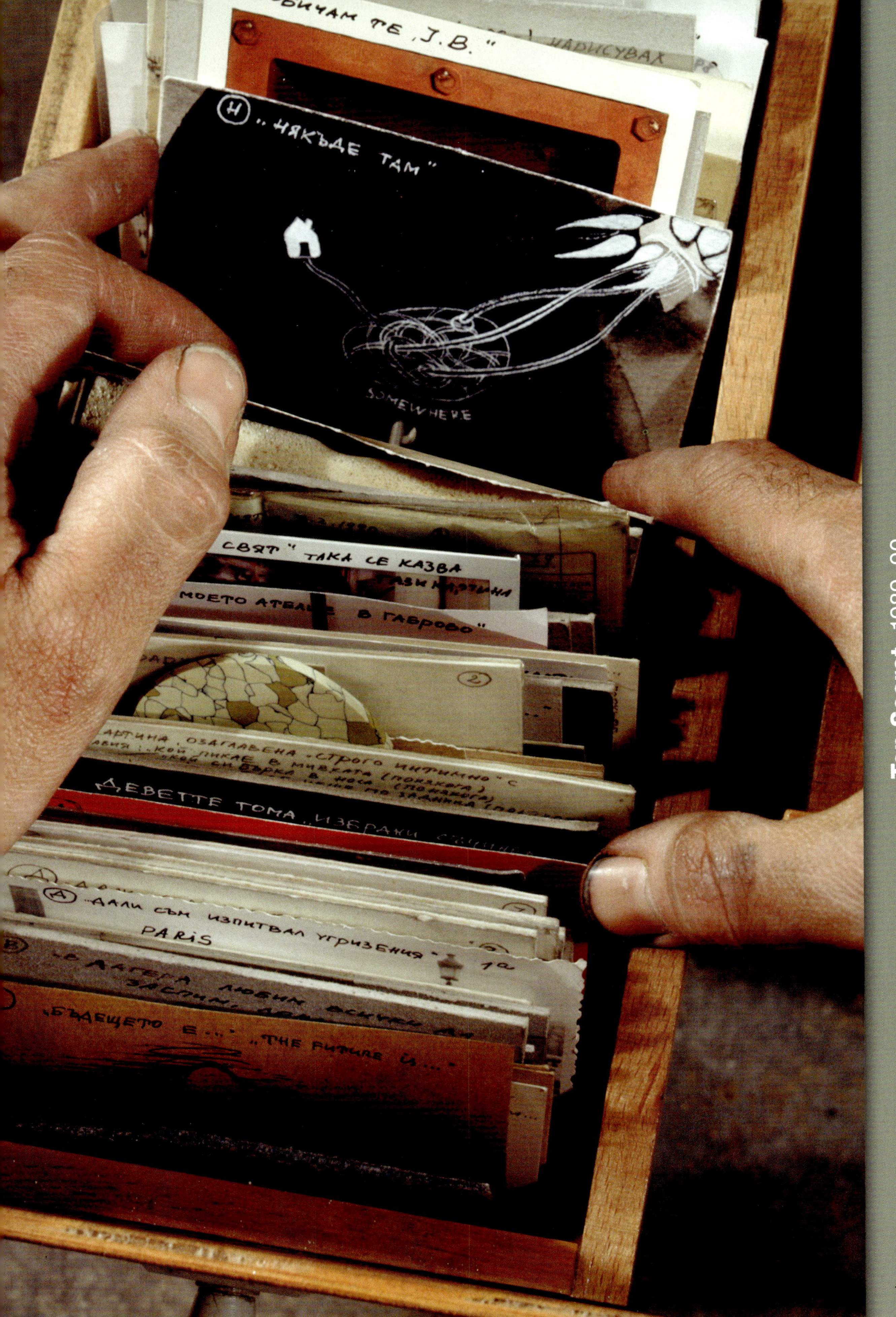

Top Secret, 1989–90

that a work of mine has caused such a scandal. The whole of it turned into a sort of happening (that is, an action where you don't really know what's going to happen next). But I am its author and it is up to me to put the tag with the right title and content of the work when its "finale" comes about.

I would like to believe that the artists in the Union of Artists and above all the audience, which I treasure the most, will understand.

Text written in 1990
Originally published in **Kultura** weekly newspaper (Sofia), June 22, 1990

*This was the day the Bulgarian government first disclosed to the public the Chernobyl nuclear disaster, which had occured on April 26.

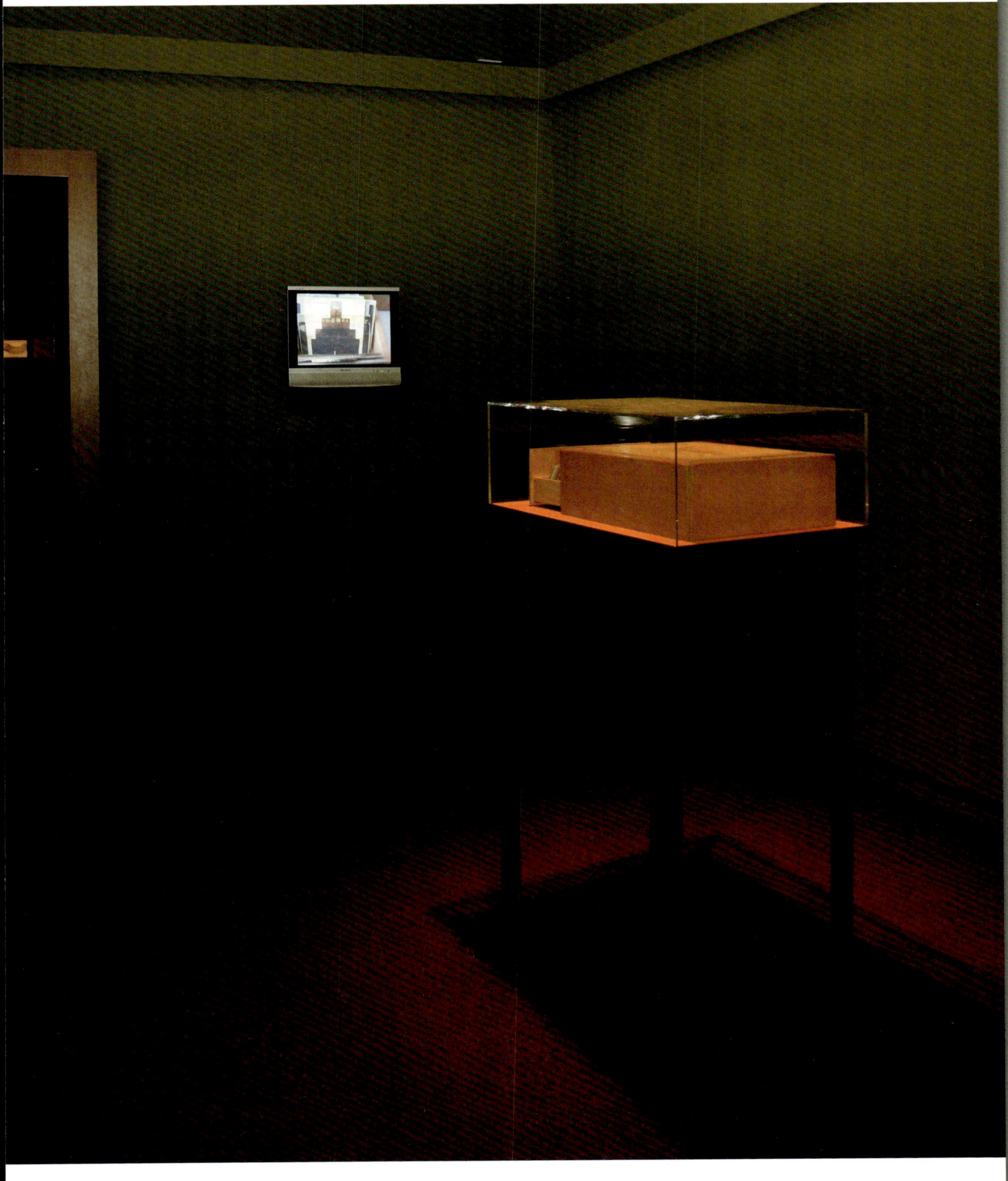

An inoperative AK-47 assault rifle, metal, wood; 26 x 87 x 7 cm / twelve life-size drawings of recently manufactured Bulgarian assault rifles, executed by Mihaela Vlaseva and Svetozara Alexandrova, charcoal and white chalk on paper; 76 x 112 cm each / The **MP-44 ("Sturmgewehr"),** graphite, black and white ink wash on paper; 16 x 24 cm / two videos on DVD, color, sound, looped, duration: **An Interview in Bulgarian,** 1'04"; **The Russian Embassy,** 5'43", one monitor, one plasma screen, two DVD players / **Lactobacillus Bulgaricus,** wall drawing, acrylic; dimensions variable / **A Cyrillic Alphabet,** vinyl lettering on wall; dimensions variable / felt-tip pens, handwritten texts

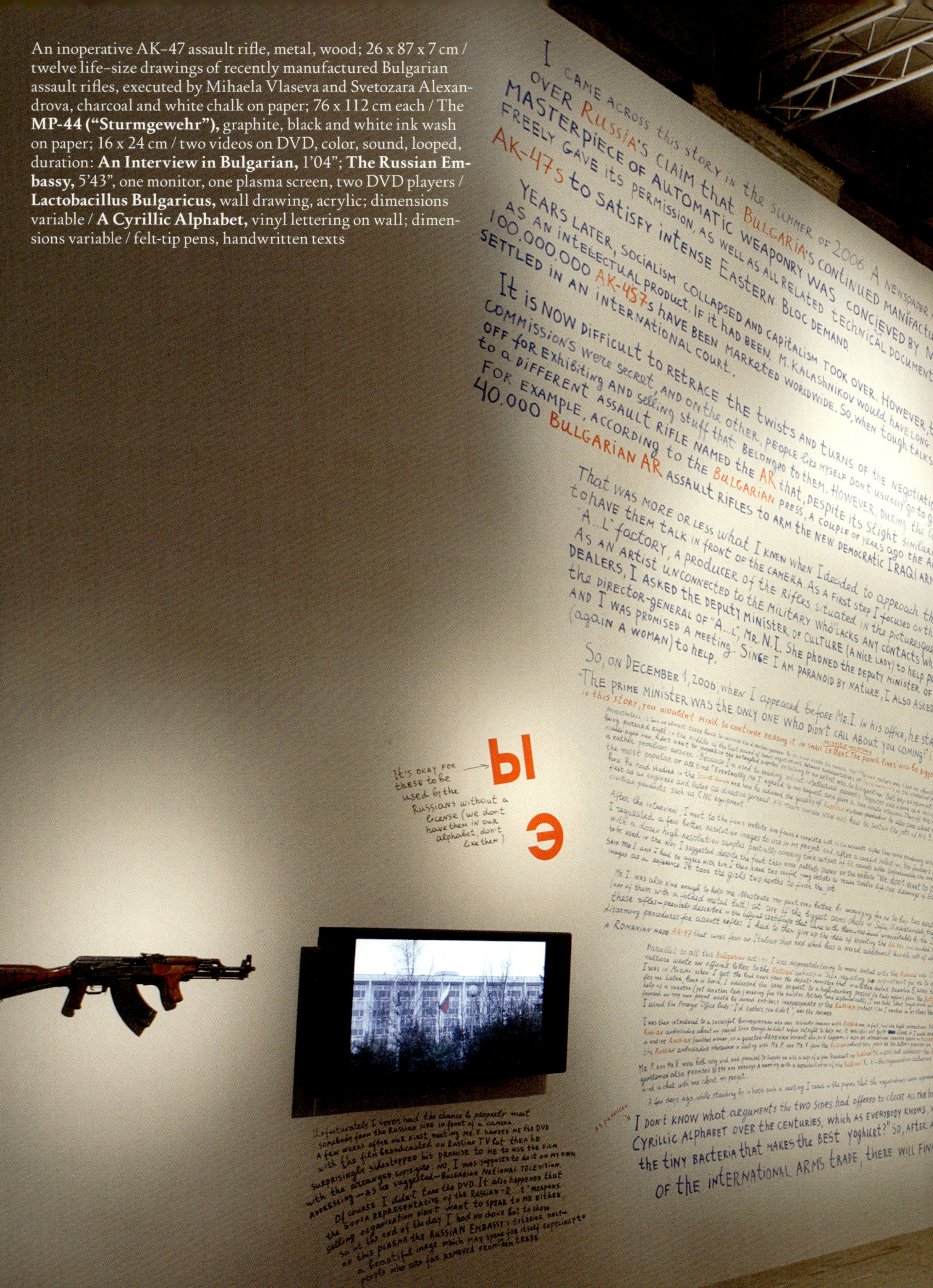

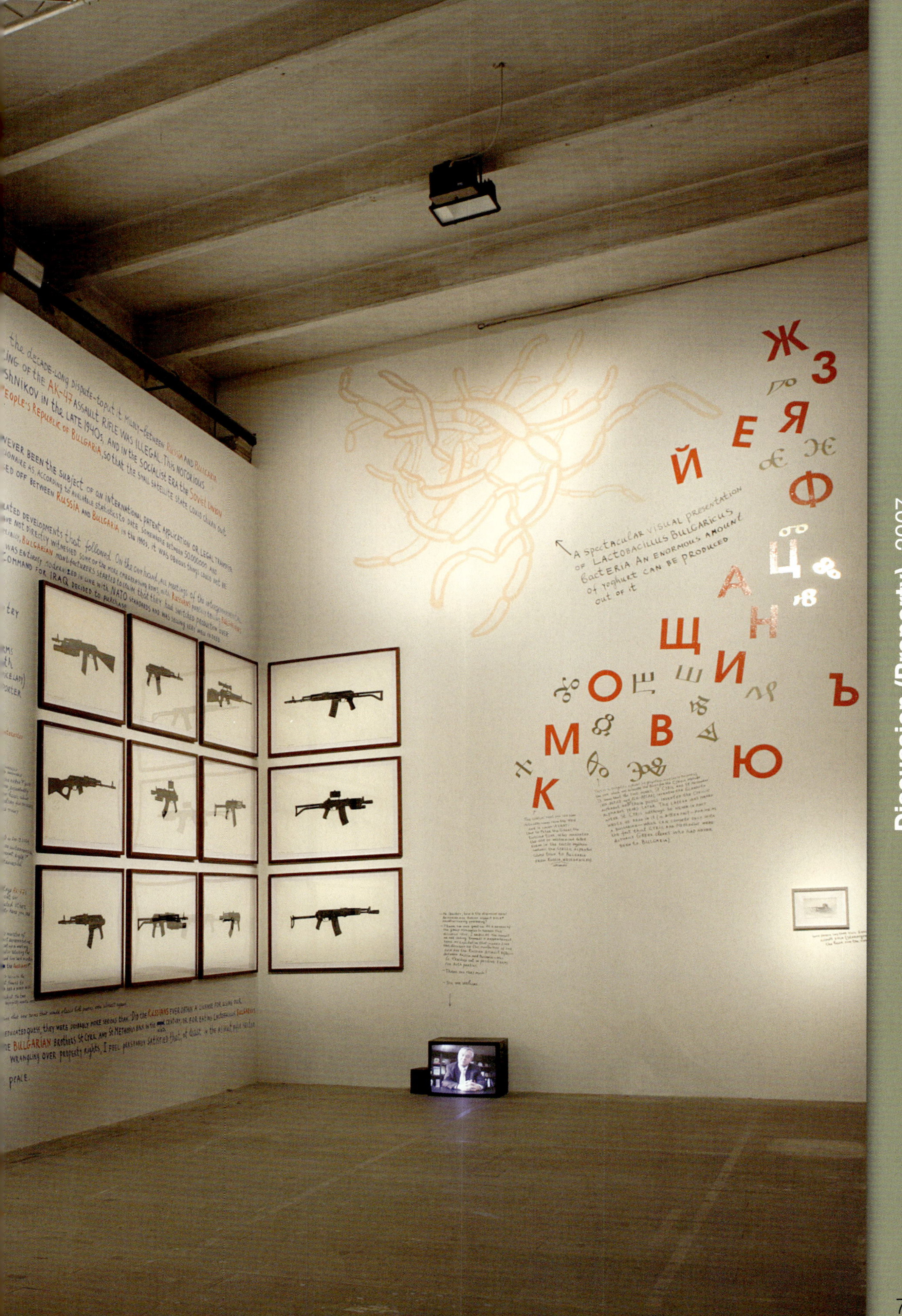

Discussion (Property), 2007

Deutsche Übersetzung siehe Seite 203

Discussion (Property)

I came across this story in the summer of 2006. A newspaper article described the decade-long dispute —to put it mildly—between Russia and Bulgaria over Russia's claim that Bulgaria's continued manufacturing and selling of the AK-47 assault rifle was illegal. This notorious masterpiece of automatic weaponry was conceived by Mikhail Kalashnikov in the late 1940s and, in the socialist era, the Soviet Union freely gave its permission, as well as all related technical documentation, to the People's Republic of Bulgaria, so that the small satellite state could churn out AK-47s to satisfy intense Eastern Bloc demand.

Years later, socialism collapsed and capitalism took over. However, the AK-47 had never been the subject of an international patent application or legal transfer as an intellectual product. If it had been, M. Kalashnikov would have long ago become a billionaire as, according to available statistics to date, somewhere between 50,000,000 and 100,000,000 AK-47s have been marketed worldwide. So, when tough talks on the issue kicked off between Russia and Bulgaria in the 1990s, it was obvious things could not be settled in an international court.

It is now difficult to retrace the twists and turns of the negotiations and other related developments that followed. On the one hand, all meetings of the intergovernmental commissions were secret and, on the other, people like myself don't usually go to gun shows and so have not directly witnessed some of the more embarrassing rows, with Russians publicly telling Bulgarians off for exhibiting and selling stuff that belonged to them. However, during the last few years especially, Bulgarian manufacturers have started to claim that they have switched production over to a different assault rifle, named the AR that, despite its slight similarity to the AK-47, has been entirely modernized in line with NATO standards and is selling very well indeed. For example, according to the Bulgarian press, a couple of years ago, the American Central Command for Iraq decided to purchase 40,000 Bulgarian AR assault rifles to arm the new democratic Iraqi army.

That was more or less what I knew when I decided to approach the two sides and try to have them talk in front of the camera. As a first step, I focused on the Bulgarian "A...l" factory, a producer of the rifles situated in the picturesque city of K. As an artist unconnected to the military who also lacks any contacts whatsoever with arms dealers, I asked the deputy minister of culture (a nice lady) to help put me in touch with the director-general of "A...l," Mr. N.I. She phoned the deputy minister of defense (another nice lady), and I was promised a meeting. Since I am paranoid by nature, I also asked a well-known reporter (again a woman) to help.

So, on December 1, 2006, when I appeared before Mr. I. in his office, he started by saying: "The prime minister was the only one who didn't call about you coming!" Nevertheless, it took me almost three hours to convince the director-general to say a few words on camera. Why? The main problem was that my attempt to get both sides to talk was simultaneously being pursued right in the middle of the last round of heavy negotiations between representatives of Russia and Bulgaria on the intellectual property of military items. Obviously Mr. I., a reasonable middle-aged man, didn't want to jeopardize the entangled disputes by talking to an artist who, to his question: "But why do you—not a journalist—have an interest in this matter?!" gave a rather peculiar answer: "Because I'm used to reading about intellectual property disputes over a book or a musical score, but never over a weapon,

tohave t
"A...L" fo
As an A
DEALERS
the DIREC
AND I WA
(again

So, on
"The p
in this

It's okay for these to be used by the Russians without a license (we don't have them in our alphabet, don't like them)

ы

э

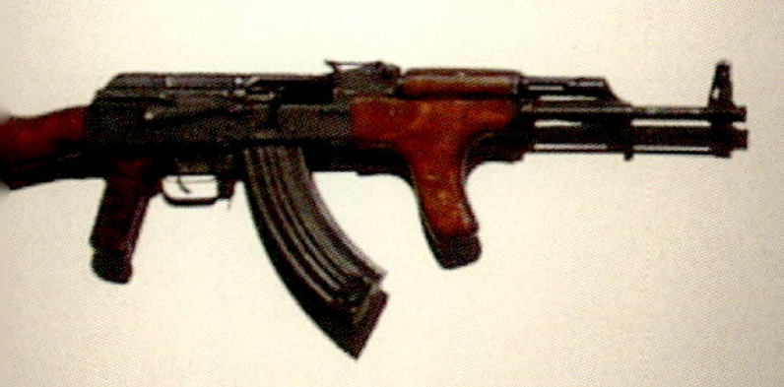

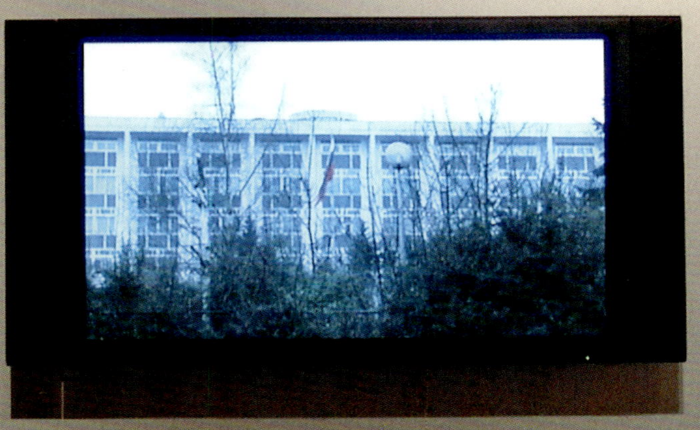

Unfortunately I never had the chance to properly meet somebody from the Russian side in front of a camera.
A few weeks after our first meeting Mr. V. handed me the DVD with the film broadcasted on Russian TV but then he surprisingly sidestepped his promise to me to use the film with the arranged copyrights: no, I was supposed to do it on my own, addressing — as he suggested — Bulgarian National Television.
Of course I didn't take the DVD. It also happened that the Sofia representative of the Russian "R...t" weapons-selling organization didn't want to speak to me either, so at the end of the day I had no choice but to show on this plasma the Russian Embassy's exterior only — a beautiful image which may speak for itself especially to people who are far removed from the arm trade.

Discussion (Property), 2007

reportedly the most popular of all time." Eventually, Mr. I. agreed to my request and gave a one-minute interview. Then, off the record, he spoke for more than an hour about how he had studied in the Soviet Union and how he admired the quality of Russian military production. He also spoke about having worked in that "A...l" factory for decades, first as an engineer and later as director-general. His main concern now was how to sustain the jobs of his 5,500 employees, who also produce many civilian products such as CNC equipment.

After the interview, I went to the firm's website and found a complete list of the assault rifles they were producing with photographs of each one. I requested a few better quality images to use in my project and, after a careful selection, the factory's design department sent me a CD on December 19, 2006, with a dozen high-resolution samples partially covering their output of AR assault rifles. Unfortunately, the ones I most wanted were deemed "too controversial" to be used in the way I suggested, despite the fact they were publicly shown on the website. "We don't want to piss the Russians off with your project, right?" said Mr. I., and I had to agree with him. I then hired two skillful young artists to make twelve life-size drawings of the AR rifles, using the less controversial images as a reference. It took the girls two months to finish the job.

Mr. I. was also kind enough to help me illustrate my point even better by arranging for me to buy two real, but inoperative, 1960s vintage AK-47s (one of them with a folded metal butt) at one of the biggest arms shops in Sofia. Unfortunately, the disarming technique carried out on these rifles—precisely described in the official certificate that came with them—was found unacceptable by the Italian authorities, who mandated other disarming procedures for assault rifles. I had to then give up the idea of exporting the AK-47s and decided to buy one in Italy. Consequently, here you see a Romanian-made AK-47 that comes from an Italian shop and which has a weird additional handle, all of which I can live with.

Parallel to all this Bulgarian activity, I was desperately trying to make contact with the Russian side. On November 21, 2006, the same deputy minister of culture wrote an official letter to the Russian embassy in Sofia, requesting an appointment for me to discuss the issue with a government representative. I was in Miami when I got the bad news from the deputy minister that, in a letter dated December 5, 2006, the Russian embassy had declined to set up a meeting for me. Later, back in Sofia, I addressed the same request to a high-ranking person (a lady again) from the Bulgarian Ministry of Foreign Affairs, also soliciting the help of a curator (yet another lady) working for the ministry. Politely and diplomatically, I was told about negotiations going on right then on the same subject and how such a letter focused on my own project would be deemed entirely inappropriate by the Russian embassy. "Can I mention in my story that you are anxious to approach the Russians?" I asked the Foreign Office lady. "I'd rather you didn't," was the answer.

I was then introduced to a successful businesswoman who was seriously involved with Russia and, in fact, had the right connections. She kindly took up my cause and finally managed to talk with the Russian ambassador about my project. Even though he didn't refuse outright to help me, it was still not quite clear if I could really meet someone from their side. At last, thanks to a native Russian (another woman, of a quarter-Armenian descent who, as it happens, is also an international curator based in Bulgaria), the Armenian ambassador in Sofia had a word with the Russian ambassador,

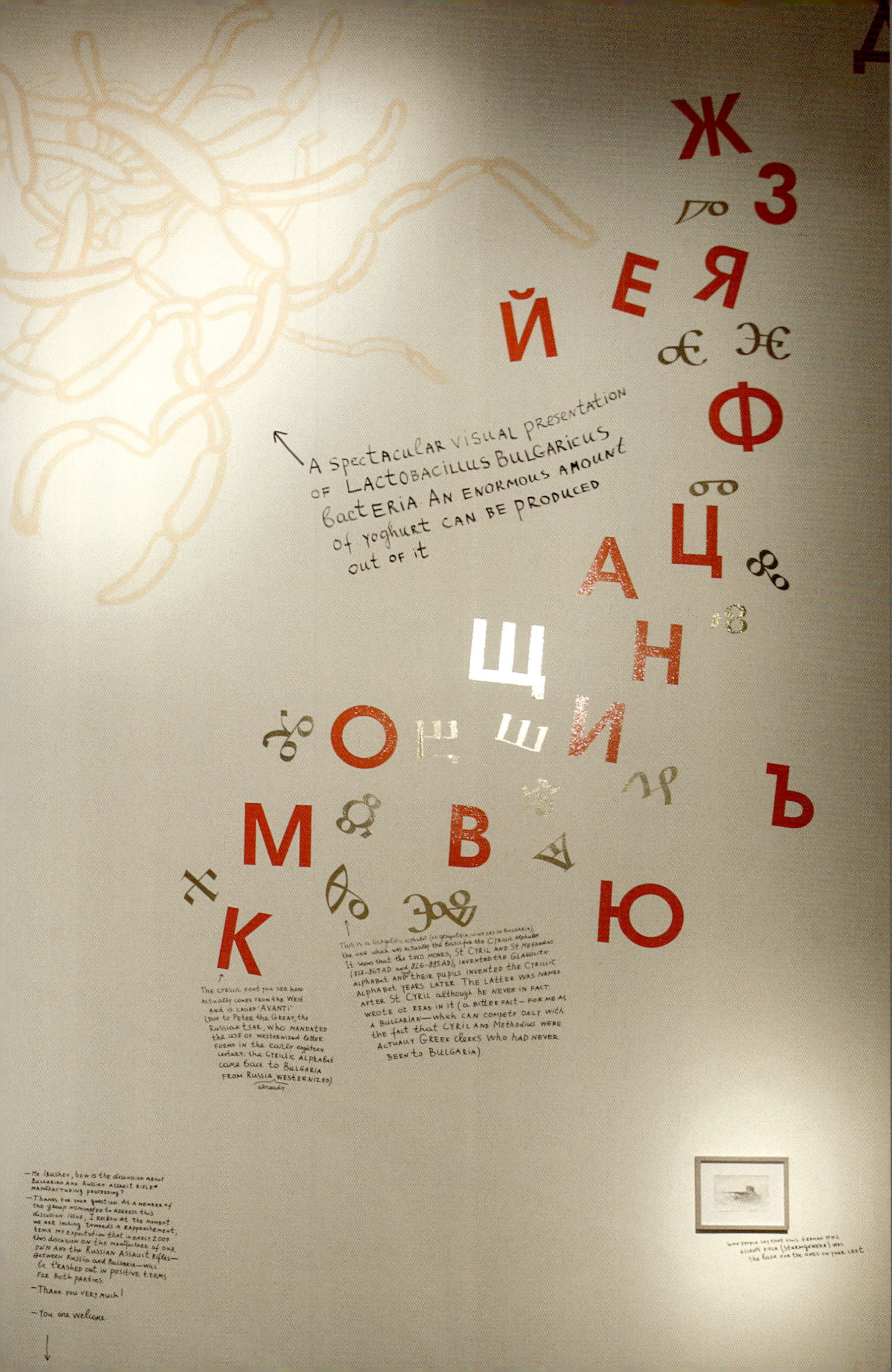

A spectacular visual presentation of Lactobacillus Bulgaricus bacteria. An enormous amount of yoghurt can be produced out of it

The Cyrillic font you see here actually comes from the West and is called "AVANTI" (due to Peter the Great, the Russian tsar, who mandated the use of westernized letter forms in the early eighteen century, the Cyrillic alphabet came back to Bulgaria from Russia already westernized)

This is a Glagolitic alphabet (or glagolitsa, as we say in Bulgaria), the one which was actually the basis for the Cyrillic alphabet. It seems that the two monks, St Cyril and St Methodius (827–869 AD and 826–885 AD), invented the Glagolitic alphabet and their pupils invented the Cyrillic alphabet years later. The latter was named after St Cyril although he never in fact wrote or read in it (a bitter fact – for me as a Bulgarian – which can compete only with the fact that Cyril and Methodius were actually Greek clerks who had never been to Bulgaria)

– Mr Ibushev, how is the discussion about Bulgarian and Russian assault rifle manufacturing proceeding?

– Thanks for your question. As a member of the group nominated to address this discussion issue, I reckon at the moment we are inching towards a rapprochement, hence my expectation that in early 2007 this discussion on the manufacture of our own and the Russian assault rifles – between Russia and Bulgaria – will be thrashed out in positive terms for both parties

– Thank you very much!

– You are welcome

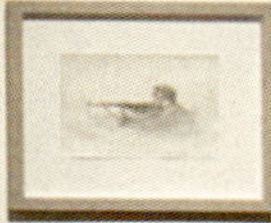

Some people say that this German WW2 assault rifle (Sturmgewehr) was the base for the ones on your left.

Discussion (Property), 2007

whereupon a meeting with Mr. P. and Mr. V. from the Russian embassy took place at the latter's premises on January 24, 2007.

Mr. P. and Mr. V. were both very kind and promised to supply me with a copy of a film broadcast on Russian TV in 2006 that addressed "the-Bulgarians-and-our-own-Russian-weapons" subject. The two gentlemen also promised to try and arrange a meeting with a representative of the Russian "R...t"—the organization authorized to sell weapons internationally—who hopefully would not mind a chat with me about my project.

A few days ago, while standing-by in hope of such a meeting, I read in the papers that the negotiations were apparently taking a turn for the better and that new terms that would please both parties were almost agreed upon.

I don't know what arguments the two sides had offered to clear all the hurdles. If I can make an educated guess, they were probably more serious than: "Did the Russians ever obtain a license for using our Cyrillic alphabet over the centuries, which, as everybody knows, was invented by the Bulgarian brothers Cyril and Methodius back in the ninth century, or for eating *Lactobacillus bulgaricus,* the tiny bacteria that makes the best yoghurt?" So, after all those years of wrangling over property rights, I feel personally satisfied that, at least in the assault rifle sector of the international arms trade, there will finally be relative peace.

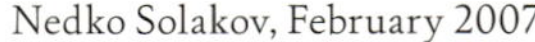

Nedko Solakov, February 2007

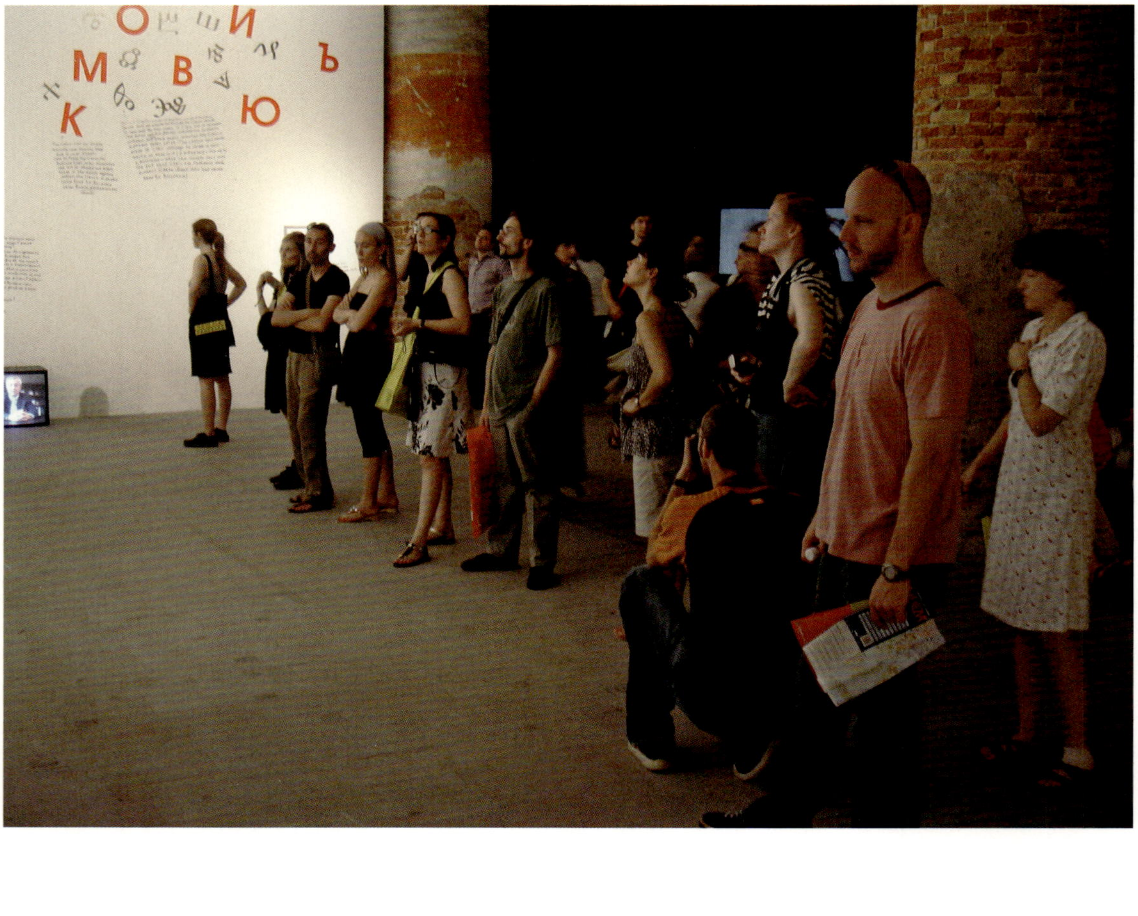

—Mr. Ibushev, how is the discussion about Bulgarian and Russian assault rifle manufacturing proceeding?

—Thanks for your question. As a member of the group nominated to address this discussion issue, I reckon at the moment we are inching towards a rapprochement, hence my expectation that in early 2007 this discussion on the manufacture of our own and the Russian assault rifles—between Russia and Bulgaria—will be thrashed out in positive terms for both parties.

—Thank you very much!

—You are welcome.

↓

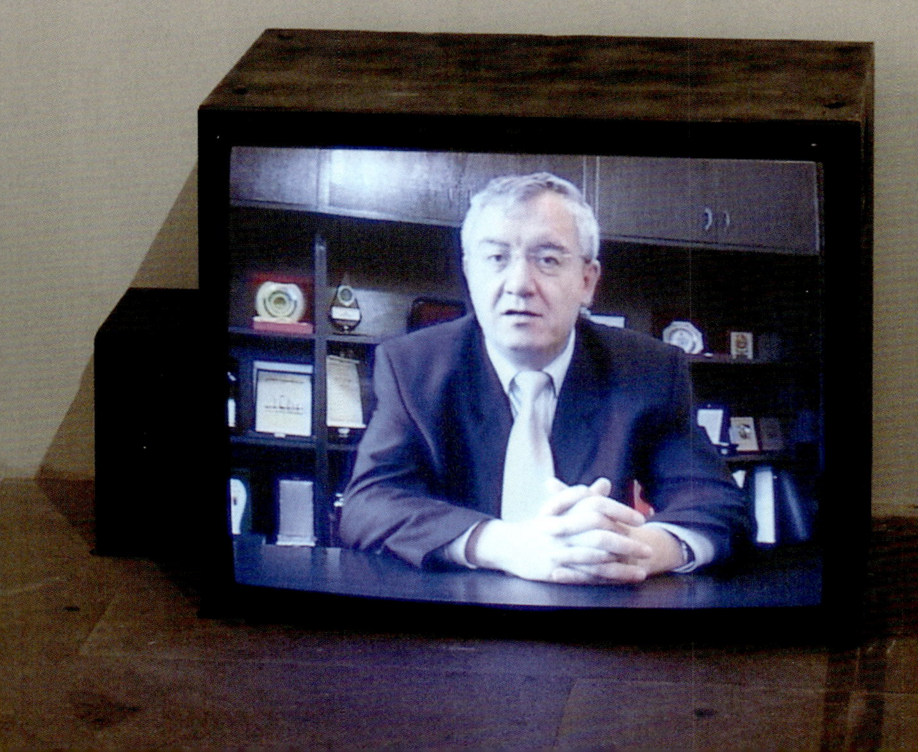

Discussion (Property), 2007

Cyrillic and Kalashnikov
Nedko Solakov's Methodical Game with the World

Ralf Beil

"Every second there is a long line of people in this world weeping and a shorter one of people laughing. But there is also a third line who are no longer weeping and no longer laughing."[1]

Georgi Gospodinov

Nedko Solakov makes us laugh and cry at the same time. He successfully achieves the feat of opening up a fourth line and getting it to grow ever longer: that of tragicomedy. It is undoubtedly the most truthful attitude to the world. Especially from the point of view of a Bulgarian. It was not for nothing that Solakov's fellow countryman Georgi Gospodinov wrote: "The Apocalypse can also happen in just one country."[2]

Bulgaria is the country on the Balkan peninsula where Nedko Solakov was born in 1957 and still lives and works today in the capital city Sofia, named after the antique goddess of wisdom. It is regarded on the one hand as a heartland of old Europe, as the cradle of Western culture: music, theater, and dance have their origins here. The mythical cultural hero and singer Orpheus is believed to have come from the Rhodopes, a mountain range in southern Bulgaria, and the cult of Dionysus is supposed to have originated in the region where the Thracians settled. On the other hand, this territory has been determined by its geographical position at the edge of Southeast Europe, five hundred years of Ottoman foreign rule, and the Russian dominance of the last century and a half. In 1877 the Russians marched in as liberators and created a monarchy; in 1944 they returned as an occupying force and set up a people's republic. After all these ups and downs of history, it has only been since the end of Socialism in 1989 that Bulgaria has again been on the path to Europe—and artists like Nedko Solakov have become visible.

The Hedgehog's Lesson

In a big, darkened room, twelve spotlights illuminate an equal number of places on the floor. Visitors have to go right up to them and bend down to take in the events spread out there. A toy octopus has lost one of its eight tentacles to a swarm of plastic ants. Written in black on the octopus's back are the words: *"The good news: in some way he liked more the uneven numbers (figures)."* There is an orange plastic flower lying in the spotlight, and on the floor beside it we read: *"The bad news: he was dead. The good news: the flower on his grave will last forever."*

Or a small, curled-up ceramic hedgehog has this comment: *"It was so nice: the same lady with the soft tender hand was caressing him. The bad news: he was dreaming again."*[3]

The installation Good News, Bad News (1998–present) introduces us in a paradigmatic way to Solakov's humor and worldview. Here Solakov lays out absurd micro-stories and snippets of thought before us—stories where laughter literally sticks in our throats. Disillusioning, tragicomic, sometimes sarcastic, and at the same time just as strange as they are true. They shift our viewpoint by way of drastic changes of perspective. "What kind of novel would in fact take shape if we could get a fly to tell it?" the first-person narrator wonders in Gospodinov's prose piece Natural Novel.[4] Solakov replies to exactly such questions with his fables, where—as in the case of the hedgehog—dream and reality quite frequently collide.

They are simultaneously stories of a socialization in state socialism, a system whose constant claim to, and breaking of, ideals virtually forced people towards tilted pictures, gallows humor, and strange improvisation. Nor do dialectics here generate any conclusive syntheses, but rather time and time again only loose ends and mixed motivations. The Bulgarian curator and art critic Iara Boubnova confirms this when she says, "After all, isn't this the way we live here? Good is never totally good, bad never totally bad."[5]

The Nonsense of Money Value

"The sense of the absurd in my work gets stimulated and fed by the absurdity of the Bulgarian reality," Solakov states frankly—this applies also, and particularly, to the time after 1989.[6] It is the same form of absurdity that likewise appears in the work of the Bulgarian writer Alek Popov, a contemporary of Gospodinov's. One of the protagonists in his novel Die Hunde fliegen tief, a New York stock exchange speculator of Bulgarian descent, goes as far as to say regarding his philosophy of money: "Just imagine you're a door through which money goes in and out. It isn't important which direction it goes in. What's important is the movement. Anyone who has once understood that will never worry again about whether he's winning or losing…"[7]

In 2002, in response to a "business-meets-art-and-creates-things-together event,"[8] Nedko Solakov implemented his action The Deal in Herning in Denmark. At the same place where, forty years before, Piero Manzoni had created his famous Socle du Monde—on which the world has seemed to rest ever since—Nedko Solakov visualized what the world of the twenty-first century rests on: the generally invisible movements of money and global financial transactions and the fluctuation of monetary value, down to its total loss.

A video documents how a one-thousand kroner note, "part of the project budget," can turn into a few coins within half an hour simply through changing the money into different currencies: "The US dollars were then changed back into Danish kroner, and then back into US dollars (or euros), and then back into Danish kroner, and so on and so forth, until the money melted away into small change, eaten up by all the commissions and the buy and sell currency rates. During the course of these transactions, a few of the best students at the Business Institute—Marlene, Monica, Robert, and Vibeke—were taking notes."[9]

Perhaps in developing this idea and carrying out his absurd money deal, Nedko Solakov felt something similar to another protagonist in Alek Popov's novel: "I felt safe… as in an escape capsule, and it was clear to me that I couldn't buy that feeling for all the money in the world. For there are recesses in which the market economy doesn't work."[10] Nedko Solakov's art is such a recess. And against this background, we also understand the artist's statement: "I can't make mistakes."[11] For mistakes, whether they are immanent in or foreign to the system, are always already part of his strategy and art.

The Home Country of the Lactobacillus

"What it means to set down pictures of the past or question collective pictures that have been stylized into national myths was ... demonstrated by the case of a young Bulgarian art historian. Because she found out that The Batak Massacre by the Polish painter Antoni Piotrowski is based not on authentic, but on staged photographs and therefore supposedly cast doubt on a Bulgarian national myth, she was threatened with death and had to leave her country. Radical nationalists stigmatized her as an 'enemy of the state' and 'pseudo-Bulgarian,' and even wanted to impale her. Here the power of pictures and the responsibility of those who deal with them is palpable. Who is the master of memory? Who establishes how things were? Historians? Politicians? Bureaucrats? Archivists? Poets? Photographers? Television, even?"[12]

Involvement with political questions in art and art history can become thoroughly dangerous in Bulgaria—up to the present day, as this 2007 case demonstrates. Nedko Solakov has not allowed himself to be frightened off. On the contrary, he has made the very recent history of Bulgaria a theme, even at the time of the collapse of Communism, taking himself as an example when he admitted in a work of art that, until the summer of 1983, he had acted as an informer for the Bulgarian secret police: "I think my fears have gone since the day I showed Top Secret (1989–90), the filing cabinet with the story of my life. That was the only time I was afraid. When I was writing these cards telling the story of my connection to the State Security Services,... a lot of scandals were emerging."[13] His political-moral self-revelation created a scandal and became a mirror—for both historical and contemporary Bulgaria.

Nedko Solakov knows that he cannot change the world fundamentally. But—as in the case of his work Discussion (Property) for the 2007 Venice Biennale—he can let it know that the Kalashnikov as well as the Cyrillic alphabet and *Lactobacillus bulgaricus* are Bulgarian, not Russian, achievements, while at the same time the ambivalent choice of the sublime aspects of national pride shows how groundless that pride ultimately is.

"I'm ironical about the feeling of freedom of the artist, who is, of course, not free at all."[14] And under one of the cheap gold frames of his Romantic Landscapes with Missing Parts are the words: *"I am a Bulgarian and this is not good at all."*[15]

1 Georgi Gospodinov, Natürlicher Roman, Graz and Vienna 2007, p. 7. Translated as Natural Novel (Normal, IL, 2005).

2 Ibid., p. 9.

3 See pp. 64–67 in this volume.

4 Gospodinov 2007 (see note 1), p. 99.

5 Nedko Solakov, interview by Iara Boubnova, in Nedko Solakov: A 12 1/3 (and even more) Year Survey, exh. cat. Casino Luxembourg: Forum d'art contemporain, Luxembourg; Rooseum Center for Contemporary Art, Malmö; O.K Centrum für Gegenwartskunst, Linz (Vienna and Bolzano, 2003), p. 80.

6 Nedko Solakov, quoted after Doug Black, "Nedko Solakov" (accessed on April 10, 2008), in http://www.coolhunting.com/archives/2008/02/nedko_solakov.php.

7 Alek Popov, Die Hunde fliegen tief (Salzburg, 2008), pp. 395–96.

8 Nedko Solakov, "The Deal," in Nedko Solakov 2003 (see note 5), p. 168.

9 Ibid.

10 Popov 2008 (see note 7), p. 267.

11 Nedko Solakov in conversation with the author at his studio in Sofia, November 2, 2007.

12 Thomas Wagner, "Laudatio auf Heribert C. Ottersbach" (unpublished manuscript, winner of 2007 Wilhelm-Loth Prize, Mathildenhöhe Darmstadt exhibition building, September 26, 2007).

13 Nedko Solakov, interview by Iara Boubnova, in Nedko Solakov 2003 (see note 5), p. 83.

14 Ibid., p. 79.

15 Wall notice and comment on the picture by the artist at the Madrid exhibition Romantic Landscapes with Missing Parts, 2003. See illustration of detail in Nedko Solakov: Paisajes románticos (con elementos ausentes), exh. cat. Museo Nacional Centro de Arte Reina Sofía (Madrid, 2003), p. 34.

Kyrill und Kalaschnikow
Nedko Solakovs methodisches Spiel mit der Welt

Ralf Beil

»In jeder Sekunde gibt es auf dieser Welt eine lange Schlange weinender Menschen und eine kürzere solcher, die lachen. Aber es gibt auch eine dritte Schlange, die nicht mehr weint und nicht mehr lacht.«[1]

Georgi Gospodinov

Nedko Solakov lässt uns zugleich lachen und weinen. Ihm gelingt das Kunststück, eine vierte Schlange aufzumachen und immer länger werden zu lassen: die der Tragikomik. Es ist die wohl wahrhaftigste Haltung zur Welt. Gerade auch aus der Sicht eines Bulgaren. Nicht umsonst schreibt Solakovs Landsmann Georgi Gospodinov: »Die Apokalypse ist auch in einem einzelnen Land möglich.«[2]

Bulgarien, das Land auf der Balkanhalbinsel, in dem Nedko Solakov 1957 geboren wurde und wo er bis heute in der Hauptstadt Sofia, benannt nach der antiken Göttin der Weisheit, lebt und arbeitet, gilt einerseits als Kernland des alten Europa, als Wiege der abendländischen Kultur: Musik, Theater und Tanz haben hier ihren Ursprung. Der mythische Kulturheros und Sänger Orpheus soll aus den Rhodopen, einem Gebirge im Süden Bulgariens, stammen, der Dionysos-Kult im Siedlungsgebiet der Thraker entstanden sein. Andererseits wird dieses Territorium bestimmt durch seine geografische Randlage in Südosteuropa, 500 Jahre ottomanisch-türkischer Fremdherrschaft und die russische Dominanz der letzten eineinhalb Jahrhunderte: 1877 marschierten die Russen als Befreier ein und schufen eine Monarchie. 1944 kehrten sie als Besatzer zurück und errichteten eine Volksrepublik. Erst seit dem Ende des Sozialismus 1989 ist Bulgarien nach all diesen Wechselfällen der Geschichte erneut auf dem Weg nach Europa – und Künstler wie Nedko Solakov werden sichtbar.

Die Lehre des Igels

In einem großen, abgedunkelten Saal beleuchten zwölf Punktstrahler ebenso viele Stellen am Boden. Die Besucher müssen nahe herangehen und sich tief herunterbeugen, um das dort ausgebreitete Geschehen zu erfassen. Da verliert ein Spielzeugoktopus einen seiner acht Fangarme an einen Trupp Plastikameisen. Auf dem Rücken des Tintenfisches steht in Schwarz geschrieben: *»The good news: in some way he liked more the uneven numbers (figures).«* Da liegt eine orangefarbene Plastikblüte im Scheinwerferlicht, und auf dem Boden daneben liest man:

»The bad news: He was dead. The good news: The flower on his grave will last forever.« Oder ein kleiner, in sich gerollter Keramikigel erhält den Kommentar: *»It was so nice: the same lady with the soft tender hand was caressing him. The bad news: he was dreaming again.«*[3]

Die Rauminstallation Good News, Bad News (seit 1998) führt paradigmatisch in Solakovs Humor und Weltsicht ein. Es sind absurde Mikrogeschichten und Denkstücke, die Solakov hier vor uns ausbreitet – Geschichten, bei denen einem das Lachen wortwörtlich im Halse stecken bleibt. Desillusionierend, tragikomisch, bisweilen sarkastisch und dabei stets ebenso kurios wie wahr. Sie verschieben unseren Blickwinkel durch drastische Perspektivenwechsel. »Was für ein Roman würde wohl entstehen, wenn wir eine Fliege dazu bringen könnten zu erzählen«, fragt sich der Icherzähler in Gospodinovs Prosatext Natürlicher Roman.[4] Solakov antwortet auf ebensolche Fragen mit seinen Fabeln, in denen, wie im Fall des Igels, nicht selten Traum und Realität kollidieren.

Es sind zugleich Geschichten einer Sozialisation im Staatssozialismus, dessen steter Anspruch und Abbruch der Ideale geradezu zu Kippbildern, Galgenhumor und kurioser Improvisation zwingt. Dialektik erzeugt auch hier keine schlüssigen Synthesen, sondern immer wieder nur lose Enden und gemischte Motivationen. Die bulgarische Kuratorin und Kunstkritikerin Iara Boubnova bestätigt dies mit den Worten: »Unser Leben hier ist nun mal so: Das Gute ist nie nur gut, das Schlechte nie nur schlecht.«[5]

Der Nonsens des Geldwertes

»The sense of absurd in my work gets stimulated and fed by the absurdity of the Bulgarian reality«, konstatiert Solakov unumwunden – dies gilt auch und gerade für die Zeit nach 1989.[6] Es ist jene Form der Absurdität, die ebenso bei dem bulgarischen Schriftsteller Alek Popov, einem Generationsgenossen Gospodinovs, aufscheint. Einer der Protagonisten seines Romans Die Hunde fliegen tief, ein New Yorker Börsenspekulant bulgarischer Abstammung, holt dort zu einer Philosophie des Geldes aus: »Stell dir vor, du bist eine Tür, durch die das Geld ein und aus geht. Es hat keine Bedeutung, in welche Richtung. Wichtig ist die Bewegung. Wer das einmal begriffen hat, wird sich niemals wieder Sorgen machen, ob er gewinnt oder verliert…«[7]

2002 führt Nedko Solakov als Antwort auf ein »Business-begegnet-Kunst-und-schafft-gemeinsam-Kreatives Event«[8] seine Aktion The Deal im dänischen Herning durch. Ebendort, wo Piero Manzoni vierzig Jahre zuvor seinen berühmten Socle du Monde realisiert hatte, auf dem seitdem die Welt zu ruhen scheint, visualisiert Nedko Solakov das, worauf die Welt des 21. Jahrhunderts beruht: die zumeist unsichtbaren Geldbewegungen und globalen Finanztransaktionen sowie die Fluktuation des Monetären bis hin zu dessen gänzlichem Verlust.

Ein Videofilm dokumentiert, wie innerhalb einer halben Stunde aus einem 1000-Kronen-Schein, »einem Teil des Projektbudgets«, ein paar Stücke Münzgeld werden, allein durch den Umtausch des Geldes in andere Währungen: »Die US-Dollar wurden dann wieder in dänische Kronen gewechselt, dann wieder in US-Dollar (oder Euro) und danach wieder in dänische Kronen und so weiter und so fort, bis dieser Betrag zu Kleingeld zusammengeschmolzen war, aufgefressen von den Provisionen und den Devisen- und Valutenkursen. Einige der besten Studierenden des Betriebswirtschaftsinstituts – Marlene, Monica, Robert und Vibeke – machten während dieser Transaktionen Notizen.«[9]

Vielleicht hat Nedko Solakov bei der Entwicklung dieser Idee und der Durchführung seines absurden Geldgeschäftes Ähnliches verspürt wie ein anderer Protagonist aus Alek Popovs

Roman: »Ich fühlte mich geborgen [...] wie in einer Rettungskapsel, und mir war klar, dass ich mir dieses Gefühl für kein Geld der Welt kaufen konnte. Es gibt eben Nischen, in denen die Marktwirtschaft nicht funktioniert.«[10] Nedko Solakovs Kunst ist so eine Nische. Und vor diesem Hintergrund versteht man auch das Diktum des Künstlers: »I can't make mistakes.«[11] Denn Fehler, ob nun systemimmanent oder systemfremd, sind immer schon Teil seiner Strategie und Kunst.

Die Heimat des Lactobacillus

»Was es bedeutet, Bilder der Vergangenheit zu fixieren oder kollektive, zu nationalen Mythen stilisierte Bilder zu hinterfragen, hat [...] der Fall einer jungen bulgarischen Kunsthistorikerin gezeigt. Weil sie herausgefunden hat, dass das Gemälde Das Massaker von Batak des polnischen Malers Antoni Piotrowski nicht auf authentischen, sondern auf inszenierten Fotografien beruht und damit angeblich einen bulgarischen Nationalmythos in Frage gestellt hat, wurde sie mit dem Tod bedroht und musste ihr Land verlassen. Radikale Nationalisten beschimpften sie als ›Staatsfeindin‹ und ›Pseudobulgarin‹ und wollten sie sogar pfählen. Hier ist sie mit Händen zu greifen, die Macht der Bilder und die Verantwortung derer, die mit ihnen umgehen. Wer ist Herr über die Erinnerung? Wer legt fest, wie es gewesen ist? Historiker? Politiker? Bürokraten? Archivare? Dichter? Fotografen? Das Fernsehen gar?«[12]

Die Beschäftigung mit politischen Fragen in Kunst und Kunstgeschichte kann in Bulgarien durchaus gefährlich werden – bis heute, wie dieser Fall von 2007 belegt. Nedko Solakov hat sich davon nicht abschrecken lassen, im Gegenteil. Er hat die jüngste Geschichte Bulgariens schon in der Wendezeit an seinem eigenen Beispiel thematisiert, als er in einem Kunstwerk bekannte, bis Sommer 1983 Informantendienste für die bulgarische Geheimpolizei geleistet zu haben: »Seit ich Top Secret (1989/90), das Aktenfach mit Karteikarten aus meiner Lebensgeschichte, ausgestellt habe, habe ich keine Angst mehr. Nur damals war mir ziemlich bange. Als ich damals die Karteikarten über meine Beziehungen zur Staatssicherheit schrieb, [...] sorgte dieses Werk für einen Rieseneklat.«[13] Seine politisch-moralische Selbstentblößung war skandalös und wurde zum Spiegel – für das historische ebenso wie für das zeitgenössische Bulgarien.

Nedko Solakov weiß, dass er die Welt nicht grundsätzlich ändern kann. Aber er kann ihr – wie im Fall seiner Biennale-Arbeit Discussion (Property) von 2007 – beibringen, dass die Kalaschnikow ebenso wie das kyrillische Alphabet und der Lactobacillus bulgaricus bulgarische und nicht etwa russische Errungenschaften sind, wobei die ambivalente Auswahl der hehren Aspekte des Nationalstolzes zugleich anzeigt, wie bodenlos dieser Stolz letztlich ist.

»Meine Ironie richtet sich gegen das Freiheitsgefühl des Künstlers, der im Grunde gar nicht frei ist.«[14] Unter einem der billigen Goldrahmen seiner Romantic Landscapes with Missing Parts steht denn auch: *»I am a Bulgarian and this is not good at all.«*[15]

1 Georgi Gospodinov, Natürlicher Roman, Graz und Wien 2007, S. 7.

2 Ebd., S. 9.

3 Siehe S. 64–67 in vorliegender Publikation.

4 Gospodinov 2007 (wie Anm. 1), S. 99.

5 Iara Boubnova im Gespräch mit Nedko Solakov, in: Nedko Solakov. A 12 1/3 (and even more) Year

Survey, Ausst.-Kat. Casino Luxembourg. Forum d'art contemporain, Luxemburg; Rooseum Center for Contemporary Art, Malmö; O.K Centrum für Gegenwartskunst, Linz; Wien und Bozen 2003, S. 79.

6 Nedko Solakov, zit. nach: Doug Black, »Nedko Solakov«, in: http://www.coolhunting.com/archives/2008/02/nedko_solakov.php, Stand 10.4.2008.

7 Alek Popov, **Die Hunde fliegen tief,** Salzburg 2008, S. 395 f.

8 Nedko Solakov, »Das Geschäft«, in: **Nedko Solakov** 2003 (wie Anm. 5), S. 202.

9 Ebd.

10 Popov 2008 (wie Anm. 7), S. 267.

11 Nedko Solakov im Gespräch mit dem Autor in seinem Atelier in Sofia, 2.11.2007.

12 Thomas Wagner, »Laudatio auf Heribert C. Ottersbach«, Wilhelm-Loth-Preisträger 2007, 26.9.2007, Ausstellungsgebäude Mathildenhöhe Darmstadt, unveröffentlichtes Manuskript.

13 Nedko Solakov im Gespräch mit Iara Boubnova, in: **Nedko Solakov** 2003 (wie Anm. 5), S. 83.

14 Ebd., S. 79.

15 Wandnotiz und Bildkommentar des Künstlers in der Madrider Ausstellung **Romantic Landscapes with Missing Parts** 2003. Vgl. die Detailabbildung in: **Nedko Solakov. Paisajes románticos con elementos ausentes,** Ausst.-Kat. Museo Nacional Centro de Arte Reina Sofia, Madrid 2003, S. 34.

Deutsche Übersetzung siehe Seite 206

Some time ago I asked five of the best Bulgarian art curators and critics to calm down for a while and to imagine somebody (or something) related to the historical city of Weimar. And after having the image in their mind, to try to seduce it...

S. H. #1—Jaroslava Boubnova, 10'56"
In general, she had Schiller in her head because he was more romantic than Goethe (and died younger, too). While she was watching herself as the video replayed, she made some remarks:
- "If I could keep this expression on my face, I will succeed in the world (art)"
- "There are men who make associations (sexual, we guess) too directly—it's very easy to deal with them."
- "Oh, no..."
- "My students told me that I was not looking in their eyes while lecturing."

S. H. #2—Boris Danailov, 5'30"
Mr. Danailov was inspired by some of the nudes from Lucas Cranach. We had a small argument with him: I expressed my concern that according to my own taste, I don't think these nudes are sexy enough, but Mr. Danailov said they were perfect—a bit perverse looking.
One of his remarks: "What a hypocrite I am!"

S. H. #3—Maria Vassileva, 2'57"
We agreed that the subject would be Goethe, even though the connection to the great poet is somewhat unusual: While she appeared to be highly emotionally involved, Ms. Vassileva actually was recalling the memory of the extremely delicious cherry cake (with cream), that she got to eat in a café after visiting the (slightly dusty) Goethe's house in 1983 (or so) during a study trip to the DDR that was organised by the Academy of Fine Arts in Sofia where she was studying Art History.
"It was very, very delicious..." she said.

S. H. #4—Philip Zidarov, 5'9"
Mr. Zidarov was short:
"Goethe's Lotte in Weimar!"

S. H. #5—Ilina Koralova, 7'34"
She was thinking of Franz Liszt, although in a strange way. A few months before, she had seen a feature movie dedicated to Chopin's life in Paris (Hugh Grant was playing Chopin) on Bulgarian television. George Sand and Liszt were there, too. So she actually had in her mind Julian Sands—the actor who was playing Liszt and who had played the surgeon in **Boxing Helena** as well.

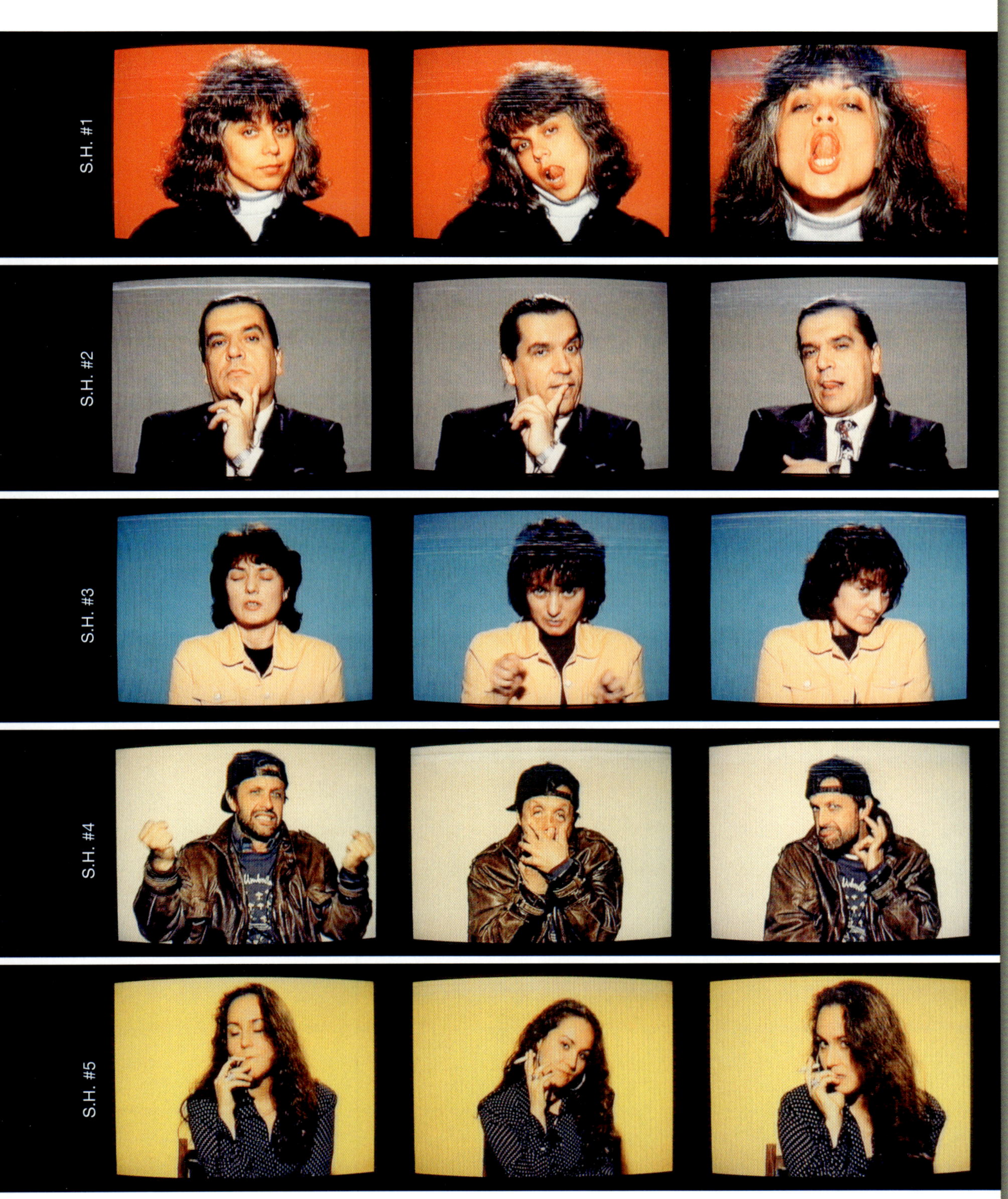

Sexual Harassment, 1997

Five video films on DVD, color, silent, looped; five monitors; handwritten texts; shelf with performers's CVs; dimensions variable

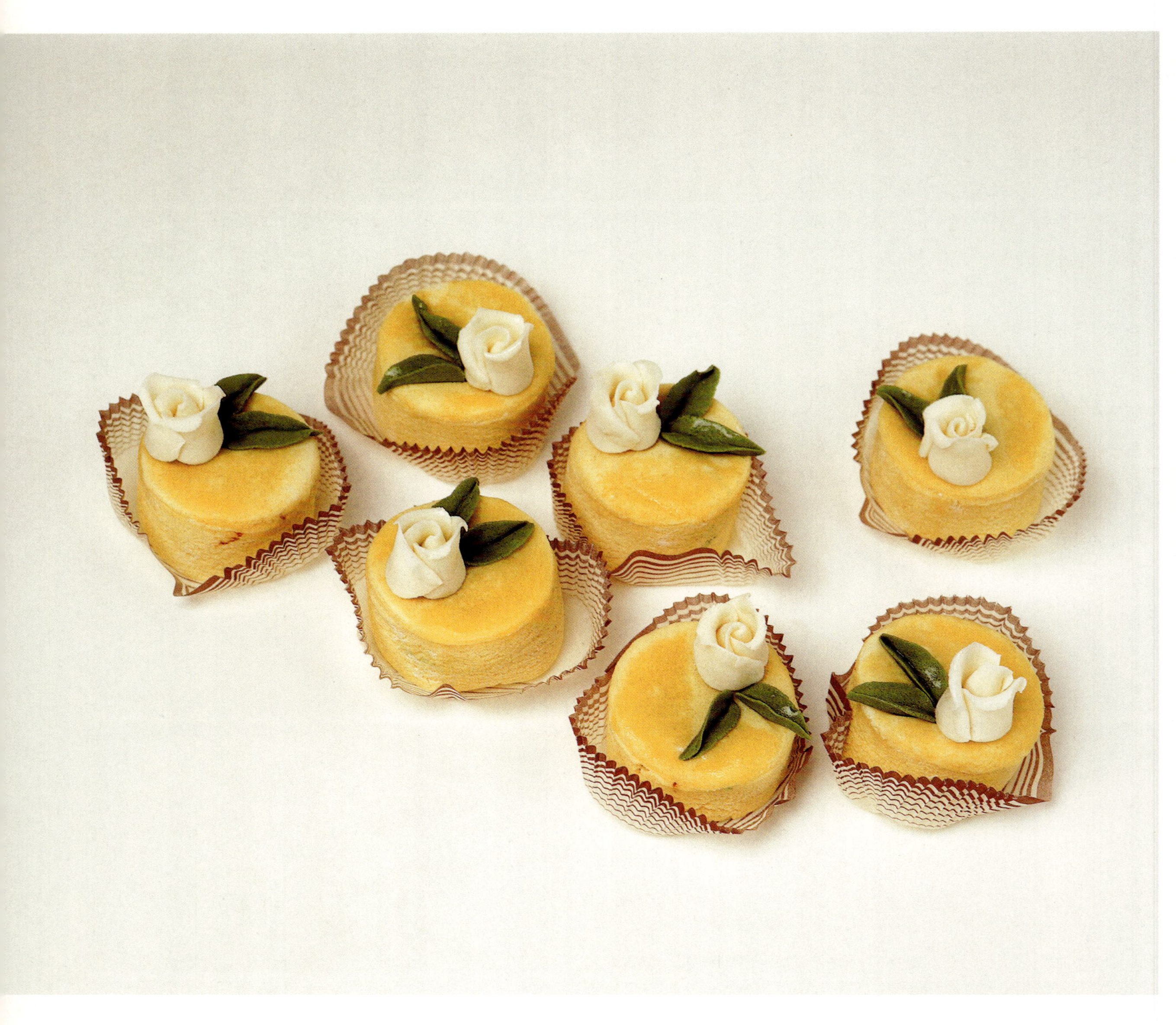

Sugar, coloring agents, flour, chocolate, pleated paper;
seven pieces (the artist's clipped-off nails inside one of them);
5 x 5 x 5 cm each

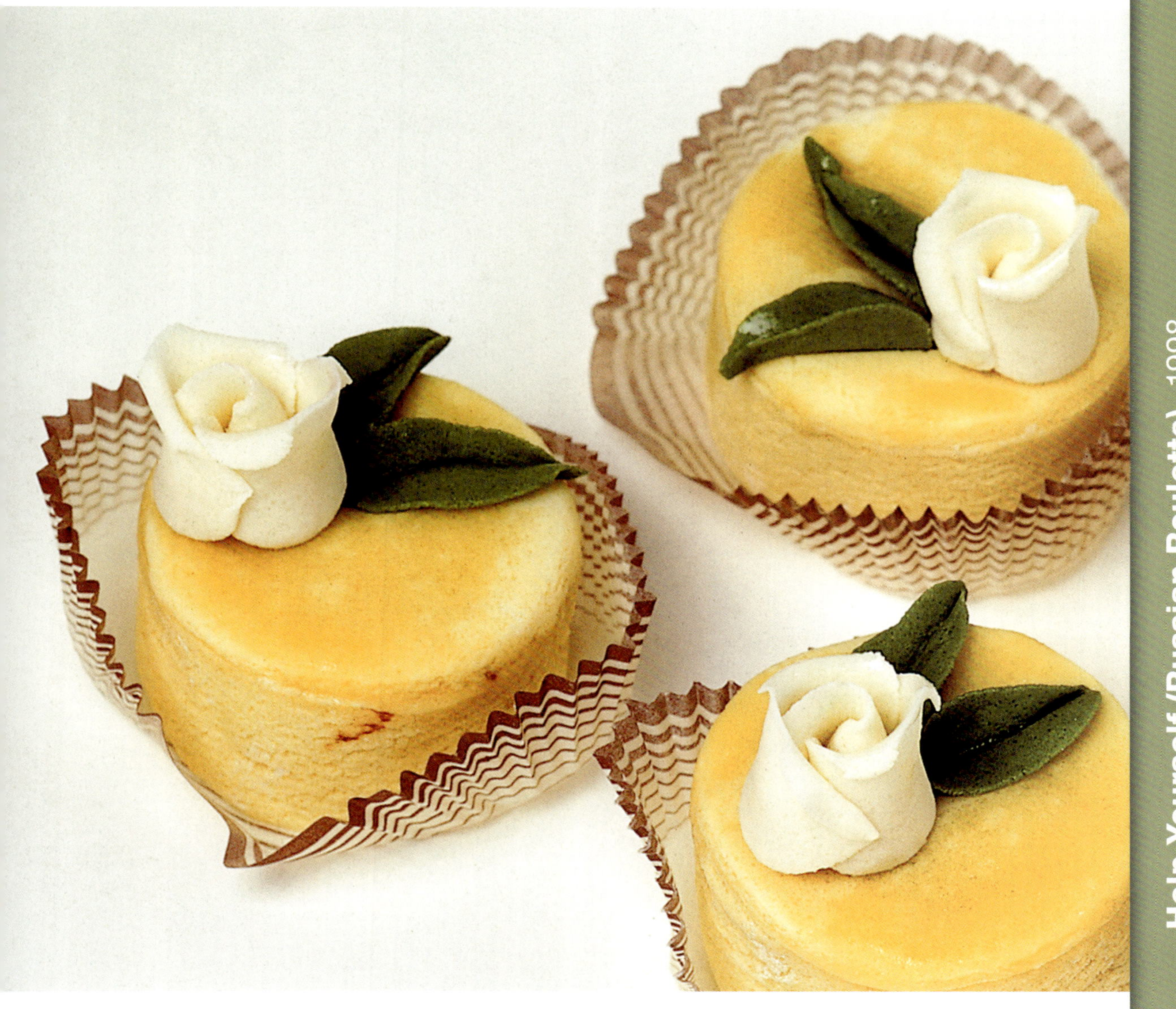

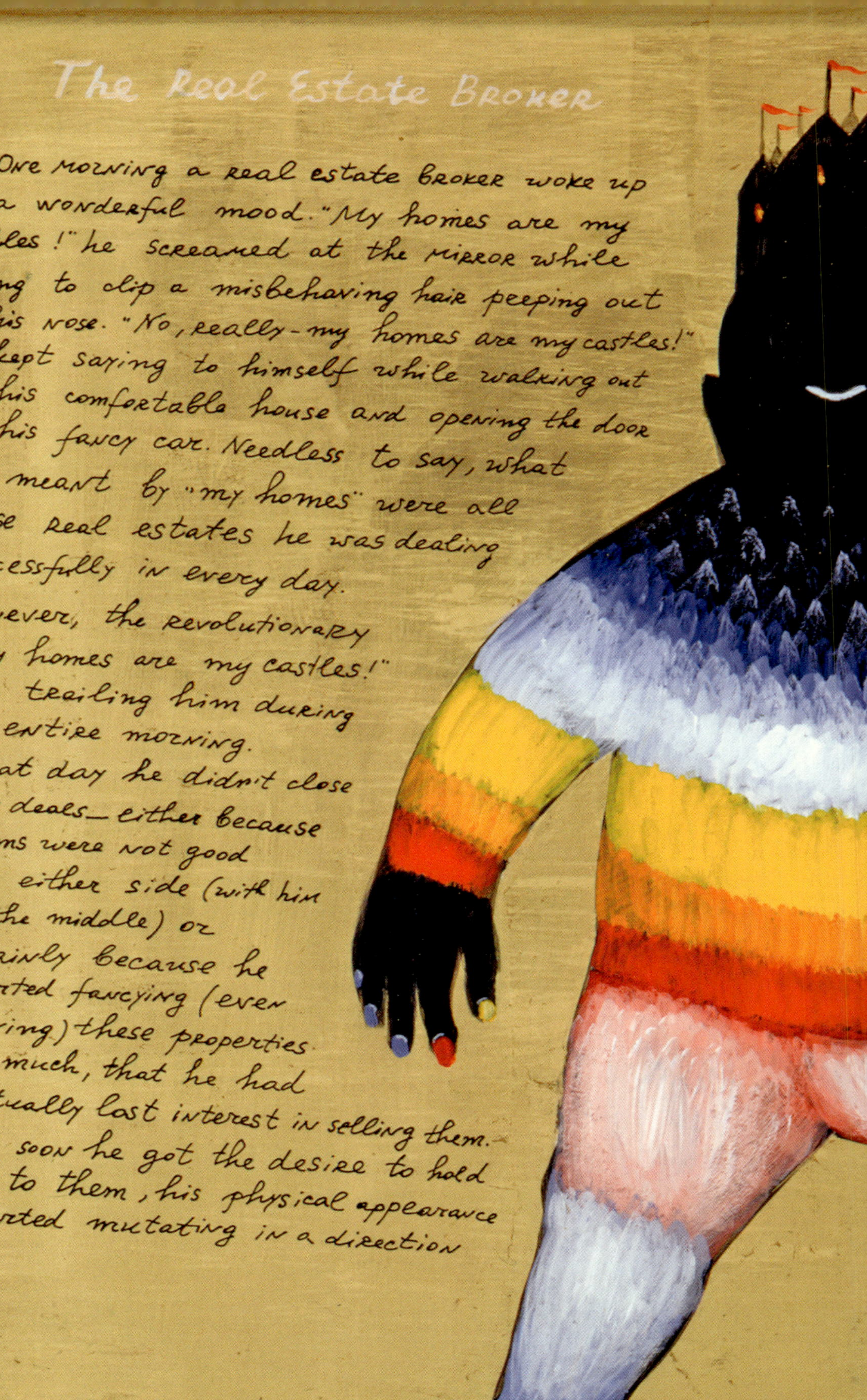

Acrylic and black drawing ink on gilded lime wood; 40 x 50 x 4 cm

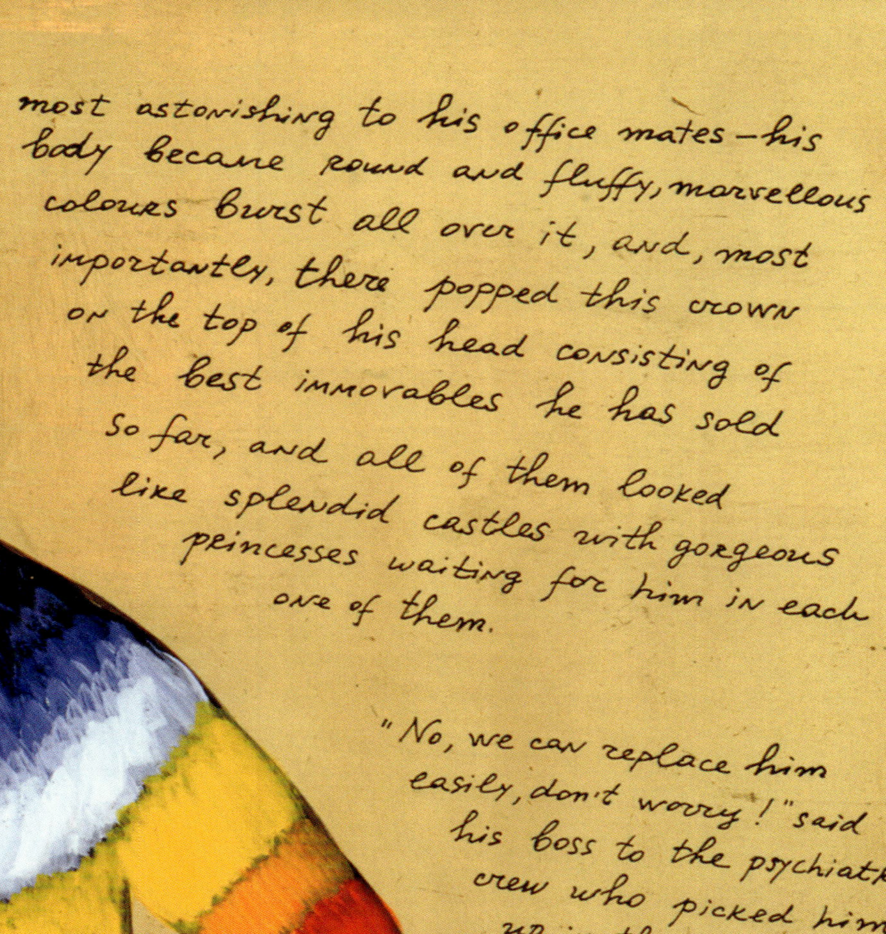
most astonishing to his office mates – his
body became round and fluffy, marvellous
colours burst all over it, and, most
importantly, there popped this crown
on the top of his head consisting of
the best immovables he has sold
so far, and all of them looked
like splendid castles with gorgeous
princesses waiting for him in each
one of them.
"No, we can replace him
easily, don't worry!" said
his boss to the psychiatric
crew who picked him
up in the early afternoon
and brought him
well fastened to
that grey, big
building with high
walls and barred
windows which looked
like a castle, too.
He is still happy, that broker.
CONAK '07

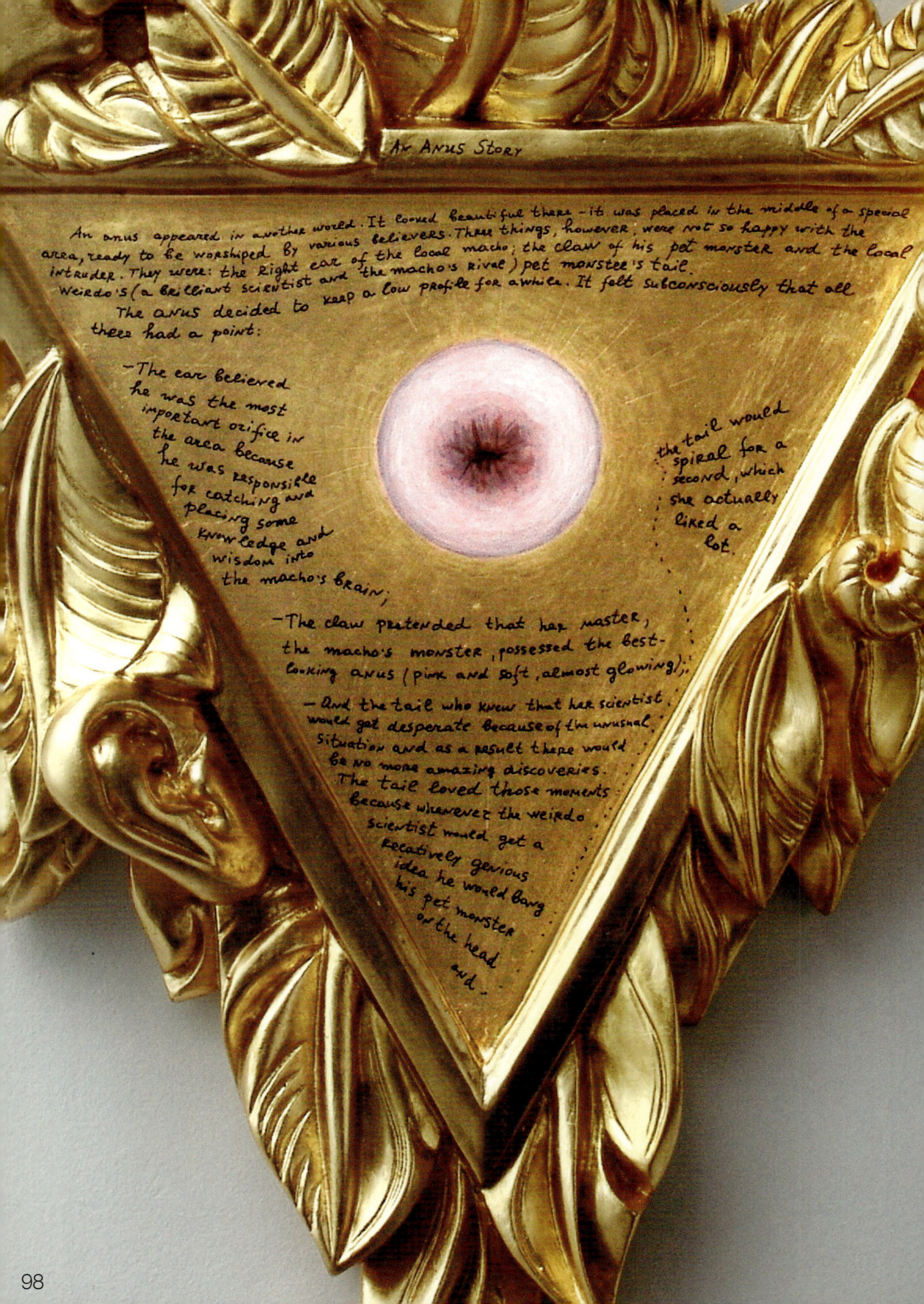

An Anus Story
An anus appeared in another world. It looked beautiful there – it was placed in the middle of a special area, ready to be worshiped by various believers. Three things, however, were not so happy with the intruder. They were: the right ear of the local macho; the claw of his pet monster and the local weirdo's (a brilliant scientist and the macho's rival) pet monster's tail.
The anus decided to keep a low profile for awhile. It felt subconsciously that all three had a point:
– The ear believed he was the most important orifice in the area because he was responsible for catching and placing some knowledge and wisdom into the macho's brain;
– The claw pretended that her master, the macho's monster, possessed the best-looking anus (pink and soft, almost glowing);
– And the tail who knew that her scientist would get desperate because of the unusual situation and as a result there would be no more amazing discoveries. The tail loved those moments because whenever the weirdo scientist would get a creatively genious idea he would bang his pet monster on the head and...
...the tail would spiral for a second, which she actually liked a lot.

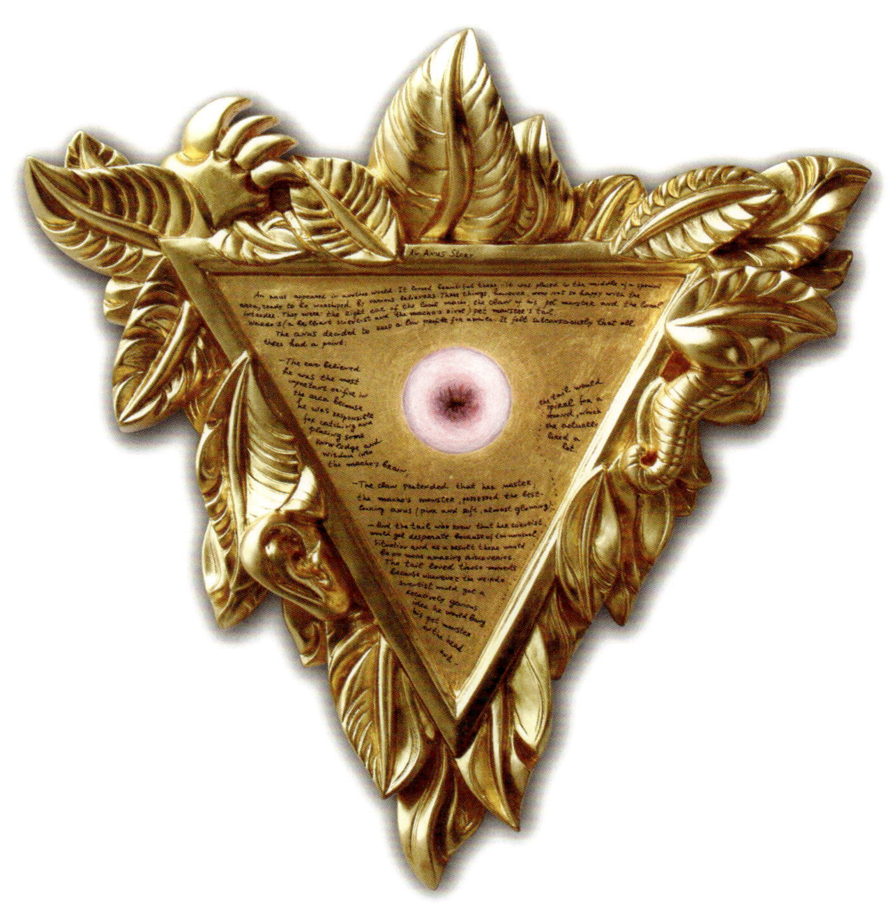

Acrylic and black drawing ink on gilded carved lime wood;
61 x 61 x 8 cm

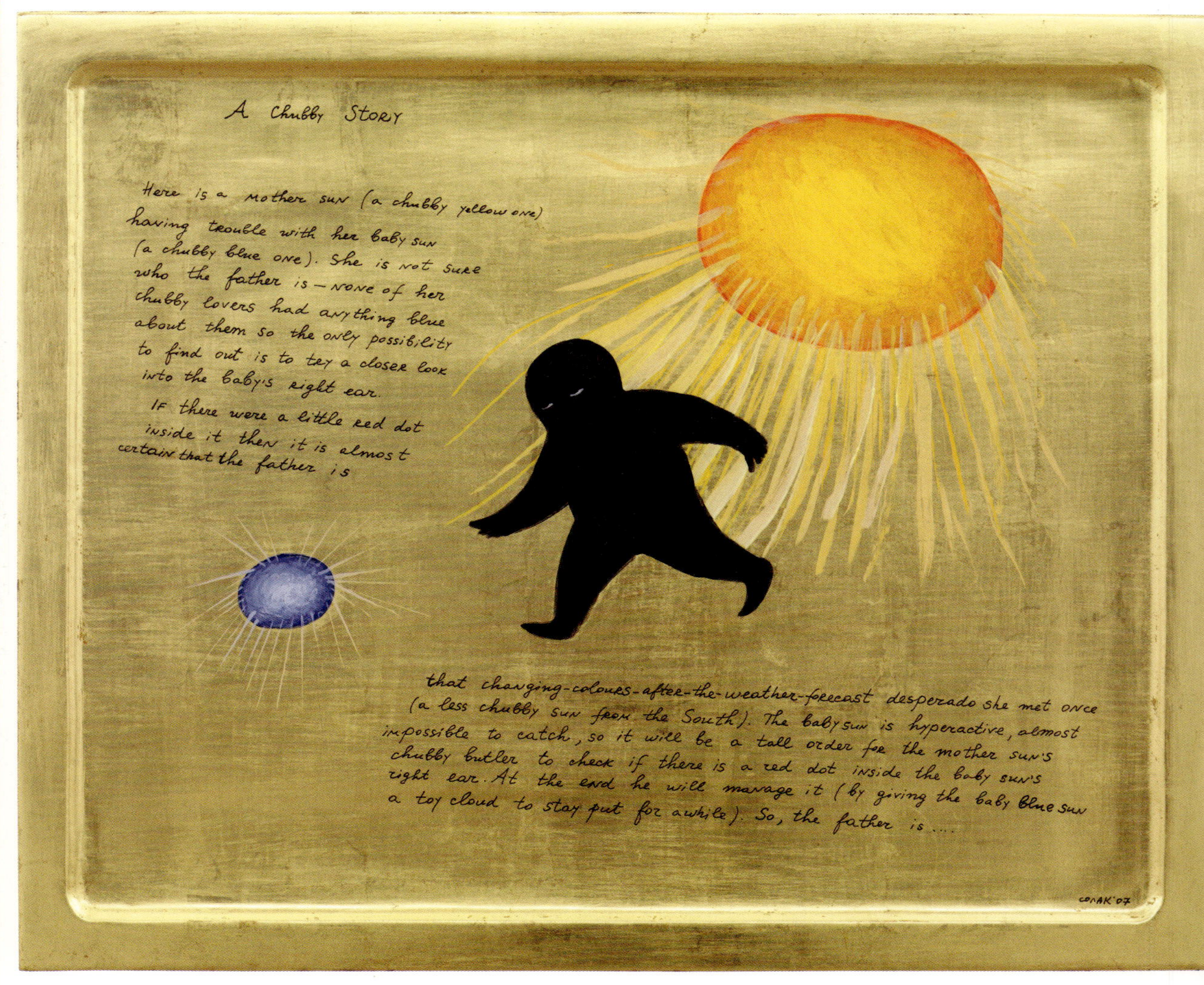

Acrylic and black drawing ink on gilded lime wood;
40 x 50 x 4 cm

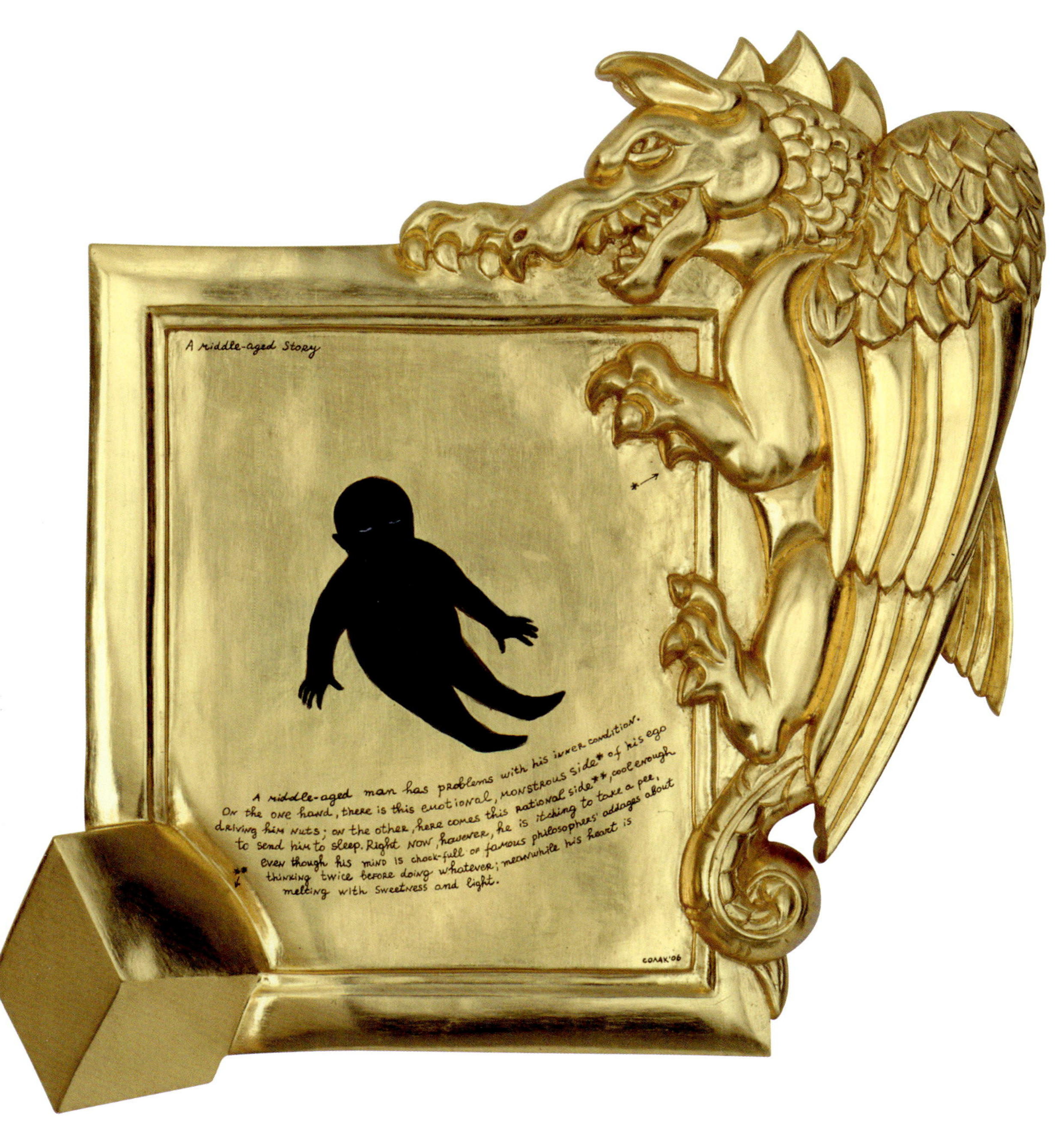

Acrylic and black drawing ink on gilded carved lime wood;
61 x 60 x 8 cm

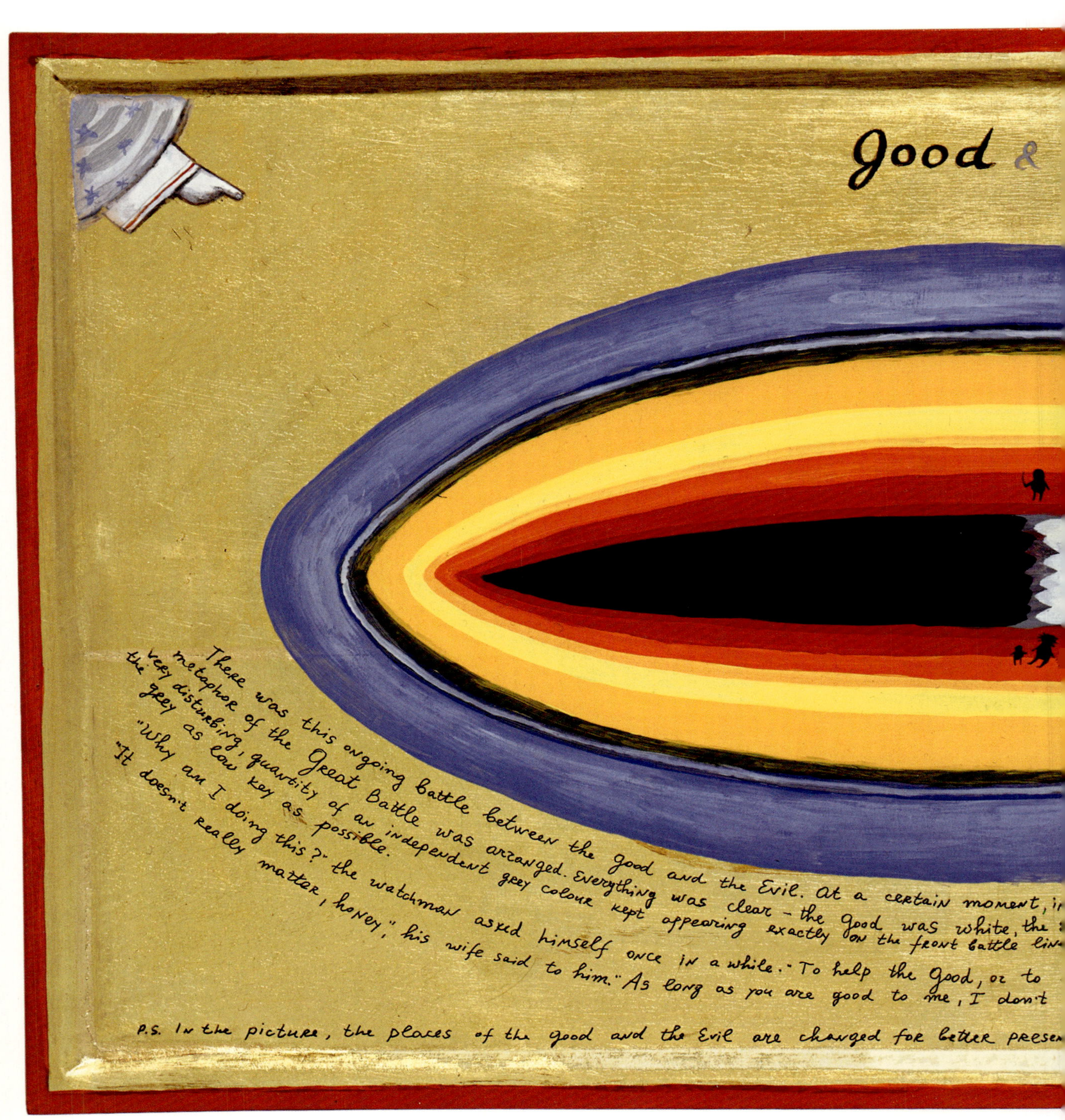

Acrylic and black drawing ink on gilded carved walnut wood; 34 x 65 x 3 cm

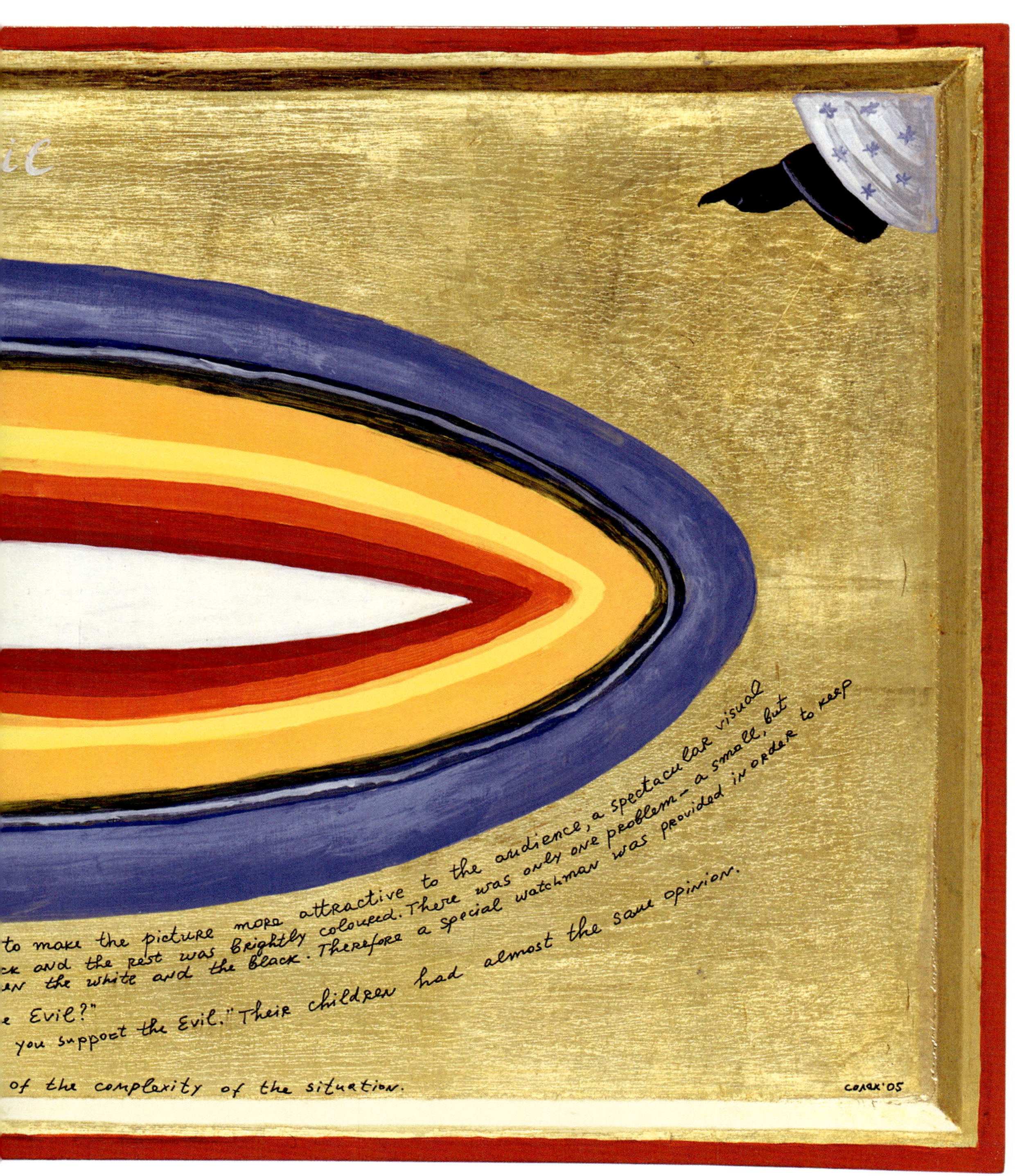
to make the picture more attractive to the audience, a spectacular visual
and the rest was brightly coloured. There was only one problem – a small, but
the white and the black. Therefore a special watchman was provided in order to keep
Evil?"
you support the Evil." Their children had almost the same opinion.
of the complexity of the situation.
colak'05

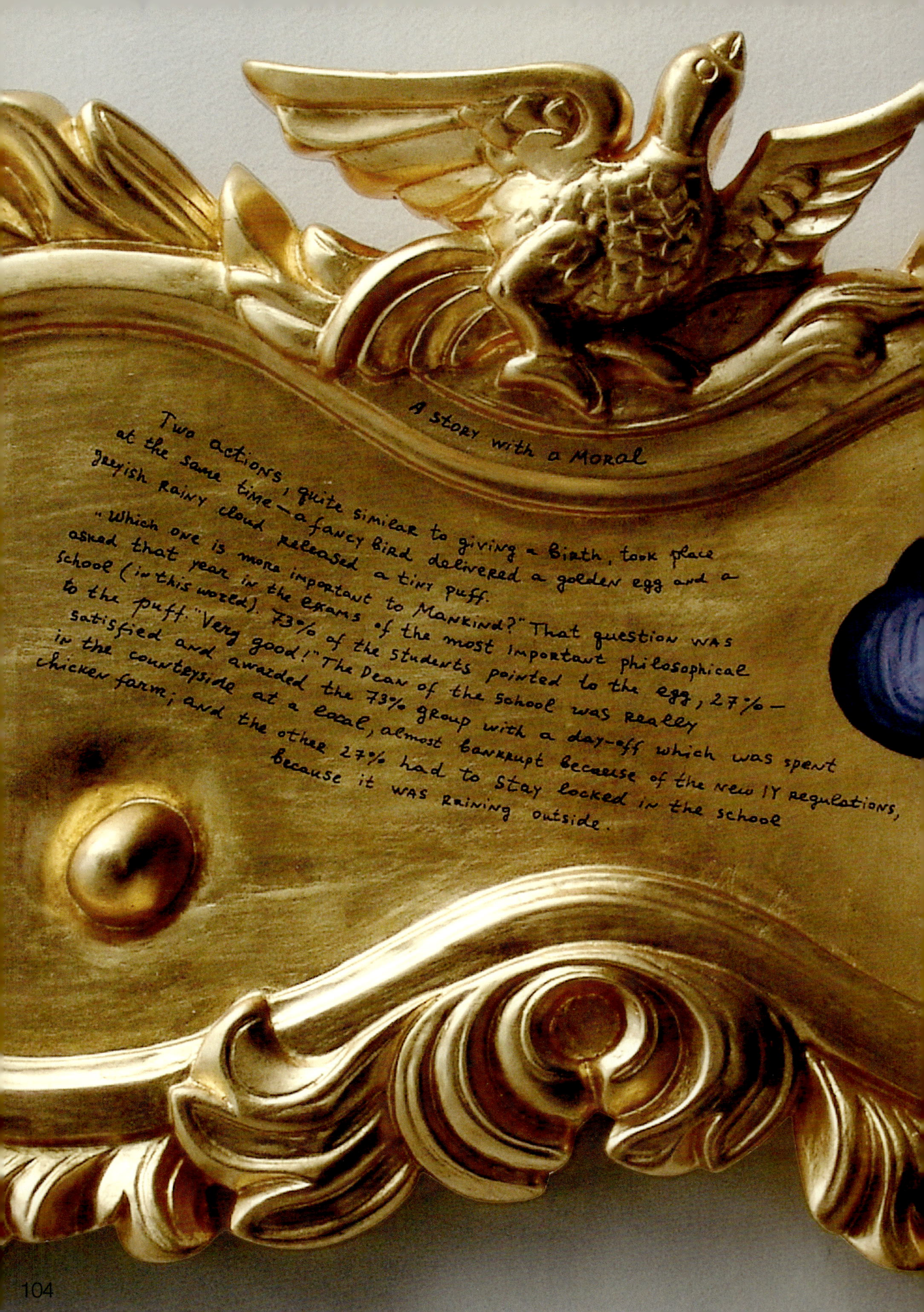
A STORY with a MORAL
Two actions, quite similar to giving a Birth, took place
at the same time – a fancy bird delivered a golden egg and a
greyish rainy cloud released a tiny puff.
"Which one is more important to Mankind?" That question was
asked that year in the exams of the most important philosophical
school (in this world). 73% of the students pointed to the egg, 27% –
to the puff. "Very good!" The Dean of the school was really
satisfied and awarded the 73% group with a day-off which was spent
in the countryside at a local, almost bankrupt because of the new IY regulations,
chicken farm; and the other 27% had to stay locked in the school
because it was raining outside.

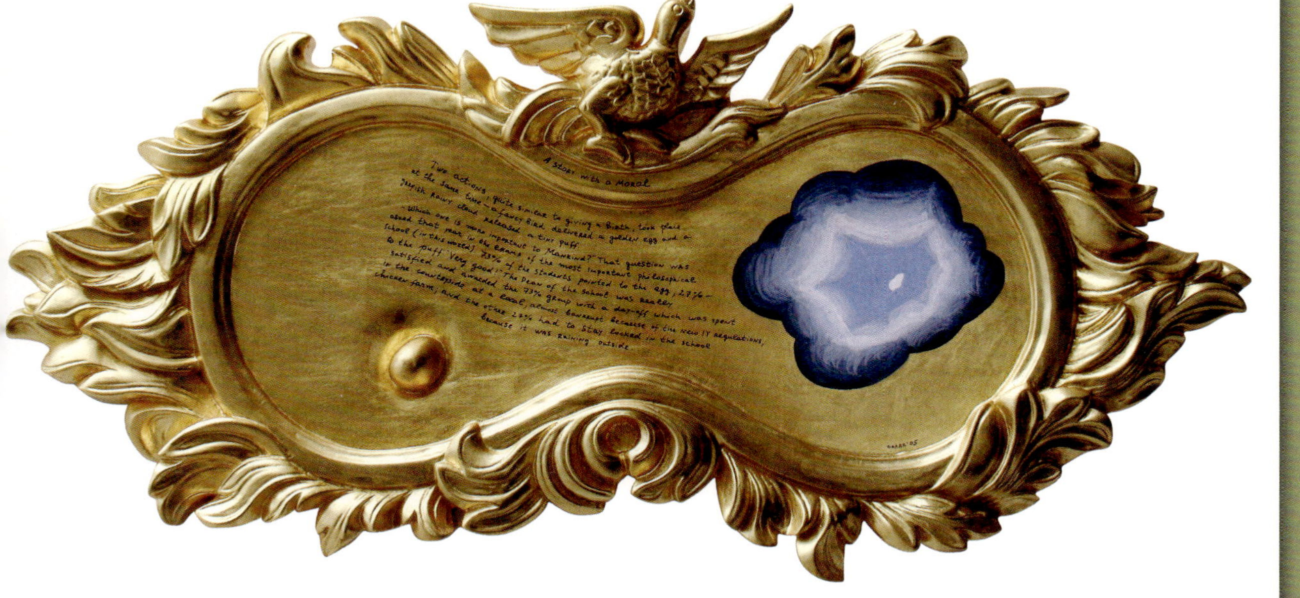

Acrylic and black drawing ink on gilded carved lime wood;
38 x 81 x 9 cm

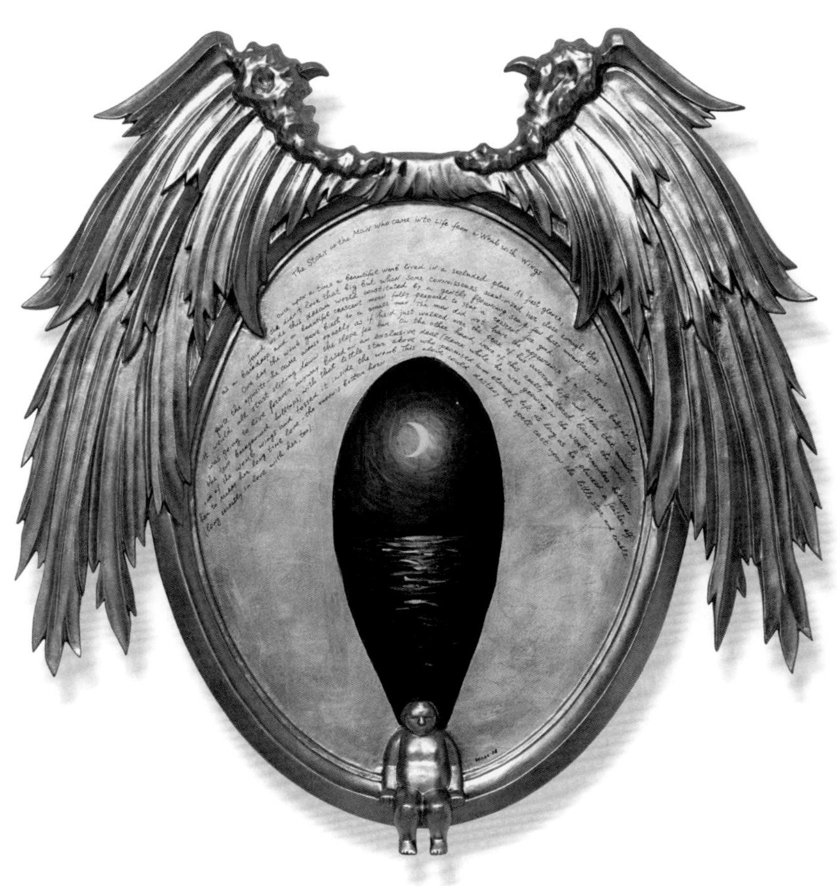

Acrylic and black drawing ink on palladium gilded carved lime wood;
71 x 71 x 9 cm

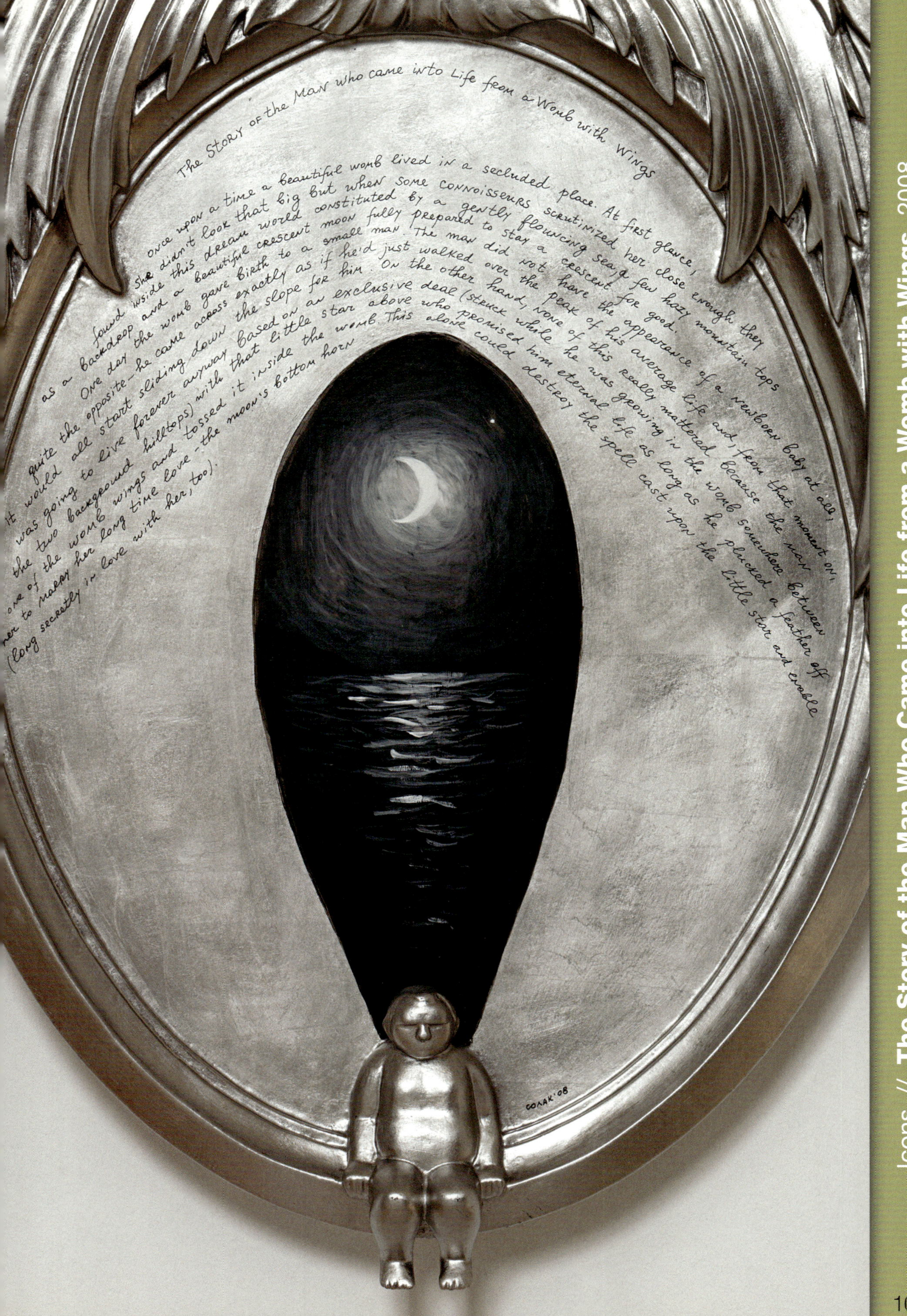

Icons // **The Story of the Man Who Came into Life from a Womb with Wings,** 2008

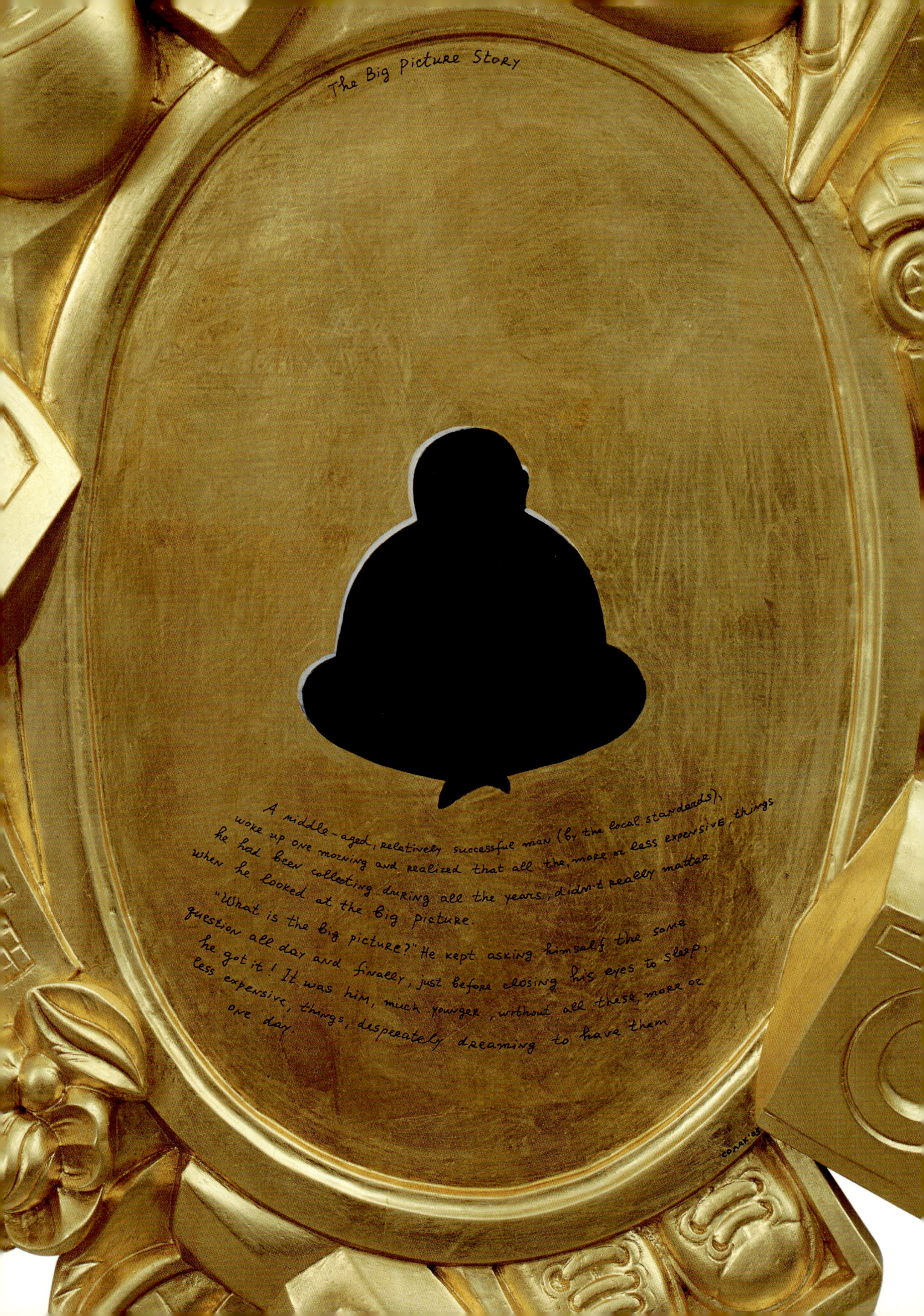
The Big Picture Story
A middle-aged, relatively successful man (by the local standards), woke up one morning and realized that all the, more or less expensive, things he had been collecting during all the years, didn't really matter when he looked at the big picture.
"What is the big picture?" He kept asking himself the same question all day and finally, just before closing his eyes to sleep, he got it! It was him, much younger, without all these, more or less expensive, things, despeeately dreaming to have them one day.
COЛAK '05

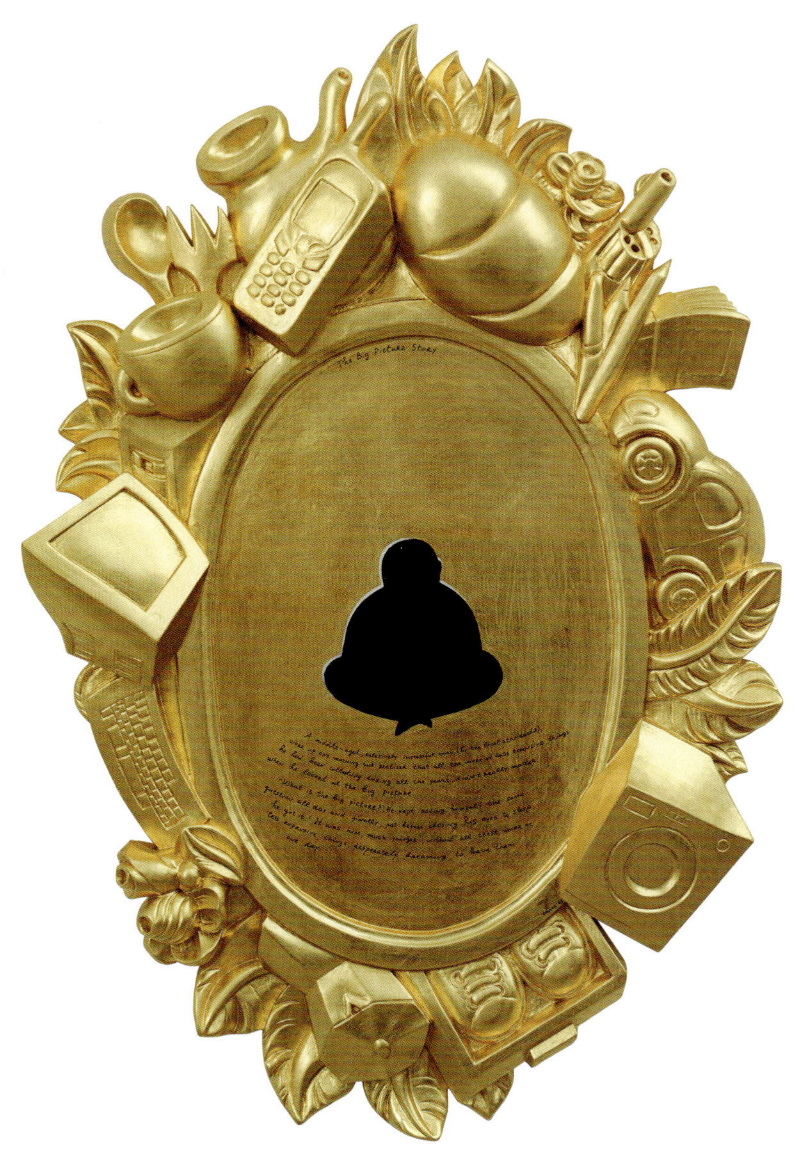

Acrylic and black drawing ink on gilded carved lime wood;
92 x 62 x 9 cm

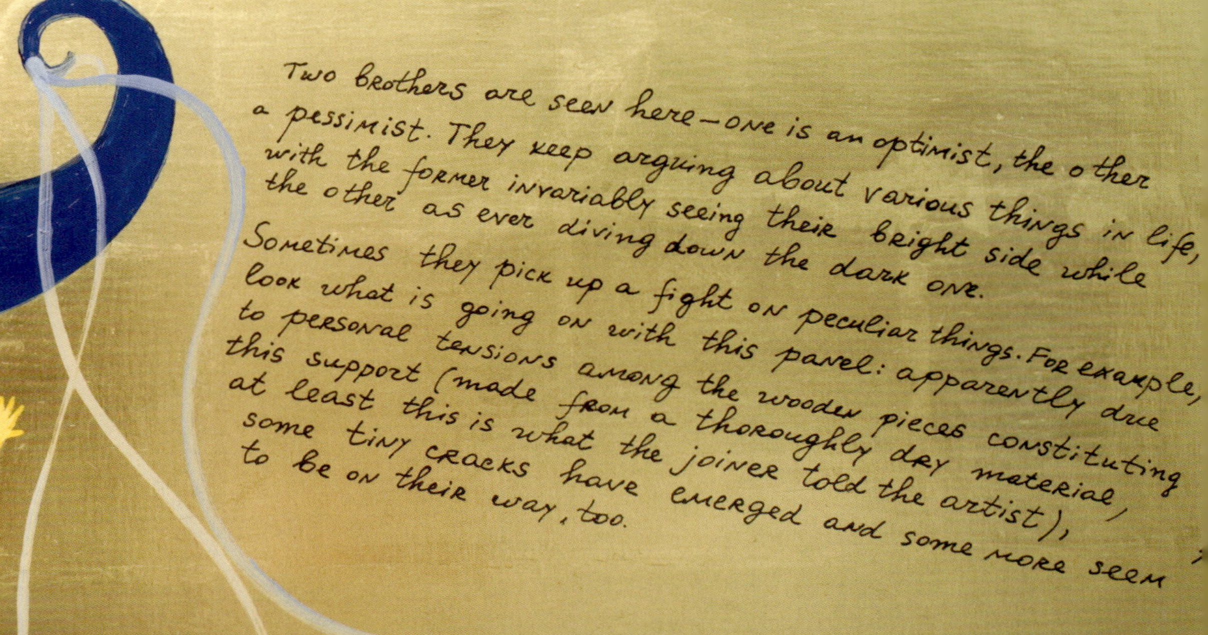

maybe the paint will peel off to

And here they go: the optimistic brother enthusiastically sends some troopers to hold the cracks together, prevent them from opening even further and thus secure the status quo; while the pessimist insists that since this is an entirely lousy support, the beautiful story meant to be drawn and written on the panel better be sealed within that black triangular envelope and put up for better times.

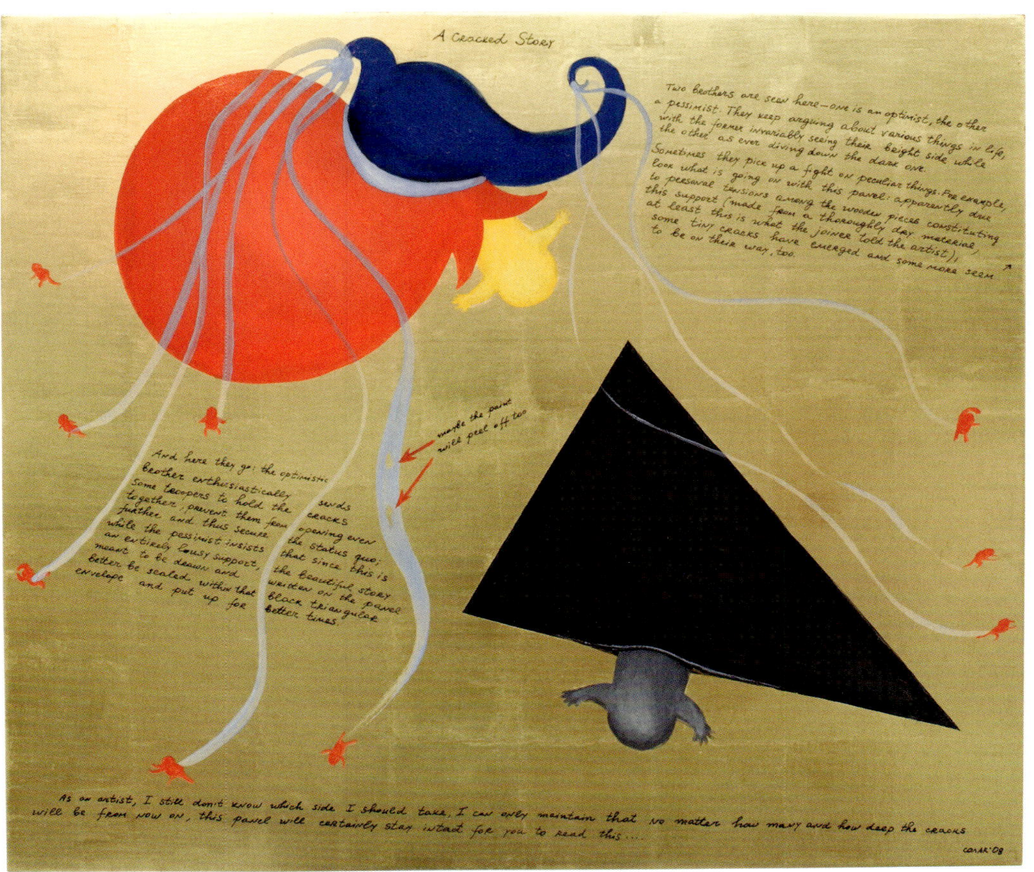

Acrylic and black drawing ink on gilded sycamore wood;
49.5 x 59.5 x 4.5 cm

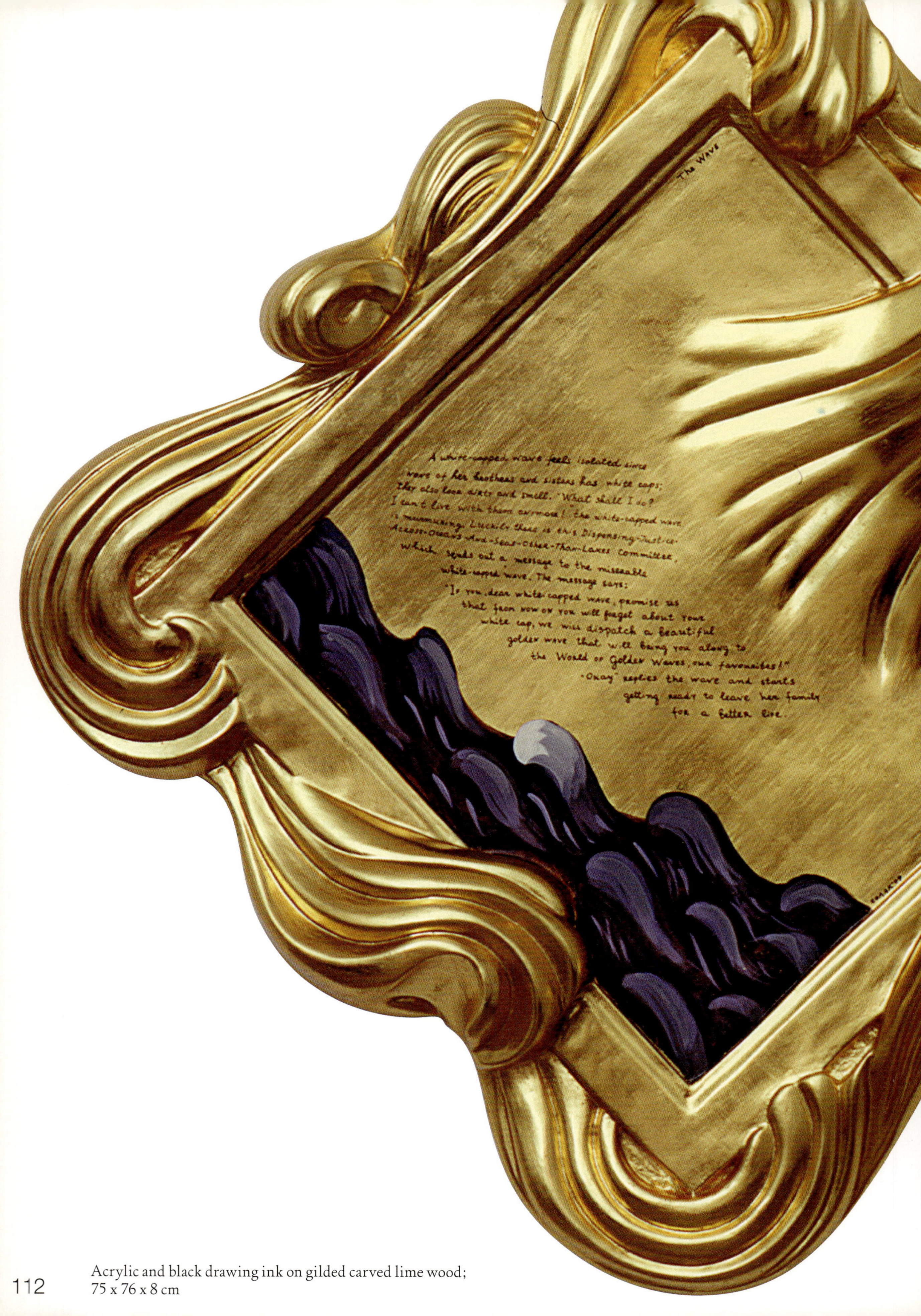

Acrylic and black drawing ink on gilded carved lime wood;
75 x 76 x 8 cm

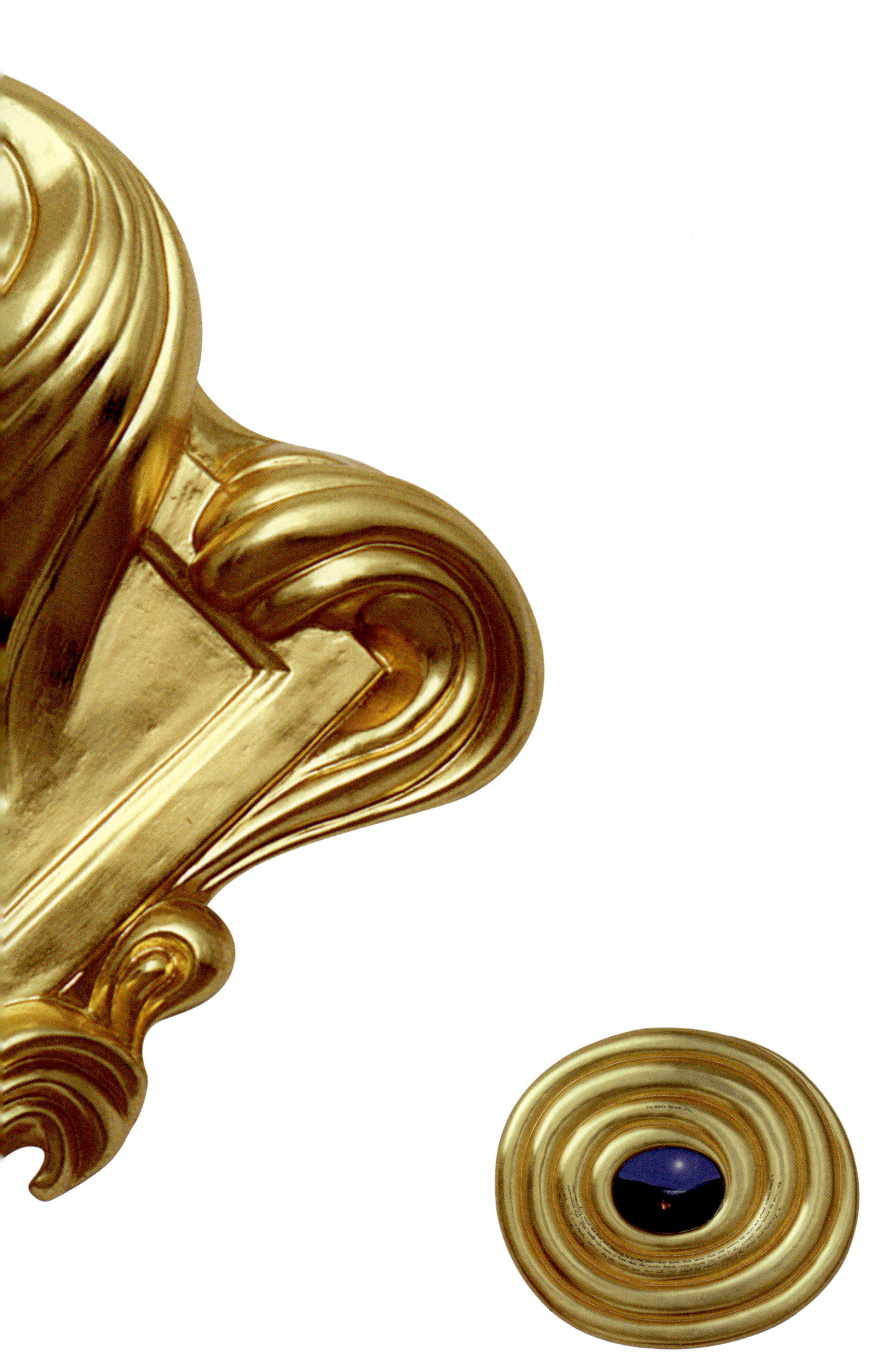

They were sitting around the fire and listening to an old story—that
accommodate them after death. "Is there a hope that the world be
"I still don't know. Maybe." replied the old man and they all
the fire's friendly cracking.

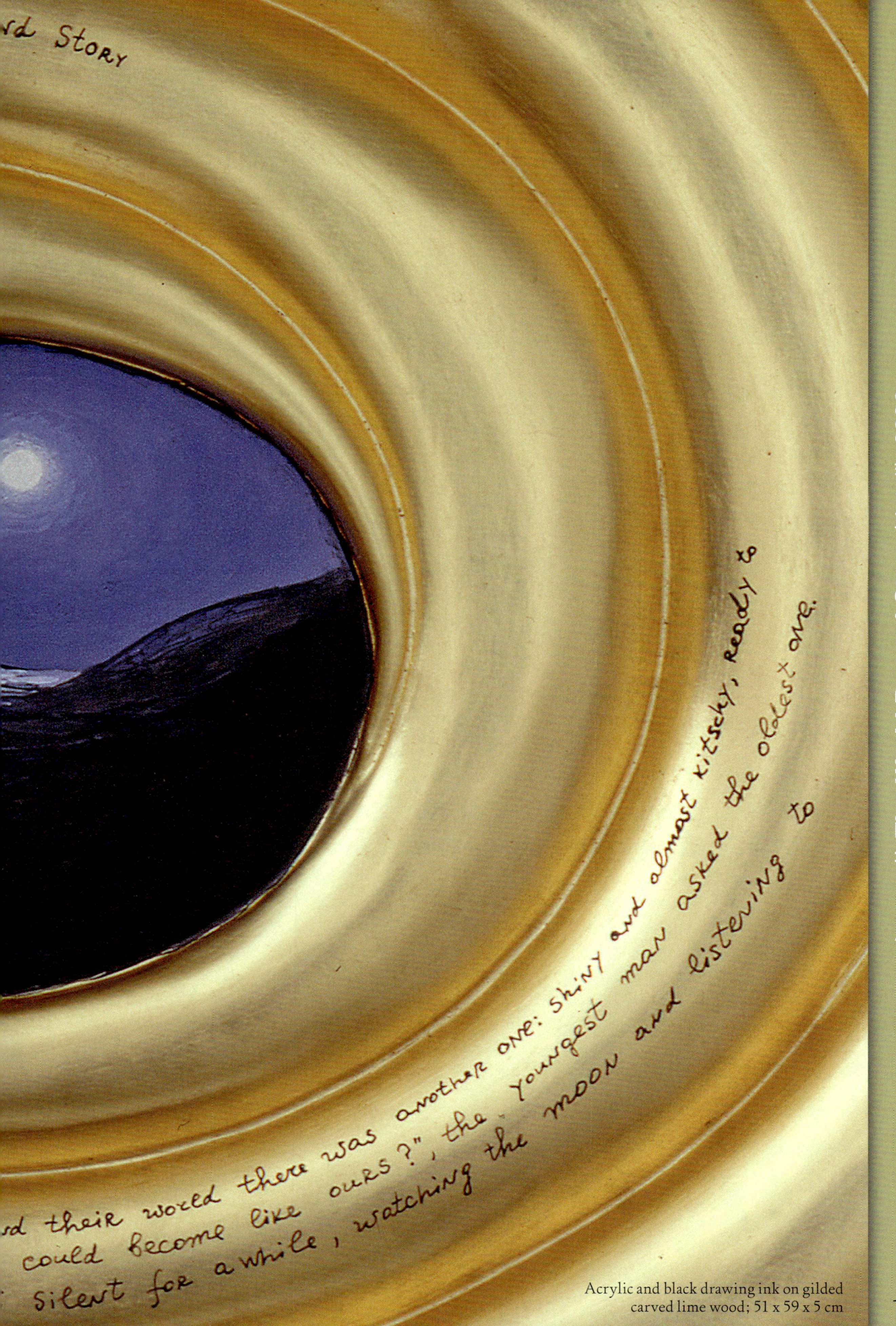

Icons // **The World Beyond Story** (detail), 2006

Acrylic and black drawing ink on gilded carved lime wood; 51 x 59 x 5 cm

Some Nice Things to Enjoy... and Other Fears (Stories from the Breaking Point)

Georgi Gospodinov

Caption: PC written text, words, letters, grammar signs, 20,000 characters (with spaces), 3,195 spaces, forty-four cups of coffee, some drawings, schemes, and hesitations.

The things we like (shall I say, the good things) invariably drive us to reflect on ourselves. And this process works without a hitch. There is no better sign, agent, marker showing whether something is good (in our opinion) than when it urges us to reflect on ourselves. In this sense, liking is an egocentric feeling, pulling the world (the artwork) towards oneself. All of this can of course be articulated using another, more elevated style. Now it suffices to say that Nedko Solakov's works urge me to reflect on myself, my fears, and my pleasures.

If global fear is a constant, then its dispersal among a larger number of people reduces the share due to each of us. At the same time, there are people like Nedko Solakov who choose to bear a more serious piece of this fear pie chart. Sponging on us, they happily set us free from our piece of the pie or at least reduce it. The pleasure of someone else experiencing our fears.

The ninety-nine drawings in the series entitled **Fears** (2006–07) are perfectly simplified in terms of vision and stories. The fears have a color: their realm is in sepia tone and black and white. My first impression—whether it is because of the technique, or the paper, the size which I recognize from old sketchpads from school—so my first impression that won't go away is an impression of something close and cozy. An impression of fear with a small *f*, with soft ears and warm paws, a feeling of everyday small fears, though with "great potential for growth" (Drawing 17). Fears that are simply doing their job (*"A little fear was trying to do his job—spreading fear vibes around,"* [Drawing 1]) and are sometimes trembling from fear of being alone.

In **Fears**, fears are everywhere; these are not only the personal obsessions of the artist (otherwise the series would be much scarier). But when you realize that fear is a universal feeling (or quality), when fears themselves share their own fears, things cease to be so scary.

Nedko Solakov does not simply tell stories about his fears. His trick is different. He makes his fears tell their own stories. This is true of the first drawing of the series. It is true in Drawing 54 about a very expensive firework afraid of not being able to explode in all its colors as everybody expects it to because it was mistakenly made in black and white, or even gray (this fear is so close to home).

I like those seven frantically dancing fat men, who are desperately trying to postpone death (Drawing 63). And the difference between their dance—or fear—and that of the two figures in Drawing 4, who put aside their everyday fears while on the dancing floor. There is a special type of humbleness in them. Fear as a coat, as a purse that we carry all the time. We can put it down on the chair while we are dancing, but it will be waiting for us: *"They will collect the fears back later."* Everyday, small, imperceptible, but always with us. Just like death. Making fear and death part of everyday life with all their coziness and irony is Solakov's trademark.

In fact, the most oppressive and scary drawing is the one where fear is absent. The old university professor from an Eastern European country who has no more fears: *"He is only starving."* (Drawing 12). And vice versa, with a particular ease and self-irony, Drawings 20 and 21 draw the fears closer to a sensation of being lively. Fear becomes a sign, a major evidence of our existence, even part of the pleasures in life.

Drawing 20: *"I am extremely scared of flying tomorrow. If there is a Drawing 21, I'll be able to be scared in the future, too."* And, then, relieved: *"I will be able to be scared in the future too..."* (Drawing 21). I am afraid, therefore I am.

I personally feel great relief from Drawing 17 with the two crossing lines: *"Two lines are... are... are... (here the artist-me gets stuck because he doesn't know how to develop the story). A fear appears on this sheet of paper. Not a big one but with a good potential for future growth."* Relief that someone else shares my fear. What's more, someone else dares to talk about it with the lightness of a black-and-white drawing with a format of 19 x 28 cm.

Another, different fear appears in **Fear** (2002–03), a work with small clay sculptures and the big fear of flying. For several months, while flying and being afraid of it, the artist gripped a ball of good clay from Albisola. *"The sophisticated material captured the nervous convulsions of my terrified hands, triggered by all that bumping, babies crying and the moments of relatively quiet cruising..."* This text and all the other texts of his work—all his instructions, explanations, and descriptions—are a key part of the Solakov event. In the specific case of **Fear,** the manner in which the author describes the method leading to the end result (some of the figurines are in pieces) is truly disarming.

The story, such as we read it, seems to "disenchant" the entire project. Honestly and with discreet, yet conscious naiveté, it discloses the entire construct, its technology and errors. Nothing is concealed. The clay figurines are broken not because of some higher conceptual plan, but from ordinary carelessness. The story is marvelous in its details: the potter father, the mother's oven, and the trouble with firing the ceramic figurines. Only to calm his worried parents does he explain to them that in this way the artwork became even better and more conceptual. Then comes the sentence: *"Luckily, the second batch of clay sculptures ... was undamaged..."* Is the artist really not aware of what the broken pieces contribute to the artwork? Few artists would walk that fine line of complete "disenchanting" transparency and openness, would accept chance with its conceptualization. And that is exactly the quality that sets Nedko Solakov apart: "one of his capabilities." The most significant of his talents. It is this openness that pieces like **The Yellow Blob Story** (1997–present) rely on with that clean-fingered and beguiling *"...I completely forgot the reason for this."* And, of course, the drawings in **Fears** (2006–07) and **Leftovers** (2005). Probably to the greatest extent in **Top Secret** (1989–90).

The breaking point, the zone of personal failure, of personal fear, of cracking is the site from which Nedko Solakov tells his stories. Often they are broken stories, and not only stories of breaking. Just like the clay figurines—special totems of and against fear. And yet the breaking of the story, as an act and event, gives it new quality and new density. To instill your fear in clay, to deposit it in there when you are afraid while flying (flying while you are afraid) is one thing. The breaking of the figurines, however, is yet another level of completion. Fear is beyond form; it refuses to be harnessed, to be closed in. Isn't it rather volatile and fluid, filling every crack, able to penetrate everywhere? Its destructive force can implode each of those clay totems of our ostensibly harnessed fear.

The undamaged figurines are the lighter version, according to which we set ourselves free from our inner monsters, taming them through art. This, as Nedko Solakov himself would say, is the good news. But it never comes alone. The bad news is that no art can overcome our fears, our monsters, our loneliness, death. It just teaches us to live with them. Not that this is a small solace.

Many of the many people who have written about Nedko Solakov point out storytelling as a central strategy of his work. He himself defines the type of his art as "narrative installations." To say that Nedko Solakov is constantly telling stories seems obvious and indisputable. Just like a white wall when seen from afar is simply a white wall. Yet, when we discuss this artist, we need to be very suspicious of the obviousness of appearances and to keep in mind that, seen up close, no wall is all that white.

I believe in storytelling (it is my job after all). Or rather I believe in its idle moves. Storytelling creates the consoling (and illusory) feeling of putting off the inevitable. The chess game is lost even before the figures are arranged, even before the first move. Such are the rules of the game. We were born on the losing side of the board. We do not have many chances to confront our fears, to face the speed at which things vanish, to confront death. Seems like we only hope with every story to buy one more night, and then one more, so that it will eventually be one thousand and one...

Yes, Nedko Solakov tells stories all the time. This is the bright side of the moon. And it is not by accident that we all quickly see it and enjoy it.

Yes, Nedko Solakov always starts with "Once upon a time..." those words that unlock the beginning, that "open sesame" for the cave of the fairy tale. But his stories begin where fairy tales usually end. In the no man's time of life after the fairy tale ends, in the dismal and hopeless no man's land. The battery of miracles (or of our childhood) is already growing weak; the tape has begun to wow and flutter. And this distortion becomes a new manner of storytelling. Exhaustion and distortion. Exhaustion, distortion, scraping. A wonderful example of this is the piece **...and they lived happily ever after** (1999), where there is a felicitous overlap of topic and narrative technique.

Here is how I imagine the background to this installation: once upon a time there was a boy who used to play fairy tales on his gramophone. The records would crack and skip. One day a record with fairy tales got stuck on "...and they lived happily ever after... and they lived happily ever after... and they lived happily ever after..." An unbearably long and happy life. Who knows why the boy felt sad and weary.

The exhaustion, the distortion, the scraping are subject, plot, story and, at the same time, they are a storytelling strategy. From Drawing 6 to Drawing 40, that is, to the end, the prince and the princess never leave their places. Nothing happening for unbearably long, thirty-four frames in a row. The intense adventure (in terms of color as well), the killing of the dragon, the betrothal, etc., makes up only five images. What continues to happen, ever after, is the unbearably static monotony and the parallel thinning and fading both of the drawing and the story.

When we say that Nedko Solakov is constantly telling stories, we need to add that it is often a story about the impossibility of storytelling. The impossibility of telling a story as it is in the fairy tales. The problematic storytelling, the collapse of the classic story are all strengths of Nedko Solakov's narrative strategies. We can already see this in **Encyclopaedia Utopia** (1989–90) and **Top Secret**. The catalogue as an (impossible) mode of storytelling. Vulnerable exactly for its pretense of being orderly and consistent. Because the will for wholeness, the desire to encompass everything is incompatible with the hierarchies of the story. On the other hand, this dispersed storytelling via a catalogue is in a way more authentic. It includes those details, pieces, routines that we—and our past—are made of. It tells of the chaos that reflects the chaos in our personal stories.

It seems to me that, beyond its aesthetic quality, **Top Secret** will become a more and more ethically and politically significant work. Because it begins a story in which we always get stuck at the beginning and refuse to move on. But that is another story and another text.

To turn their own real and invented fears (who knows which ones are scarier) into a powerful source of energy driving the machinery of art is something that many try to do, but very few succeed.

Most installations by Nedko Solakov are centaur-like creatures with visual fore parts (head and neck) and textual croups. No matter how hard you try, you cannot separate one from the other and keep the centaur alive. And since I am on the textual side, i.e., the losing side, I will make a bold proposal. Text is back. Very slowly, centimeter by centimeter, it is coming back. The lightness of the image has gradually begun to be annoying. Text is back, but not for the better. The things that happen to us need a slower medium; they need the classical instrument of words.

I have no particular evidence of this, but the success of the works we are discussing is a sign. Paradoxically or not, it is through text that the visual artist Nedko Solakov is what he is.

I have been to his exhibitions, I have approached them, I have seen esteemed people crouching and crawling on their rheumatic knees, assuming improper postures only to read the text, which is often disrespectful of these efforts. Nedko Solakov's works with text, with scribblings on walls, change the convention of art perception. They change the ritual. We not only look at the installation, we also have to read it. And reading is a different type of effort, a different discipline of looking. "Please look closer," as the author himself urges. Other distances, other proximities. What is the right thing to say—I saw Nedko Solakov's exhibition or I read Nedko Solakov's exhibition?

Nedko Solakov works with a ready made world. We all work with and in such a world, of course. But he imprints his stories and corrections directly on its surface. Thus destroying once and for all its pretense of completeness and wholeness. He strips bare all its crevices, grooves, bumps, shades, spots. And just when we think he will unleash all his scathing sarcasm because he has seen the frailty of this world, this home, this body, just then… then Solakov does something completely different. He populates this zone of frailty, of error, of failure with his small figures and stories. They live somewhere there in the defects of the masonry, which might turn out to be an entrance *to another, better, dimension* (Dead-Lock Stories, 2005). Or in the withering orchids (are they really orchids?) of the old wallpaper (Wallpaper, 1993–present). Or on the pipe of the cast iron radiator because *she loves cozy and warm places* (A [not so] White Cube, 2001–present).

Nedko Solakov's discovery is that when this defective spot is bared and "insolently" pointed out, this same damaged spot suddenly becomes cozy and tells stories. After seeing his works, all bare white surfaces appear suspicious to us. A (not so) white world.

This is me, too: Tribute to N.S.

Nedko Solakov's This is me, too.... encourages transformations. If he can be a snowflake, then why can't I be an artist? For a while, in this text at least. Just like the snowflake is a snowflake, for a while, with a temporary identity. During the few months I have been watching, reading, and exploring Nedko Solakov's works and compiling this text—all the while doing a myriad of other things as well (because there is never time for only one thing)—I have caught myself starting to think in terms of installations. Here are three of them, my debut and tribute to Nedko Solakov:

A Life (Black & White) ... in Progress

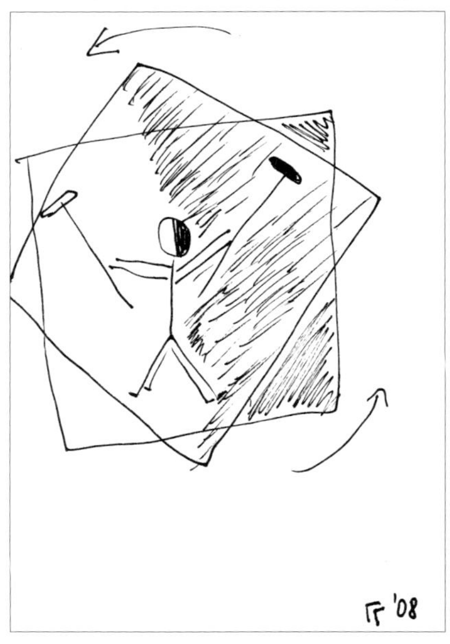

Everything is as in Nedko Solakov's work **A Life (Black& White)** (1998), with only one exception... Black and white paint; two workers/painters constantly repainting the walls of the exhibition space in black and white for the entire duration of... life, day after day (following each other); dimensions variable

Once upon a time, there were two young workers who used to live in a visual artist's project. Here is what they had to do: they had an unlimited amount of (water-based) paint, but only in two colors—black and white. And there was one room painted half white, and half black. The task was simple (so simple that both constantly racked their brains over it): one had to paint the black white, and the other, the white black. And so, day after day, they did this, following each other. The pay was good, the paint was enough, and the evenings were free. Sometimes there were visitors, sometimes not. The workers were allowed (according to instructions they always kept on them) to talk to the visitors. But the instructions did not say what they should talk about and how far they could go. The period they were hired for was five months. But when the five months expired, nobody came to replace them or dismiss them. The paint kept coming. Money kept coming. The painters (because after the fifth month, they felt they were now painters) did not mind. They did not even ask what this extension was for and how long it would take. They perceived it as part of the visual artist's higher plan. They never saw him, by the way, but they always kept the instructions in the pockets of their overalls. Instructions made life clear and simple (black and white). Follow the instructions and you will never get in trouble.

The years passed, the painters were no longer young—they got tired faster. Even their dreams lost color, they dreamed only in black and white. But they did not complain and did not avoid work. In the beginning, there was a sort of competition between them.

Each one wanted to expand the promised land of his color by a few inches. It was not just a rivalry; it was a clash of two worlds (colors). The white against the black. White was now a mission, a philosophy for one of the workers. And black for the other as well. But they were equal, and the instructions were strict. The balance was preserved.

Both grew old together, simultaneously and equally, in exactly the same way as they painted. They were always back-to-back, communicating through their backs. They no longer needed to talk. From the very beginning, there had been one question nagging them. That's right, the question was "Why?" (As if there are other questions.) Neither of the two could remember how much time had passed since the start. White would replace the black; black would replace white, black, white, black, white... Layer after layer, paint on paint, inch by inch the room got smaller and smaller.

They felt their backs getting closer and closer. At one point, their backs were leaning against each other and they could only revolve around a common axis. They were now one person with a joint back, four hands, and two paintbrushes... They looked like a weird insect caught in the amber of water-based paint. One half white, the other half black.
A Death (White & Black).

Vertical Reading

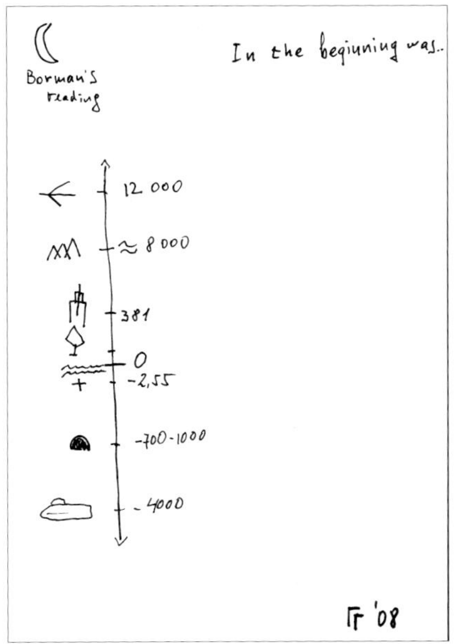

A holy text, an airplane, the Himalayans, the Empire State Building, a cherry tree, an ocean, a crypt, a cave, a submarine, volunteers for reading.

One and the same excerpt from a Holy Book (the Bible, the Qur'an, the Talmud, the Vedas...) is read at four different vertical points. The reader may be different. Only the text that is to be read aloud is important. In this case, we start with the first chapter of Genesis from the King James Version. We have a recording of the text being read while orbiting the moon. On Christmas morning, 1968, the astronaut Frank Borman read the first verses aloud in space:

"In the beginning God created the heaven and the earth. And the earth was without form, and void; and darkness was upon the face of the deep. And the Spirit of God moved upon the face of the waters."

The other altitudes for the readings: 12,000 meters (in an airplane); Himalayan peaks higher than 8,000 meters; the roof of the Empire State Building (381 meters); reading from a cherry tree (three meters); reading on the shore of the Atlantic (zero meters above sea level); reading in an old cemetery (2.55 meters under ground); from a cave (700–1,000 meters deep); reading in a submarine at the bottom of the Arctic Ocean (4,000 meters underwater).

Does the text preserve its sublime and profound nature at different altitudes and depths? This technique could be used both to test the sacred (vertically) and to do something more important: to read the story of the Creation to Creation itself in heaven and on earth (and beneath it).

From my series Captions

The starting point for the aesthetic and strategy of Captions is to transform the captions from a supporting role into a central role by relying on extreme and radical delicacy, ecology (environmental correctness), and noninterference in the internal (and external) affairs of the environment. To name, denote, describe is the only act with which the artist works, and it is sufficient.

My Favorite 3 p.m. Afternoon
Three ordinary houseflies *(Musca domestica)* with moderate, slightly weary buzzing; August; a cool stone room with a low ceiling; the glowing light of a switched-on radio, a forecast about the water level of the Danube in Bulgarian, Russian, and French; an old humming fridge; the quiet chatting of relatives outdoors, under the trellis.
Owned by the artist.

Some Nice Things to Enjoy... and Other Fears
(Stories from the Point of Breaking)

Georgi Gospodinov

Caption: PC written text, words, letters, grammar signs, 20,000 characters (with spaces), 3,195 spaces, forty-four cups of coffee, some drawings, schemes, and hesitations.

Die Dinge, die wir mögen (soll ich sagen: die guten Dinge?), stiften uns unweigerlich an, uns selbst und unsere eigenen Geschichten zu reflektieren. Diese Prozedur vollzieht sich mit größter Unfehlbarkeit. Wir besitzen kein deutlicheres Zeichen, Feedback, keinen besseren Hinweis, ob wir etwas für gut halten oder nicht, als eben dies: Provoziert es uns dazu uns selbst zu reflektieren? In diesem Sinne ist »Gefallen« eine egozentrische Empfindung, ein Zu-sich-Heranziehen der Welt oder eines Kunstwerkes. Man könnte dies natürlich auch in einer elaborierteren Sprache ausdrücken, doch an dieser Stelle genügt es mir, zu sagen, dass die Werke Nedko Solakovs mich dazu anstiften, »mich zu denken«, meiner Ängste und meiner Lustempfindungen gewahr zu werden.

Wenn die Summe der Angst auf der Welt eine konstante Größe ist, so sinkt der Anteil eines jeden von uns an ihr umgekehrt proportional zur wachsenden Weltbevölkerung. Gleichzeitig gibt es Leute wie Nedko Solakov, die sich entschieden haben, sich einen deutlich größeren als den ihnen zufallenden Anteil von dieser »Torte der Angst« auf den Teller zu legen. So befreien sie uns glücklich von dem uns zugemessenen Teil oder verringern ihn zumindest. Es ist angenehm für uns, wenn jemand anderes unsere eigenen Ängste durchlebt...

Die 99 Zeichnungen aus dem Zyklus **Fears** (2006/07) sind visuell und narrativ vollkommen aufs Wesentliche reduziert. Die Ängste haben eine Farbe: Sepia und Schwarz-Weiß sind ihr Reich. Mein erster Eindruck – hervorgerufen durch die Technik, durch die Papiersorte oder gar das Format, das ich von den Zeichenblöckchen meiner Grundschulzeit kenne –, der auch nicht völlig verschwinden wollte, war der von etwas Nahem und Gemütlichem: Angst mit kleinem »a«, die eher Assoziationen an weiche Ohren und warme Pfoten weckt; an unsere kleinen Alltagsängste, wenn auch »mit großen Wachstumspotenzial« (Zeichnung Nr. 17). Ängste, die einfach ihre Pflicht tun *(»A little fear was trying to do his job – spreading fear-vibes around«,* Zeichnung Nr. 1) und manchmal selbst vor Angst zittern, weil sie so allein sind.

In **Fears** sind die Ängste allgegenwärtig, und dabei handelt es sich nicht nur um die persönlichen Obsessionen des Künstlers (sonst wäre der Zyklus deutlich erschreckender ausgefallen). Offenbar ist es so, dass – wenn man versteht, dass die Angst ein kosmisches Gefühl ist, eine kosmische Größe, und wenn man sieht, wie die Ängste selbst ihre Ängste mitteilen – die Dinge nicht mehr ganz so furchtbar zu sein scheinen.

Nedko Solakov erzählt nicht einfach die Geschichten seiner Ängste. Sein Trick besteht in etwas Anderem. Er provoziert die Ängste, ihre eigenen Geschichten selbst zu erzählen. So ist es in der bereits erwähnten ersten Zeichnung der Serie; so ist es auch in Zeichnung Nr. 54, einem sehr kostspieligen Feuerwerk, das sich davor fürchtet, nicht – wie es alle von ihm erwarten – im vollen Farbenspektrum zu explodieren, da es versehentlich in Schwarz-Weiß hergestellt wurde, ja, genau genommen sogar in Grau... (was für eine mir vertraute Angst).

Mir gefallen die sieben wild tanzenden dicken Männer, die verzweifelt versuchen, den Tod hinauszuzögern (Zeichnung Nr. 63) – und der Unterschied zwischen ihrem Tanz, respektive ihrer Angst – und dem der beiden Figuren auf der vierten Zeichnung, die ihre alltäglichen Ängste abschütteln, solange sie sich auf der Tanzfläche befinden. Sie strahlen eine gewisse Demut aus. Die Angst als übergeworfene Kleidung, als Tasche, die wir immer bei uns tragen. Wir können sie für eine Weile auf dem Stuhl abstellen, ja, sie dort sogar vergessen, während wir tanzen, doch sie wartet auf uns: *»They will collect the fears back later.«* Alltäglich, klein, unbemerkbar, doch immer bei uns. Wie der Tod. Und diese Veralltäglichung der Angst und des Todes, inklusive aller menschlichen Wärme, aller Ironie, ist ein Markenzeichen Solakovs.

Die bedrückendste und schrecklichste Zeichnung von allen ist denn auch die, in der die Angst abwesend ist. Über den alten Universitätsprofessor aus einem osteuropäischen Land, der keine Ängste mehr hat, heißt es: *»He is only starving«* (Zeichnung Nr. 12). Umgekehrt wiederum nähern die Blätter Nr. 20 und 21 mit einer gewissen Leichtigkeit und Selbstironie die Ängste dem Empfinden an, lebendig zu sein. Die Angst verwandelt sich in ein Zeichen, einen fundamentalen Beweis, dass wir existieren, teils sogar auf der angenehmen Seiten des Lebens.

Zeichnung Nr. 20: *»I am extremely scared of flying tomorrow. If there is a drawing 21, I'll be able to be scared in the future, too.«* Dann, erleichtert: *»I will be able to be scared in the future, too...«* (Zeichnung Nr. 21). Ich habe Angst, also bin ich.

Ich persönlich empfinde wahre Erleichterung bei Zeichnung Nr. 17 mit den beiden sich schneidenden Linien: *»Two lines are... are... are... (here the artist-me gets stuck, because he doesn't know how to develop the story). A fear appears on this sheet of paper. Not a big one but with a good potential for future growth.«* Erleichterung, dass ein anderer meine Ängste teilt. Mehr noch, er erkühnt sich, von ihr mit der Leichtigkeit einer Schwarz-Weiß-Zeichnung im Format 19 x 28 cm zu sprechen.

Anders und unterschiedlich zeigt sich die Angst in Solakovs Arbeit **Fear** (2002/03), kleine tönerne Skulptürchen, in die sich die große Angst vor dem Fliegen eingegraben hat. Im Verlauf einiger Monate, während er fliegt und sich ängstigt, drückt der Künstler je ein Klümpchen schönen Albisola-Tons in seinen Händen. *»The sophisticated material captured the nervous convulsions of my terrified hands, triggered by all that bumping, babies crying and the moments of relatively quiet cruising...«,* wie Solakov im Begleittext schreibt. Dieser Text, wie überhaupt die Kommentare zu seinen Arbeiten – all seine Anweisungen, Erläuterungen und Beschreibungen – sind ein essenzieller Bestandteil des »Ereignisses Solakov«. In unserem konkreten Fall mit **Fear** ist die Art und Weise, in welcher der Künstler den Entstehungsprozess bis zum Endresultat nacherzählt (einige der Figürchen sind zerbrochen), wirklich entwaffnend.

Die Geschichte, so wie wir sie zu lesen bekommen, scheint das ganze Projekt eher zu »entzaubern«. Aufrichtig und mit dezenter, aber bewusster Naivität enthüllt sie das ganze Konstrukt, seine Technologie und seinen Mangel. Keinerlei Geheimnistuerei. Die Tonfigürchen sind nicht zerbrochen aufgrund eines höheren gedanklichen Konzeptes, sondern durch schlichte Nachlässigkeit – diese in ihren Einzelheiten so wundervolle Erzählung vom Vater, der Keramiker ist, vom Backofen der Mutter und dem Pech beim Brennen der Tonfigürchen. Um seine verlegen-besorgten Eltern zu beruhigen, sagt er ihnen, dass sein Werk nun sogar noch besser, noch konzeptueller geworden sei. Es folgt der Satz: *»Luckily, the second batch of clay sculptures ... was undamaged...«* Ob der Künstler wirklich nicht weiß, was die zerbrochenen Figürchen zu dieser Arbeit beitragen? Wenige Künstler würden wohl auf dem schmalen Grat der vollständigen »Entzauberung«, sprich der Transparenz und Offenheit wandeln, würden den Zufall als konzeptuelles Prinzip akzeptieren. Genau darin besteht die Qualität, die Nedko Solakov unterscheidet: »Eine seiner Fähigkeiten.« Das Wichtigste unter seinen Talenten. Auf dieser Offenheit basieren Arbeiten wie **The Yellow Blob Story** (seit 1997), unbestechlich und bestechend zugleich *»...I completely forgot the reason for this«* und natürlich die Zeichnungen aus **Fears** (2006/07) und **Leftovers** (2005). Vermutlich auch in hohem Maße **Top Secret** (1989/90).

Die Zone des Zerbrechens, des persönlichen Scheiterns, der eigenen Angst, des Zerspringens ist der Ort, von dem aus Nedko Solakov seine Geschichten erzählt. Oft sind das zerbrochene Geschichten, nicht nur Geschichten vom Zerbrechen. Ganz wie die Tonfigürchen – eigentümliche Totems der Angst und gegen sie. Doch das Zerbrechen der Geschichte, als Akt wie als Ereignis, gibt ihr eine neue Qualität, eine neue Dichte. Dem Ton seine Angst hinzuzufügen, sie darin zu verstecken, während man – fliegend – Angst empfindest, ist das eine. Das Zerbrechen der kleinen Skulpturen aber ist ein anderes, neues Niveau der Realisierung. Die Angst ist jenseits der Form, weigert sich, festgehalten, eingesperrt oder gesammelt zu werden. Ist sie nicht eher flüchtig, fluktuierend, und deswegen jeden Spalt oder Riss ausfüllend, fähig, überall einzudringen? Ihre destruktive Kraft kann jenen tönernen Totem unserer angeblich gut kontrollierten Angst von innen heraus zerstören.

Die heil gebliebenen Figuren sind die eine, die lichte Version, derzufolge wir uns von unseren Schreckgespenstern befreien können, indem wir sie durch die Kunst bannen. Dies, so würde Nedko Solakov sich ausdrücken, ist doch schon eine gute Nachricht. Doch sie kommt leider nicht allein. Die schlechte Nachricht nämlich ist, dass keine Kunst unsere Ängste, unsere Schreckgespenster, unsere Einsamkeit und unseren Tod vertreiben kann. Sie hilft uns nur, irgendwie damit zu leben. Das ist ja auch nicht wenig.

Vieles von dem Vielen, das über Nedko Solakov geschrieben wurde, rückt das Geschichtenerzählen in den Mittelpunkt seiner künstlerischen Strategie. Er selbst hingegen bezeichnet das Feld seiner künstlerischen Arbeit als »narrative Installationen«. Dass Nedko Solakov ununterbrochen Geschichten erzählt, ist nun wirklich offensichtlich und unterliegt keinem Zweifel. Auch eine weiße Wand, von Weitem betrachtet, ist nichts als eine weiße Wand. Doch gerade wenn wir von diesem Urheber sprechen, sollten wir vorsichtig sein mit den Offensichtlichkeiten des Augenscheins und uns ins Gewissen rufen, das von Nahem betrachtet keine Wand vollkommen weiß ist.

Ich glaube schon an das Geschichtenerzählen (letzten Endes besteht darin ja meine Arbeit). Genauer gesagt, glaube ich an ihre Leerläufe. Das Geschichtenerzählen erzeugt das rettende (und täuschende) Empfinden, dass ein unausweichliches Ende vertagt wird. Die Schachpartie ist schon verloren, wenn die Figuren aufgebaut werden, schon vor dem ersten Zug. So sind die Spielregeln. Wir werden auf der Seite des Schachbrettes geboren, auf der die Partie verloren wird. Wir haben nicht viele Möglichkeiten, etwas gegen unsere Ängste zu tun, gegen die Geschwindigkeit, mit der alles vergeht, gegen den Tod. Wir hoffen bloß, uns mit jeder Erzählung noch eine weitere Nacht, und noch eine, und noch eine zu erschleichen, damit es am Ende wenigstens tausendundeine Nacht werden…

Ja, Nedko Solakov erzählt pausenlos. Das ist die helle, uns zugewandte Seite des Mondes. Und es ist kein Zufall, dass wir alle sie sofort bemerken und uns an ihr erfreuen.

Ja, Nedko Solakov sagt immer wieder »Once upon a time…«, jene die Tür des Beginns aufschließenden Worte, jenes »Sesam, öffne dich« vor der Märchenhöhle. Doch seine Geschichten beginnen dort, wo die Märchen normalerweise enden. In der Niemandszeit des Lebens nach dem Märchenende, auf dem finsteren und hoffnungslosen Niemandsland. Die Batterien des Wunders (oder unserer Kindheit) werden bereits schwach, der Filmprojektor beginnt zu leiern. Das Leiern wird zur neuen Erzählweise. Erschöpfung und Leiern. Erschöpfung, Leiern und Ruckeln. Ein wunderbares Beispiel dafür ist eine Arbeit wie **…and they lived happily ever after** (1999), wo wir den glücklichen Zusammenfall von Topos und Erzähltechnik sehen können.

Ich stelle mir die Vorgeschichte dieser Installation wie folgt vor: Es war einmal eine Zeit, in der ein Junge Märchenschallplatten hörte. Die Schallplatten knackten und die Nadel sprang die ganze Zeit zurück. Eine der Schallplatte drehte sich den ganzen Tag lang immer wieder auf der Rille »und sie lebten glücklich bis… und sie lebten glücklich bis… und sie lebten glücklich bis…« Unerträglich, ein so langes glückliches Leben, nicht wahr? Wer weiß, warum dem Jungen alles so dumm und traurig vorkam.

Erschöpfung, Leiern und Ruckeln sind ein Thema, ein Sujet, eine Erzählung und zugleich eine Erzählstrategie. Von Zeichnung Nr. 6 bis Zeichnung Nr. 40, sprich: bis zum Ende, stehen der Prinz und die Prinzessin nicht von ihren Plätzen auf. Eine unerträglich lange Ereignislosigkeit, geschlagene vierunddreißig Bilder lang. Die (auch farblich) gesättigte Zeit des Abenteuers zuvor mit der Erschlagung des Drachens, der Verlobung und so weiter dauert nur ganze fünf Bilder. Das, was sich danach so lange hinzieht, ist die unerträgliche Statik des immer gleichen Einerlei, begleitet vom Ausdünnen und Verblassen der Zeichnung und der Erzählung.

Wenn wir sagen, dass Nedko Solakov unaufhörlich Geschichten erzählt, so müssen wir hinzufügen, dass es sich dabei häufig um eine Erzählung von der Unmöglichkeit des Erzählens handelt. Von der Unmöglichkeit, wie im Märchen zu erzählen. Das problematische Erzählen, der Zerfall der klassischen Geschichte sind jeweils Dinge, die einen beträchtlichen Teil der Erzählstrategien Nedko Solakovs bilden. Wir werden das noch an seiner **Encyclopaedia Utopia** (1989/90) und bei **Top Secret** sehen. Der Katalog als (unmögliche) Erzählweise. Verletzbar gerade aufgrund des Anscheins, ordentlich und konsistent zu sein. Weil der Wille zur Ganzheit, das Verlangen, alles zu umfassen, nicht einhergeht mit den Hierarchien der Erzählung. Auf der anderen Seite ist gerade dieses sich entziehende Erzählen mittels Katalog in gewissem Sinne authentischer. Es schließt jene Details, Einzelheiten, Alltäglichkeiten mit ein, aus denen wir letzten Endes gemacht sind – wir und unsere Vergangenheit. Es erzählt in jenem Chaos, das dem Chaos unserer persönlichen Geschichten adäquat ist.

Mir scheint, **Top Secret** wird – ganz abgesehen von seinen ästhetischen Qualitäten – immer bedeutender als moralistisch-politische Arbeit. Denn es ist der Anfang einer Geschichte, bei der wir zu Beginn immer stocken und uns weigern, fortzufahren. Doch das ist ein anderes Thema und ein anderer Text.

Seine eigenen Ängste, die echten wie die synthetisch erzeugten – könnten wir auf Anhieb sagen, welche schrecklicher sind? –, in eine Energiequelle zu verwandeln, die die Maschinerie der Kunstproduktion antreibt, das ist etwas, was alle versuchen, aber nur wenigen gelingt.

Die überwiegende Mehrzahl der Installationen Nedko Solakovs sind zentaurische Geschöpfe mit einem visuellen Vorderteil (Kopf und Hals) und dem Text als hinterem Teil. Man kann das eine nicht vom anderen trennen und den Zentauren am Leben erhalten. Da ich persönlich mehr auf der Seite des Textes stehe, der Verliererseite, möchte ich direkt einen kühnen Vorschlag machen. Der Text kehrt zurück. Sehr langsam, Zentimeter für Zentimeter. Die Leichtigkeit des Gebildes hat dezent begonnen, auf die Nerven zu gehen. Die Rückkehr des Textes verheißt nichts Gutes. Die Dinge, die uns zustoßen, benötigen ein langsameres Medium, ein klassischeres Instrument, wie die Worte.

Ich habe dafür keine besonderen Beweise. Doch der Erfolg der Arbeiten, über die wir hier reden, ist ein Zeichen dafür. Paradox oder nicht, gerade durch den Text ist der visuelle Künstler Nedko Solakov das, was er ist.

Ich war auf seinen Ausstellungen, habe mich genähert, habe hochanständige Leute gesehen, die sich hinhocken, auf ihren rheumatischen Knien herumrutschen, in unziemliche Posen verfallen, nur um den Text zu lesen, der sich diesen Bemühungen gegenüber nicht immer achtungsvoll verhält. Die Arbeiten Nedko Solakovs mit dem Text, den Aufschriften auf den Wänden, verändern unsere Sehgewohnheiten. Sie verändern das Ritual. Wir betrachten die Installation nicht mehr nur, wir müssen sie auch lesen. Das Lesen aber ist eine andere Art der Bemühung, eine andere Disziplin des Blicks. »Please look closer«, wie der Künstler uns direkt auffordert. Andere Installationen, andere Formen der Nähe. Wie muss man richtig sagen: »Ich habe die Ausstellung von Nedko Solakov gesehen« oder »Ich habe die Ausstellung von Nedko Solakov gelesen«?

Nedko Solakov arbeitet mit einer Welt, der bereits vorgegebenen Welt. Das tun wir natürlich alle. Doch er trägt seine Geschichten und Korrekturen direkt auf ihre Oberfläche auf. Wodurch er automatisch seinen Anspruch auf Ein-für-allemal-Vollendet-sein-und-Ganzheitlichkeit zerstört. Er entblößt all ihre Risse, Untiefen, Vorsprünge, Schatten und Flecken. Und während wir erwarten, dass er seinen ganzen vernichtenden Sarkasmus ergießt, weil er die Schwachpunkte dieser Welt, dieses Heims, dieses Körpers gesehen hat, genau dann... Genau dann macht Nedko Solakov etwas völlig anderes. Er bevölkert diese Orte der Schwäche, des Fehlerhaften, des Scheiterns mit seinen Männchen und Geschichten. Genau dort leben sie: In den Schadstellen des Verputzes, die sich als Eingang *to another, better, dimension* erweisen könnten (**Dead-Lock Stories**, 2005). Oder in den verwelkten Orchideen (sind es wirklich Orchideen?) alter Tapetenmuster (**Wallpaper**, seit 1993). Oder auf den Rohren eines gusseisernen Heizkörpers, *she loves cosy and warm places* (**A [not so] White Cube**, seit 2001).

Die Entdeckung Nedko Solakovs besteht darin, dass, wenn er »nassforsch« auf eine fehlerhafte Stelle hinweist, genau diese beschädigte Stelle auf einmal Wärme ausstrahlt und Geschichten erzählt. Nachdem wir seine Arbeiten gesehen haben, erscheinen uns alle leeren und weißen Oberflächen verdächtig. A (not so) white world.

This is me, too: Tribute to N.S.

Das solakovsche »This is me, too« ermutigt zu Transformationen. Wenn er eine Schneeflocke sein kann, warum kann ich dann kein Künstler sein? Wenigstens für ein Weilchen, im Rahmen dieses Textes. So, wie auch die Schneeflocke nur für kurze Zeit Schneeflocke ist, mit temporärer Identität. Die Monate, in denen ich mich schauend und lesend in die Arbeiten Nedko Solakovs vertiefte und diesen Text hinwarf, wie alle anderen auch unterbrochen von hundert anderen Dingen – warum haben wir nie so etwas wie »reine Arbeitszeit«? –, ertappte ich mich dabei, dass ich begann, in Installationen zu denken. Hier sind die drei Erstlinge, gedacht als Hommage an Nedko Solakov.

A Life (Black & White)... in Progress

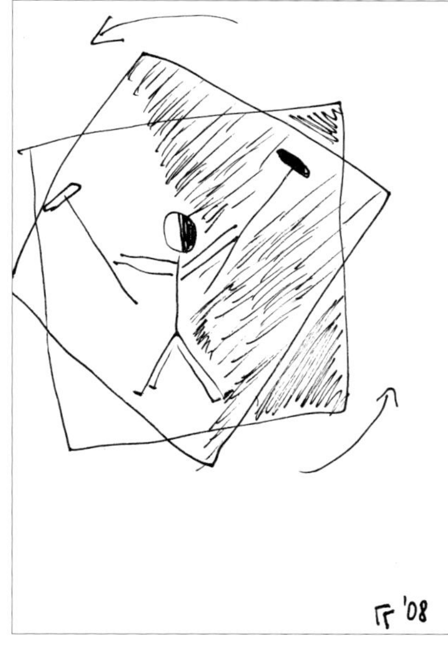

Everything is as in Nedko Solakov's work **A Life (Black & White)** (1998), with only one exception... Black and white paint; two workers/painters constantly repainting the walls of the exhibition space in black and white for the entire duration of... life, day after day (following each other); dimensions variable

Es waren einmal zwei Anstreicher, die lebten im Projekt eines bildenden Künstlers. Die Sache war die: Es gab eine unbegrenzte Menge Wandfarbe, aber nur in zwei Farben – schwarz und weiß. Und ein Zimmer, zur Hälfte in Weiß, zur Hälfte in Schwarz gestrichen. Ihre Aufgabe war einfach, so einfach, dass beide sich unaufhörlich den Kopf darüber zerbrachen: Der eine sollte das Schwarze weiß streichen, der andere das Weiße schwarz. Und so Tag für Tag. Die Bezahlung war gut, Farbe war da, so viel sie wollten, den Abend hatten sie frei. Gelegentlich kamen Besucher, manchmal auch nicht. Die Arbeiter hatten das Recht (gemäß den Anweisungen, die sie nie missachten durften), mit den Besuchern ins Gespräch zu kommen. Doch in den Instruktionen stand nicht, was genau sie sagen sollten, wie weit sie gehen durften. Die Zeitspanne, für die sie engagiert worden waren, betrug fünf Monate. Doch als die Zeit abgelaufen war, kam niemand, um sie abzulösen oder nach Hause zu schicken. Stattdessen wurden ihnen immer wieder neue Farbeimer gebracht. Sie bekamen auch ihr Geld weiter. Die Künstler (im fünften Monat entschieden sie, selbst auch Künstler zu sein) hatten nichts dagegen. Sie fragten noch nicht einmal, warum es plötzlich diese Verlängerung gab und wie lange sie andauern würde. Sie nahmen sie einfach als höhere Vorsehung vonseiten des bildenden Künstlers hin. Den sie im Übrigen nie zu Gesicht bekamen; doch sie trugen immer das Blatt mit den

Arbeitsanweisungen in den Taschen ihrer Latzhosen. Damit war das Leben klar und einfach (schwarz und weiß). Folge den Anweisungen und du wirst keinerlei Schwierigkeiten bekommen.

Die Jahre vergingen. Sie waren schon nicht mehr ganz jung, wurden schneller müde. Sogar ihre Träume verloren die Farbe und wurden schwarz-weiß. Doch sie beklagten sich nicht und drückten sich auch nicht vor der Arbeit. Am Anfang gab es so etwas wie einen Wettstreit zwischen ihnen. Jeder versuchte, wenn auch nur um einige Zentimeter, das gelobte Land seiner Farbe zu vergrößern. Das war nicht bloß ein Kräftemessen, sondern ein echter Kampf der Kulturen (Farben). Weiß gegen Schwarz. Weiß war für den Weißmaler so etwas wie eine Mission, eine Philosophie. Schwarz für den Schwarzmaler ebenfalls. Doch ihre Kräfte waren ausgeglichen und die Instruktionen streng. Das Gleichgewicht blieb erhalten.

Und so wurden die beiden gemeinsam alt, gleichzeitig und so gleichmäßig, wie sie anstrichen. Immer einer mit dem Rücken zum anderen waren sie durch ihre Rücken in Kontakt. Längst hatten sie es nicht mehr nötig, miteinander zu reden. Von Anfang an, während der ganzen Zeit, nagte eine und immer wieder dieselbe Frage an ihnen. Genau, es war die Frage »warum?« (Als gäbe es überhaupt andere Fragen.) Keiner der beiden konnte sich noch daran erinnern, wie viel Zeit seit dem Anfang verstrichen war. Immer wieder ersetzte das Weiße das Schwarze, das Schwarze das Weiße, schwarz, weiß, schwarz, weiß... Und so, Schicht für Schicht, Farbe um Farbe, Millimeter um Millimeter wurde der Raum immer kleiner und kleiner.

Jeder der beiden spürte, wie der Rücken des anderen immer näher kam. Irgendwann stießen ihre Rücken zusammen, und sie konnten sich nur noch um eine gemeinsame Achse drehen. Sie waren jetzt ein Mensch mit einem gemeinsamen Rücken, vier Armen und zwei Anstreicherrollen... Sie sahen aus wie ein seltsames Insekt, eingeschlossen im Bernstein der Wandfarben. Die eine Hälfte weiß, die andere Hälfte schwarz.
A death (White & Black).

Vertical Reading

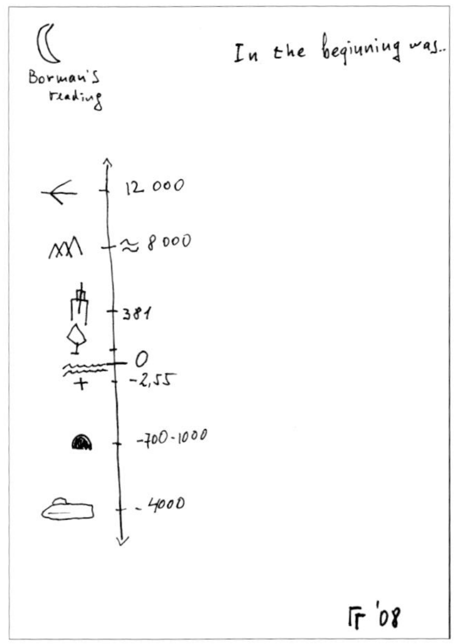

A holy text, an airplane, the Himalayans, the Empire State Building, a cherry tree, an ocean, a crypt, a cave, a submarine, volunteers for reading.

Ein und derselbe Ausschnitt aus einem heiligen Buch (Bibel, Koran, Talmud, Veden…) wird an unterschiedlichen Punkten der Vertikalen gelesen. Der Vorleser kann unterschiedlich sein. Wichtig ist, dass laut gelesen wird. In diesem Fall beginnen wir mit dem Ersten Kapitel der King-James-Bibel. Wir verfügen über eine Aufzeichnung des Textes, die in der Umlaufbahn des Mondes gelesen wurde. Am Weihnachtsmorgen 1968 las der Astronaut Frank Borman aus dem Weltraum laut die ersten Verse:

»In the beginning God created the heaven and the earth. And the earth was without form, and void; and darkness was upon the face of the deep. And the Spirit of God moved upon the face of the waters.«

Die nächsten Höhenstufen der Lesung: 12 000 Meter (im Flugzeug); von einem Achttausender im Himalaya; vom Dach des Empire-State-Buildings (381 Meter); aus der Krone eines Kirschbaums (3 Meter); am Ufer des Atlantischen Ozeans (0 Meter über dem Meeresspiegel); in einer alten Gruft (2,55 Meter unter der Erde); in einer Höhle (700–1 000 Meter Tiefe); in einem U-Boot in den Tiefen des arktischen Meeres (4 000 Meter unter dem Meeresspiegel).
Bewahrt der Text seine Erhabenheit und Tiefe in den unterschiedlichen Höhen und Tiefen? Diese Technik kann angewandt werden für das Testen des Sakralen (in der Vertikalen) wie auch von etwas noch Wichtigerem. Die Schöpfungsgeschichte, vorgetragen vor der Schöpfung, des Himmels, der Erde (und unter der Erde).

Aus meiner Serie Captions

Die Ästhetik und Strategie von Captions geht aus von der Verwandlung dieses Hilfsgenres in ein Hauptgenre, indem es auf eine extreme, radikale Behutsamkeit, auf Ökologie (Öko-Korrektheit) und Nicht-Einmischung in die inneren (äußeren) Angelegenheiten unserer Umwelt setzt. Aufrufen, Zeigen und Beschreiben – das ist der einzige und ausreichende Akt, mit dem der Künstler arbeitet.

My Favorite 3 p.m. Afternoon
Three ordinary houseflies *(Musca domestica)* with moderate, slightly weary buzzing; August; a cool stone room with a low ceiling; the glowing light of a switched-on radio, a forecast about the water level of the Danube in Bulgarian, Russian, and French; an old humming fridge; the quiet chatting of relatives outdoors, under the trellis.
Owned by the artist.

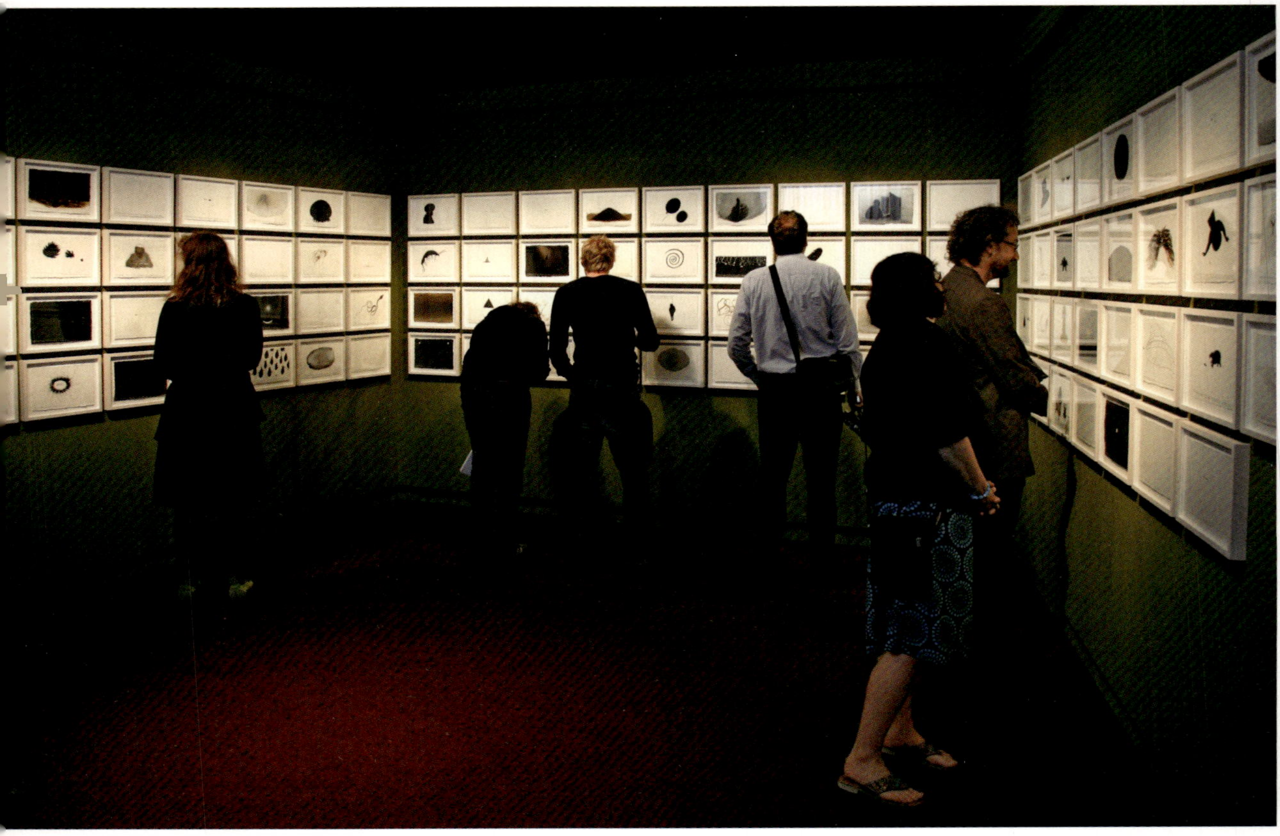

FROM "Fears" #1

A little fear was trying to do his job – spreading fear vibes all around. Unfortunately no one got affected just because there was nobody around. "Sometimes it is pretty scary to be alone" said the little fear to himself and slowed down a bit.

conax '06

FROM "FEARS" #5

Two people are dancing. They feel especially happy because they left all their daily fears aside in order to feel more free and relaxed. They will collect the fears back later.

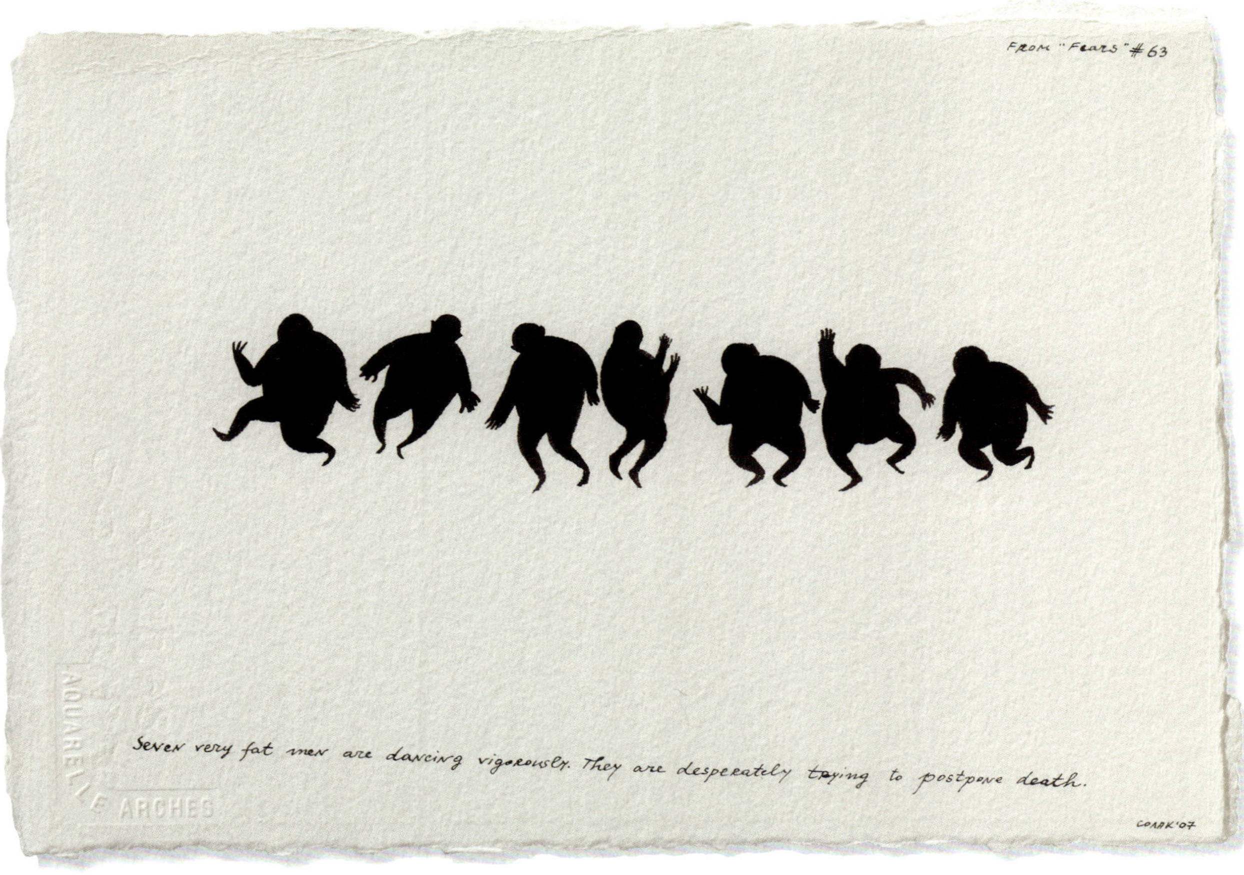

CORAK'06

FROM "FEARS" #63

Seven very fat men are dancing vigorously. They are desperately trying to postpone death.

CORAK'07

Fears, 2006–07

Series of Ninety-nine drawings
Sepia, black and white ink and wash on paper; 19 x 28 cm each

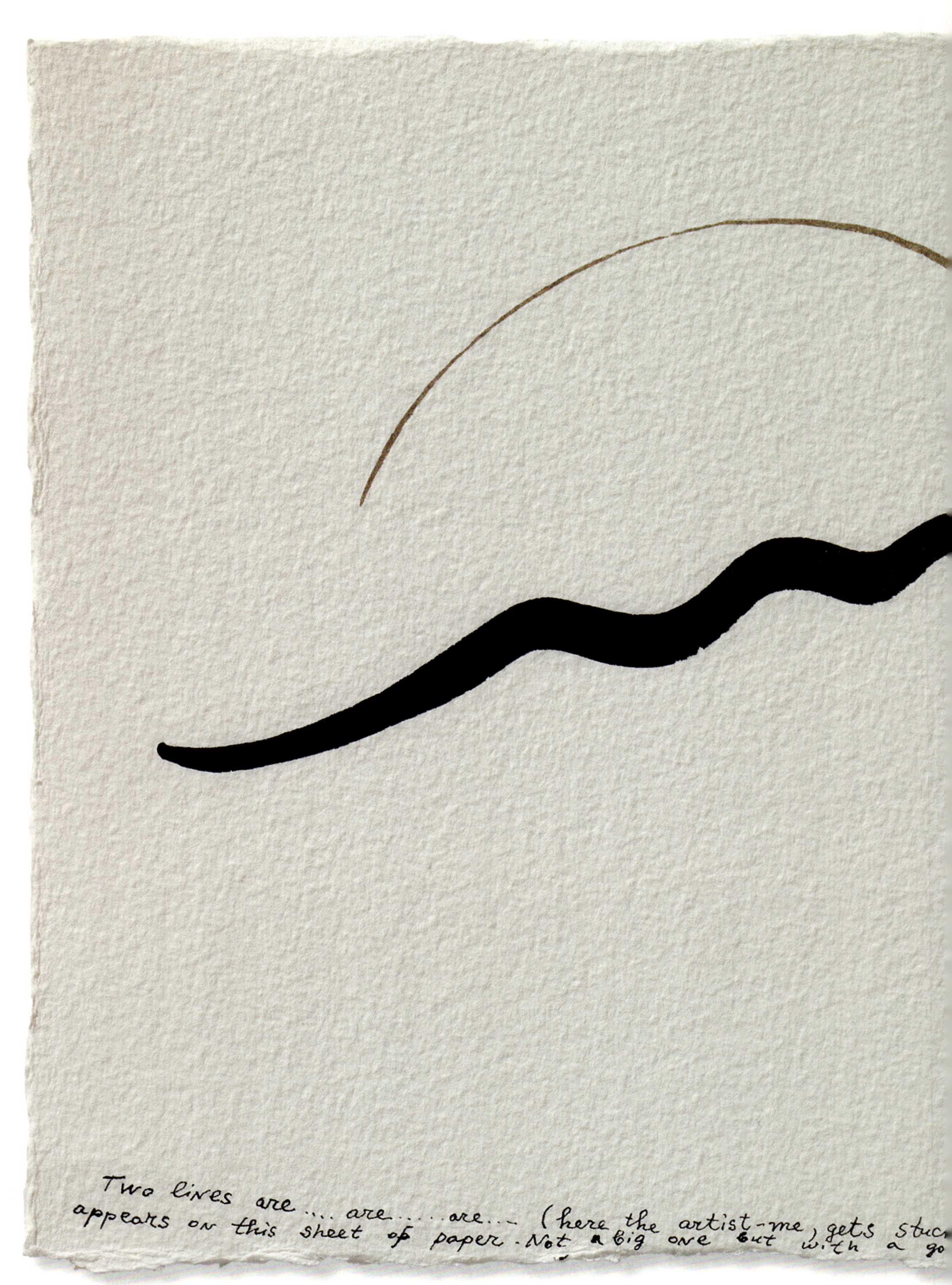
Two lines are .... are ..... are ... (here the artist-me, gets stuc
appears on this sheet of paper. Not a big one but with a go

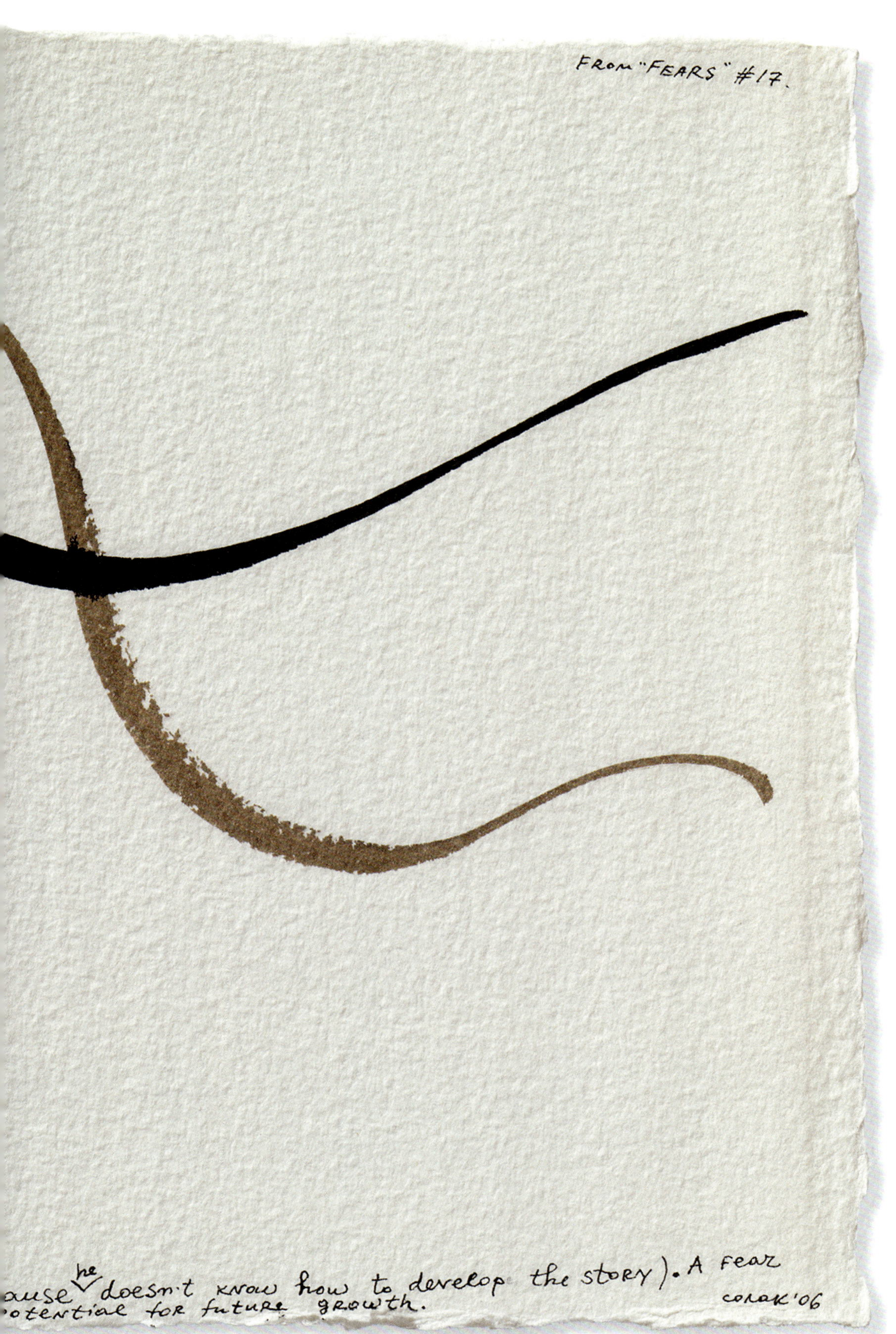

Fears // **#17,** 2006–07

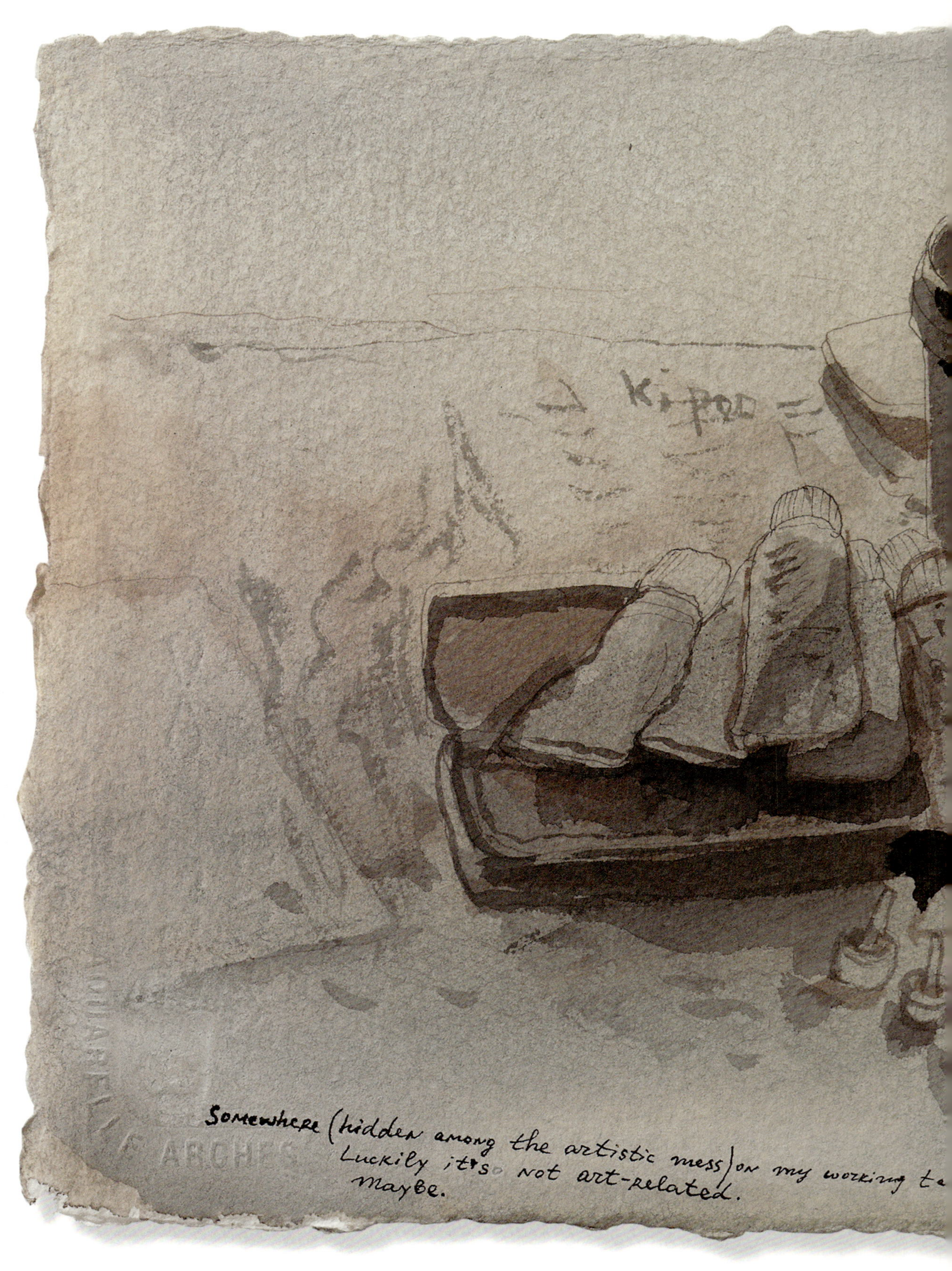
Somewhere (hidden among the artistic mess) on my working ta
Luckily it's not art-related.
Maybe.

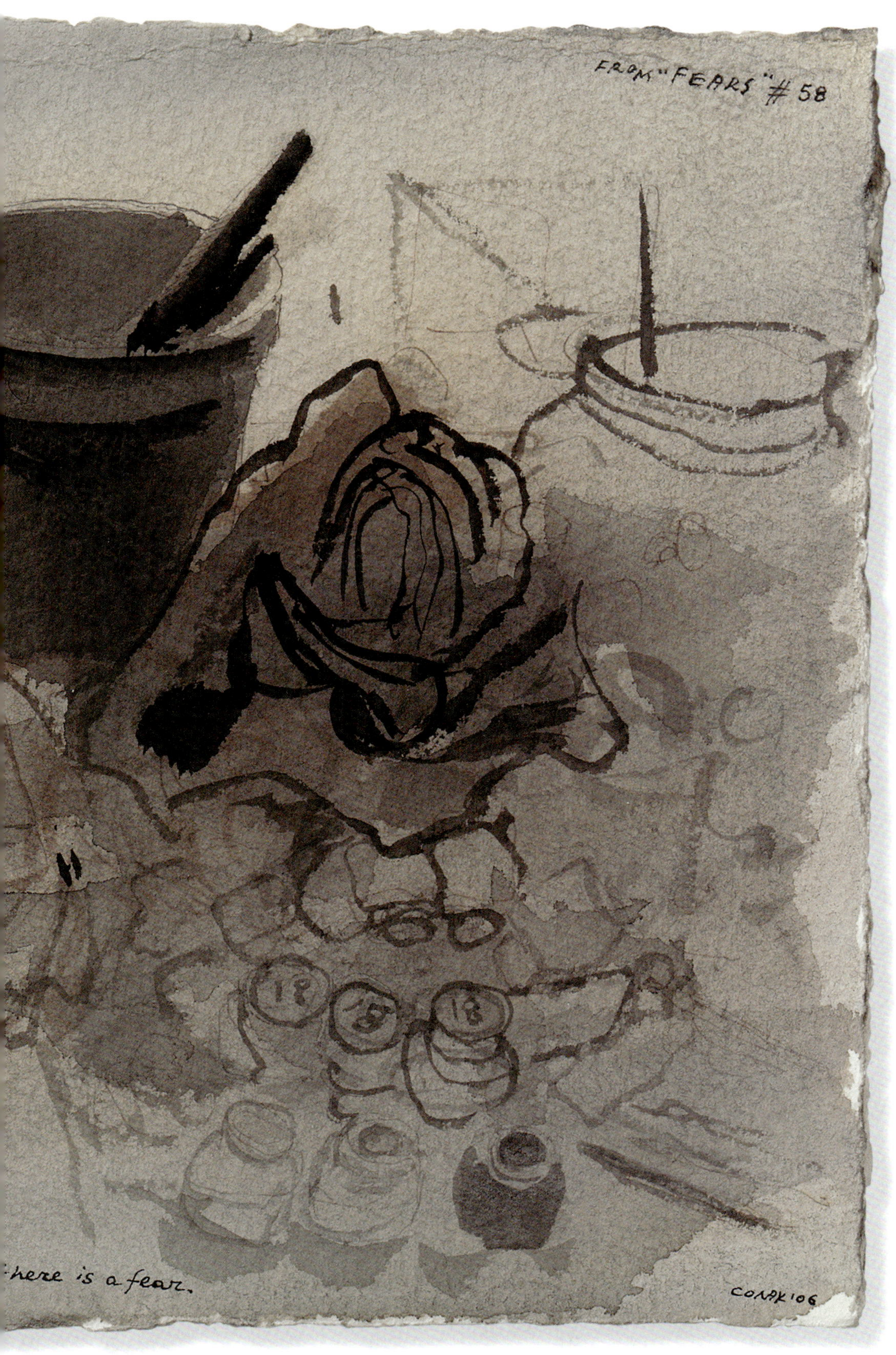

Fears // **#58,** 2006–07

Today is my birthday. Now I'm 49. I still have mos
That's why the thumbs-up-for-good-luck-to-my-belove
Seem to have disappead. For example, when I was you
Nowadays, when my CV is really huge, that part

FROM "Fears" #50.

f my fears that have been with me over the years.
ople position of my hands. However, some old fears
I had that fear that my penis was too small.
r fears vanished.
28.12. COLAK '06

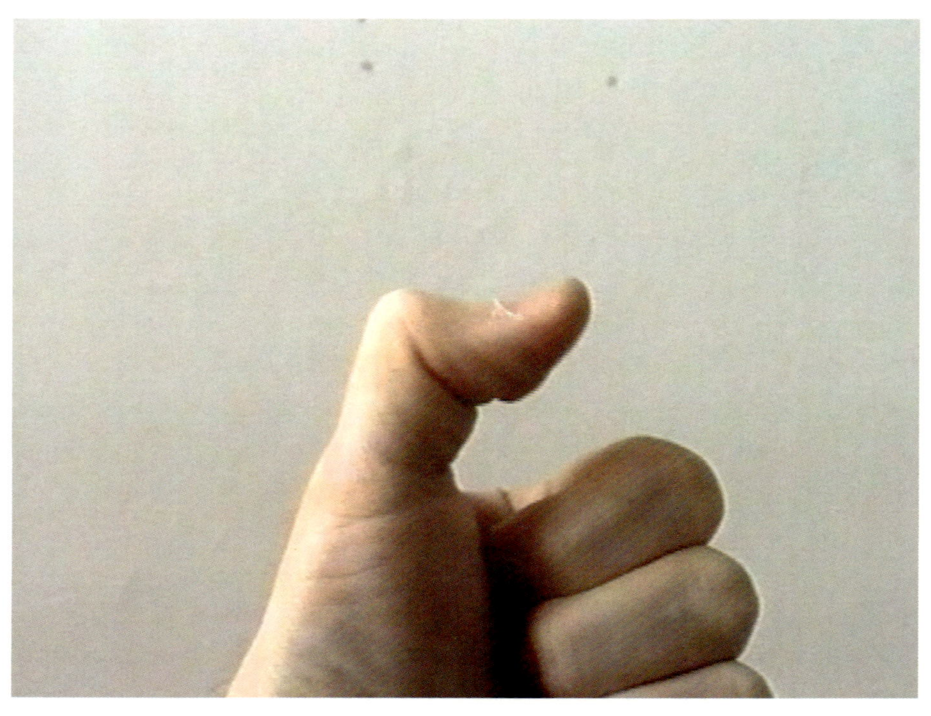

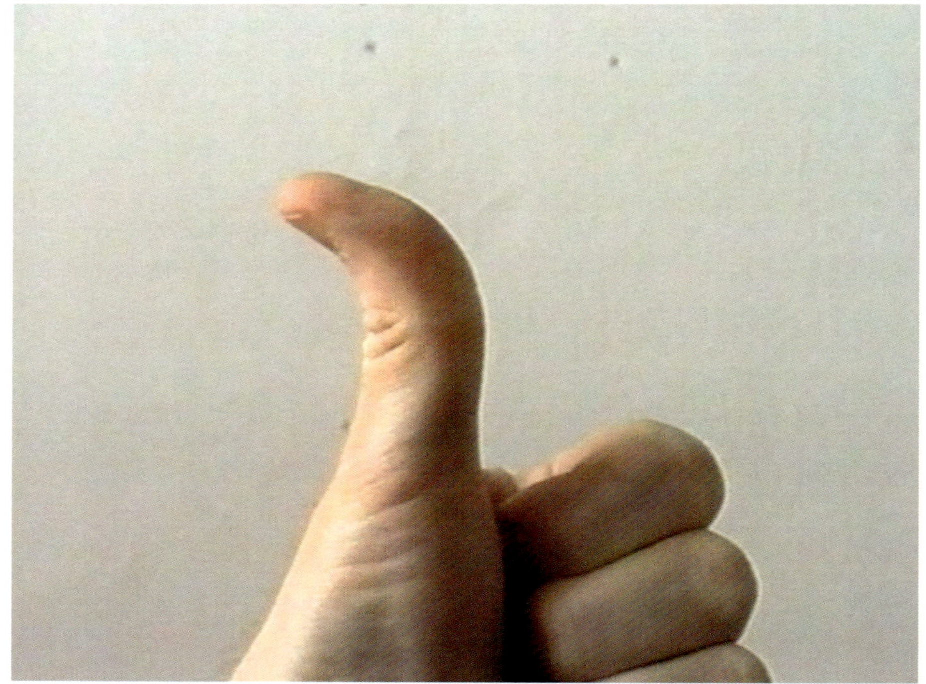

 Video on DVD, color, sound, 1'38'', looped

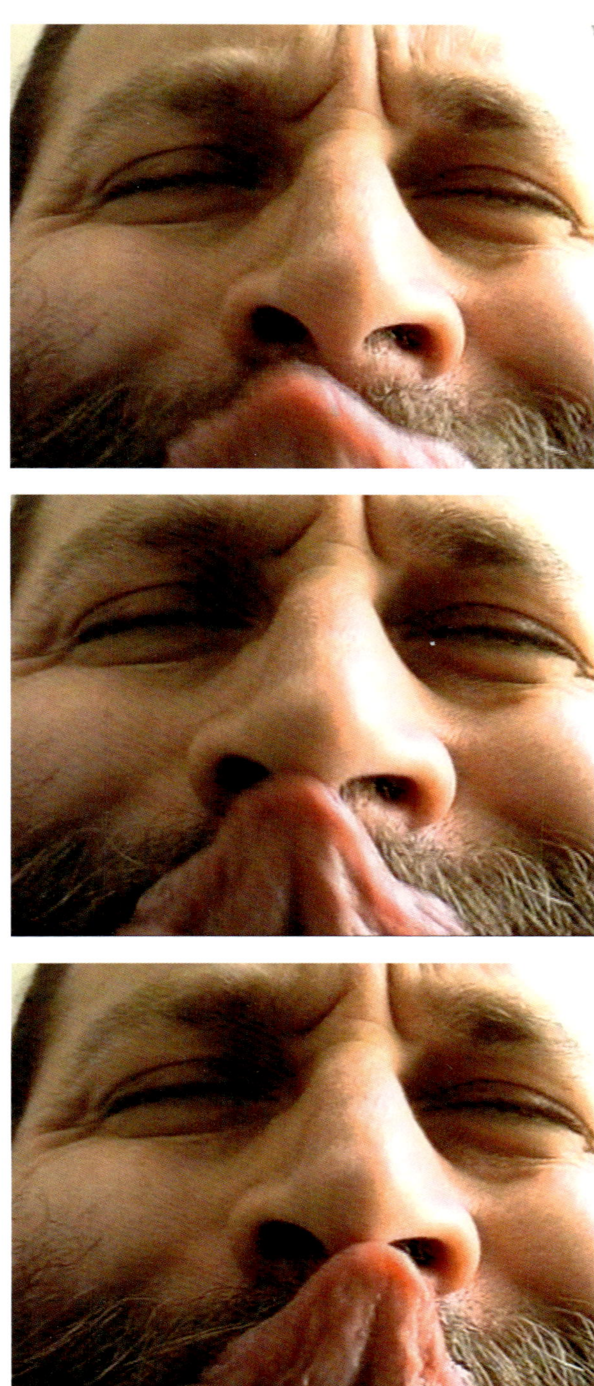

Some of My Capabilities, 1995

Deutsche Übersetzung siehe Seite 207

Fear

I am scared of flying. Really scared. And, for the time being, I have to fly all the time.

Before every departure, I take a pill. Sometimes, if it is an overseas flight, I take two. Naturally, this is not enough to block my fear. While I am on board, I constantly pray my own words in a kind of very personal mantra. That is not enough either. Most of the time, almost all the time, I keep my fists tight with thumbs up for good luck. I touch the plane with them too. For good luck.

When I was invited to create a ceramic sculpture for the Biennale of Ceramics in Albisola, I was not quite sure if I should accept. But then one day, while airborne on my way to the next exhibition, with my fiercely and painfully squeezed fists, I realized what would possibly make me interested in doing something with that overtly classical material—clay.

I asked the organizers, and they sent me some balls of the finest Albisola clay.

Between July 3 and September 15, 2002, I carried small balls of clay in my hands during all the flights I took to various destinations. To transform these balls into works of art was very easy. I just exploited my natural (and acquired) fear of flying and kept squeezing them all the time in my fists. Some of them were held for three hours, some for one. The sophisticated material captured the nervous convulsions of my terrified hands, triggered by all that bumping, babies crying, and the moments of relatively quiet cruising (which are the worst because I expect something—For God's sake, no!—to happen every minute). I stopped the **Fear** series when I was supposed to repeat a flight, which happened to be Sofia–Munich. Meanwhile, while visiting Albisola, I left the first three pairs of **Fear** sculptures to be fired by a professional ceramicist. The other seven pairs remained in my Sofia studio for several months to dry.

Needless to say, I have other fears too. One of them manifested itself with the very specific concern that if I was going to send the raw clay sculptures to Italy by courier, they might be damaged. So, I decided to fire them in Bulgaria and to ship them safely later as more robust fired terracotta pieces. However, my knowledge with regards to the firing of ceramics is pretty vague. After asking around for a reliable kiln, I finally decided to use the rather unprofessional kiln in which my father bakes his own extremely beautiful little abstract sculptures. He was happy to help me. Even though he was unfamiliar with that particular clay, he suggested that we should proceed as he normally does and bake the figures at a low temperature in my mother's kitchen oven until all the moisture had evaporated and then fire them in a proper kiln that reaches high temperatures fairly quickly. No, I said, my **Fear** sculptures are dry enough; they have been drying for seven months. Perhaps I should mention that despite my cautiousness and doubts about everything, I do really stupid things as well. Although my father was not convinced, I pulled rank as the more famous artist of the two of us.

The laws of nature naturally made themselves felt. After twenty minutes of firing, my extremely anxious father entered the sitting room and said that there were booming sounds coming from the kiln in his studio. We switched it off, and after opening the door, a devastating sight appeared before our eyes. All of the **Fear** sculptures, the testaments to my panic up there 10,000 meters above the ground, came out in pieces, some bigger some smaller. Another

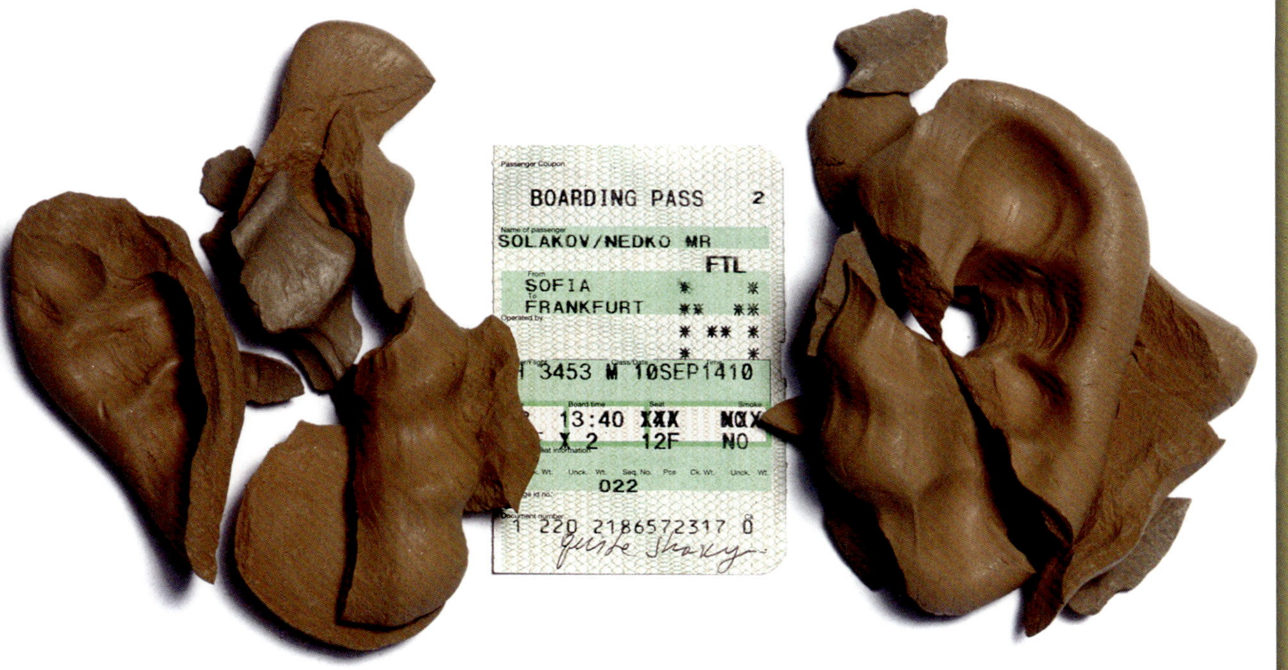

Fear, 2002–03

Terracotta, Alitalia, Austrian Airlines, and Lufthansa boarding pass stubs, ball-point pen; ten pairs of sculptures, some of them in pieces; dimensions variable

fear then took over. My parents (both with serious heart conditions) were getting extremely worried. I had to make up something and to assure them that I would be able to handle the situation. The famous Bulgarian proverb "out of bad can come good" came to mind and I convinced them that my sculptures were now looking much better and the concept was all the more profound. Luckily, the second batch of clay sculptures that was supposed to be next in the little kiln was undamaged, so my father baked it (along with the broken pieces of the first set) in his way and everything worked out fine, of course.

What you see now, my dear viewer, is a combination of unbroken and broken **Fear** sculptures. All the tiny fragments you see really belong to this or that particular piece. I spent many hours restoring their shapes. Because of my stupidity, my original idea was destroyed although all the baked clay here, no matter in how many pieces it now appears, was with me in those ten aircraft and I believe that all of them do carry elements of my fear on those ten flights.

I am superstitious too. The overwhelming thought in my mind now is this—if these so carefully prepared little **Fear** sculptures are partly broken, what about me and the future flights that I am supposed to take? What I am supposed to hold and squeeze now, while I am still on the ground, to try to overcome the newly born fear deriving from these broken **Fear** sculptures? Should I fly at all from now on?

Nedko Solakov, May 2003

Passenger Coupon
BOARDING PASS 2
Name of passenger
SOLAKOV/NEDKO MR
FTL
From
FRANKFURT
To
SOFIA
Operated by
LUFTHANSA
LH 3418 M 15SEP0955
Gate
Board time
Seat
Smoke
B31 09:25 6F NO
ZONE 2
098
Baggage id no.
Document number
2 220 2186572317 3

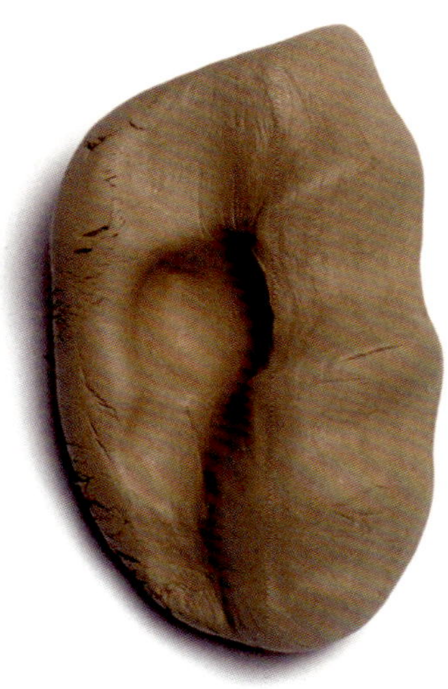

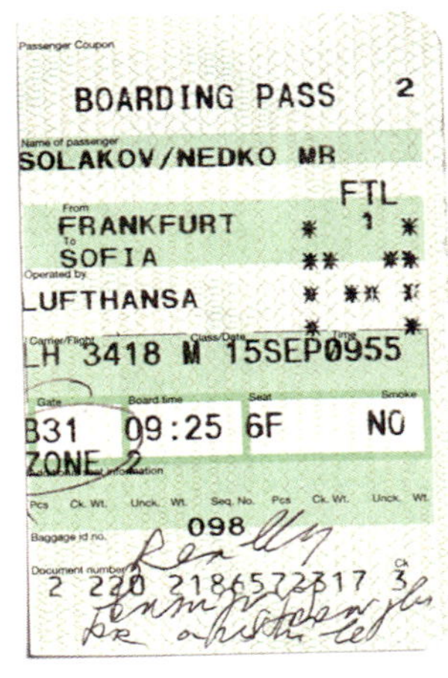

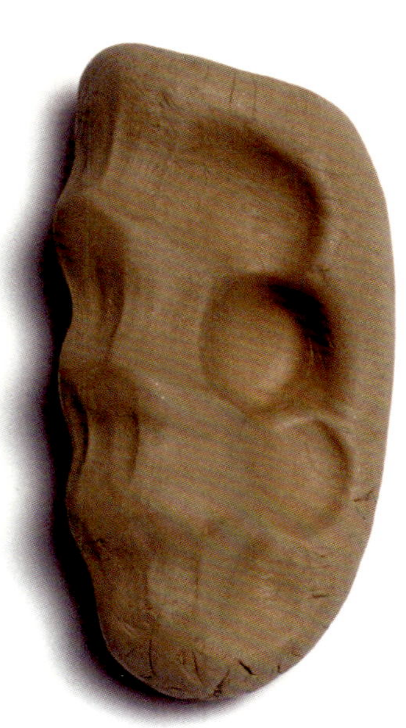

Fear, 2002–03

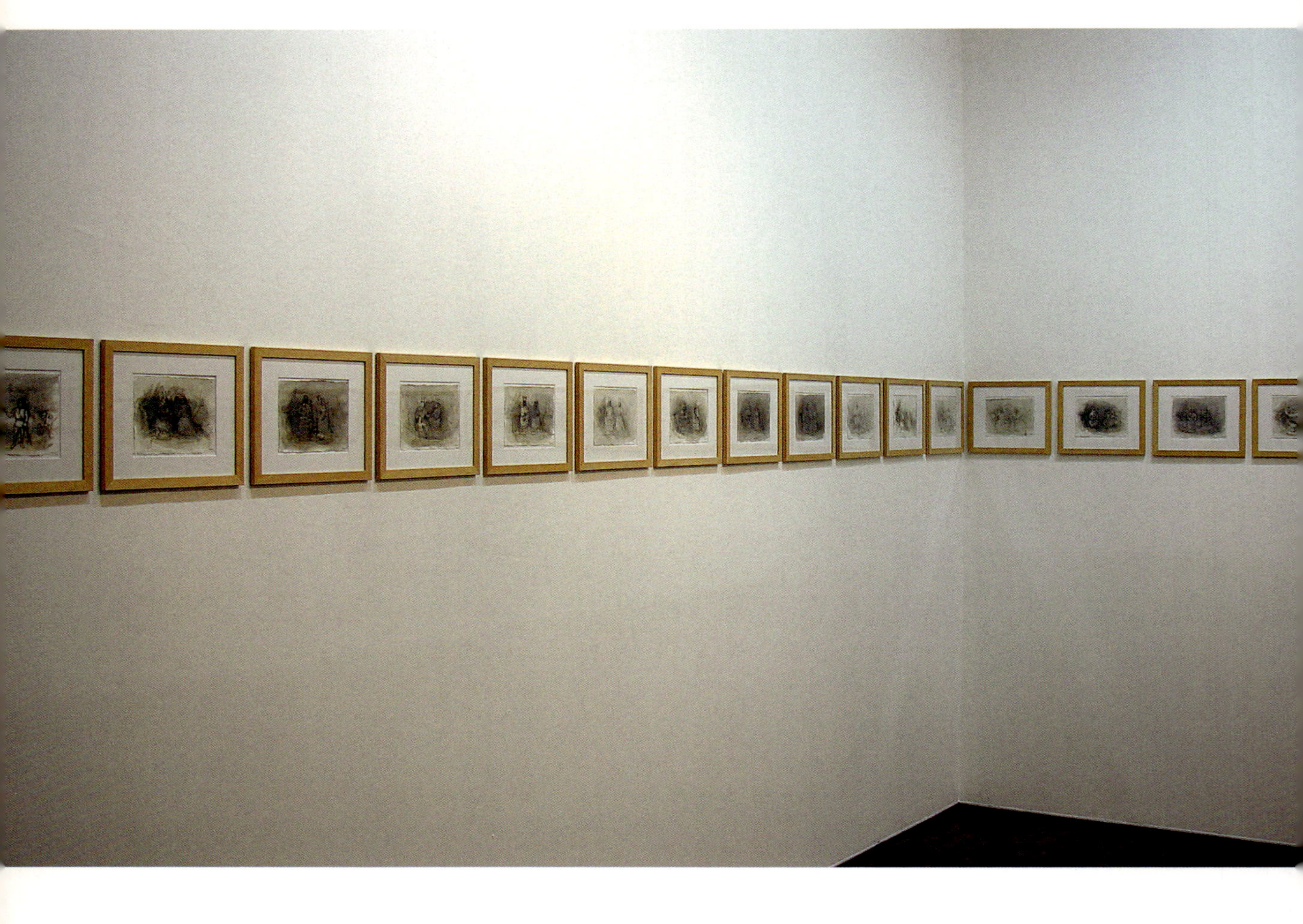

Series of forty drawings
Sepia, black and white ink and wash on paper; 14.5 x 19 cm each

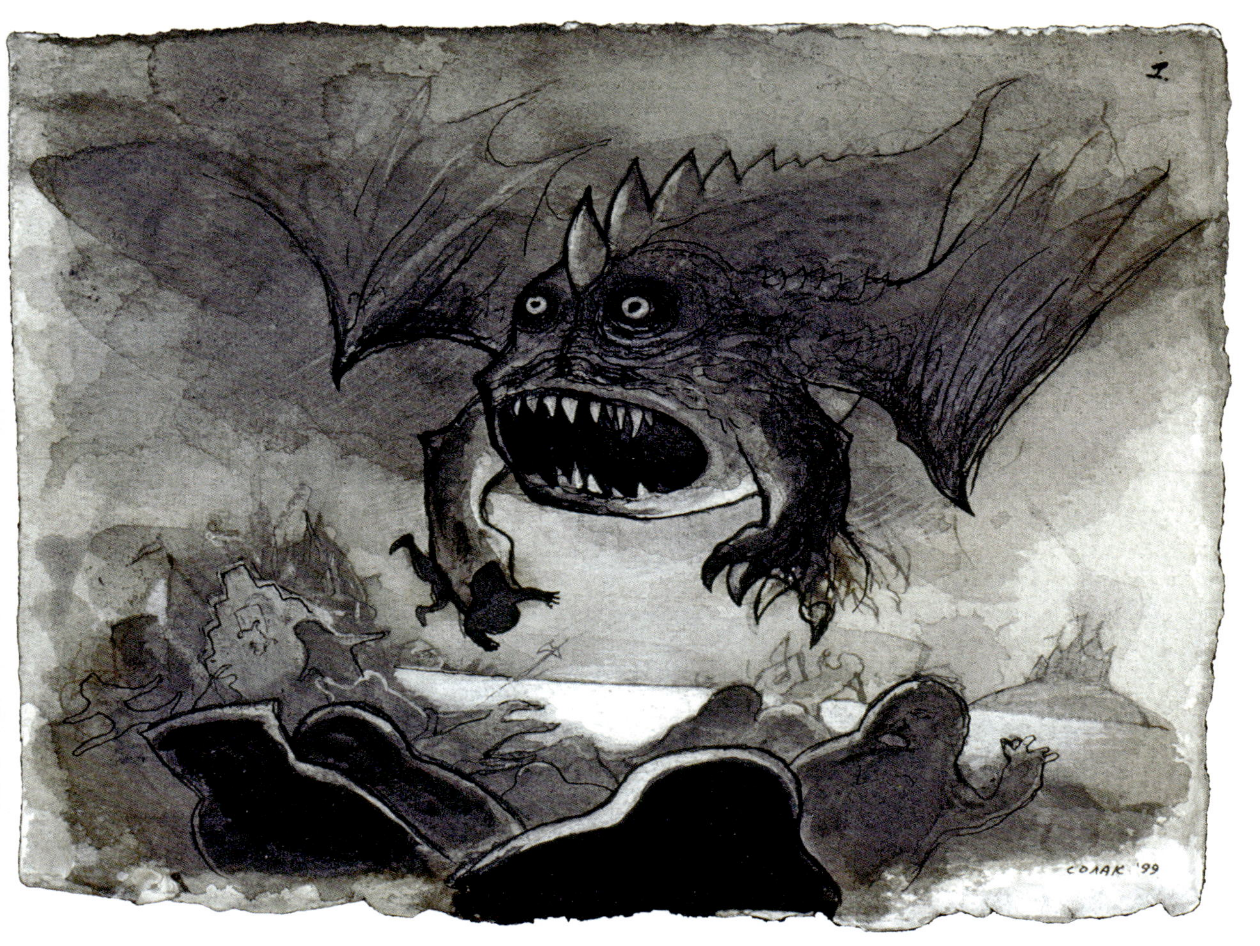

...and they lived happily ever after, 1999

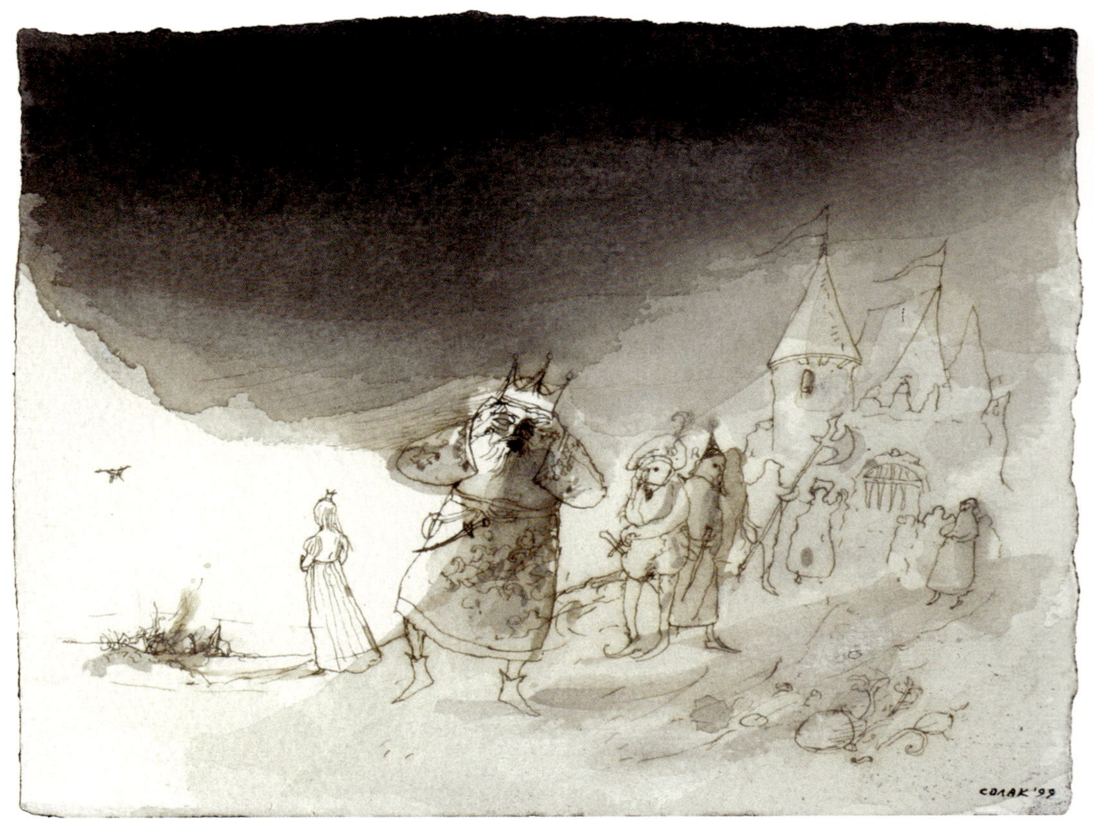
COLAK '99

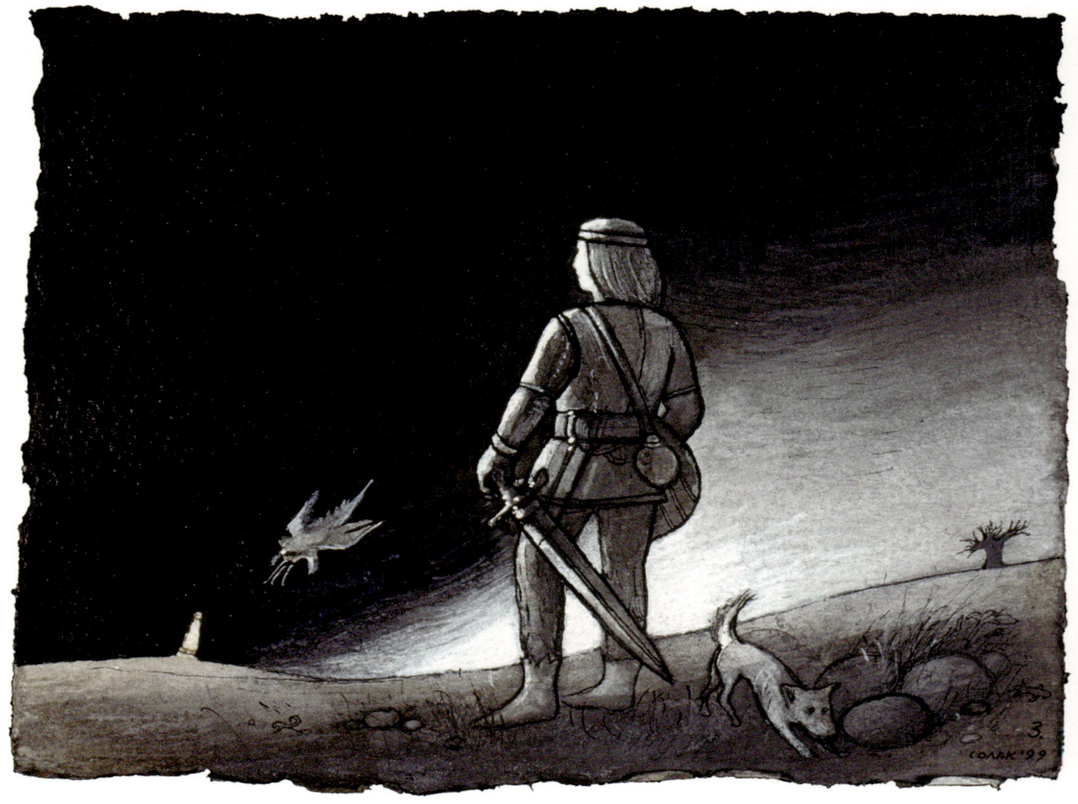
3.
COLAK '99

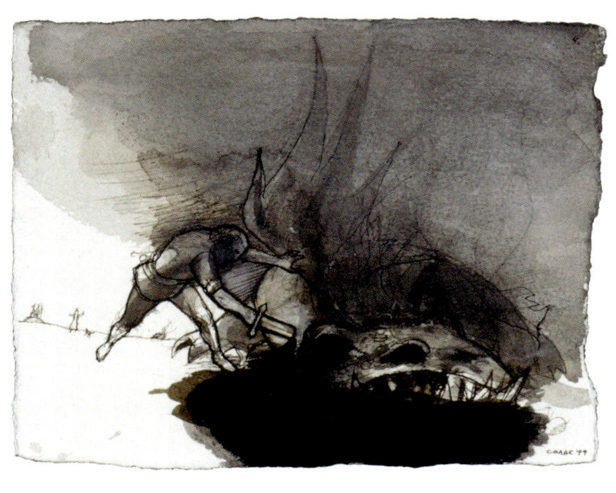

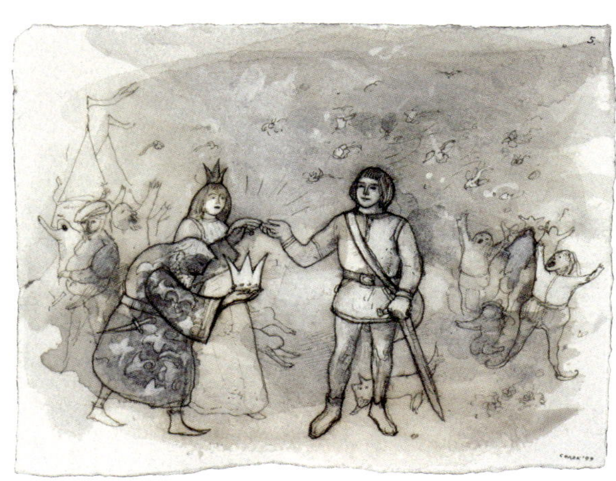

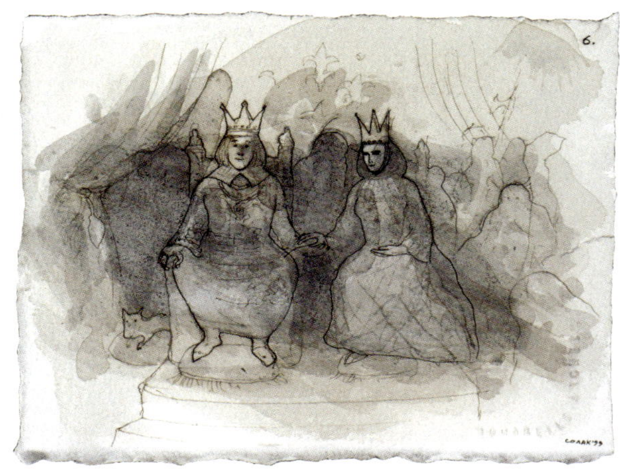

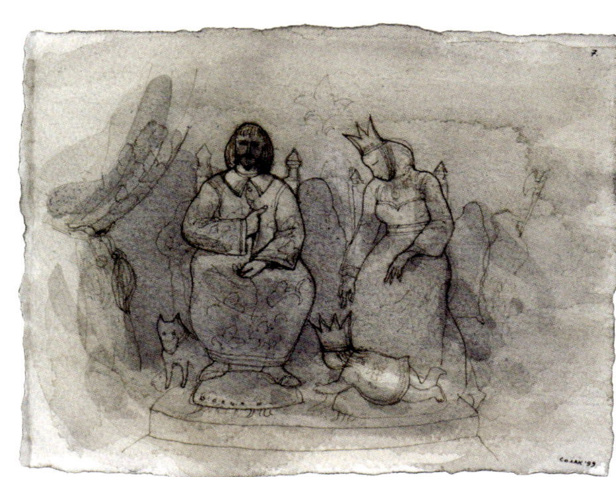

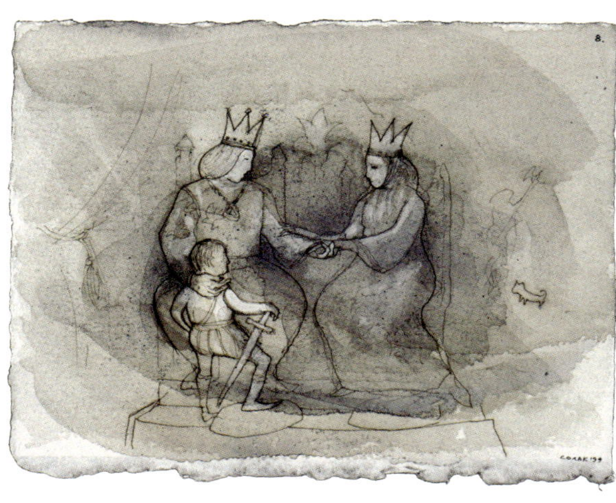

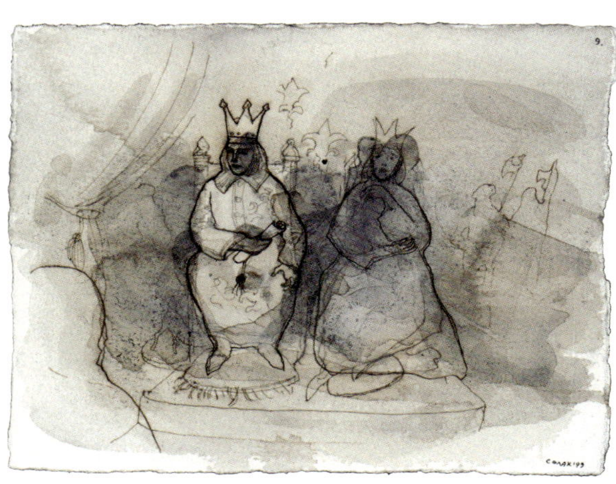

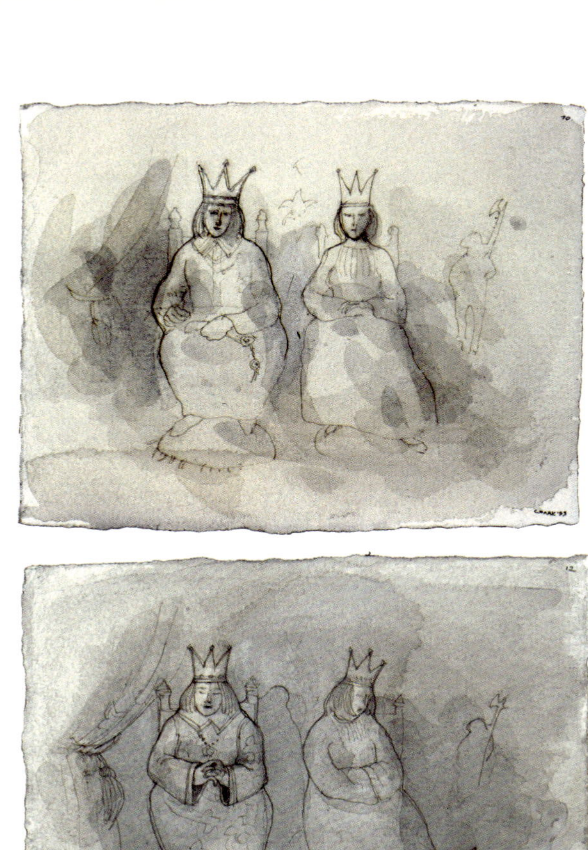
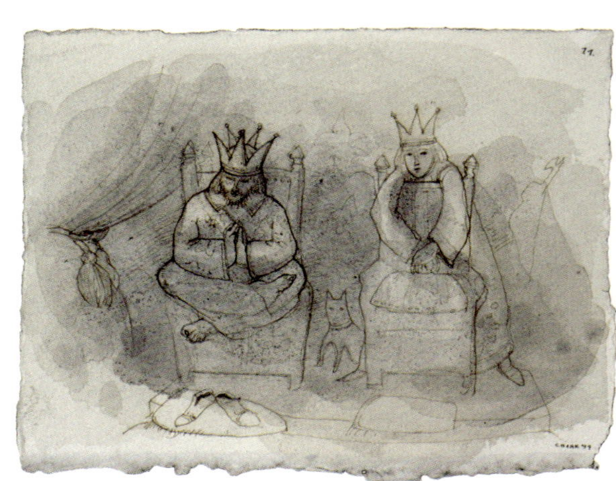
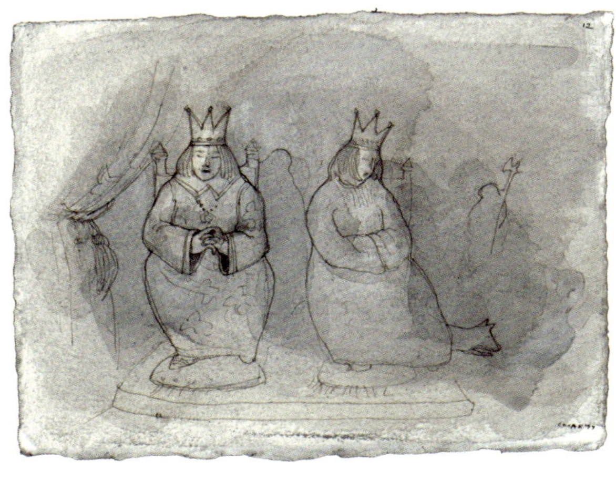
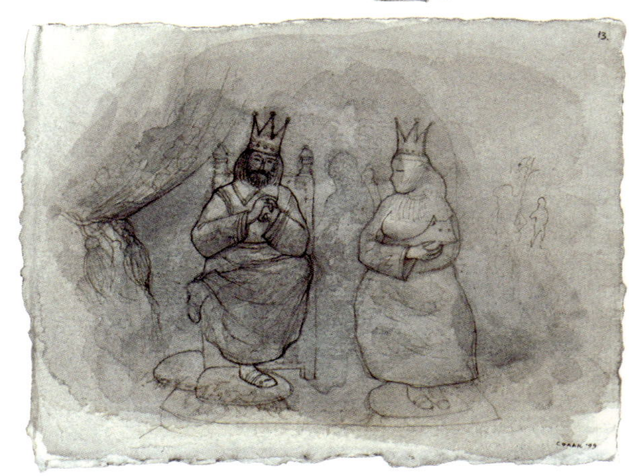
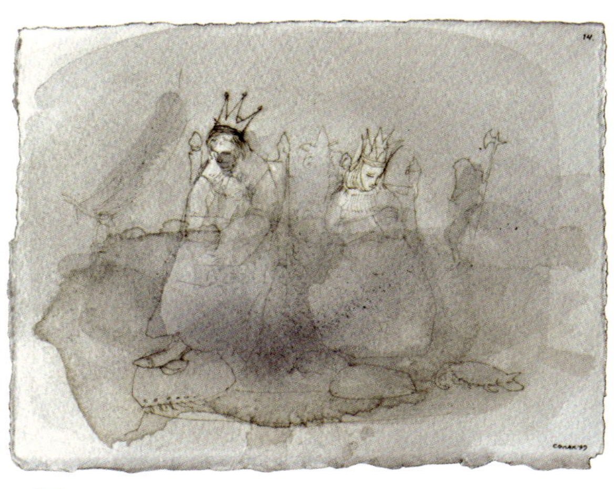
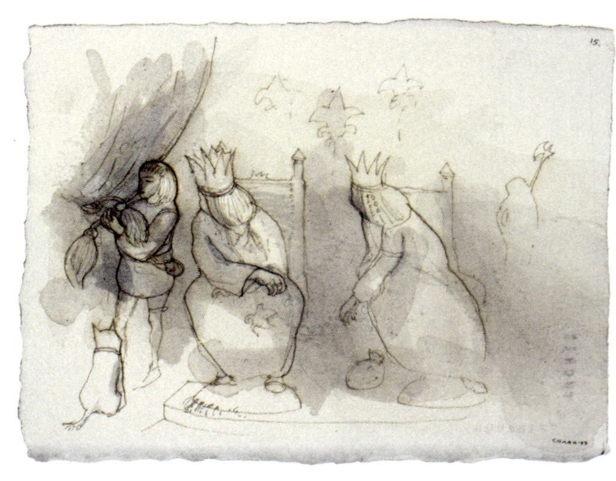
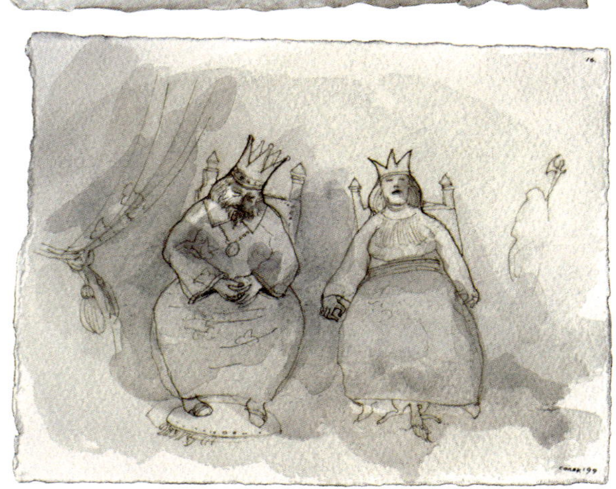
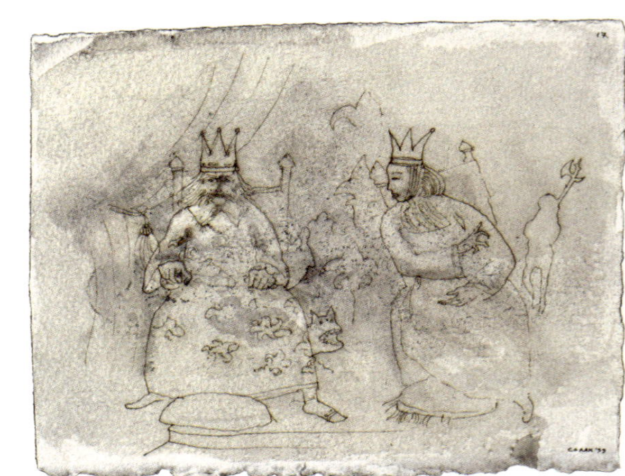

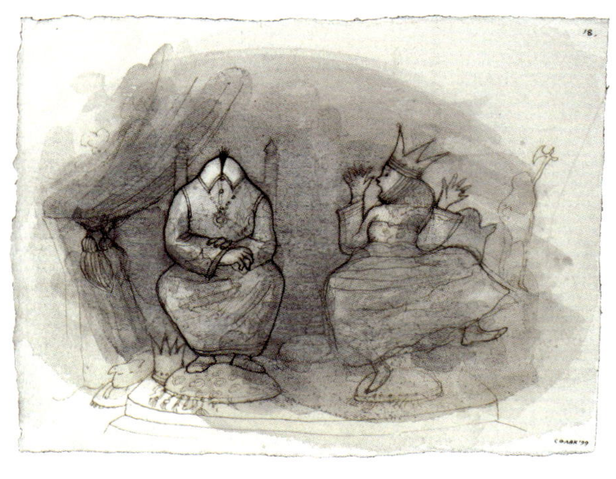

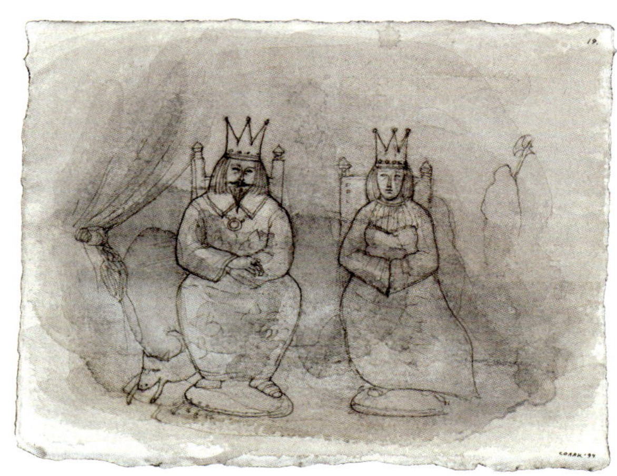

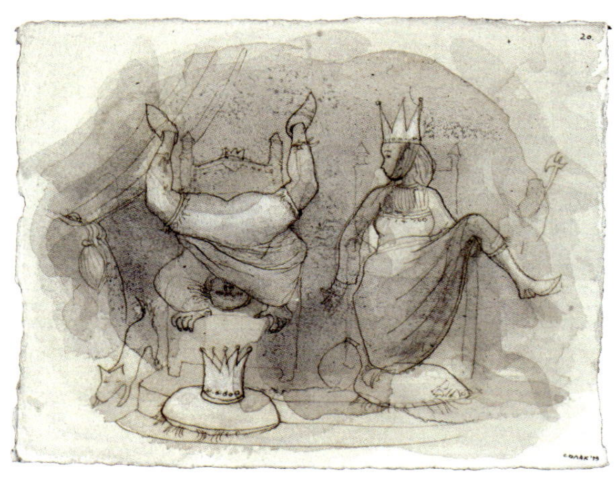

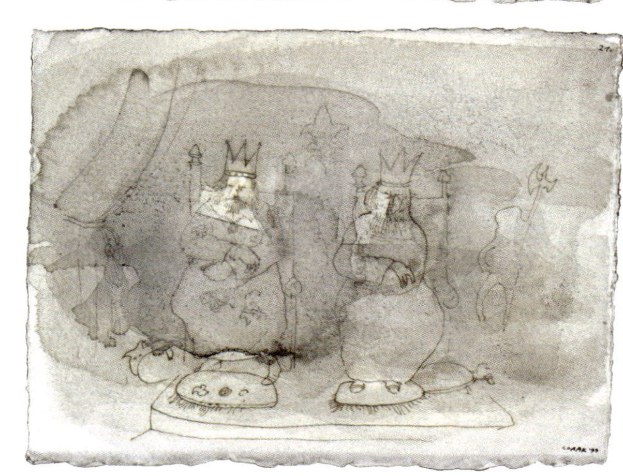

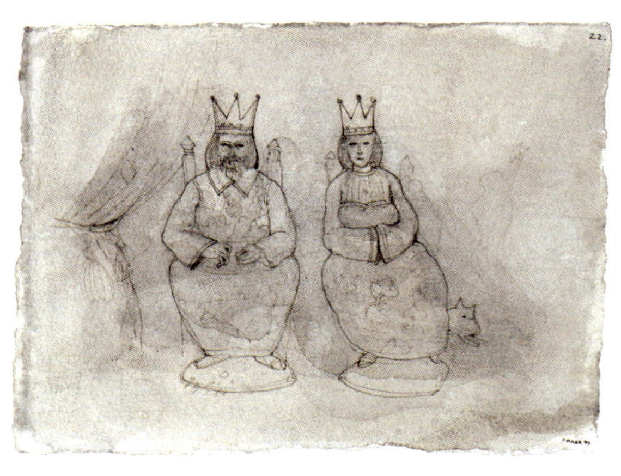

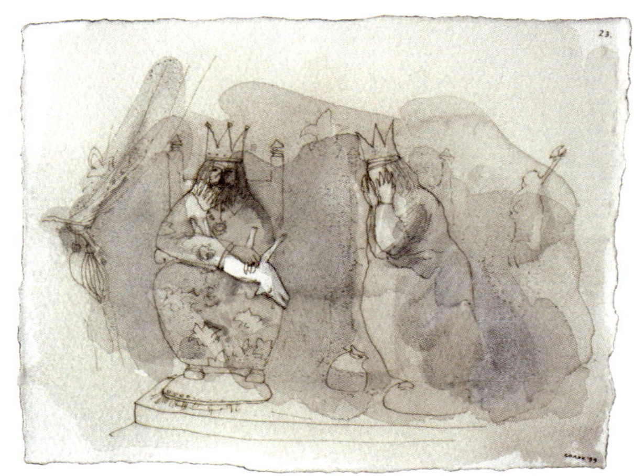

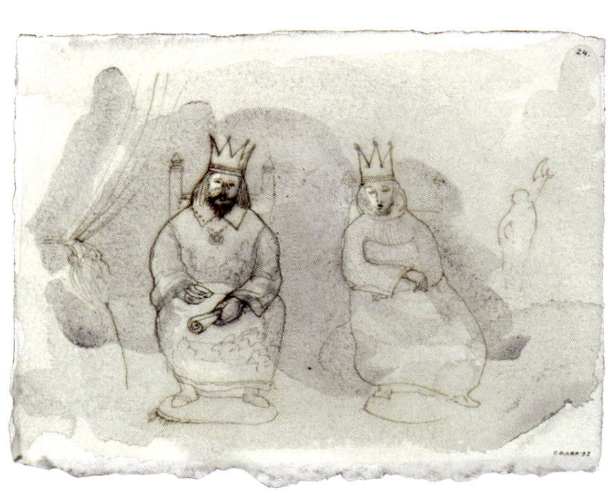

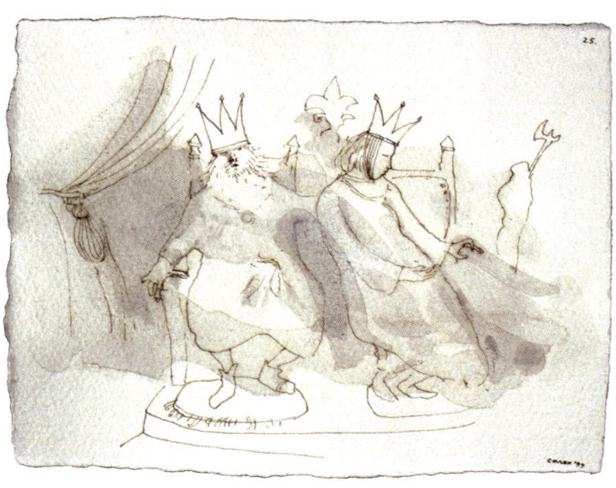

...and they lived happily ever after, 1999

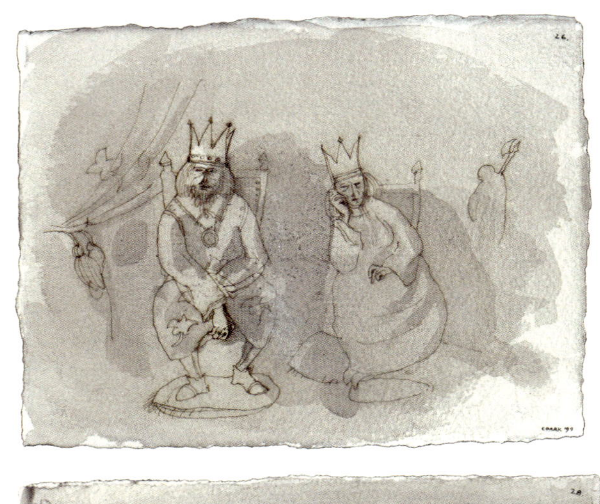
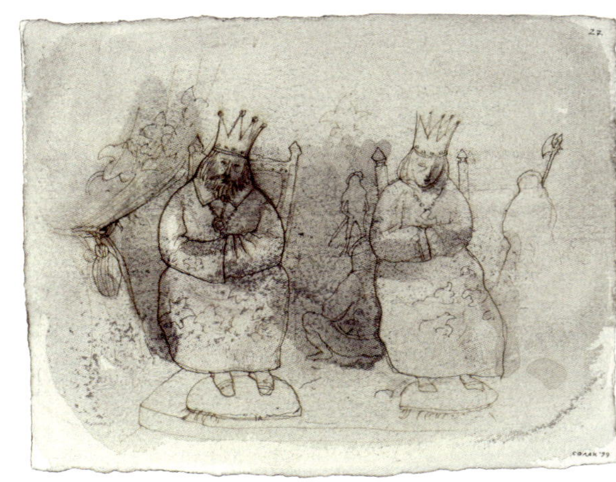
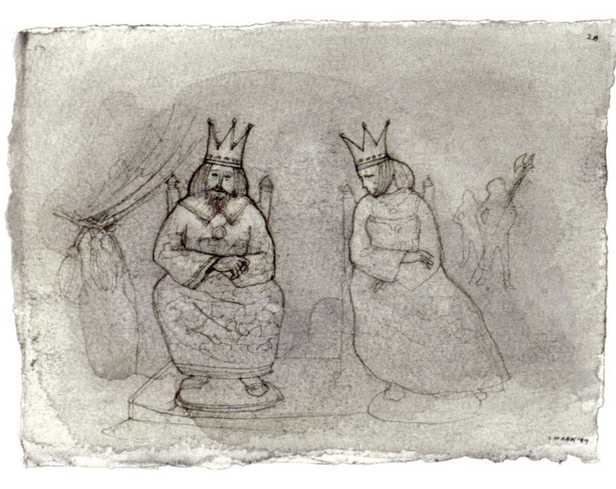
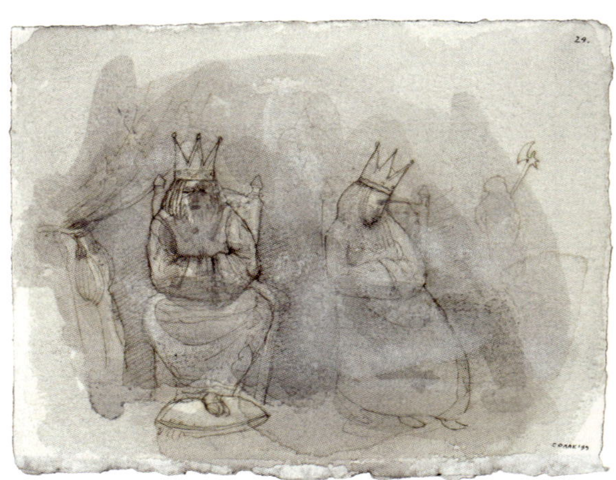
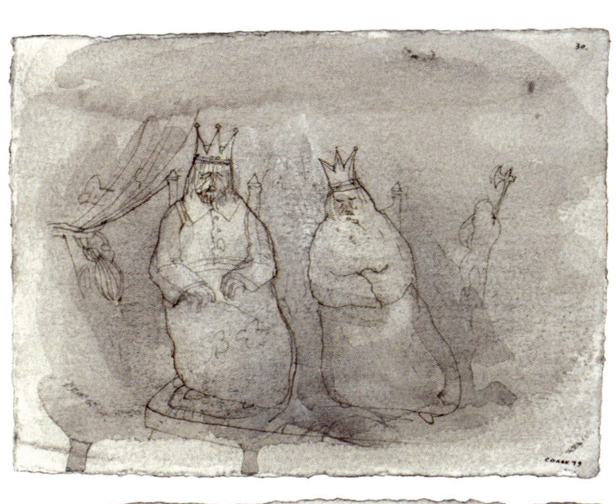
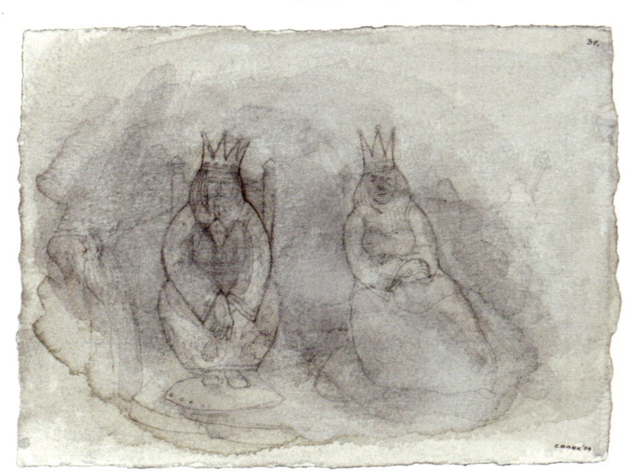
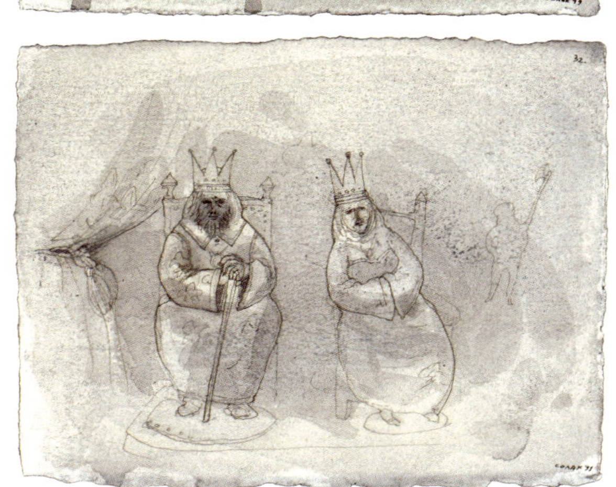
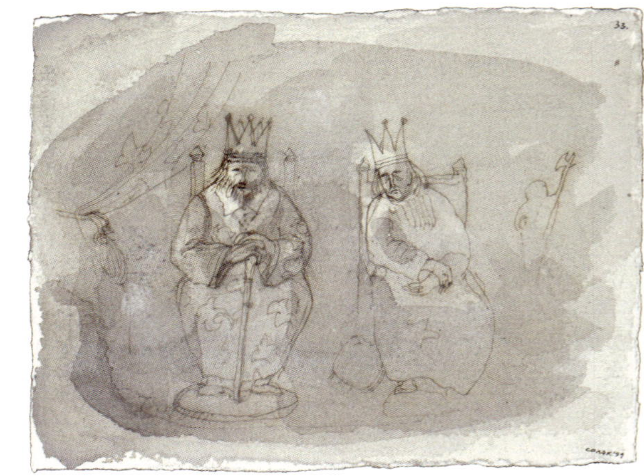

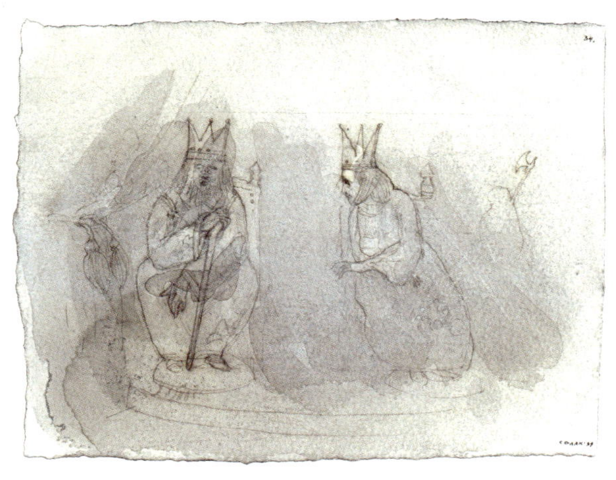
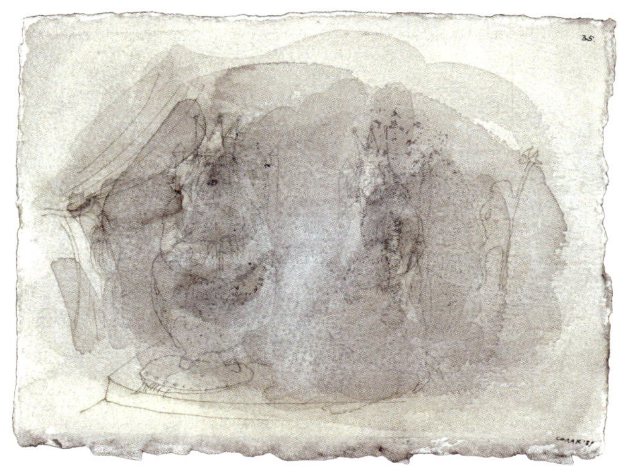
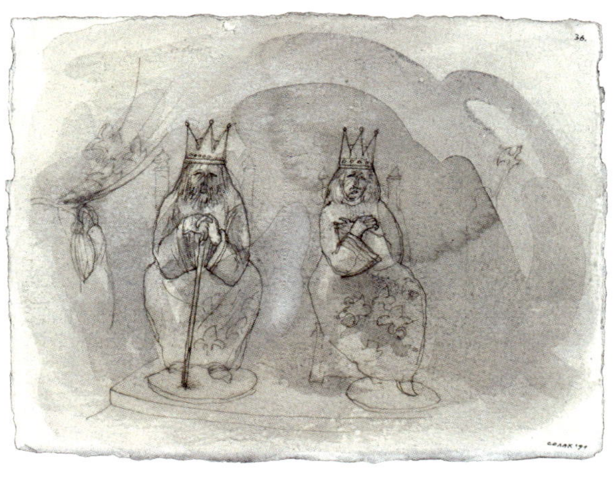
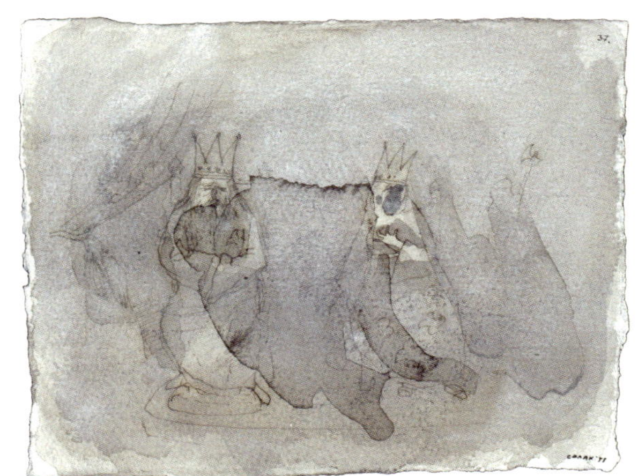
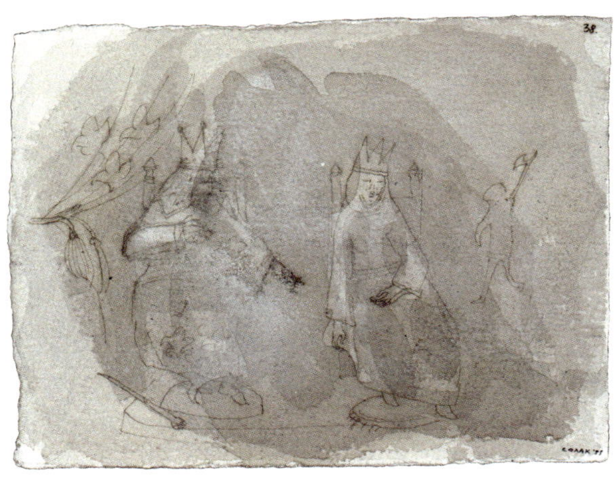
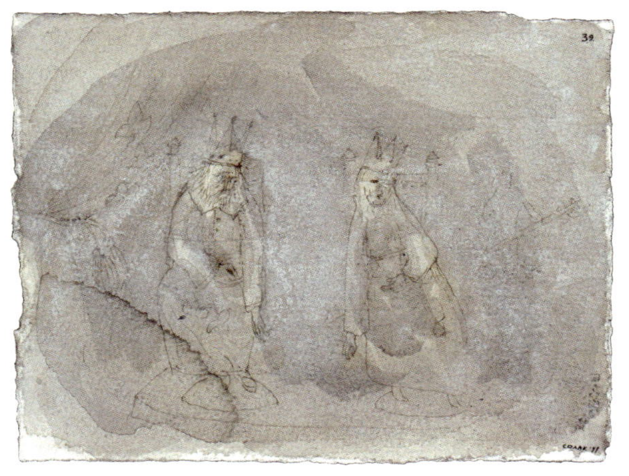
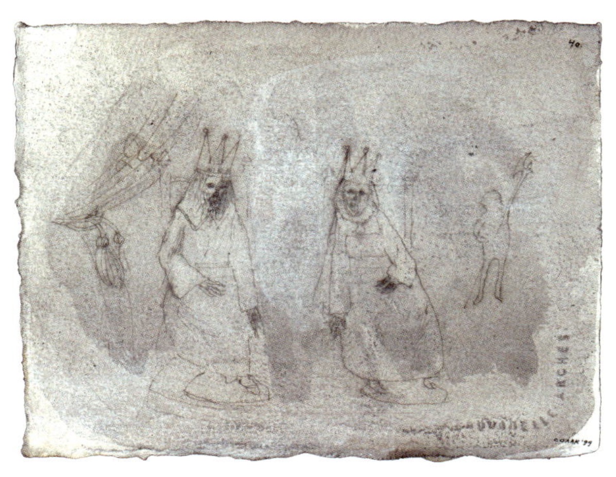

I love them

I love watching movies. It has always been like that. Ever since my childhood some of the most precious moments in my life have taken place in a cinema (often as the only spectator in the place because I love going to the movies during the day on working days) or in front of my plasma screen at home or, while traveling the world for exhibitions, lying in bed in a hotel room staring at my laptop screen. I can't really explain why I love them, I just do. Nor can I explain why I recently decided to visualize my love in a peculiar way—silently, with colors only and some odd comments. I watched seven of my favorite films—**City Lights, The Big Lebowski, Seven Samurai, Rocco fickt Rio** (my favorite porn film), **Fawlty Towers (The Psychiatrist), Amadeus,** and **Amarcord—,** and while watching them, I wrote the scripts for what you can see here now on the seven screens. I know that it is hard to make a sensible connection between a particular color and a particular time from the time code generator bars, but believe me in all those hours, minutes, seconds, and frames, I really did find myself sinking into many different emotional states, and what could be better than a color for representing the emotions of a movie fan? But because the emotions were sometimes altered by thoughts (not necessarily connected to the movies) spinning through my head, I had to add some words too.

I love them

Ich liebe es mir Filme anzusehen. Schon immer. Seit meinen Kindertagen trugen sich die kostbarsten Momente meines Lebens im Kino (oft war ich der einzige Zuschauer, weil ich gern tagsüber während der Arbeitszeit ins Kino gehe) oder daheim vor meinem Plasmabildschirm oder, wenn ich zu Ausstellungen in der Welt unterwegs war, im Hotelzimmer vor dem Bildschirm meines Laptops zu. Ich kann nicht wirklich erklären, weshalb ich Filme liebe. Es ist einfach so. Auch kann ich nicht erklären, weshalb ich mich vor kurzem entschloss, meine Liebe auf eine eigenwillige Weise zu visualisieren – leise, nur mit Farben und einigen wenigen merkwürdigen Kommentaren. Ich schaute mir sieben meiner Lieblingsfilme an – **Lichter der Großstadt, The Big Lebowski, Die sieben Samurai, Rocco fickt Rio** (mein Lieblingsporno), **Fawlty Towers (The Psychiatrist), Amadeus** und **Amarcord –,** und während ich zusah, schrieb ich die Skripts für das, was Sie jetzt auf diesen sieben Bildschirmen sehen. Ich weiß, dass es schwer ist, eine sinnvolle Verbindung zwischen einer bestimmten Farbe und einem bestimmten Zeitpunkt auf der Timecode-Anzeige herzustellen, aber glauben Sie mir, während all der Stunden, Minuten, Sekunden und Bilder bin ich in viele verschiedene Gefühlszustände eingetaucht, und was könnte sich besser eignen, die Gefühle eines Filmliebhabers darzustellen, als Farbe? Da aber die Gefühle bisweilen durch die Gedanken, die mir durch den Kopf schwirrten (und nicht unbedingt in direktem Zusammenhang zu den Filmen standen), verändert wurden, musste ich auch einige Worte beifügen.

Seven-channel video installation, silent; dimensions variable.
Duration:
City Lights, 82'52"; **The Big Lebowski,** 108'02"; **Seven Samurai,** 189'23"; **Rocco fickt Rio,** 54'05"; **Fawlty Towers (The Psychiatrist),** 36'32"; **Amadeus,** 153'36"; **Amarcord,** 118'43"

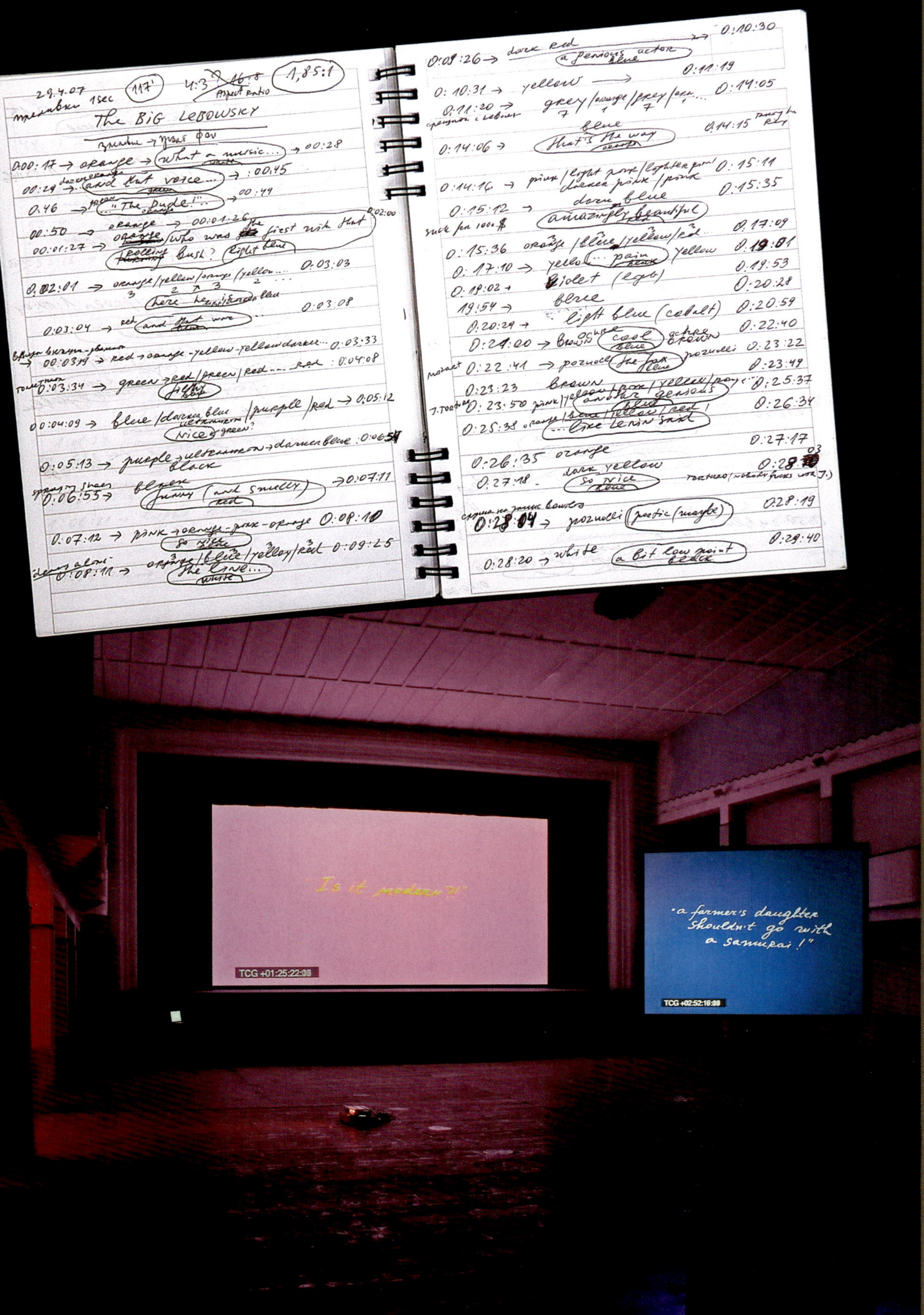
The BIG LEBOWSKY
"Is it modern?!"
"a farmer's daughter shouldn't go with a samurai!"
TCG +01:25:22:08
TCG +02:52:18:08

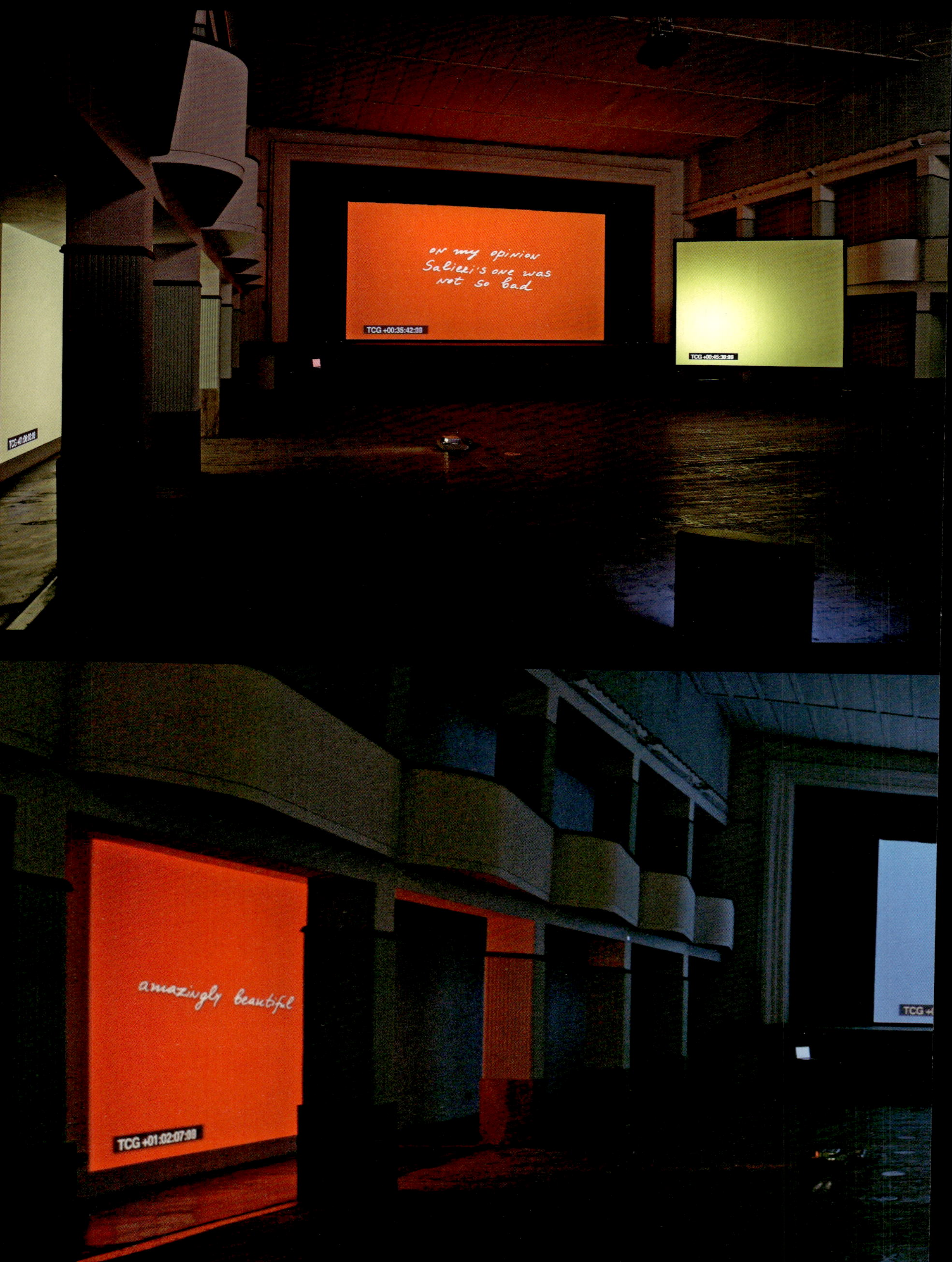
on my opinion
Salieri's one was
not so bad
amazingly beautiful
TCG +01:02:07:08

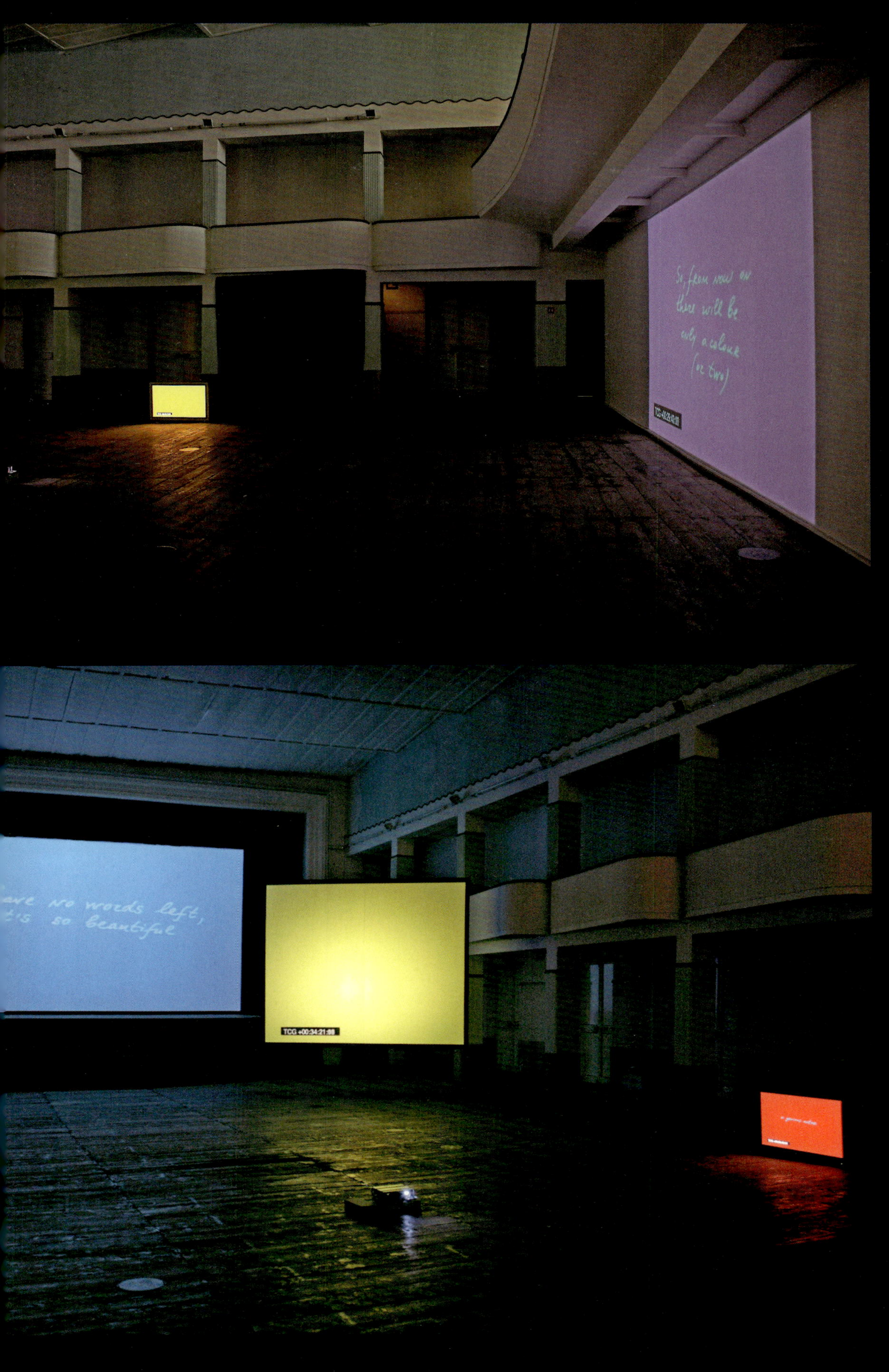
So, from now on
there will be
only a colour
(or two)
ere no words left,
t's so beautiful

Luckily, in my field, nowadays,
if an artist is mediocre
he/she still could become
a curator (presumably
possessing the feeling what
could a good art be)

TCG +02:08:52:08

it's so beautiful-
the black & white

TCG +00:26:19:18

Checking quickly the
emails while the
film is running.
Sorry!

TCG +01:12:53:15

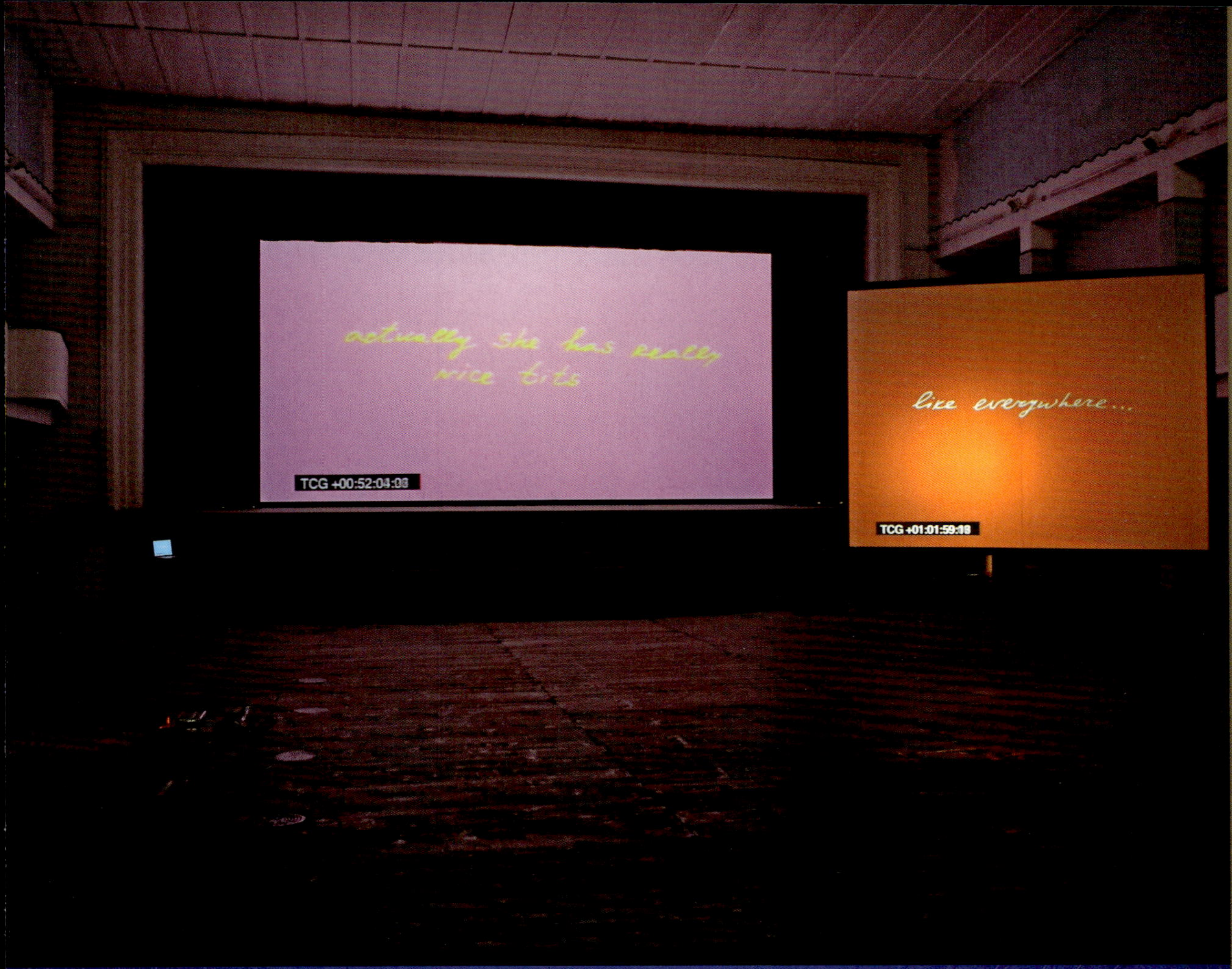

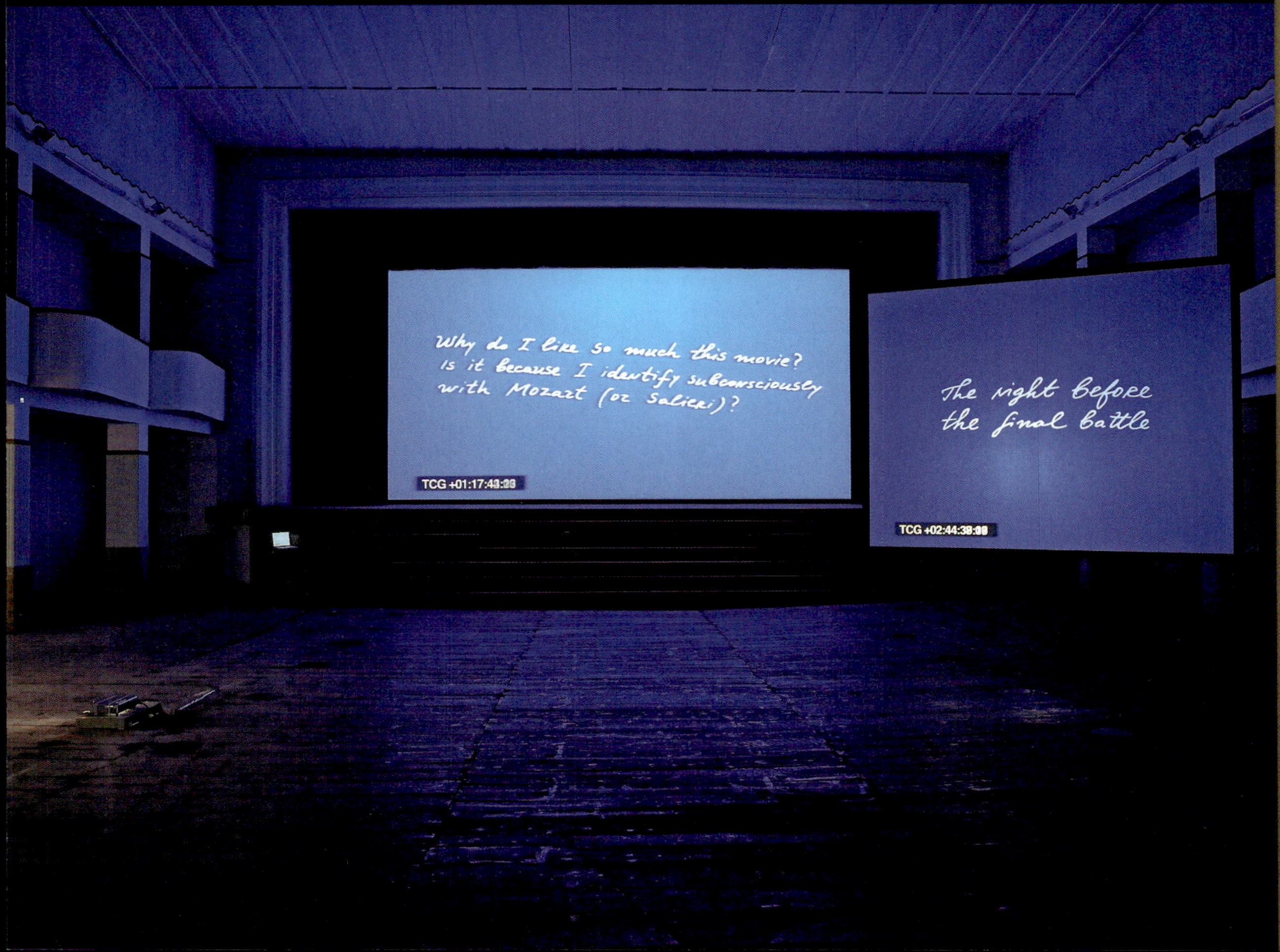

3.2.08

Some Nice Things to Enjoy when...

> page/Seite 166

Sunrise Sunset
97
150
+ wall texts

> page/Seite 192

the going-down bancrupt businessman
20 sec. looped

Nice calming you down/amusing you sounds (with several headphones) → on a very hysteric background

bright, contrast colours (wall drawing)

> page/Seite 162

the sleeping child

instructions what to do with the other visitors who must agree to accept anything as long as they are in that area

to make you very nervous (the wall drawing) and at the same time to calm you down

red
green
pink
yellow
ect.

To cuddle in
700 cm
700 cm

> page/Seite 163

to worship (just in case) a combo-icon with as many religions' symbols as possible

> page/Seite 194

"Sorry → no socially engaged video works provided for this area"

> page/Seite 180

Texts over the "inserts"

black velvet with "duck" yellow buttons
190
150 150

page/Seite 172 <

the Brussels' thieves collectors

the clock that makes your working hours run faster and your rest hours slower ?

endless supply of cardboard boxes to be thorn appart (to provide gloves because of the staples)

> page/Seite 176

a depositorium for the balls from your nose stuff

a glass jar

> page/Seite 164

on a plinth nicely exposed/lit

To mummify/embalm the worst parts of my BF life in order to keep you fresh in the world beyond

to look at the friendly cracking fire (shot in pizzeria? ....) with subtitles of the people's conversations

Мбкава за художник

Somebody to draw/paint for me

> page/Seite 174

> page/Seite 182

To raise a modern genius' art work's price in an easy way

Lucio Fontana's 1949 drawing with a "cut" framed + video

cold water machine

To enjoy an improbable story with even more improbable substories

the shoes + the market stuff

imagine how you would torture your own boss, local politician, the president of a super power, etc.

> page/Seite 190

+ manual for torture methods

the people's creations stay on the table + the wall

To spread juicy rumours about your neighbors, mates, etc. → writing on the wall or a panel or on a long roll

> page/Seite 186

in what place you would like to live in your other life? make a choice and enjoy later

"divine" places
visitors vote for the best place

By entering this particular area, you, dear visitor, have agreed to withstand (with no complaints whatsoever) any kind of harassment* other visitors may subject you to!

* like "Klaps auf den Hintern"

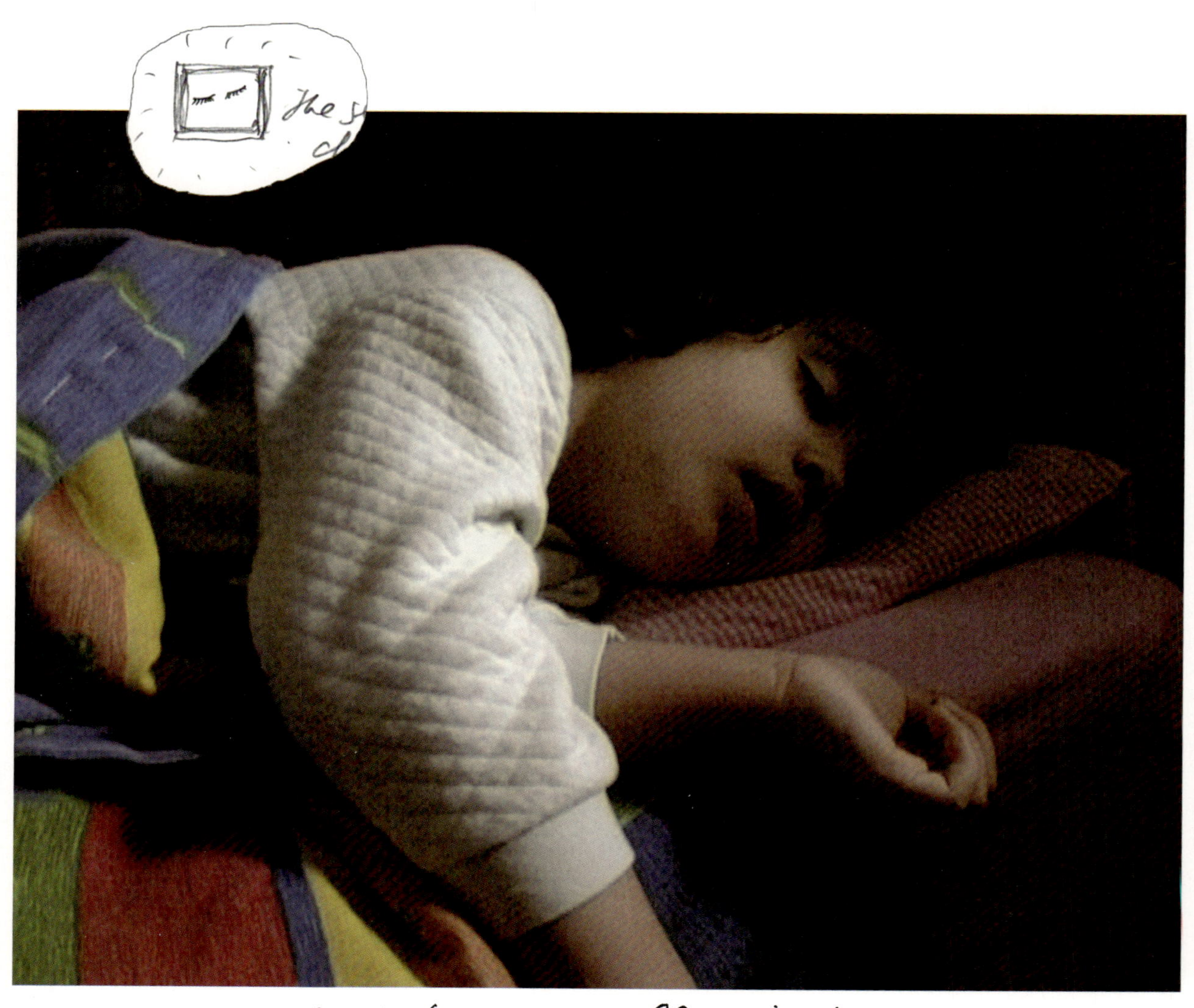

Just a sleeping child (my adorable niece).
By any standards, a lovely, enjoyable scene.

Enjoy worshiping the one-of-a-kind
Combo Icon! All major religions
are properly covered; none of
their symbols is neglected by any
other. It's an irreplaceable device
for emergency situations

Sorry for showing only part
of the life-size preparatory
drawing, made by the wood-carver
it will be shining golden

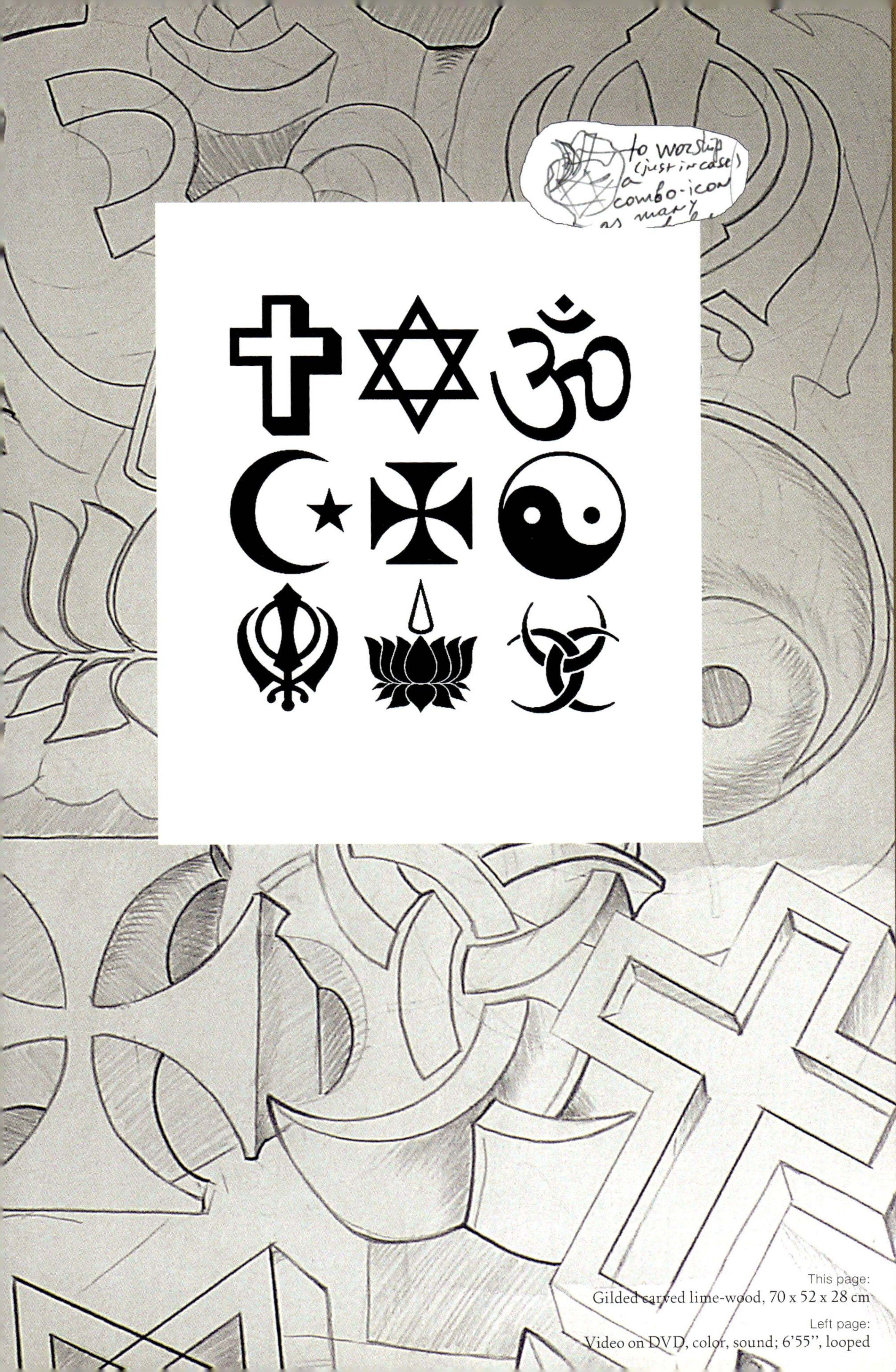

This page:
Gilded carved lime-wood, 70 x 52 x 28 cm

Left page:
Video on DVD, color, sound; 6'55", looped

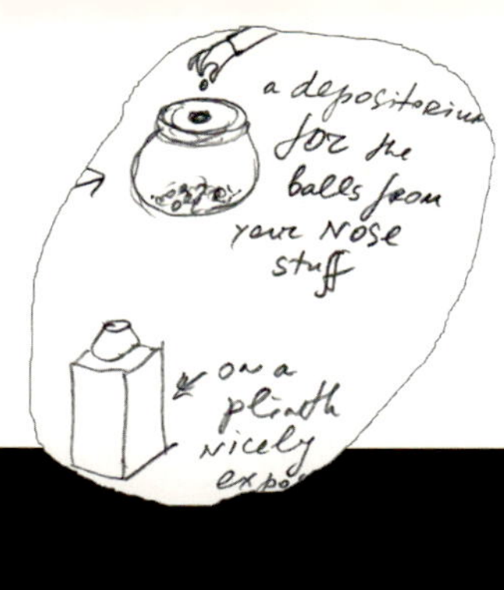

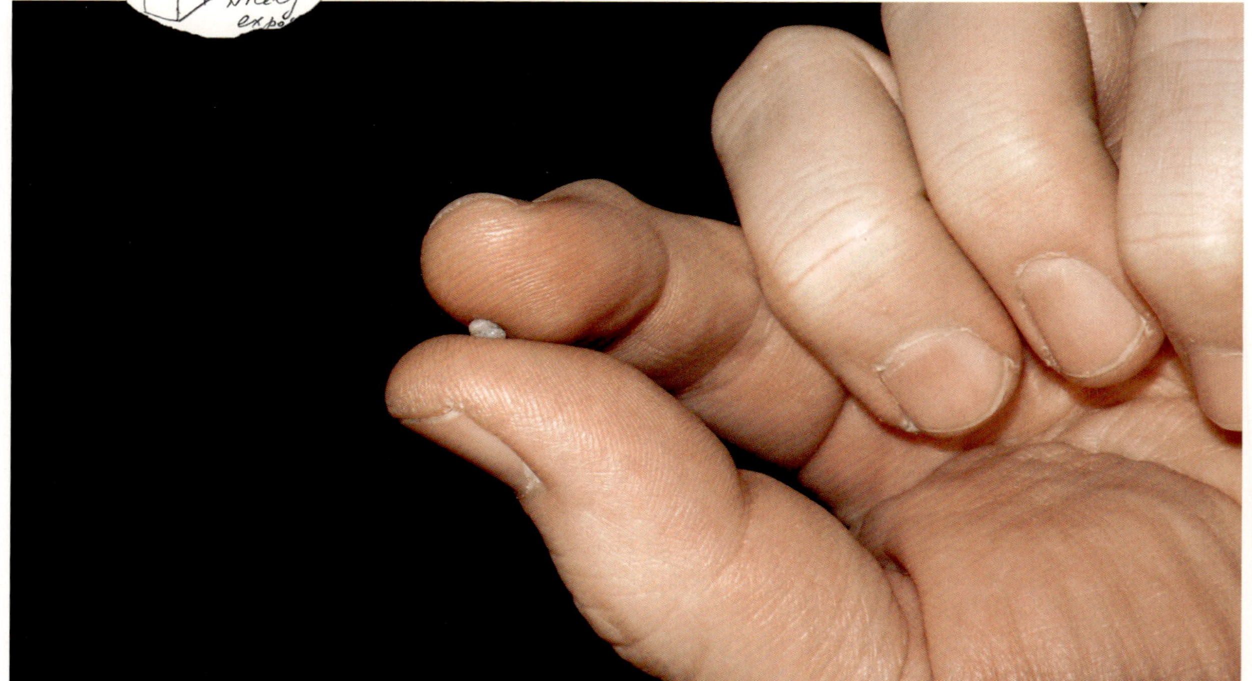

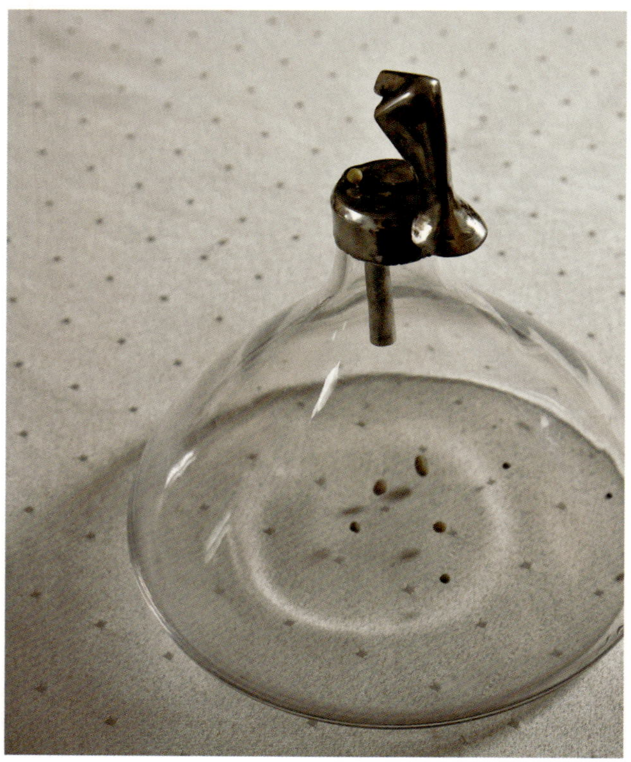

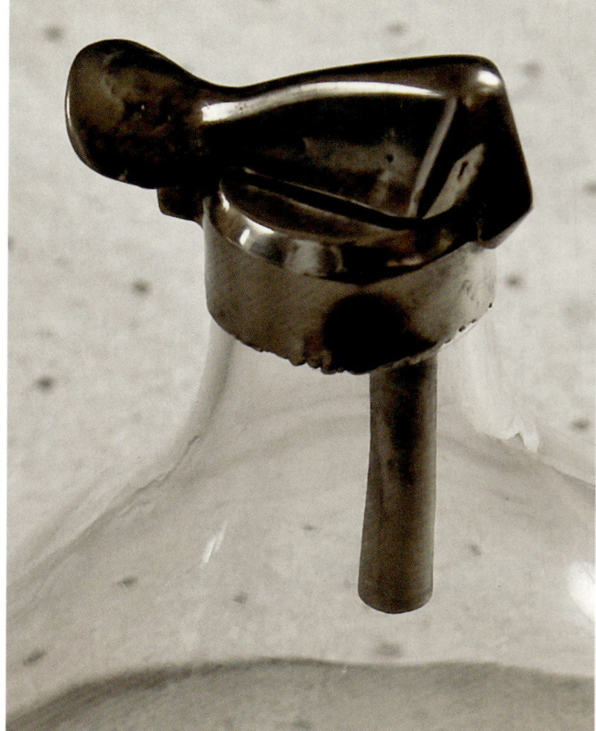

 Crystal, silver, copper, "nose stuff" little balls, 16 x 18 x 18 cm;

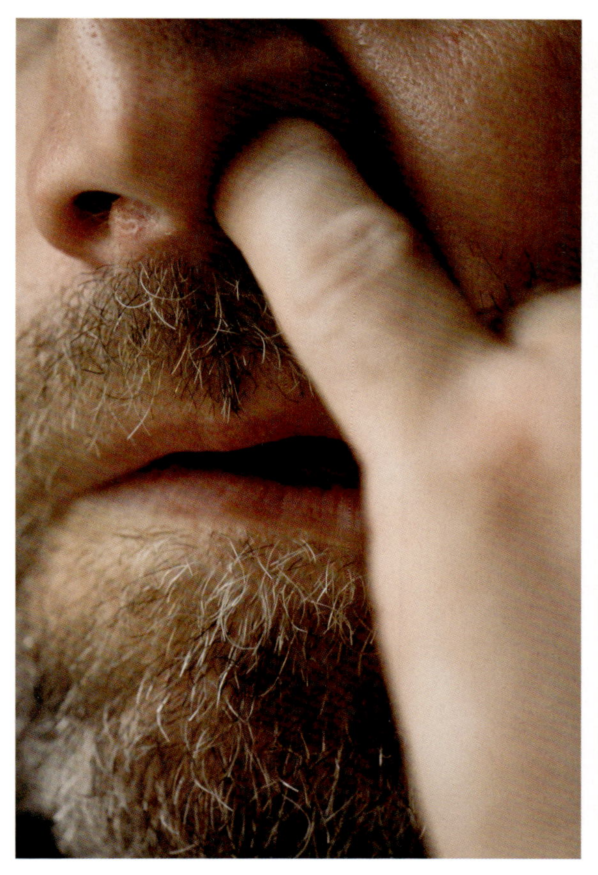

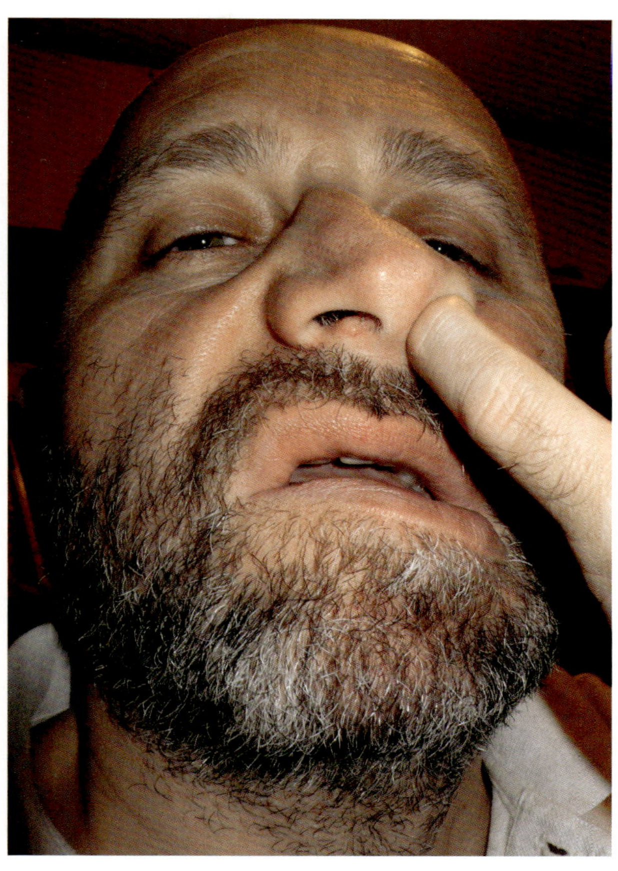

This is a nice crystal depository (with a delicate silver receptacle) for storing tiny balls which may seem to have been produced in a disgusting way (from the stuff coming out of your nostrils), but they are charged with a dense intellectual energy (we all know when we produce these balls with our fingers – in those rare moments of highest, sublime intellectual activity, stimulated by picking your nose). It is nice to have them collected to eventually reuse their energy in future brainstorming situations.

You may either complete in your head (following the artist's instructions on the canvas) the emotionally charged but still not rendered in the best possible way sunrise ....

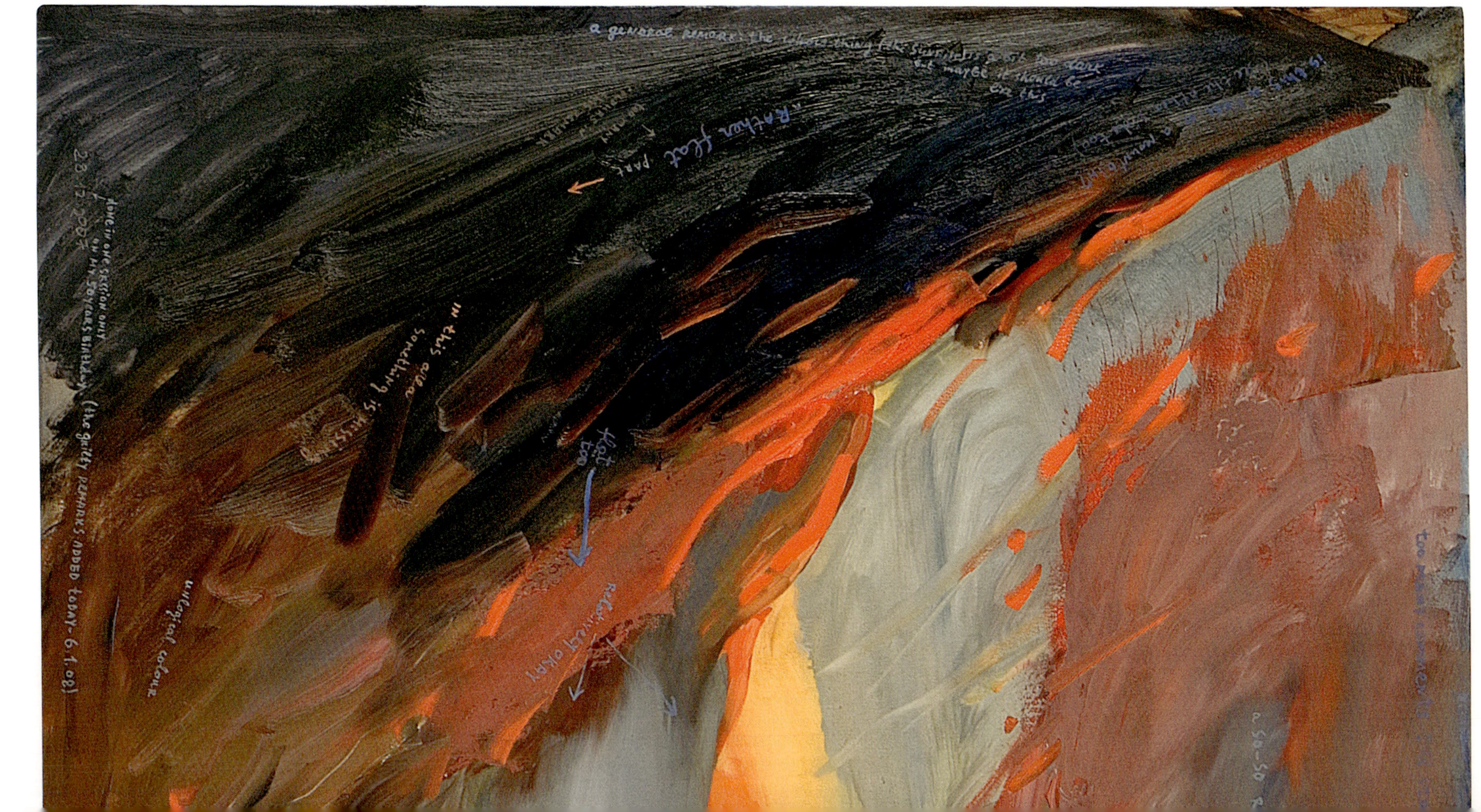

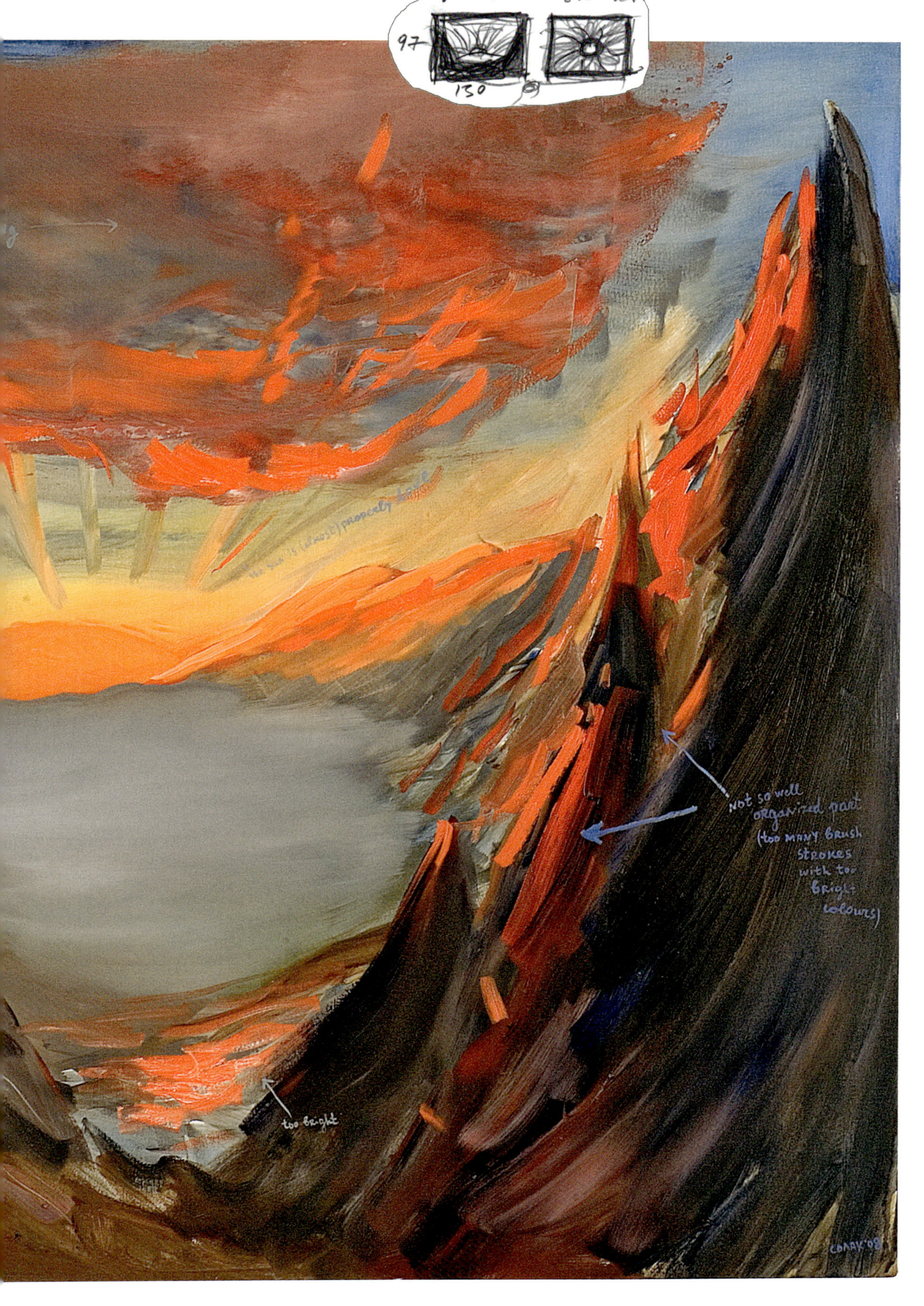

Oil on linen; 97 x 130 cm

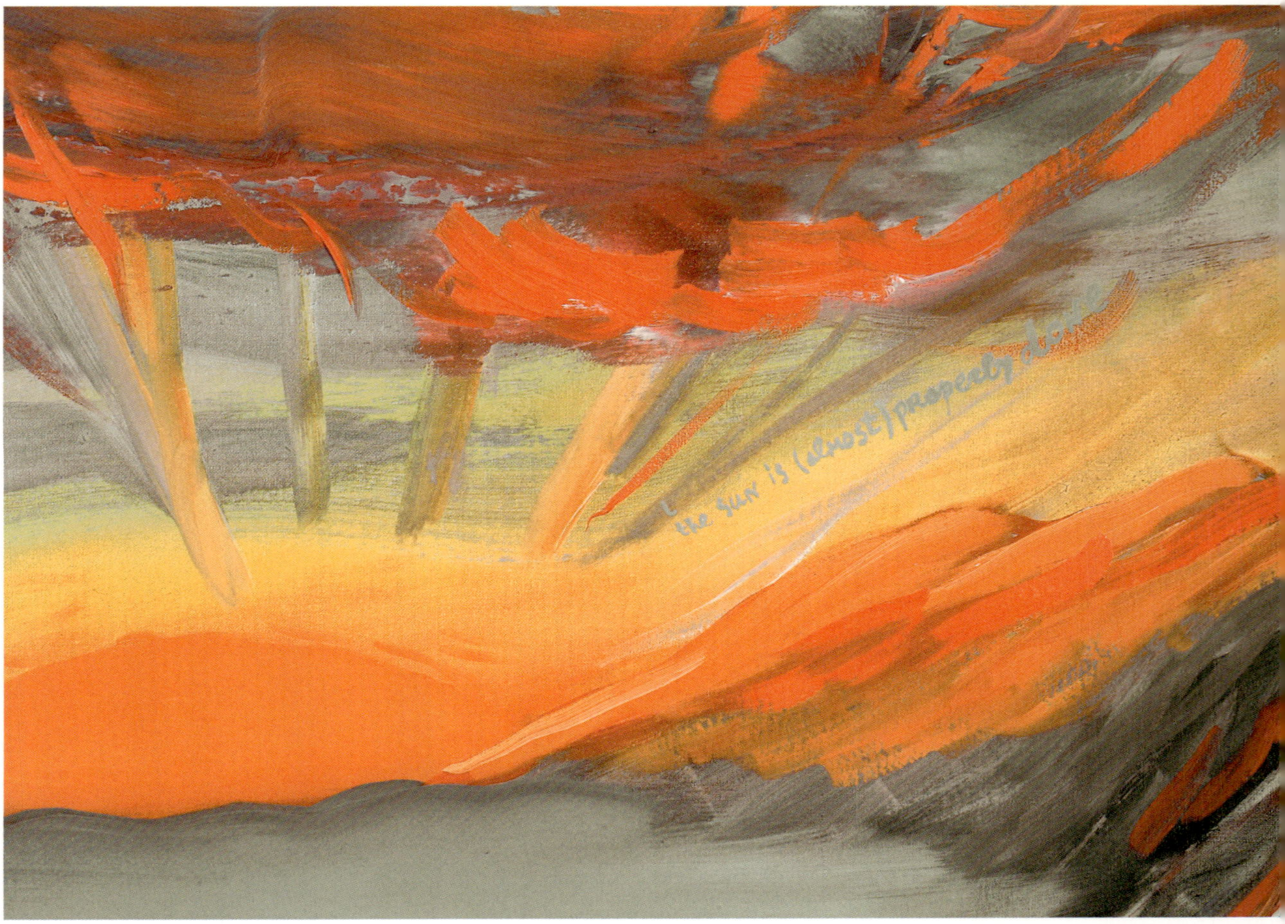
the sun is (almost) properly done

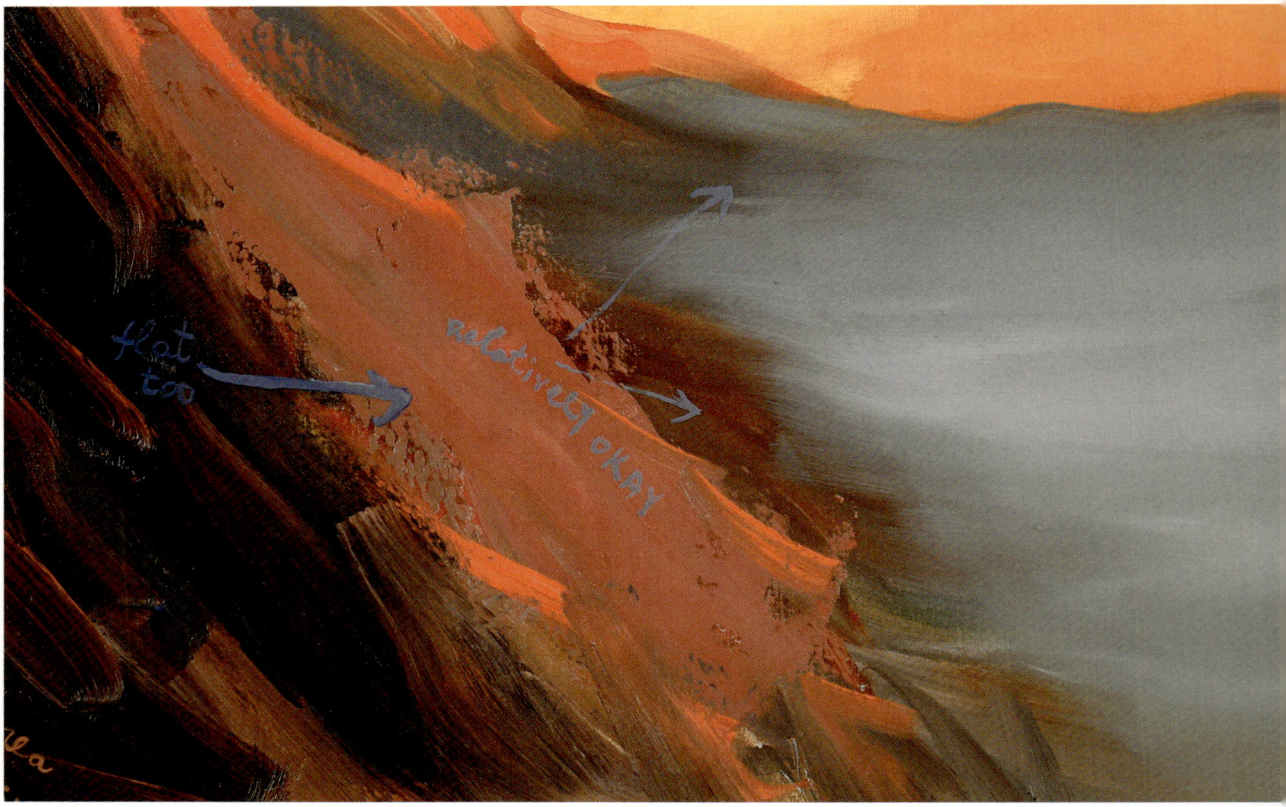
flat too
relatively OKAY

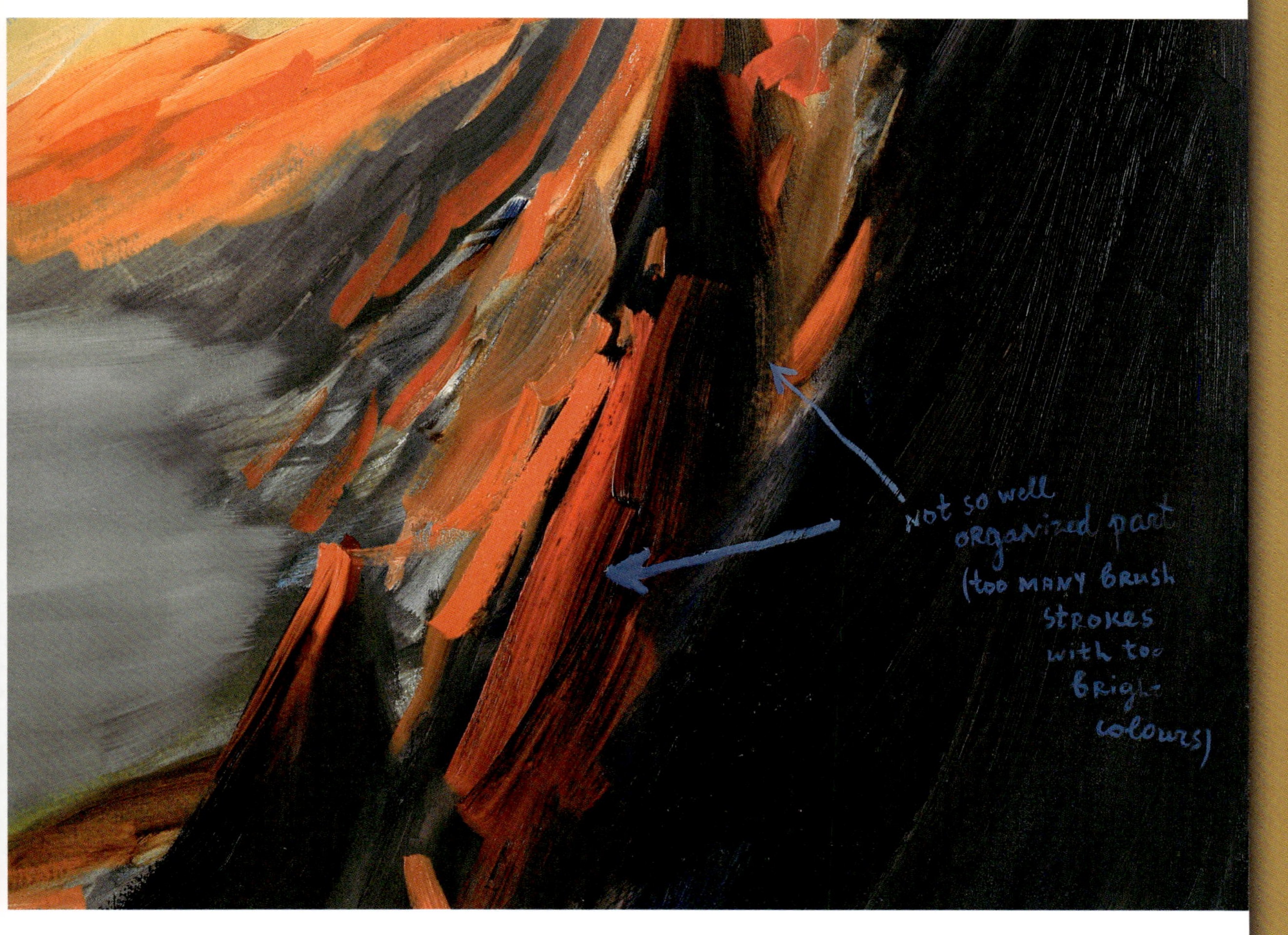

. . . OR . . . .

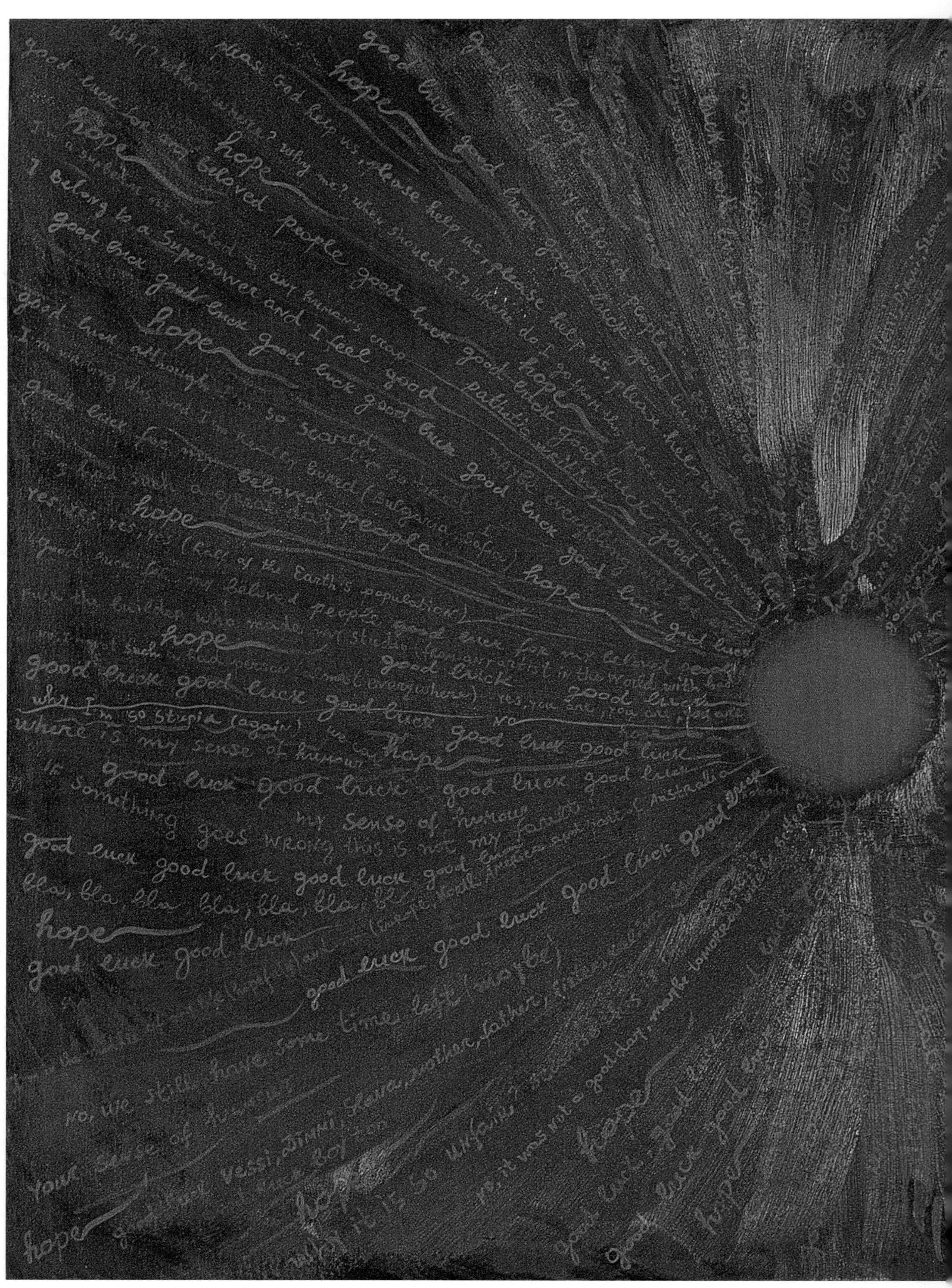

 Oil on linen; 97 x 130 cm

... you may enjoy the well executed (hopefully it really is) sunset, crowded with worries felt by people all over the world in that particular insignificant, already-vanishing day.

① the Brussels' thieves collectors

The best (a bit inappropriately obtained) art you can buy with your (black) money

Olivier
Allan's bodyguard

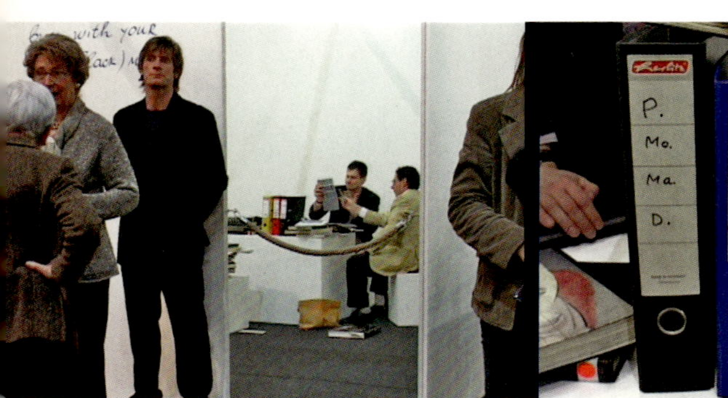

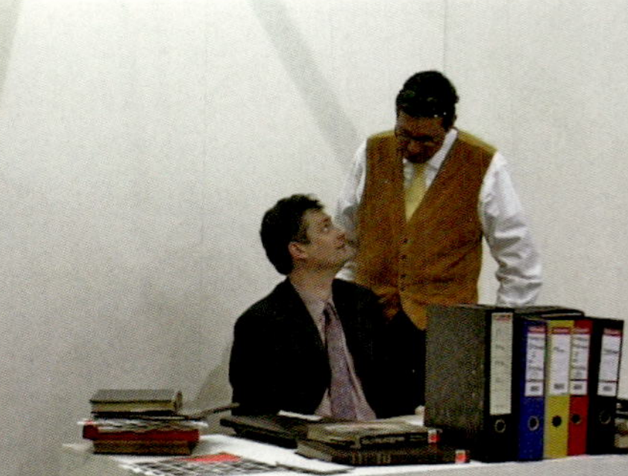

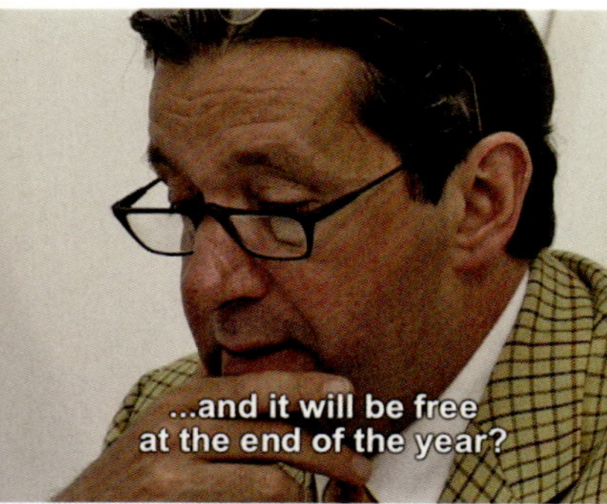

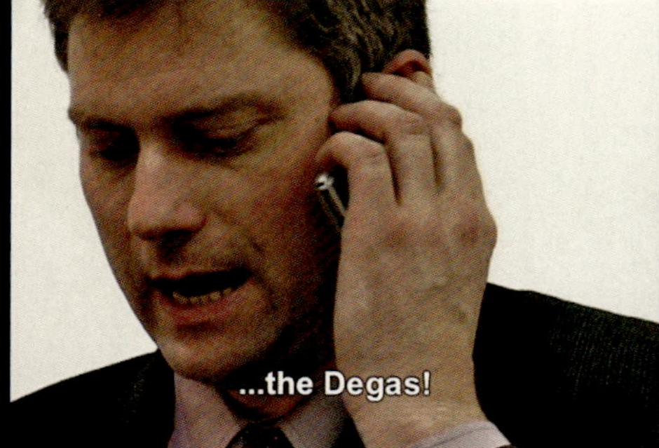

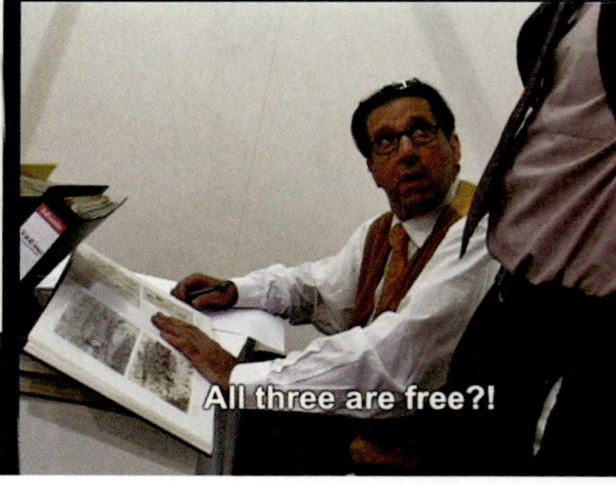

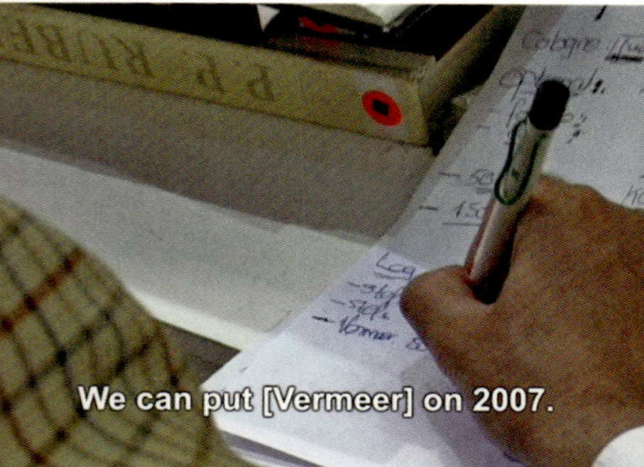

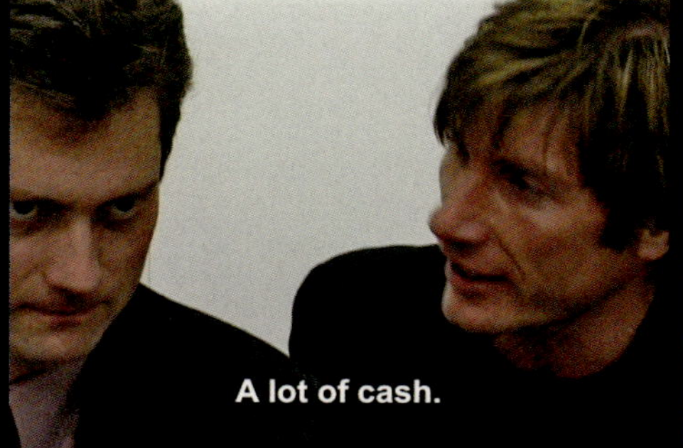

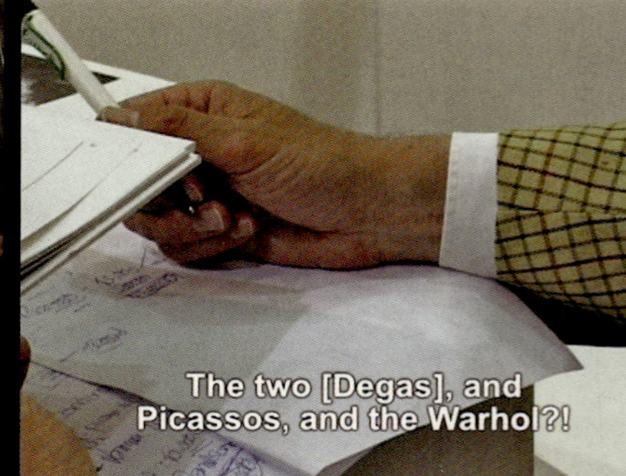

 Video on DVD, color, sound; 60'31", looped

Here is one of the ways to obtain, sell, and collect art – most certainly an enjoyable one.
If you have time, watch (for an hour) what happened recently at an art fair somewhere in Western Europe....

Allan
dealer

Luigi
collector
(and middleman)

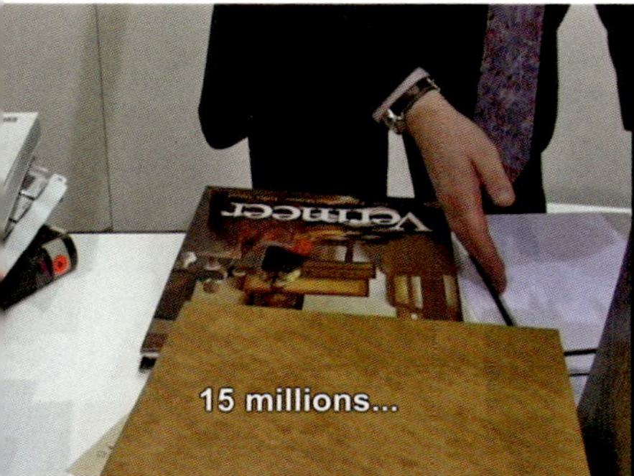

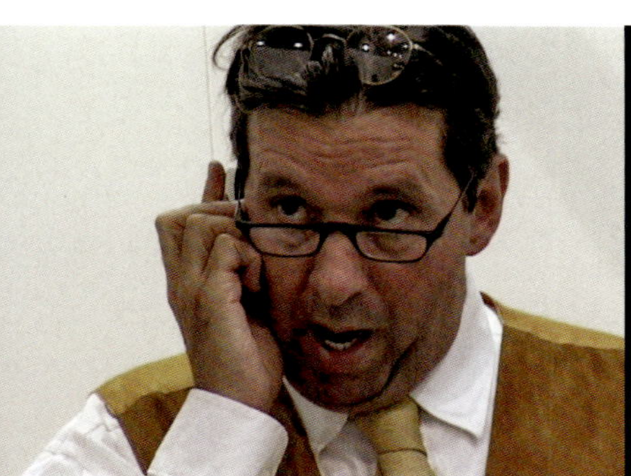

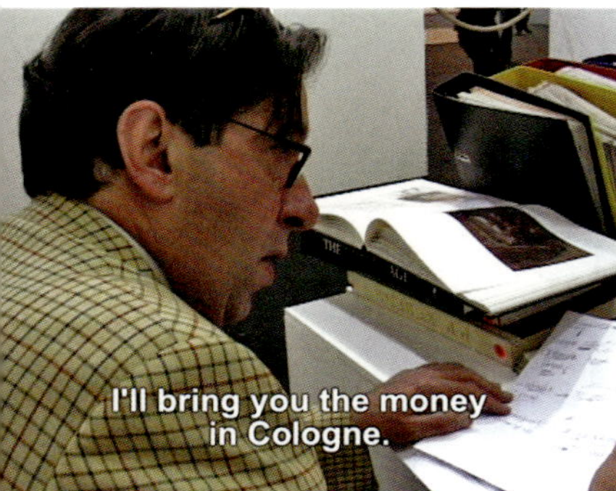

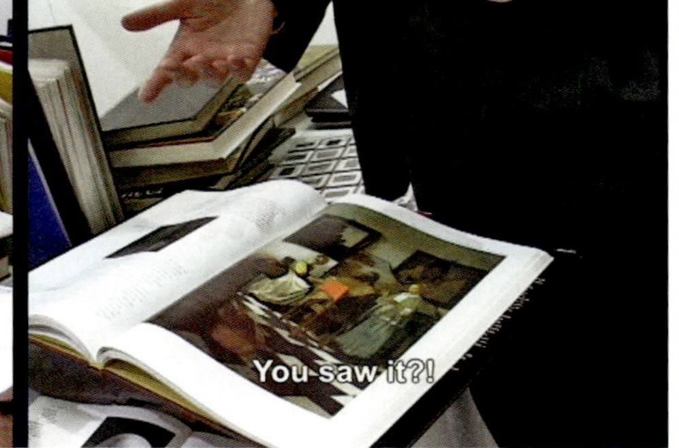

very uneven black things

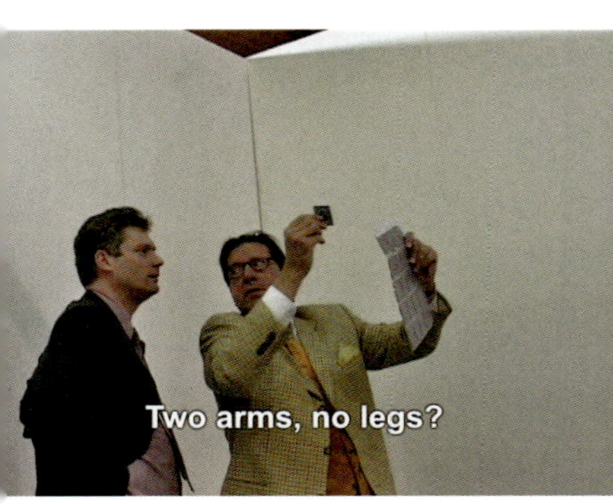

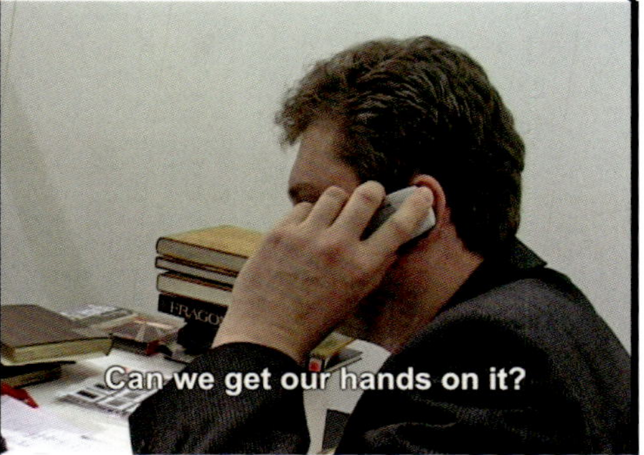

all these texts will be handwritten on the walls next to the paintings, monitor, combo-icon, etc.

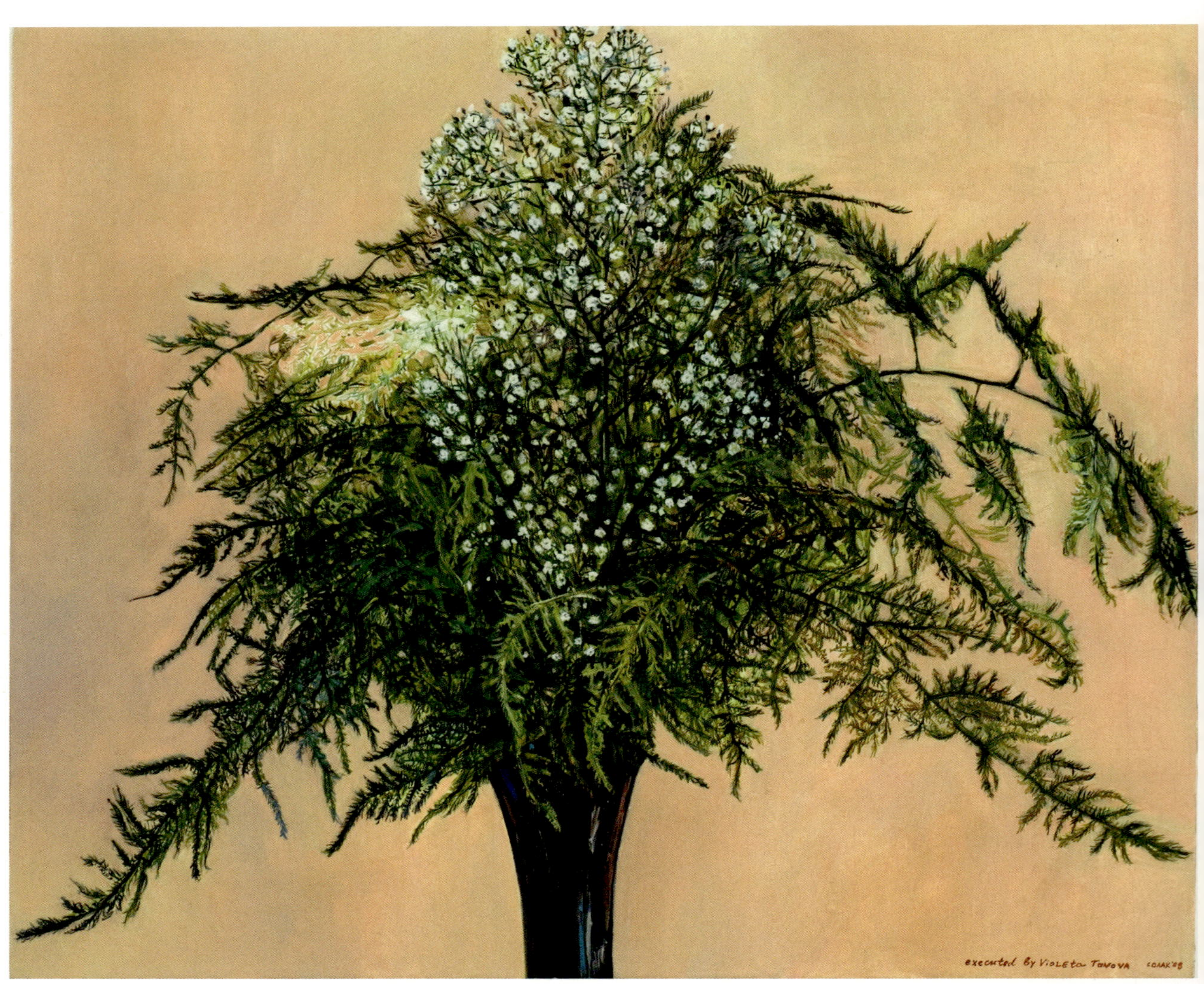

 Oil on canvas; 65 x 81 cm; executed by Violeta Tanova

Somebody to draw/paint for me

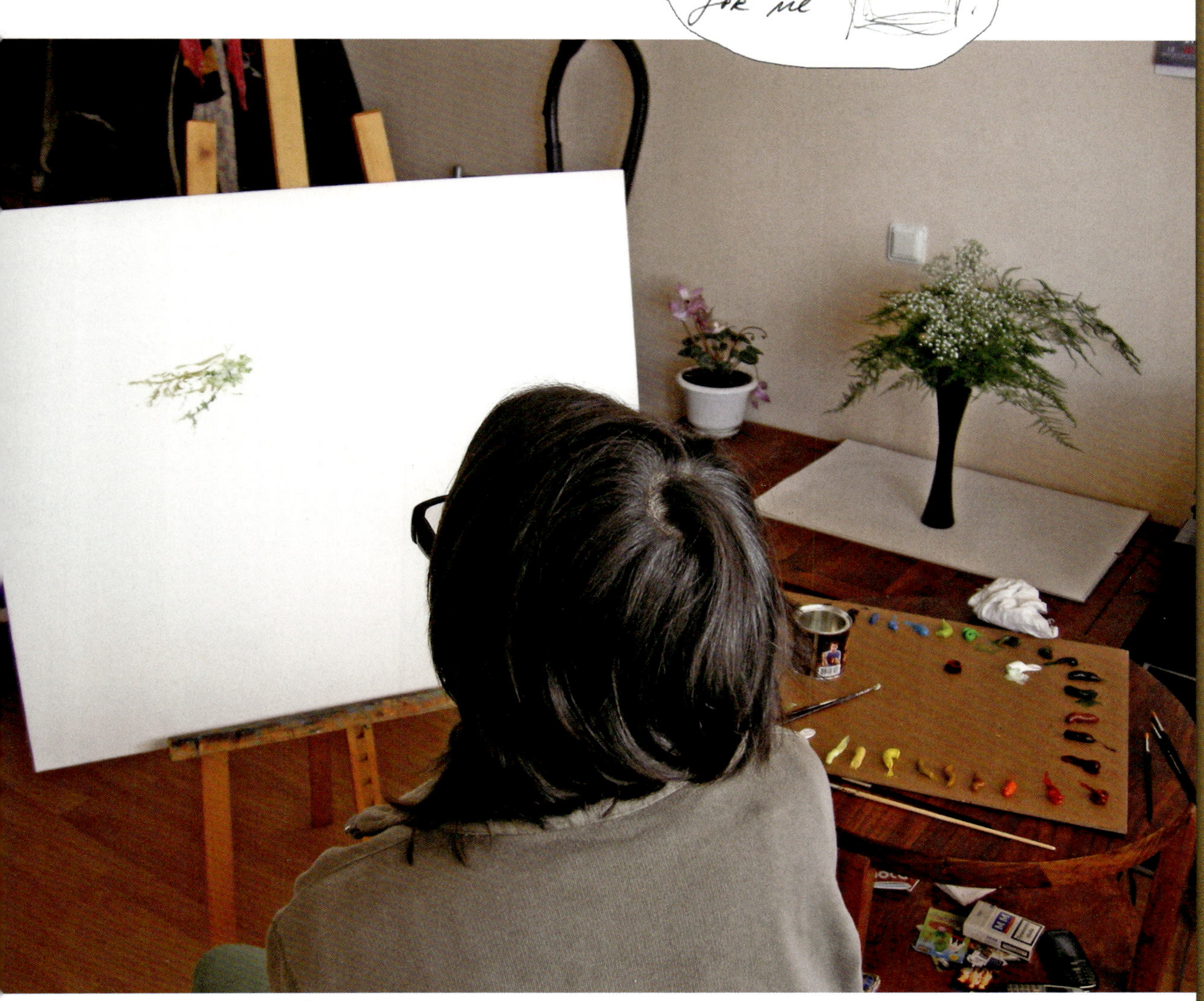

It's nice when a middle-aged artist (me) has enough means, after a one minute painting session, to hire a young artist to continue to paint and complete a bouquet of gipsophila and Asparagus (two plants usually called in Bulgarian "the artist's struggle" because of their numerous, tiny leaves and blossoms which are so hard to capture, draw and paint in a proper still-life).

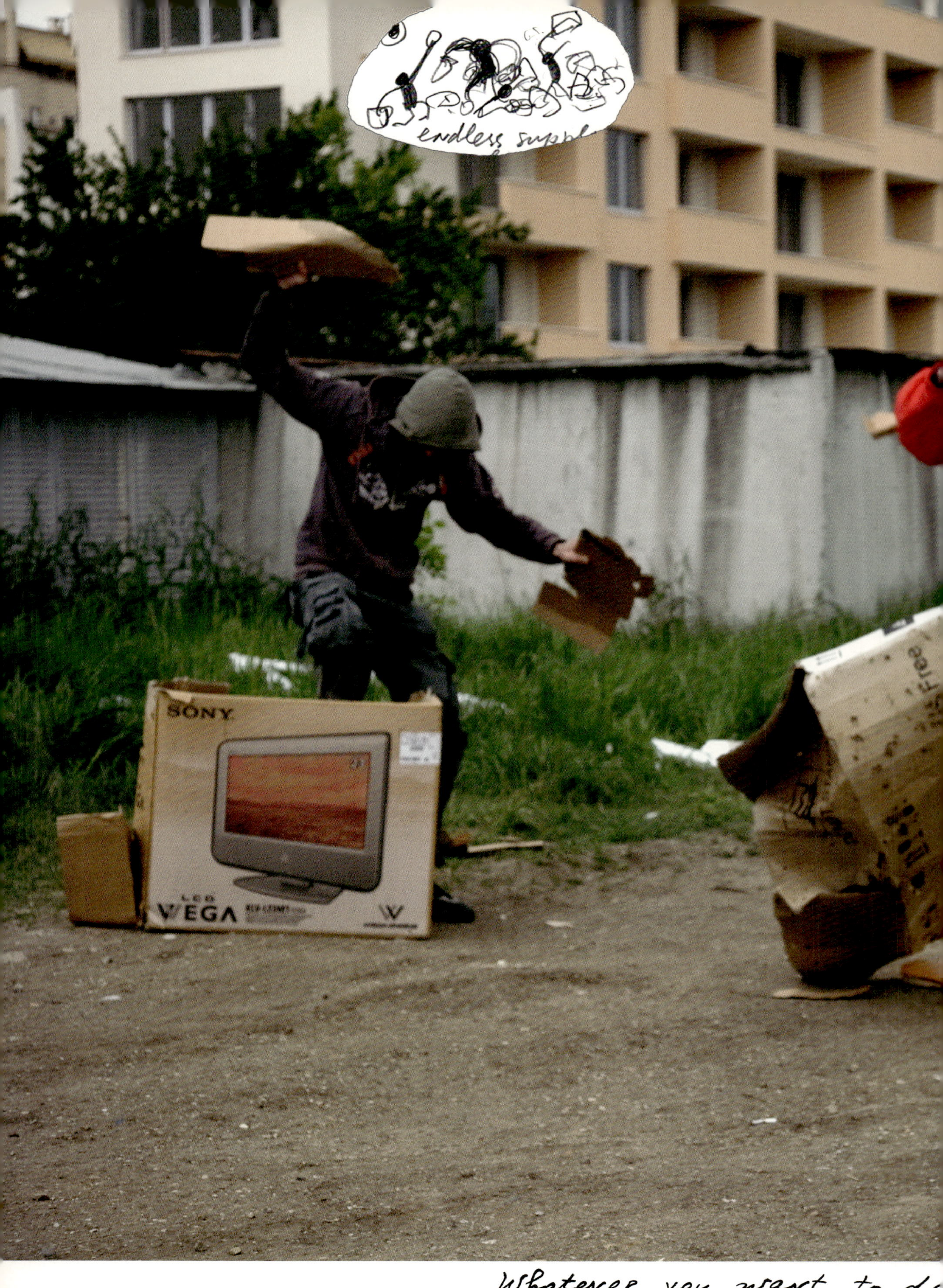

Whatever you want to d

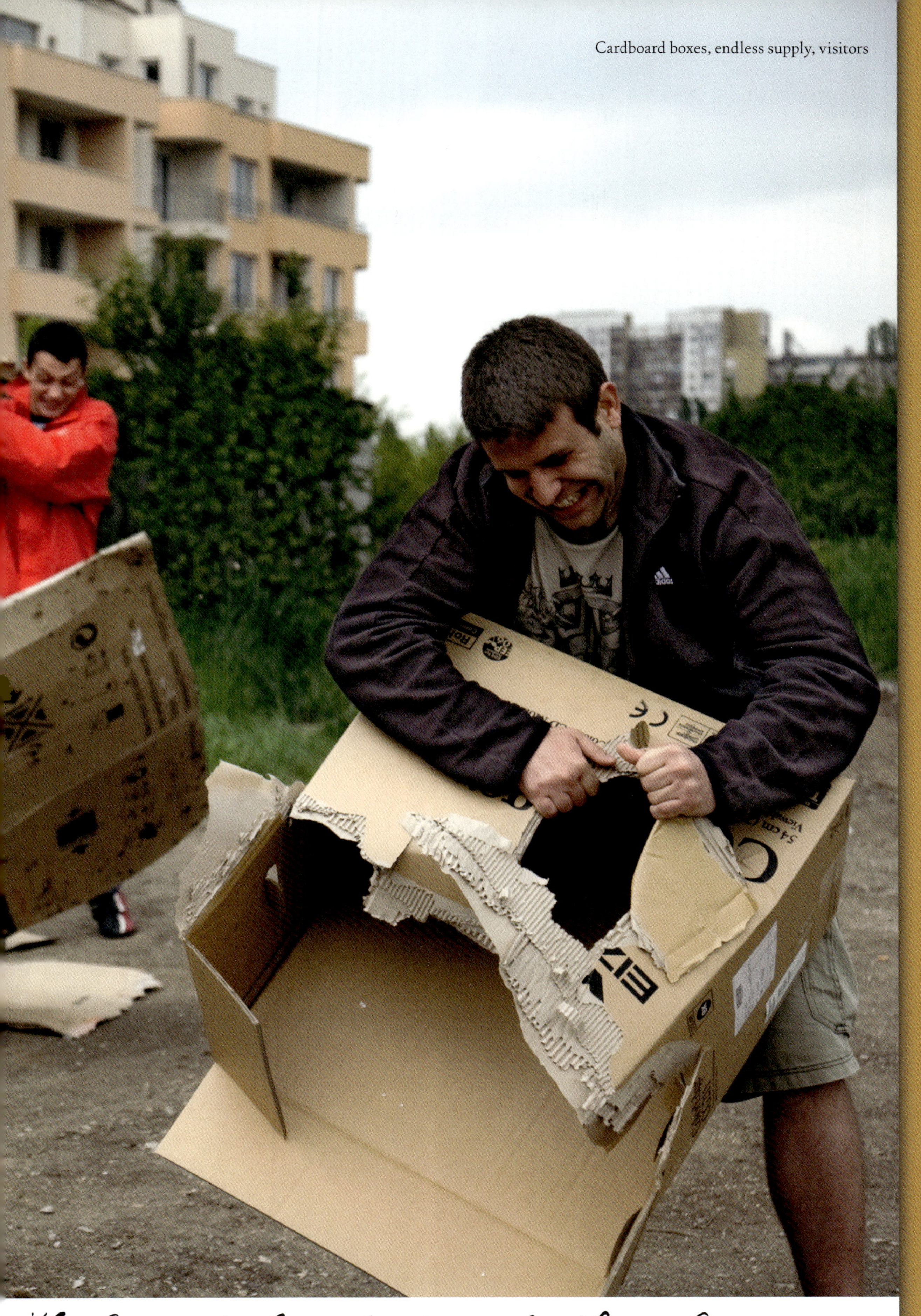

with some people, do it with these boxes.

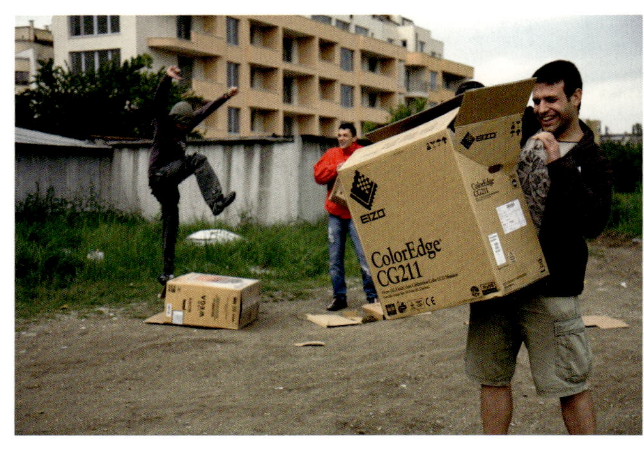
ColorEdge
CG211
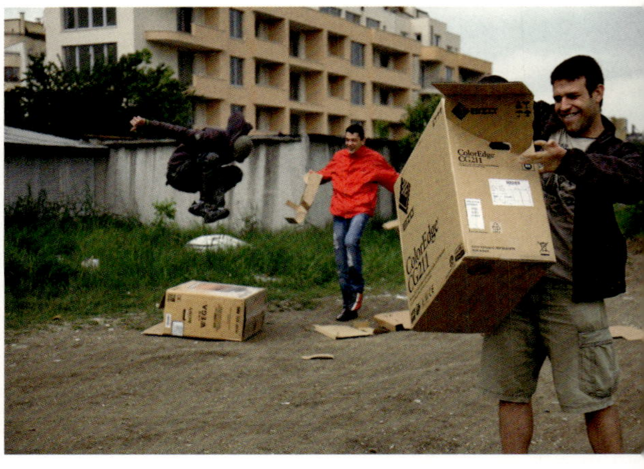
ColorEdge
CG211
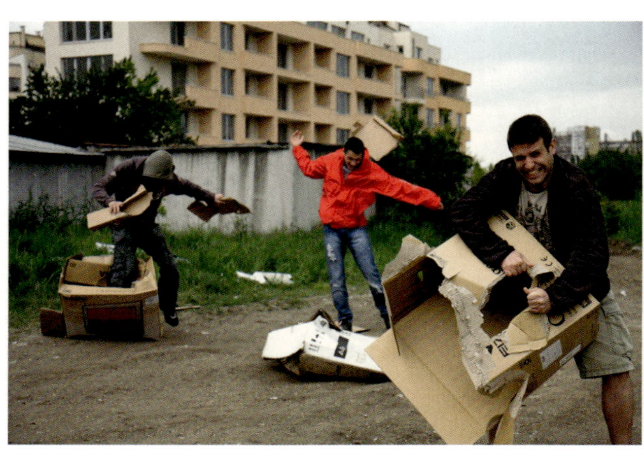
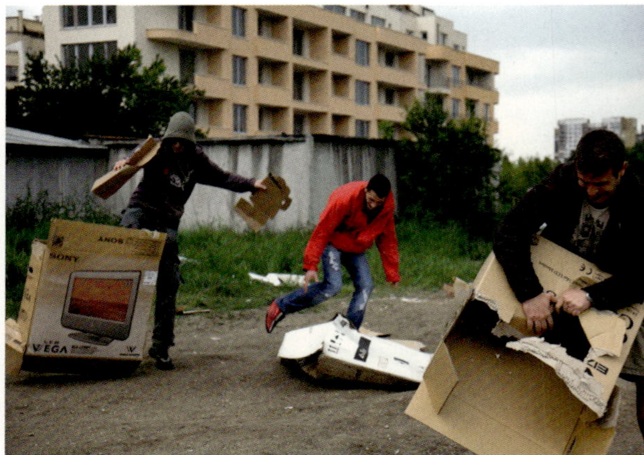
SONY
VEGA
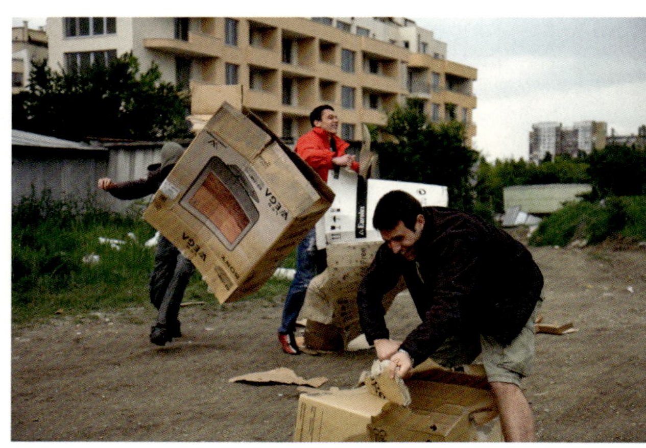
VEGA
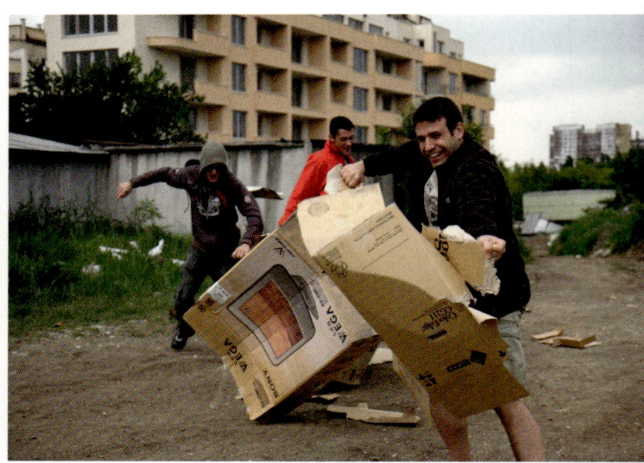
VEGA
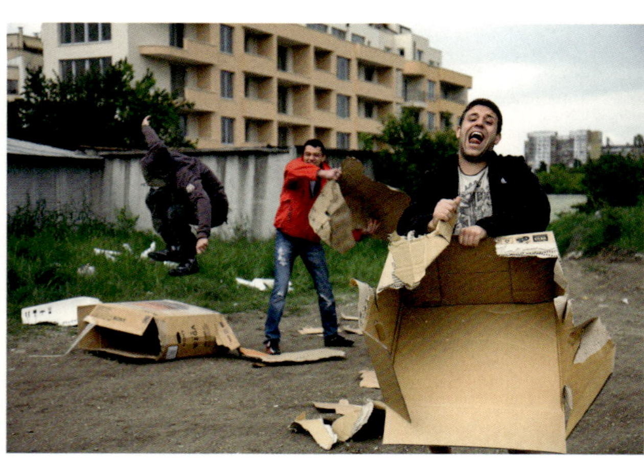
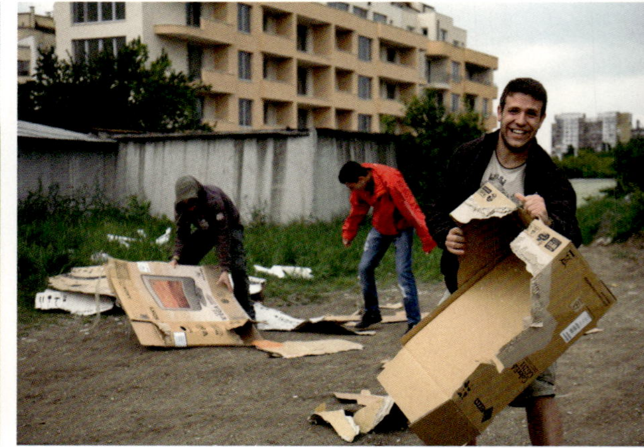

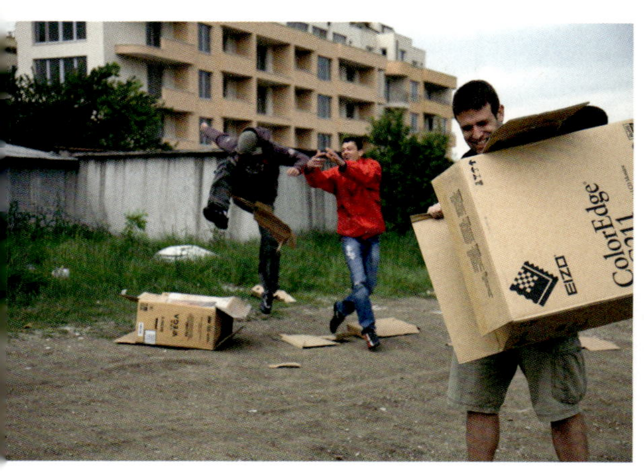
ColorEdge
EIZO

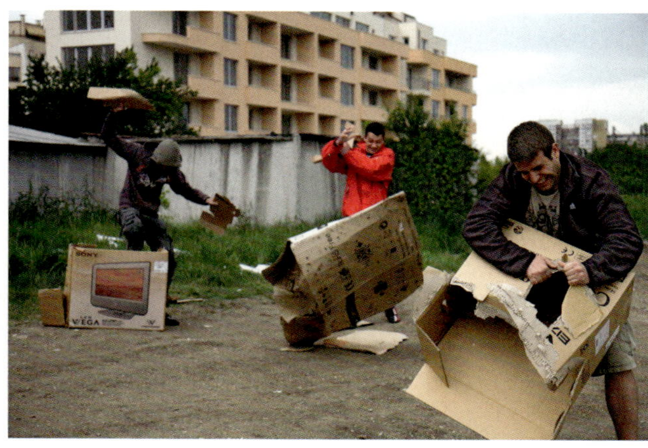

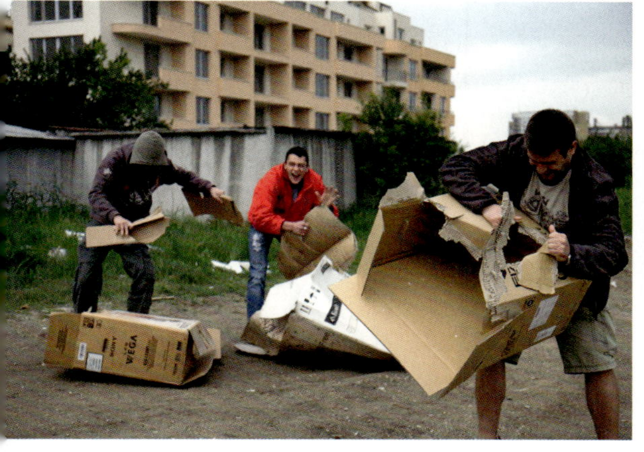

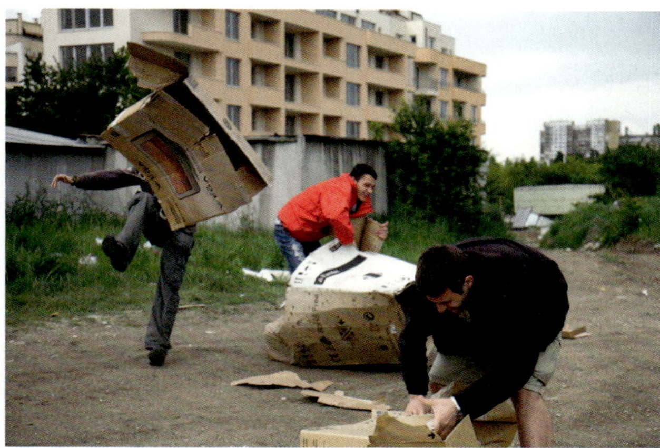

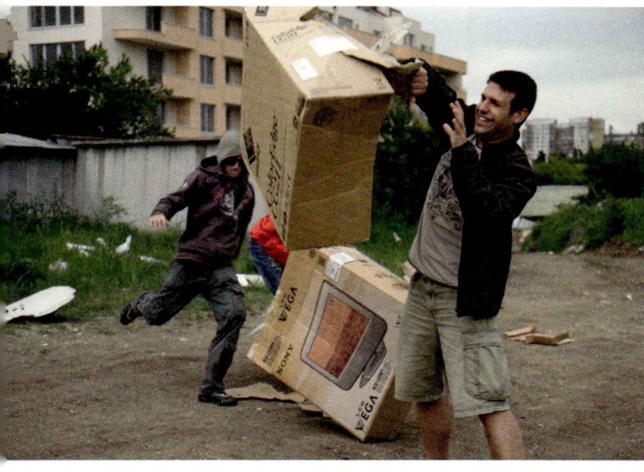

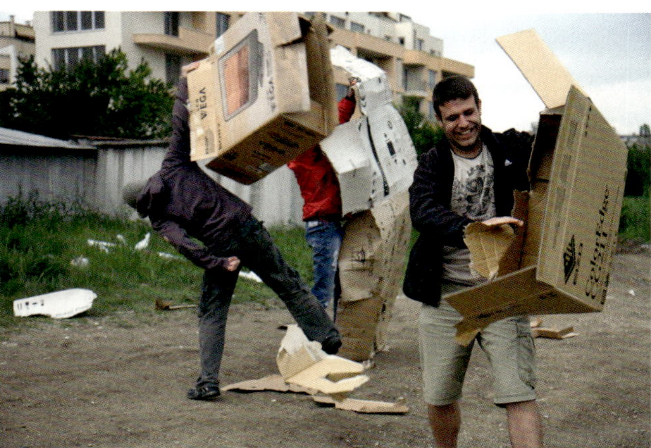

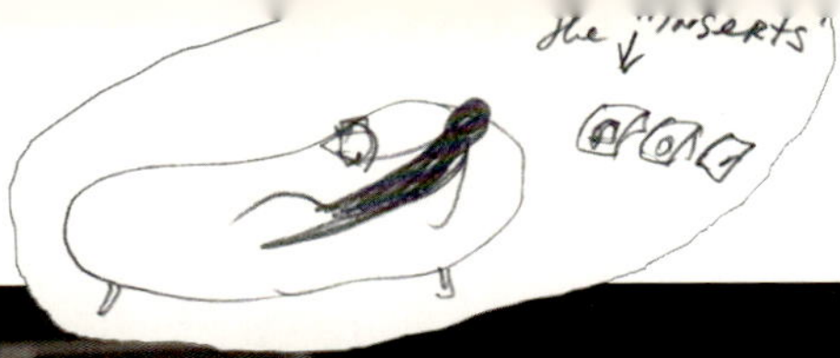

the "inserts"

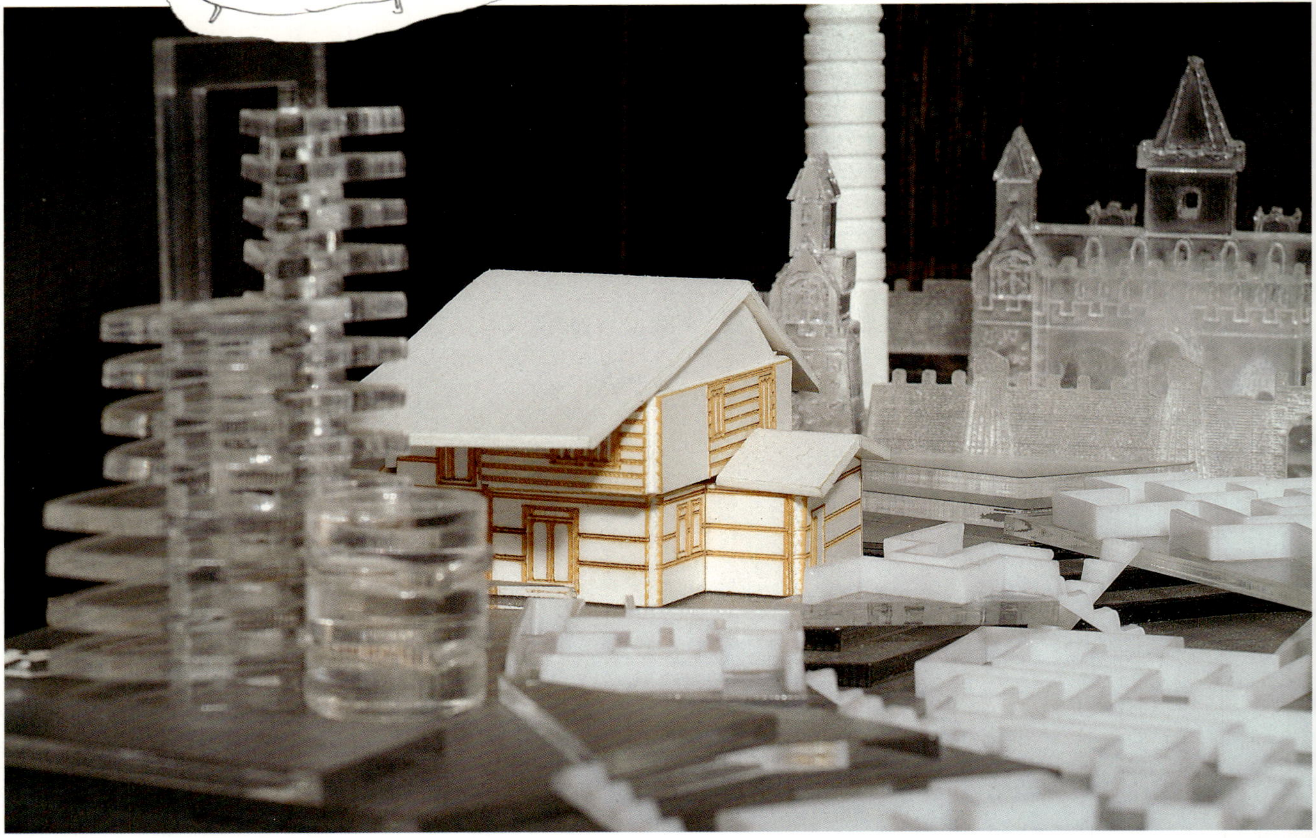

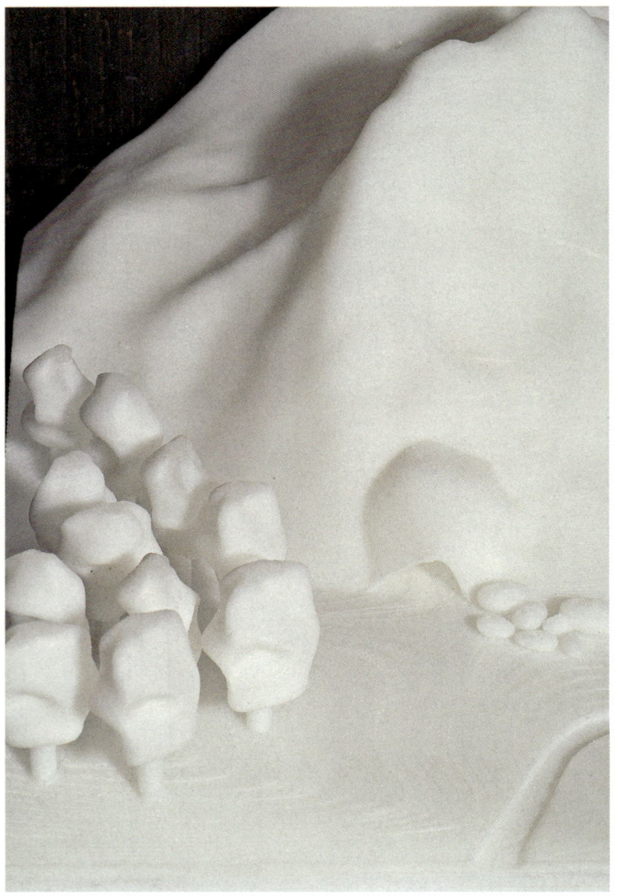

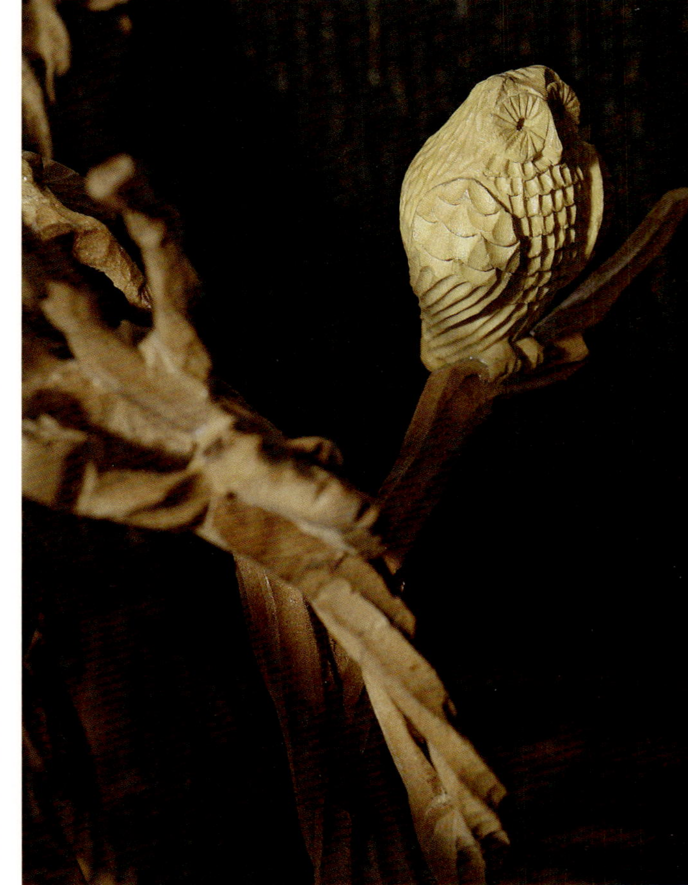

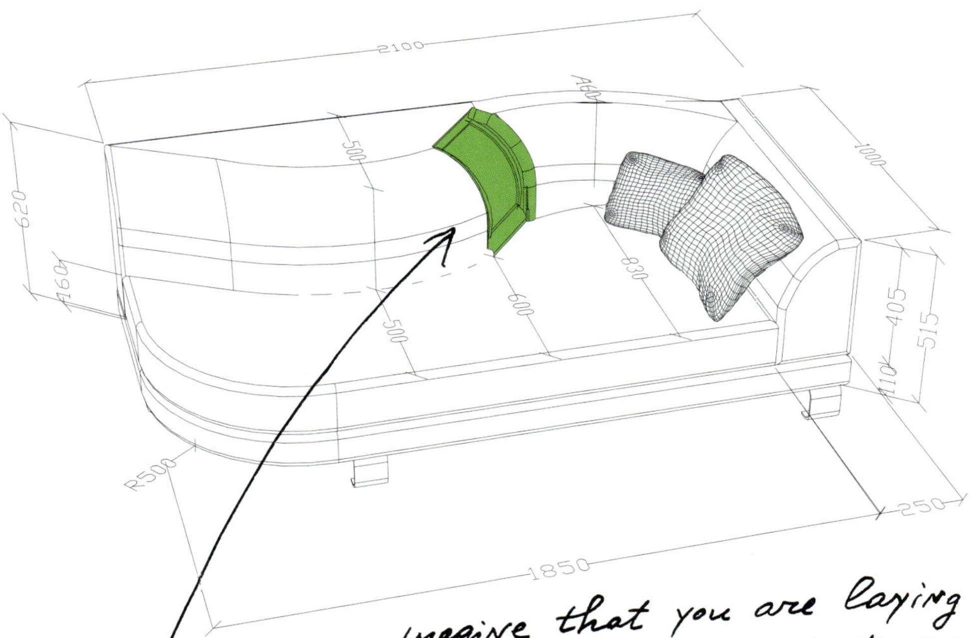

Imagine that you are laying on this sofa, whose sole purpose is to provide physical and spiritual comfort for your exhausted (and a bit lazy) body. You have at your disposal these three peculiar boxes which represent three options where your restless mind can wander temporarily: . . . .

All this is for your wellbeing – you can insert into the sofa whatever box option you want and contemplate for hours . . .

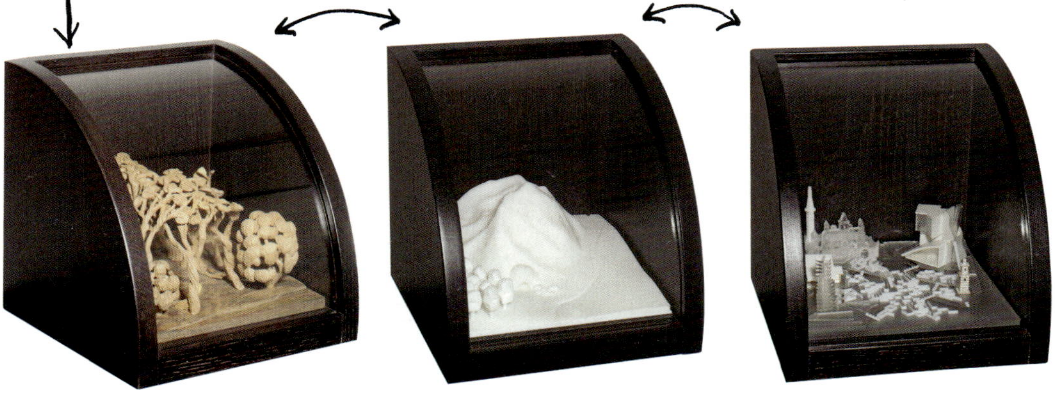

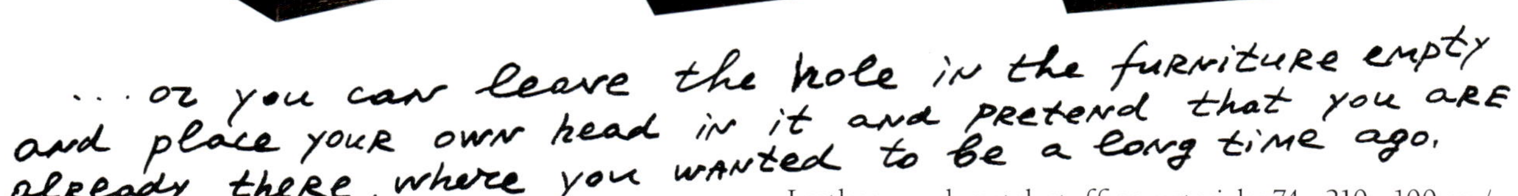

Leather, wood, metal, stuffing materials; 74 x 210 x 100 cm / the capsules's holder: leather, wood, metal, stuffing materials; 55 x 46 x 61 cm / three capsules made from oak, pear, and boxwood, ABS, PVC, Plexiglas; 25 x 25 x 24 cm each

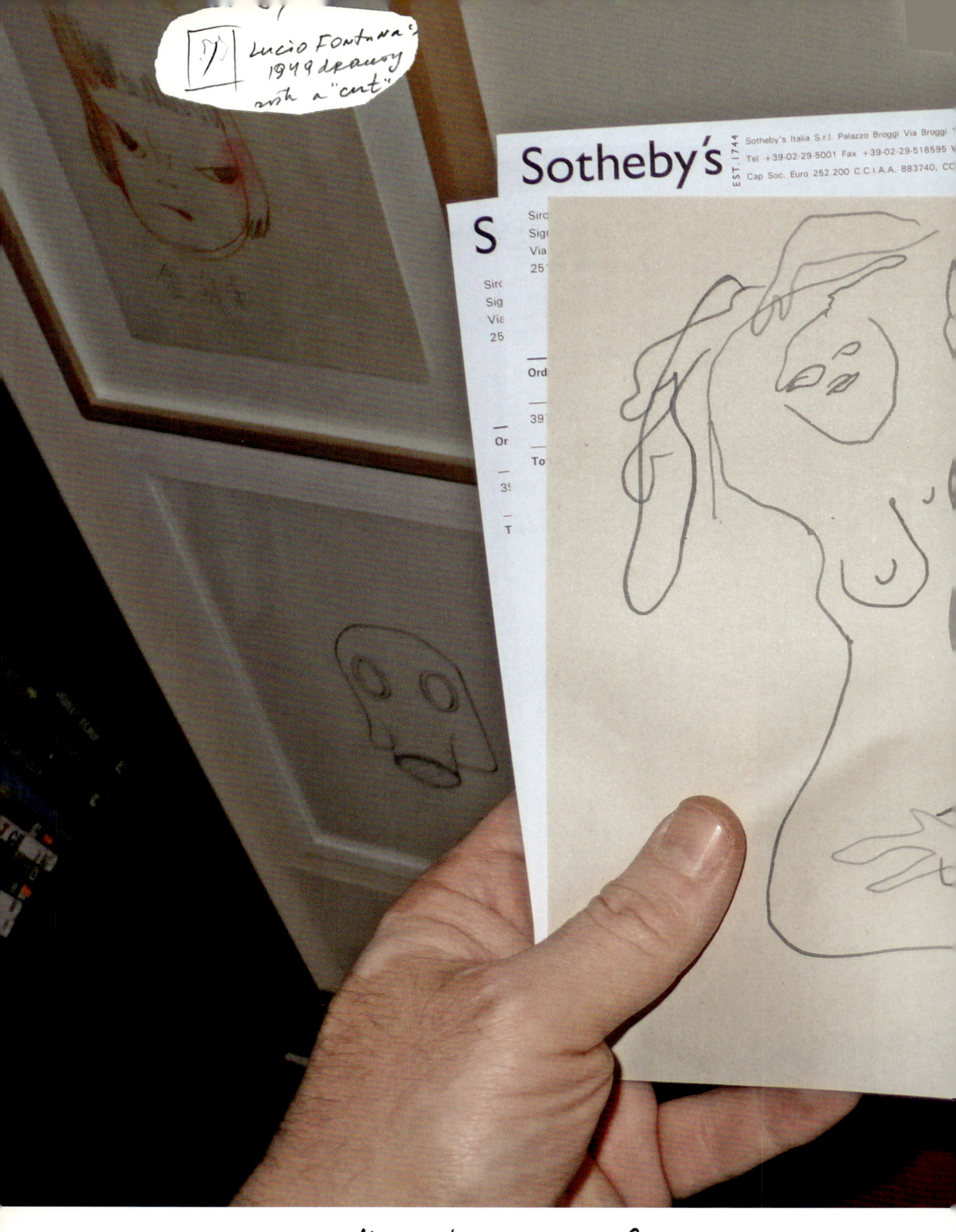

How to raise the price of a modern

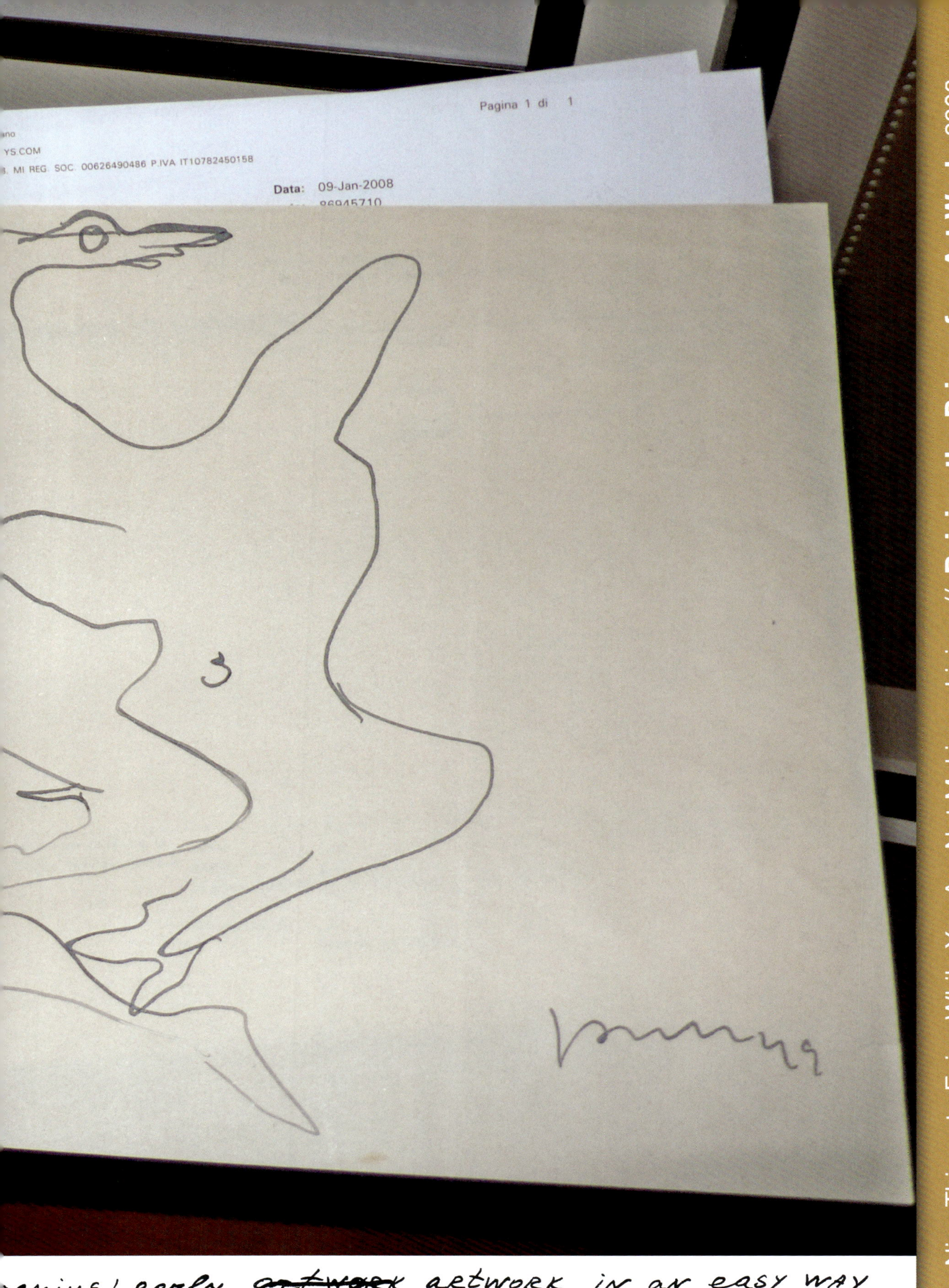

genius' early ~~artwork~~ artwork in an easy way

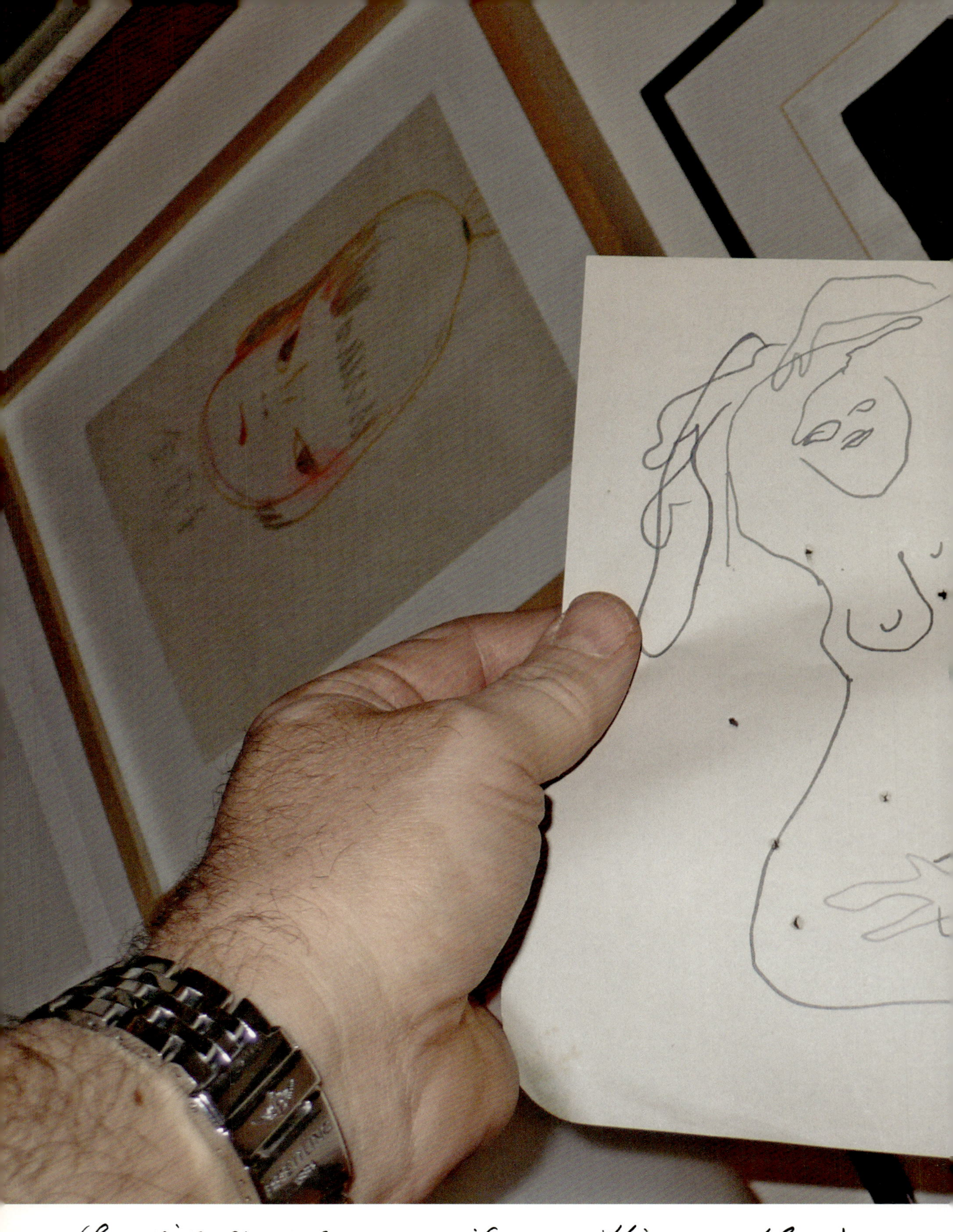

(By using one of your wife's knitting needles).

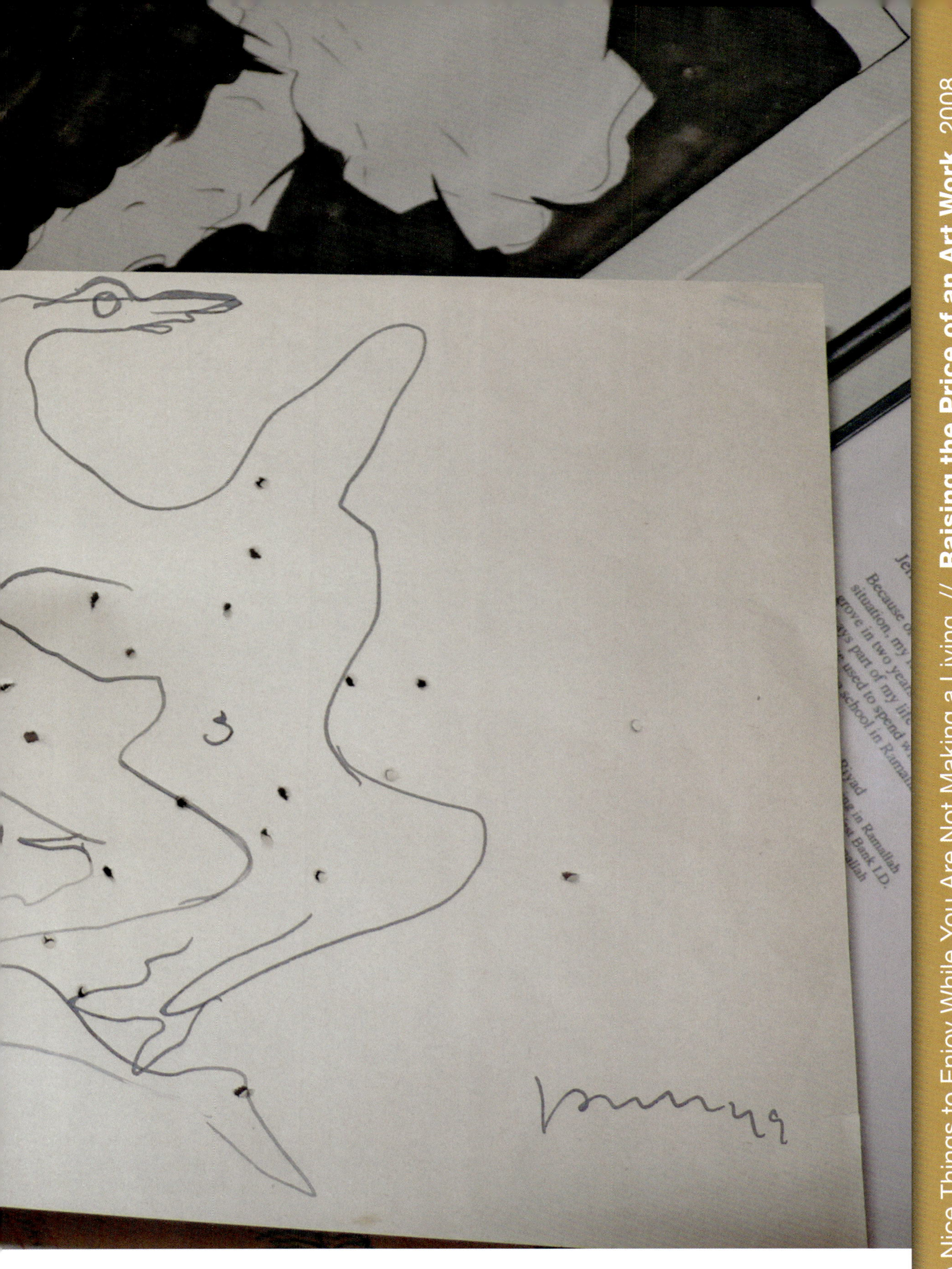

An original drawing by Lucio Fontana, 1949, ink on paper; 21 x 29 cm;
red knitting needle; 21,5 x 0,3 cm

② This is a very predictable, moody place — well known from numerous descriptions, highly recommended for people who don't want to risk;

Where would you like to spend your afterlife? pleas

Oil on canvas-board, seven pieces; 30 x 40 cm each

① Somewhere between Heaven & Hell. It's reasonable to hang around for a while (why not forever?). This will give you the security to be prepared if on the Last Judgement Day you have to go to HELL anyway;

see the page before fo.

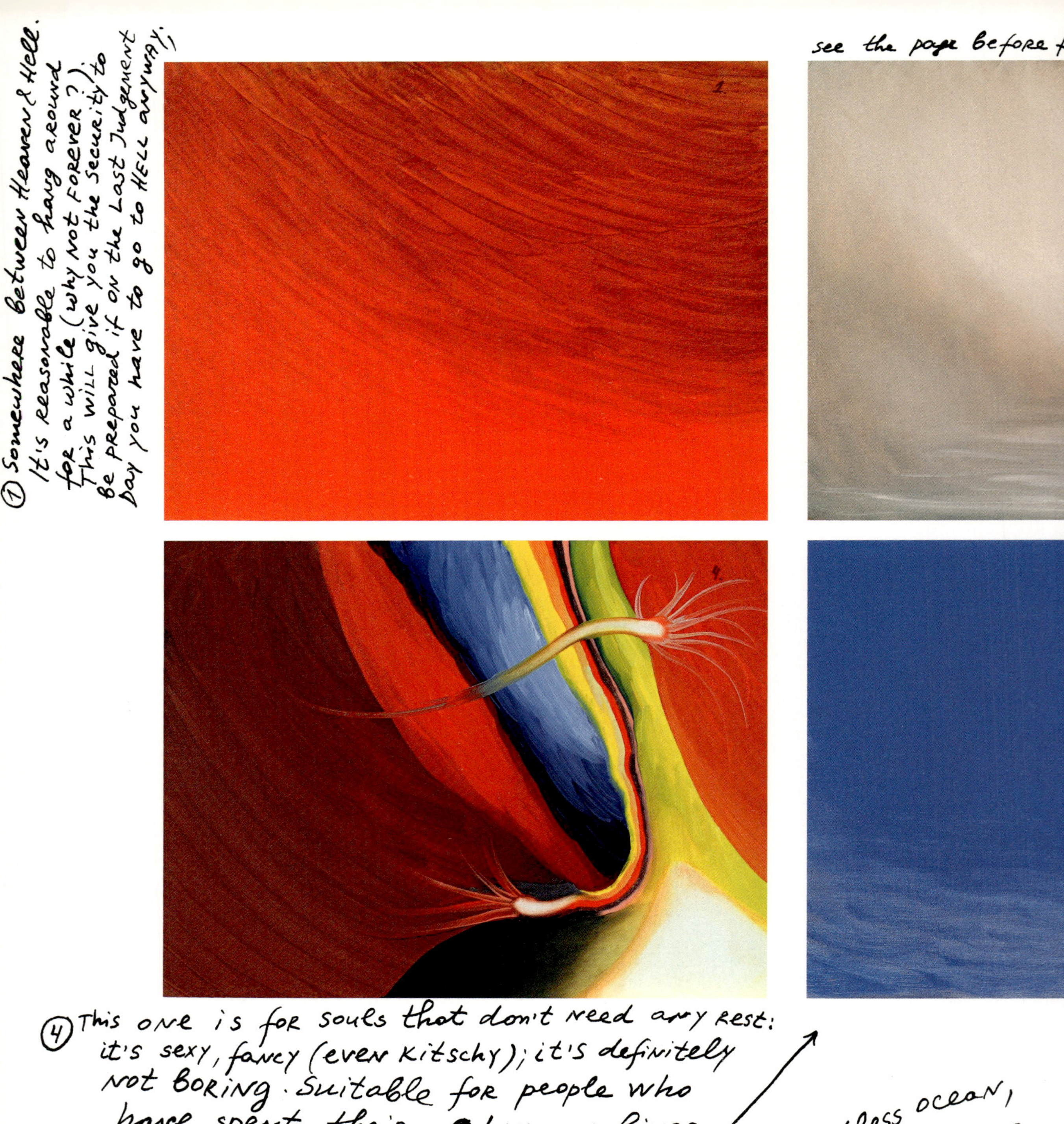

④ This one is for souls that don't need any rest: it's sexy, fancy (even kitschy); it's definitely not boring. Suitable for people who have spent their human lives alone (or have felt lonely);

⑤ Floating in an endless ocean, underwater, with closed or opened eyes;

⑦ Believe it or not, some people may prefe

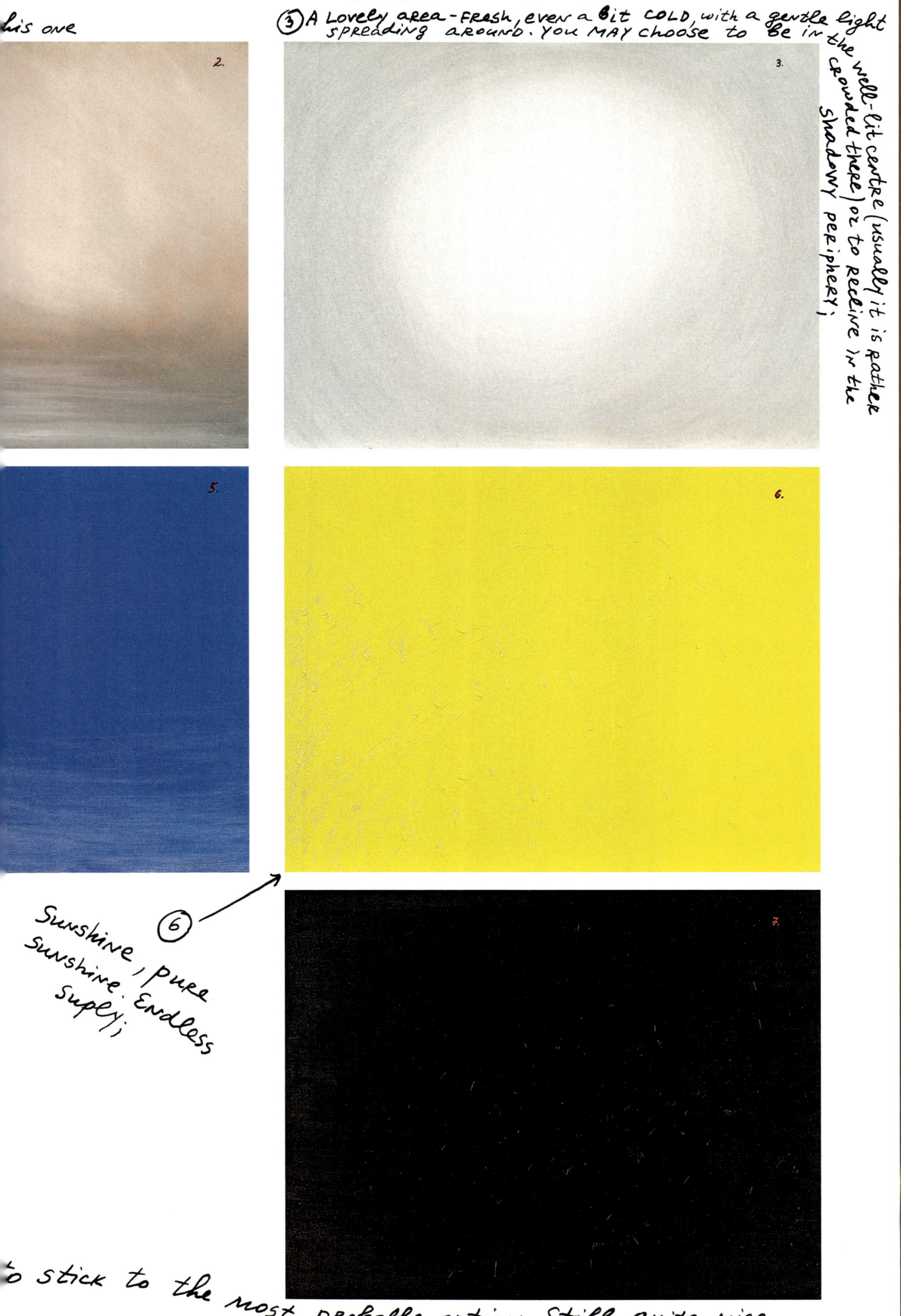
his one
③ A Lovely area - FResh, even a Bit COLD, with a gentle light spreading around. You MAY choose to Be in the well-lit centre (usually it is rather crowded there) or to recline in the shadowy periphery;
2.
3.
5.
6.
⑥ Sunshine, pure sunshine. Endless suply;
7.
o stick to the most probable option. Still quite nice, nobody's complained so far.

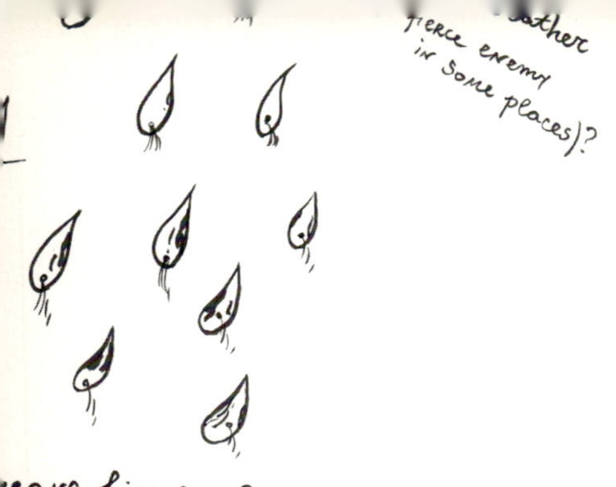

eans, hire Mr Prick-the-Rain-Drops ( ).
n all raindrops become powerless
the water-goes out through the
CONAK'08

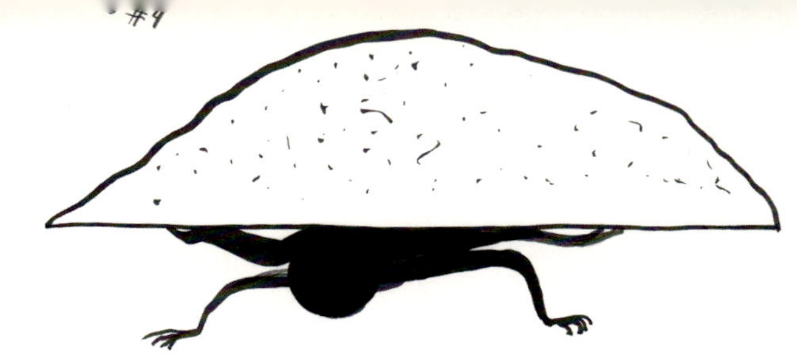

Leave your neighbour under this enormous Burden constituted by all of your complaints (for his/her Behaviour), each of them equal to 17 kilos.

CONAK'08

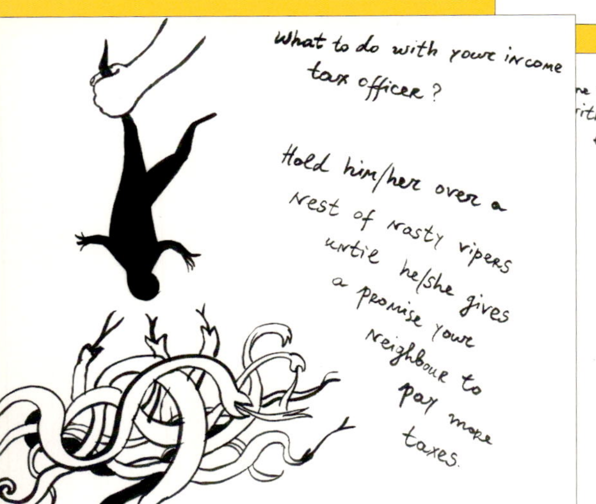

CONAK'08

e tips what to do
ith some of your
enemies #5

what to do with a bitch more beautiful than you?

Use all of your (inner) power to keep her eyes closed, so, she will not be able to see and feel people's adoration*

* Adoration, my ass!

CONAK'08

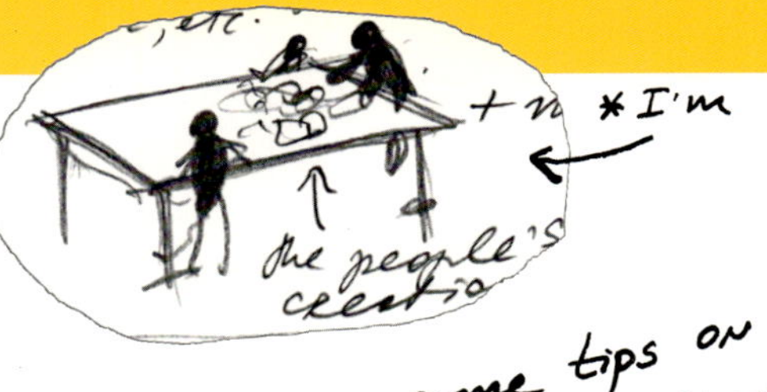

* I'm addressing these people

Here are some tips on how to torture (unfortunately in a made-up dream situation) your boss, neighbour, local (and global) politician.... Take the felt-tip pen and make a drawing* with instructions over this brightly coloured panel. Thus you may help other citizens.

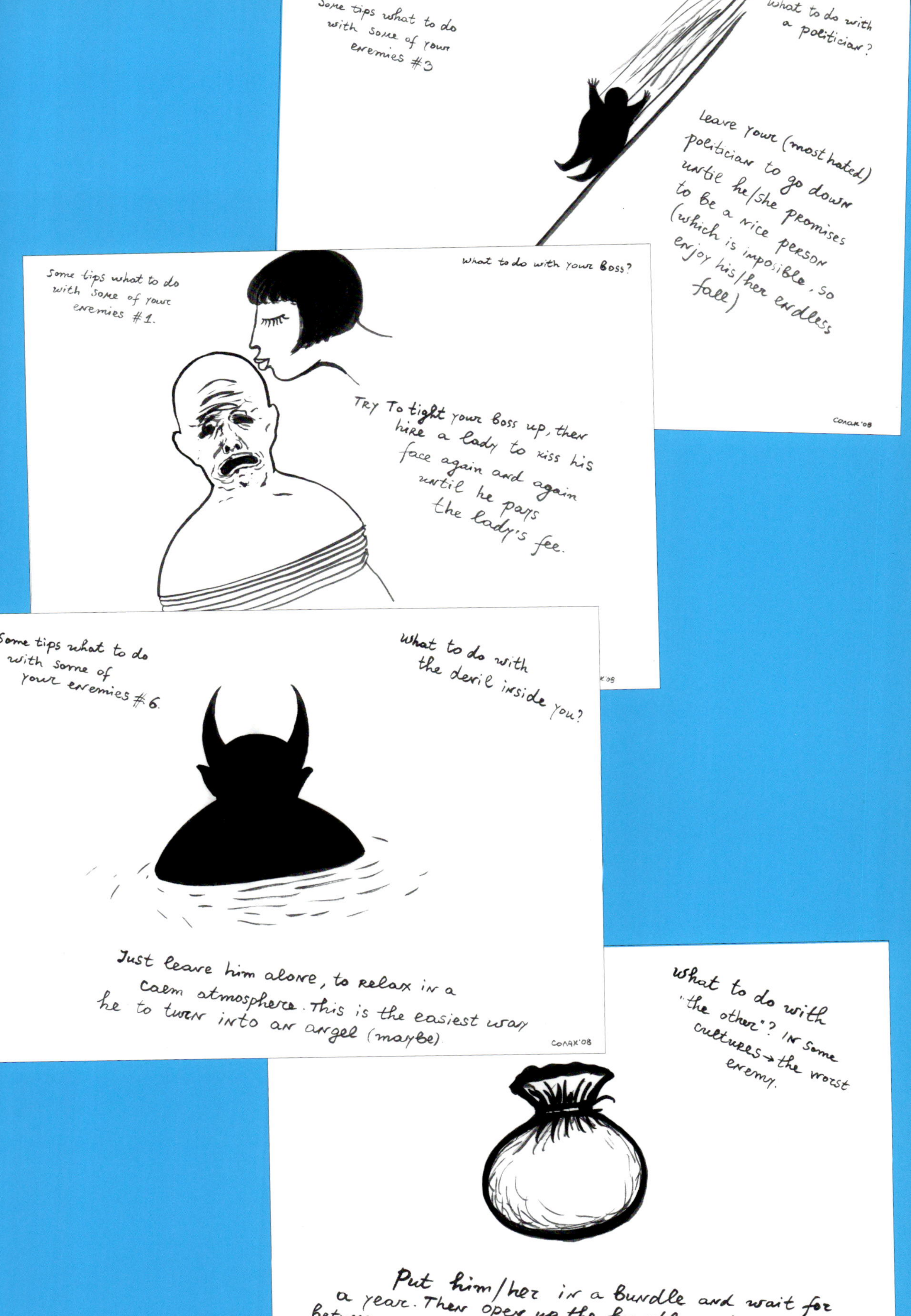

Ink on paper, a manual comprised of seven drawings; 21 x 29 cm each

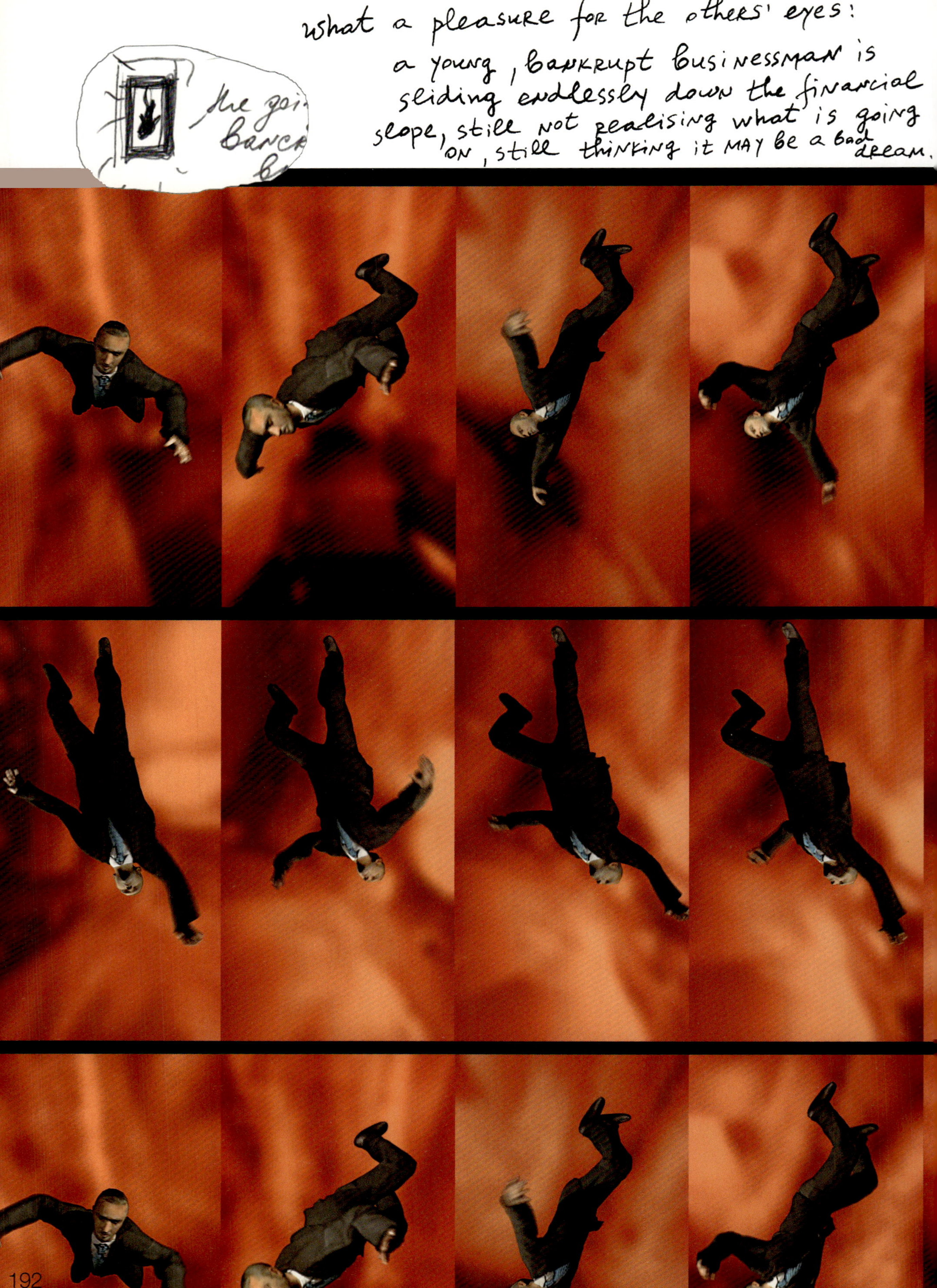
what a pleasure for the others' eyes:
a young, bankrupt businessman is
sliding endlessly down the financial
slope, still not realising what is going
on, still thinking it may be a bad
dream.

HD animation, silent; 20'', looped

"No, no, it's not (a bad dream)!" The others (we) enjoy the moment tremendously.

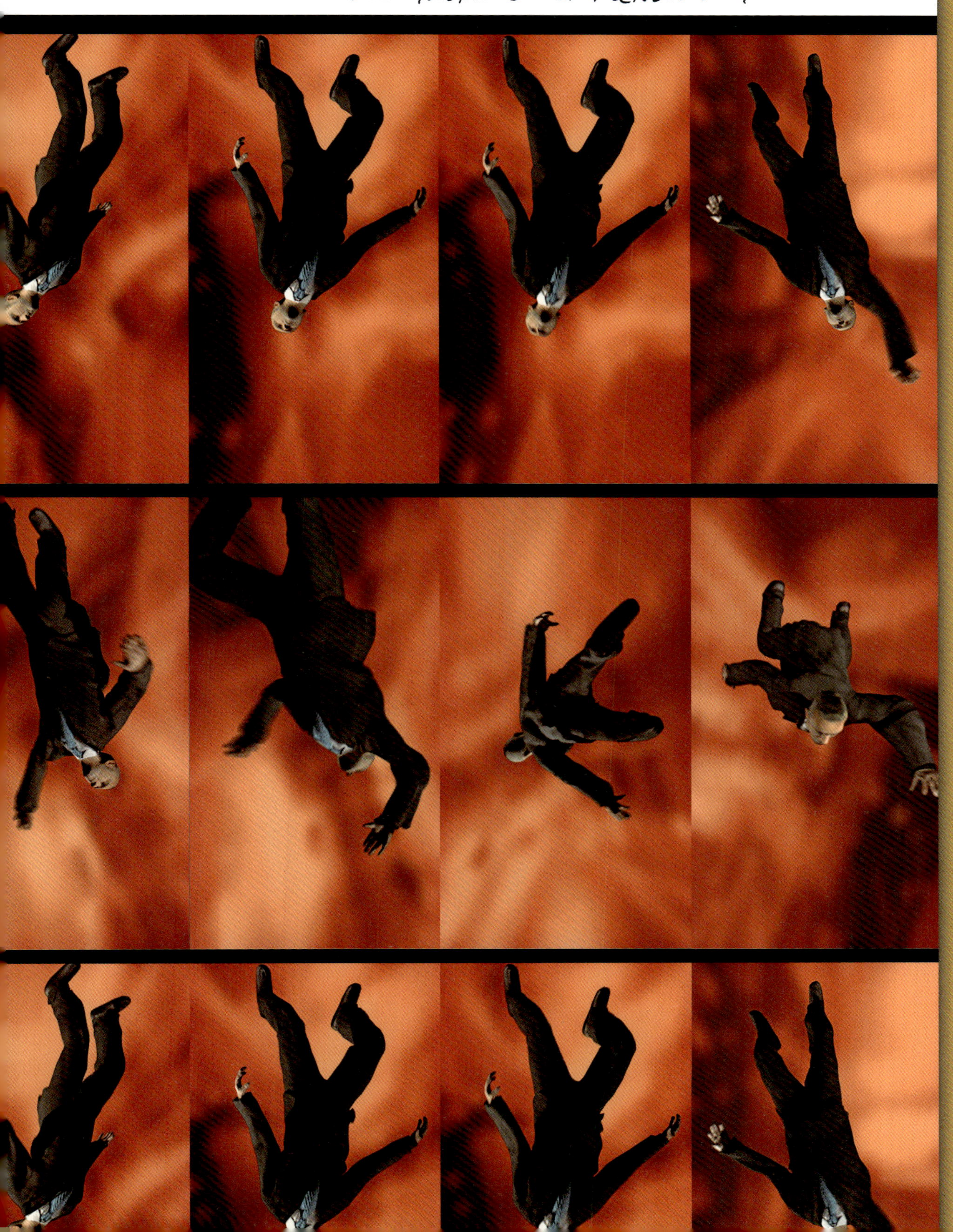

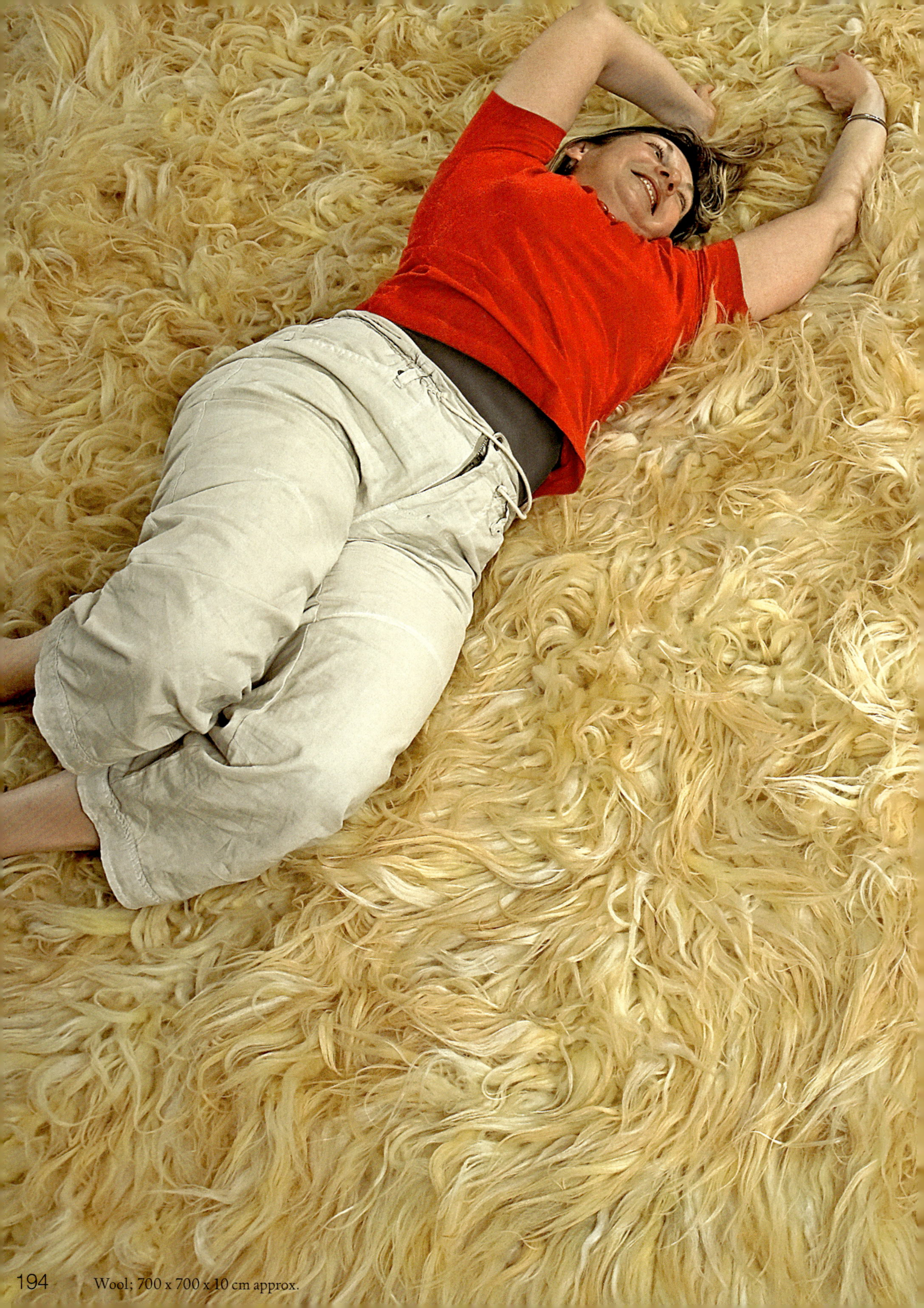

Wool; 700 x 700 x 10 cm approx.

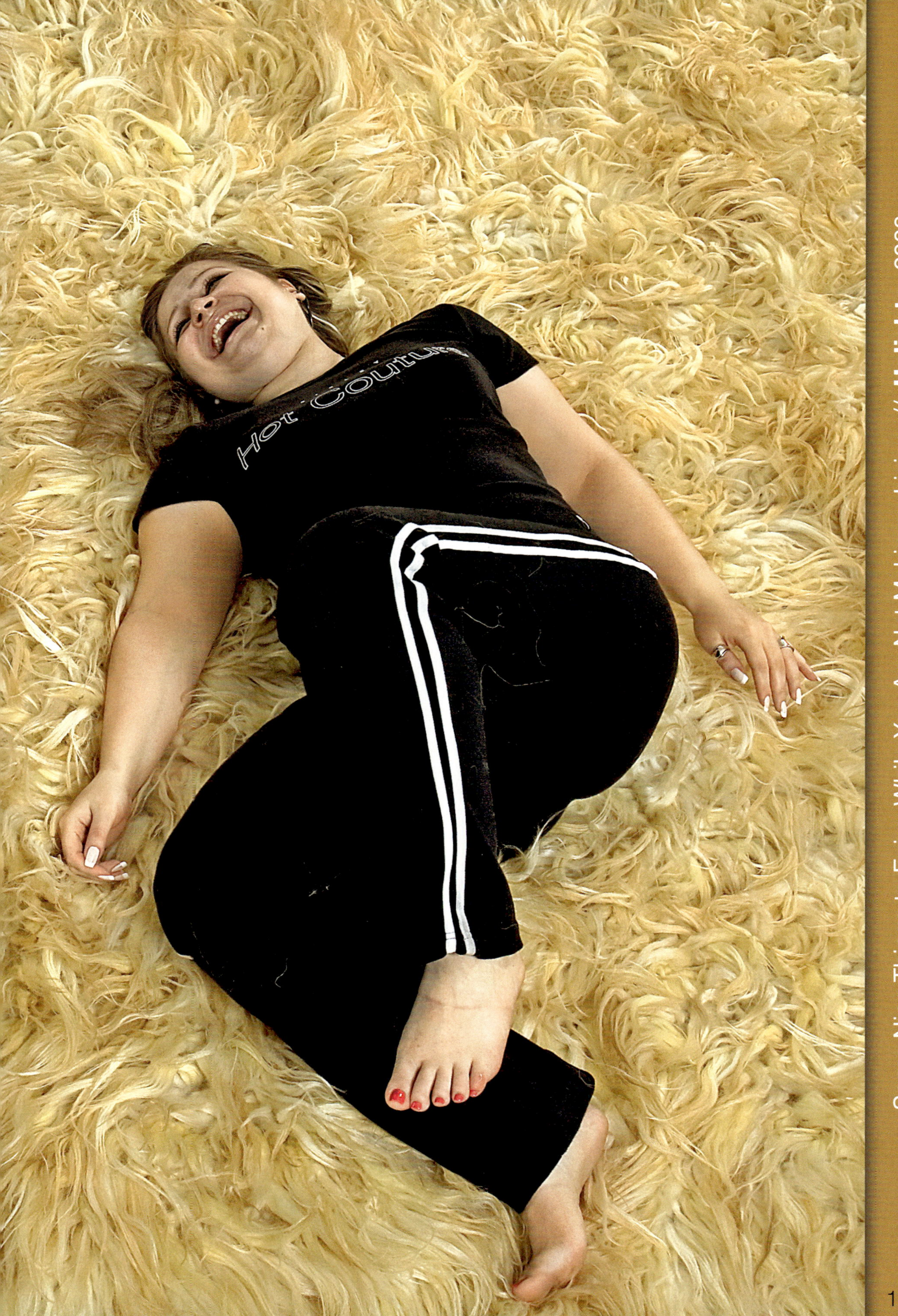

Some Nice Things to Enjoy While You Are Not Making a Living // **Halishte,** 2008

Zur Arbeit **A Life (Black & White)**, Seite 36–43

Für die vollständige Arbeit wird Folgendes benötigt:

—Ein Team aus zwei erwachsenen Malern, wobei Geschlecht, Ethnie, geografische Herkunft, gesellschaftlicher Status et cetera keine Rolle spielen. Es ist nicht notwendig, dass es sich um professionelle Maler und Anstreicher handelt; der Einsatz von professionellen Malern könnte die soziale Komponente der Arbeit einschränken, weil sich Fachleute üblicherweise nicht frei und locker mit den vorbeigehenden Besuchern unterhalten. Zudem widerspricht das ständige Übermalen der Wände mit dicker, unverdünnter Farbe in zwei Kontrastfarben, ohne dass die Wände entsprechend trocknen oder Farbschichten entfernt werden können, allen Standards professioneller Malerarbeit. Die ausgewählten Amateurmaler sollten natürlich bezahlt werden. Sie sollten Overalls oder Latzhosen und eigene Hemden in nicht zu grellen Farben tragen. Spezielles Schuhwerk ist nicht erforderlich. Der Einsatz zusätzlicher Maler in weiteren Arbeitsschichten ist zulässig, die Maler sollten aber während des Arbeitsprozesses nicht Platz oder Arbeitskleidung miteinander tauschen (es ist zum Beispiel nicht erwünscht, dass der Maler, der schwarze Farbe verwendet, während der Schicht beginnt, weiße Farbe zu verwenden).

—Ausreichende Mengen der bestmöglichen Qualität von schwarzer und weißer Farbe auf Wasserbasis (bevorzugterweise Außenfarbe, die sehr gut deckt). Es wird empfohlen, die Farbe im Voraus auf Deckfähigkeit et cetera zu testen. Weiter wird empfohlen, für die gesamte Projektdauer den geschätzten Bedarf an Farbe zusammen mit den von bereits verbrauchter Farbe zurückbleibenden leeren Eimern / Dosen in der Mitte des Ausstellungsraumes zu lagern, wo sie bis zum Ende der Ausstellung verbleiben.

—Die erforderlichen Malerutensilien: Rollen, Pinsel (für Ecken und jene Stellen, für die Rollen nicht geeignet sind), Stofffetzen, eine Unmenge an Papierhandtüchern, mobile Gerüste und Leitern (der Wandhöhe entsprechend), zwei Eimer Wasser zur Aufbewahrung der Rollen und Pinsel am Ende des Arbeitstages, vier Schilder (je zwei weiße Kartonschilder im DIN-A4-Format mit der Aufschrift »10 Minutes Break« und »Lunch Break«). Jeder Maler erhält eines von jeder Sorte. Die Schilder sind im Voraus vorzubereiten. Der Text sollte in schwarzen, zwei Zentimeter hohen Buchstaben in der Mitte der Schildhorizontale im Querformat geschrieben sein. Wird die Arbeit in einem nicht-englischsprachigen Land gezeigt, sollten die Texte in die Landessprache übersetzt werden. Alle Utensilien sollten im Ausstellungsraum, bevorzugterweise in der Mitte platziert / aufbewahrt werden.

—Ein geeigneter Raum: Einem Durchgangsraum mit zwei Eingängen wäre der Vorzug zu geben, sodass die Besucher durch den Raum hindurchgehen und sich mit der Arbeit beschäftigen können. Die Arbeit kann auch auf einer einzigen Wand oder zwei Wänden, die in einer Ecke zusammenstoßen, realisiert werden. Die Maler sollten auch in diesen Fällen denselben Grundprinzipien der Aktion folgen: hintereinander her zu arbeiten, wobei die Summe der schwarz bemalten Wandteile immer gleich der Summe der weiß bemalten Wandteile sein sollte. Wegen der erforderlichen Trockenzeit ist es nicht zu empfehlen, dass der Raum kleiner als 50 Quadratmeter ist. Die Wände sind gut mit Grundierung vorzubehandeln, die für Farben auf Wasserbasis geeignet ist. Der Malgrund aus Sperrholz sollte stark genug sein (mindestens 16 Millimeter), um dem Erfordernis des wiederholten Bemalens zu entsprechen. Mit Gipskartonplatten verkleidete Wände sind nicht zu verwenden. Raumdecke und Fußboden sind nicht zu bemalen. Alle »Kanten« des immer wieder zu bemalenden Bereichs sind wie beim normalen Ausmalen eines Raumes mit Klebeband abzukleben. Sind zusätzliche Bereiche auf den Wänden vor Farbe zu schützen, so sollten auch diese mit Band abgeklebt werden (zum Beispiel Notausgangsschilder). Es wird empfohlen, dass ein Spezialist vor Beginn die Wände inspiziert und dass dessen Anweisungen für die Vorbereitung des Malgrunds an den Wänden Folge geleistet wird. Der Fußboden sollte durch eine Plastikfolie geschützt werden, die – falls notwendig – erneuert werden kann.

—Ein Arbeitsprozess: Vor Eröffnung der Ausstellung müssen der Raum, die Materialien und Utensilien vorbereitet und die Arbeitsschichten der Maler eingeteilt werden. Bei Eröffnung der Ausstellung muss der Raum zur Hälfte schwarz und zur Hälfte weiß sein. Die grundierten Wände sind mit einer Schicht schwarzer Farbe zu bemalen, darüber wird eine Schicht weißer Farbe angebracht, welche die Hälfte der Gesamtlänge der Wände bedeckt. Dann ist der halb schwarze und halb weiße Raum für die Arbeit vorbereitet.

Zur Eröffnung der Ausstellung sollten die beiden Maler zu arbeiten beginnen (unabhängig davon, ob Besucher da sind oder nicht). Die Arbeitsrichtung sollte grundsätzlich im Uhrzeiger sinn laufen, es ist aber auch möglich, dass beide Maler gegen den Uhrzeigersinn arbeiten. Ist einmal eine Richtung festgelegt, muss sie während der gesamten Dauer der Aktion beibehalten werden. Die Maler sollten keine Eile an den Tag legen, sondern die Wände auf bestmögliche Weise mit Farbe bedecken. Sie können während der Arbeit mit den Besuchern sprechen. Sie dürfen jedoch nicht vergessen, dass immer eine Hälfte des Raumes weiß und eine Hälfte schwarz sein muss – das ist die Grundbedingung. Die Maler sollten jede Stunde zehn Minuten Pause machen, diese jedoch zu unterschiedlichen Zeiten. Bei Beginn der Pause lehnt der Maler das Schild »10 Minutes Break« an seinen Farbeimer, er kann den Raum verlassen oder die Pause im Raum verbringen. Die tägliche Mittagspause dauert dreißig Minuten und sollte wiederum nicht gleichzeitig genommen werden. Bei Beginn der Mittagspause lehnt der Maler das Schild »Lunch Break« an seinen Farbeimer, er kann den Raum verlassen oder im Raum bleiben, wenn er das wünscht. Der Maler, der während der Pause des anderen weiterarbeitet, sollte dann das Arbeitstempo verlangsamen. Die Maler sollten auch arbeiten, wenn kein Besucher im Raum ist. Fünf Minuten, bevor die Ausstellung schließt, sollten die Maler sich auf den Arbeitsschluss vorbereiten – alle Pinsel und Rollen kommen in die jeweiligen Wassereimer, die Farbbehälter werden geschlossen. Die Mal- und Übermalarbeiten müssen während der gesamten Ausstellungsdauer fortgesetzt werden – unabhängig davon, ob diese einige Tage oder mehrere Monate beträgt. Die Maler haben an jedem Werktag konstant zu arbeiten. Am Ende der Ausstellung kann der eigentliche Besitzer der Arbeit die »Erinnerungsstücke« – die leeren Farbeimer, Pinsel und Rollen, die Plastikabdeckungen und Stücke der mit Farbschichten bedeckten Wände – behalten und als visuelles / physisches Archiv dieses Teils der Arbeit verwenden.

Bitte befolgen Sie bei der praktischen Ausführung der Aktion die obigen Anweisungen und nicht die ursprüngliche handschriftliche Projektbeschreibung im DIN-A4-Format, die von den obigen Anweisungen abweicht.

Der Künstler Nedko Solakov ist berechtigt, die Foto- und Videodokumentation der verschiedenen Teile dieser Arbeit zur Schaffung neuer, eigenständiger Kunstwerke zu verwenden.

—

Zur Arbeit **On the Wing**, Seite 60–63

(Linke Tragfläche)

1. Lieber Passagier, irgendwo da unten, hinter dem zweiten Berg, am linken Ufer eines Baches, gibt es einen kleinen Hügel. In diesem kleinen Hügel ist ein kleines Loch, und in diesem kleinen Loch wohnt eine kleine Maulwurfsdame. Ganz ehrlich, sie wäre jetzt gerne an Ihrer Stelle – fast 10 000 Meter über der Erde....

2. Keine Sorge. Alles wird gut. Sie werden es schaffen. Sie werden das Geld finden....

3. Diese Tragfläche hat zwei Kanten – die Vorderkante und die Hinterkante. Sie sind Schwestern (oder so ähnlich). Manchmal wird die Hinterkante paranoid. »Ich könnte nie eine Vorderkante sein«, sorgt sie sich. Glücklicherweise kann ihre Schwester sie beruhigen: »Meine Liebe, ohne Deine Unterstützung könnte ich gar nicht existieren. Hast Du je von einer Vorderkante gehört, die alleine geflogen wäre?«

4. Unter dieser Tragfläche hängt ein ganz kleiner Regentropfen am silbrigen Metall.... irgendwo in der Nähe des Rades.... Er ist sehr froh. Warum? Weil er die Absicht hat, sich später auf diesen (manchmal verschneiten) Berg fallen zu lassen, auf dem seine geliebten Cousins und Cousinen leben. Sie gehören zu den besten Schneeflocken der Welt.

5. Der gleiche Text steht auch auf der rechten Tragfläche.... aber sehen Sie zur Sicherheit lieber nach.

6. Lieber Passagier, wollen Sie nicht versuchen, den Himmel über Ihnen zu betrachten? Ja, direkt über Ihnen.... an der Stelle, wo das noch nicht ganz tiefe Blau zum tiefen Blau wird und das ganz tiefe Blau in die stärkste Farbe des Universums übergeht.... Wenn Ihnen das gelingt, können Sie eine schöne Szene sehen – einen schlafenden außerirdischen Postboten (dort wird vielleicht ein anderer Ausdruck für »Postbote« verwendet – wer weiß?). Er wartet darauf, dass der nächstgelegene Fernsehsatellit vorbeikommt. Er hat die letzte Folge seiner Lieblingsseifenoper verpasst und wartet darauf, die Geschichte aus erster Hand zu erfahren....

(Rechte Tragfläche)

1. Mein lieber Passagier, haben Sie den Silberdollar gesehen, der ganz unten im Gepäckfach über Ihnen liegt? Ganz richtig – er liegt unter Ihrem Handgepäck. Nehmen Sie ihn später an sich! Er gehört Ihnen.

2. Lieber Passagier, sehen Sie die kleine Wolke rechts.... ganz jung und relativ klein. Dieser Bursche will so gerne wie die großen starken Kerle sein (ganz nahe am Horizont).... aber er kann noch nicht und deshalb ist er ein bisschen traurig.... aber so traurig dann doch nicht, denn er hat daher auch nicht so viel Verantwortung für das Bild, das die Atmosphäre abgibt....

3. Eigentlich würde das Ihnen am nächsten gelegene Querruder gerne »Hallo!« zu Ihnen sagen, indem es dreimal auf und ab wippt. Aber seine Mutter, das Cockpit, hat ihre Prinzipien. Es wird Sie deshalb später, beim Landen, grüßen.

4. Hi! Ja, ich war das – ich habe gerade »Hi!« gesagt.

4. (näher) Wenn Sie weiter diese Buchstaben anstarren, dann werden Sie sicherlich sehr, sehr bald einschlafen.... schauen Sie sie nur an. Schauen Sie uns an.... lesen Sie uns immer und immer wieder.... immer wieder, immer wieder.... Ihre Augen fallen zu.... das freundliche Brummen der Motoren umspielt zart Ihren Körper.... Sie schlafen schon, obwohl Ihre Augen vielleicht noch offen sind.... schlafen.... und der schöne Traum, der heute morgen so mysteriös verschwunden ist, wird zu Ihnen zurückkehren....

5. Der gleiche Text steht auch auf der linken Tragfläche.... aber sehen Sie zur Sicherheit lieber nach.

6. Sie Glücklicher! Sie haben die hübschesten Flugbegleiterinnen an Bord.

6. (näher) Wenn eine Stubenfliege (Musca domestica) Astronaut sein könnte, glauben Sie, dass sie mit der geeigneten Astronautenausrüstung für Stubenfliegen unsere Höhe erreichen könnte?

—

Top Secret *(Dezember 1989–Februar 1990) besteht aus einem Fach mit Karteikarten, die die frühere Zusammenarbeit des jungen Künstlers mit der bulgarischen Geheimpolizei thematisieren, die von Solakov 1983 beendet wurde. Neunzehn Jahre nach der Wende sind die Akten in Bulgarien nach wie vor unter Verschluss, sodass es keine öffentlichen Dokumente zur Mitarbeit von Nedko Solakov gibt. Als das Werk zuerst im Frühjahr 1990 ausgestellt wurde, auf dem Höhepunkt der politischen Wende nach jahrelanger kommunistischer Herrschaft, sorgte es für heftige kontroverse Diskussionen. Der Gestus der Selbstentblößung in diesem künstlerischen Projekt ist immer noch einmalig im Kontext des europäischen Postkommunismus. Mittlerweile ist* **Top Secret** *zu einem Symbol seiner Zeit geworden.*

Das 40-minütige Video, in dem Nedko Solakov die Inhalte des Aktenfaches nochmals liest, wurde 2007 in seinem Studio in Sofia gedreht.

Die Aktion läuft bis auf weiteres...

Es gab einmal einen Jungen.

Er sei klug und brav gewesen, erzählt man. In der Schule hat der Junge Einser geschrieben, zu Hause Bücher gelesen und gemalt. Gemalt hat der Junge Kaninchen, Jäger, Häuser mit Schornsteinen, Flugzeuge mit einem roten Stern, die andere Flugzeuge mit Hakenkreuzen abschossen... Besonders geliebt hat der Junge die Abenteuerbücher, wo die »Guten« immer die »Bösen« besiegten. Geliebt hat er aber auch die Spionagebücher. Gefallen fand er an den tapferen sowjetischen Tschekisten und deren bulgarischen Kollegen Awakum Zachow und Emil Boew, die seinen Glauben verfestigten, dass der immer angemahnte Feind seine sozialistische Heimat in Ruhe lassen würde.

Der Junge wuchs heran. Nach einem Abschluss mit summa cum laude (Goldmedaille) am Mathematik-Gymnasium seiner Heimatstadt, wurde er zum Studium an der Kunstakademie zugelassen (wegen einer schweren Krankheit in seiner Kindheit hatte er den Militärdienst aussetzen müssen). Auch hier blieb er wie gewohnt fleißig und brav.

Im Herbst 1976 (damals war er im zweiten Studienjahr) ist der Junge mit einer organisierten Gruppe nach Paris gefahren (die ihn heiß liebenden Eltern – er liebte sie auch – haben die Kosten übernommen). Alles war sehr schön – der Louvre, Rodin, die Dufy-Retrospektive, einige Pornostreifen. Die Hälfte der achttägigen Reise war vorbei, als ihm der Gruppenleiter mitteilte, jemand habe an der Hotelrezeption ein Päckchen für ihn und für B. abgegeben (B. war ein netter, älterer Herr, der Bruder eines bekannten Professors). Die Überraschung des Jungen war groß, denn im Päckchen waren feindliche Propagandaschriften. Nach einer oberflächlichen Lektüre hat er sie dem Gruppenleiter mit den Worten ausgehändigt: »Man bespuckt Bulgarien!« Der Gruppenleiter seufzte und grübelte, dann holte er aber jemanden von der Botschaft und der Junge – zufrieden, dass er seine Pflicht getan hatte – gab das Päckchen weiter.

Einige Wochen später aber wurde er von der Personalabteilung der Kunstakademie bestellt. Mit geheimnisvoller Stimme wurde ihm erklärt, ein »Genosse« möchte ihn sprechen. Der »Genosse« (ein sympathischer junger Mann) bat um eine kurze schriftliche Auskunft über die Pariser Begebenheit. Der Junge lieferte sie. Der »Genosse« war zufrieden, stellte aber unvermittelt eine überraschende Frage: »Wir sind eigentlich an jemanden interessiert…«, und nannte den Namen eines Kommilitonen des Jungen, eines bescheidenen und leisen Studenten. »Was ist er für einer, macht er sich irgendwie bemerkbar et cetera?« Der Junge (fleißig und brav) sagte zu, da es sein müsse, die Auskunft zu geben. Anschließend und stolzen Herzens erzählte er die Geschichte einem Freund und seiner eigenen Freundin.

Der sympathische junge »Genosse« tauchte aber wieder auf, diesmal geheim, »unter vier Augen«. So beschritt der Junge eine Wiese, wo die Blumen immer weniger und die Disteln immer mehr und immer dichter wurden, bis ihm die Dornen und das Gras den Blick versperrten. Eigentlich war der Junge nicht besonders aktiv. Jedes Mal aber, wenn er gefragt wurde, gab er Auskunft (und immer hatte er auch Aufzeichnungen auf einem weißen Blatt Papier mit Extrarand oben geführt): welche Ausstellung Beifall bekam und welche nicht, wer mit religiösen Sekten mitmischt und wer nicht et cetera. Ob dem Jungen bewusst war, was er tat? Ja und nein, denke ich… Er hat einfach geglaubt – an die Institutionen und daran, dass dies sein Beitrag sei für die künftige, großartige Gesellschaft, wo alles und alle wunderbar sein werden. Selbstverständlich hatte er dafür nichts bekommen, nur das seltsame Gefühl der Sicherheit vielleicht. Während seines Militärdienstes wurde er einem anderen jungen (und uniformierten) Mann zugeteilt. Auch hier hatte er anfangs geglaubt, nur seine Militärpflicht zu tun. Dieser Glaube aber wurde immer wackeliger.

So kam der Sommer 1983. Nach dem Militärdienst hatte er Kraft geschöpft (so sagt man doch, oder?) und verweigerte ausdrücklich, weiterhin ausgenutzt zu werden. Der uniformierte »Genosse« hat auf ihn eingeredet, man würde ihn an einen anderen »Genossen«, zuständig für die Intelligenz, vermitteln, der Junge aber blieb bei seiner Entscheidung.

Dies war der Anfang eines langen und qualvollen Erwachens. Der einst fleißige und brave Junge fand allmählich Gefallen an anderen Beschäftigungen, viel männlicheren. Immer noch aber hatte der Junge (der Mann?) Angst. Und seine Bilder spiegelten wohl diese Angst wider.

Als sein erstes Kind geboren wurde (es war im Sommer 1986) wurde ihm plötzlich klar, dass er sich für einen Weg entscheiden musste. Denn er wollte ja nicht immer verlegen weggucken im Angesicht dieses Kindes, das an jenem denkwürdigen 1. Mai 1986* unter blühenden Rosen noch von seiner Mutter im Leib getragen wurde. Und den Weg, für den er sich entschieden hatte, führte wohl nicht in die »helle Zukunft«.

Das Publikum hat ihm geglaubt. Es hat an die Zeichnungen **Enlighted by the Decisions** und **The Endurance of a Nation** geglaubt, die im Januar 1988 ausgestellt worden waren, es hat auch an das Karteikästchen in der Ausstellung **The City?** geglaubt, und auch an das Fernrohr **View to the West,** das von der Terrasse der Galerie Schipka 6 zum roten Stern auf dem Giebel der Parteizentrale ausgerichtet war (abgebaut wurde dieses Fernrohr unter Geheimhaltung von den zuständigen Diensten, die schon längst den jungen Mann als unzuverlässig abgeschrieben hatten). In seinem Atelier lagerten noch viele ähnliche Bilder und Objekte, deren Zeit noch nicht gekommen war.

Hätte er mit seinem Bekenntnis schon an diesem Punkt Schluss machen können?

Ja, das hätte er. Die sieben Jahre zurückliegenden Kontakte mit den sympathischen »Genossen« wären höchstwahrscheinlich nie ans Tageslicht gekommen. Keine Partei und keine politische Macht hat ein Interesse an der Veröffentlichung der ganzen Namenslisten (man weiß schon warum, oder?).

Der Mann aber traf die einsame Entscheidung, dass auch dieses Bekenntnis publik werden müsse. So entstand das Aktenfach mit den Karteikarten, die er in der Tradition der Pop-Art beschrieb und bemalte, und zwar mit allen beschämenden und bedrückenden Einzelheiten, die immer noch um sein schmerzendes Herz herumkrochen. Beschrieben hat er auch den besagten Fall.

Das Aktenfach wurde unter dem Titel **Top Secret** im Rahmen der Ausstellung **End of Quotation** im Klub der jungen Künstler vom 20. April bis 26. Mai 1990 ausgestellt. Innerlich hatte sich der Mann ein für allemal festgelegt: Ein echter Künstler ist nur der Künstler, der seine Angst bewältigt hat. Unabhängig davon, ob man sich vor einem neuen künstlerischen Weg fürchtet, wo man doch den heutigen Erfolg genießt, oder vor dem Akt der totalen Selbstentblößung, der gegen einen hohen Preis zum Kunstakt wird.

Viele der jüngeren (aber auch der älteren) Kollegen haben es richtig verstanden und dem Mann die Hand gedrückt. Einen Monat nach der Ausstellungseröffnung fand der außerordentliche Kongress der Union Bulgarischer Künstler statt. Der Mann dachte, jemand würde »die Sache« bestimmt ansprechen, aber keiner tat es. An sich hätte er ja stillhalten sollen (im Einklang mit allen Gesetzen der Vernunft), angesichts des wieder auflebenden Konservatismus, aber er hat seine freiwillig zurückgezogene Kandidatur für den Präsidentenposten erneut zur Abstimmung gestellt. Er fühlte sich moralisch verpflichtet, an dem Sturz dieser schrecklichen Maschinerie zur Unterdrückung der Künstler (der besagten Union nämlich) mitzuwirken. Er wollte seinen Kollegen dabei helfen, sich frei und mit Selbstsicherheit (und nicht mit der Sicherheit der Künstlerunion im Rücken) zu entfalten, endlich dem Publikum zu vertrauen, das ja seit Jahren darauf gewartet hatte. Er wurde zum Vizepräsidenten gewählt.

Die Geschichte ist aber noch nicht zu Ende. Die Gerüchte, dass er »der Mann der Abteilung 6 in der Künstlerunion« sei, die seit der Ausstellung **End of Quotation** kursierten, nahmen ein bedrohliches Ausmaß an. Viele Kollegen (die offenbar ungern Ausstellungen besuchten) hatten überhaupt nicht mitbekommen, dass er selbst noch einen Monat zuvor seine Vergangenheit offengelegt hatte, und dass sich diese Vergangenheit von dem Etikett »der Mann der Abteilung 6 in der Künstlerunion« sehr wohl unterscheide. Damit wurde ein Feldzug gestartet, der mit Kunst nichts zu tun hatte. Der Mann sah sich gezwungen, seinen geheimen Kasten wieder auszustellen, diesmal in der ehemaligen Parteikanzlei der Künstlerunion. In der Annahme jedoch, dass das Aktenfach wieder von vielen ungesehen bleiben könnte, die Gerüchte in den Cafés und Dienststuben aber zäh weiterlaufen würden, bot er der Redaktion einer von ihm geschätzten Zeitung diesen Text zur Veröffentlichung an.

Mit der Erklärung, dass der Junge, der Mann und ich ein und dieselbe Person sind, möchte ich abschließend noch einen Grund für die öffentliche Ausstellung von **Top Secret** erwähnen. Ich wünschte mir, dies möge eine Warnung sein für alle jungen Menschen, die irregeführt werden und ins feine Netz der »Behörde« geraten könnten. Denn in ein paar Jahren (vielleicht sogar früher), von den künftigen »zuständigen Stellen« mit der Frage konfrontiert, ob sich in ihrer Umgebung vielleicht Kommunisten, Anarchisten oder was weiß ich was versammeln, würden diese jungen Menschen vielleicht gar nicht zögern, Auskunft zu geben. Und diese Tat würde aus ihrer Sicht als ganz normal und moralisch vertretbar gelten. Ob es für mich als Künstler schmeichelhaft ist, dass mein Werk zu so einem Eklat geführt hat, weiß ich nicht. Es hat sich mittlerweile zu einer Art von »Happening« entwickelt, also zu einer Aktion, deren weiterer Verlauf unbekannt ist. Der Autor allerdings bin ich und mir steht es zu, nach dem endgültigen Finale das Etikett mit dem genauen Titel und dem Inhaltsverzeichnis darauf zu kleben.

Ich möchte glauben, dass mich die Künstler in der Künstlerunion, aber vor allem das Publikum, das ich am meisten schätze, verstehen werden.

Text aus dem Jahre 1990
Erste Veröffentlichung in der Wochenzeitung **Kultura**, 22. Juni 1990

*Erst an diesem Tag informierten die bulgarischen Behörden über den Atom-GAU in Tschernobyl, der bereits am 26. April stattgefunden hatte.

—

Zur Arbeit **Discussion (Property)**, Seite 76–83

Discussion (Property)

Im Sommer 2006 bin ich auf diese Geschichte gestoßen. Ein Zeitungsartikel berichtete über den – um es milde auszudrücken – jahrzehntelangen Disput zwischen Russland und Bulgarien, in dem Russland die Bulgaren der fortgesetzten illegalen Herstellung und des illegalen Vertriebs des Sturmgewehrs AK-47 bezichtigt. Dieses berühmt-berüchtigte Meisterwerk unter den automatischen Schusswaffen wurde in den späten 1940er-Jahren von Michail Kalaschnikow entwickelt, und während der sozialistischen Ära gab die Sowjetunion freizügig die Produktionslizenz und technische Unterlagen an die Volksrepublik Bulgarien weiter, damit der kleine Satellitenstaat massenhaft AK-47 produzieren konnte, um und die gewaltige Nachfrage im Ostblock zu befriedigen.

Jahre später brach der Sozialismus zusammen, und der Kapitalismus hielt Einzug. Für das AK-47 war nie ein internationales Patent angemeldet worden, für den Transfer des geistigen Eigentums daran bestand also keine Rechtsgrundlage. Wäre es anders gewesen, wäre Michail Kalaschnikow längst Multimilliardär, denn laut den verfügbaren Statistiken dürften bis heute weltweit zwischen fünfzig und einhundert Millionen AK-47 verkauft worden sein. Als es in den 1990er-Jahren in diesem Bereich zu den ersten Auseinandersetzungen zwischen Russland und Bulgarien kam, war klar, dass dieser Zwist nicht durch ein internationales Gericht beigelegt werden konnte.

Es ist heute schwer, das ganze Tauziehen dieser Verhandlungen und die damit verbundenen Entwicklungen nachzuvollziehen. Zum einen finden alle Treffen der zwischenstaatlichen Kommission im Geheimen statt und zum anderen gehen Leute wie ich für gewöhnlich nicht zu Waffenschauen, sodass ich selbst nie Zeuge eines jener peinlichen Auftritte wurde, bei denen die Russen die Bulgaren in aller Öffentlichkeit beschuldigten, sie verkauften Dinge, die eigentlich ihnen gehörten. Insbesondere in den letzten Jahren haben sich die bulgarischen Hersteller zunehmend damit verteidigt, dass sie ihre Produktion auf ein anderes Sturmgewehr namens AR umgestellt hätten, das trotz gewisser Ähnlichkeiten mit dem AK-47 vollständig modernisiert und den NATO-Standards angepasst worden sei, und das sich im Übrigen vorzüglich verkauft. So orderte zum Beispiel die US-amerikanische Heeresleitung im Irak laut bulgarischer Presse vor einigen Jahren 40 000 bulgarische Sturmgewehre vom Typ AR, um die neue irakische Armee damit auszurüsten.

Dies war ungefähr mein Kenntnisstand, als ich beschloss, die beiden Kontrahenten zu kontaktieren, um sie für ein Gespräch vor laufender Kamera zu gewinnen. In einem ersten Schritt konzentrierte ich mich auf die bulgarische Firma »A…l«, eine Waffenfabrik in der pittoresken Stadt K. Als Künstler ohne Verbindung zum Militär und bar jeder Verbindung zu Waffenhändlern, wandte ich mich zunächst an die stellvertretende Kultusministerin (eine nette Dame) mit der Bitte, mir bei der Kontaktaufnahme zum Generaldirektor von »A…l«, Herrn N. I., zu helfen. Sie rief die stellvertretende Verteidigungsministerin an (ebenfalls eine nette Dame), die versprach, ein Treffen zu arrangieren. Da ich von Natur aus zur Paranoia neige, bat ich auch eine bekannte Journalistin (erneut eine Frau) um Hilfe.

Als ich am 1. Dezember 2006 im Büro von Herrn I. stand, eröffnete dieser das Gespräch mit den Worten: »Der Premierminister war der Einzige, der mir Ihr Erscheinen nicht angekündigt hat!« Dennoch benötigte ich fast drei Stunden, den Generaldirektor davon zu überzeugen, ein paar Worte vor der Kamera zu sagen. Warum? Das Hauptproblem bestand darin, dass mein Versuch, beide Seiten zum Sprechen zu bewegen, zur gleichen Zeit stattfand wie die letzte schwergewichtige Verhandlungsrunde zwischen Vertretern der russischen und der bulgarischen Regierung über geistiges Eigentum an militärischen Dingen. Herr I. wollte den verstrickten Disput ganz offensichtlich nicht durch ein Gespräch mit einem Künstler gefährden, der auf die Frage »Aber weshalb interessiert Sie diese Sache überhaupt, wenn Sie kein Journalist sind?« die eher absonderliche Antwort gab: »Weil man viel von Streitigkeiten um das Eigentum an Büchern oder musikalischen Kompositionen liest, aber von einem Streit über das geistige Eigentum an einer Waffe, die anerkanntermaßen die beliebteste Waffe aller Zeiten ist, habe ich noch nie etwas gelesen.« Am Ende gab Herr I. meiner Bitte nach und gewährte mir ein einminütiges Interview. Danach sprach er, undokumentiert, über eine Stunde lang von seiner Studienzeit in der Sowjetunion und seiner Bewunderung für die Qualität der russischen Militärindustrie. Er erzählte, dass er schon seit Jahrzehnten für »A…l« arbeite, zunächst als Ingenieur, später als Generaldirektor. Seine Hauptsorge sei nun, die Arbeitsplätze seiner 5 500 Beschäftigten zu erhalten, die auch viele zivile Produkte wie CNC-Geräte herstellten.

Nach dem Interview besuchte ich die Website der Firma und fand dort eine vollständige Liste der Sturmgewehre, die dort produziert werden, ein jedes mit Abbildung. Ich forderte für mein Projekt bessere Fotos an, und nach sorgfältiger Auswahl schickte mir die Entwicklungsabteilung der Firma am 19. Dezember 2006 eine CD mit einem Dutzend Bilder in hoher Auflösung, die einen Teil ihrer Produktion an AR-Gewehren abdeckte. Leider wurden ausgerechnet diejenigen, an denen mir am meisten lag, für die von mir vorgeschlagene Nutzung als »zu kontrovers« eingestuft, und dies, obwohl sie auf der Website öffentlich gezeigt werden. »Wir wollen doch durch Ihr Projekt die Russen nicht verärgern, oder?« hatte Herr I. mich gefragt, und ich musste ihm beipflichten. Dann beauftragte ich zwei begabte junge Künstlerinnen damit, anhand der weniger kontroversen Fotos zwölf Zeichnungen von AR-Gewehren in Originalgröße anzufertigen. Für diese Arbeit brauchten die beiden Frauen zwei Monate.

Herr I. war außerdem so freundlich, mir beim Kauf von zwei echten, aber funktionsunfähigen alten AK-47 (eines davon mit gekerbtem Metallkolben) aus den 1960er-Jahren in einem der größten Waffengeschäfte in Sofia zu helfen, damit ich meinen Gedanken besser veranschaulichen konnte. Leider entsprach die Technik, mit der diese Gewehre funktionsunfähig gemacht wurden, nicht den Standards der italienischen Behörden, die ein anderes Verfahren zur Untauglichmachung von Sturmgewehren forderten. Ich gab die Idee auf, die beiden AK-47 zu exportieren und kaufte stattdessen eines in Italien. Sie sehen daher hier ein in Rumänien hergestelltes AK-47, das in einem italienischen Laden gekauft wurde und einen kuriosen Zusatzgriff aufweist, aber damit kann ich leben.

Parallel zu meinen Aktivitäten in Bulgarien versuchte ich verzweifelt, mit der russischen Seite Kontakt aufzunehmen. Am 21. November 2006 schrieb die stellvertretende Kultusministerin einen offiziellen Brief an die russische Botschaft in Sofia und bat um einen Termin, bei dem ich die Sache mit einem Regierungsvertreter besprechen könne. Ich war gerade in Miami, als mich die schlechte Nachricht der stellvertretenden Ministerin erreichte, die russische Botschaft habe mit Schreiben vom 5. Dezember 2006 ein Treffen mit mir abgelehnt. Zurück in Sofia trug ich mein Anliegen mit Unterstützung einer im bulgarischen Außenministerium tätigen Kuratorin einer hochrangigen Person in diesem Ministerium vor (es war wiederum eine Frau). Ebenso höflich wie diplomatisch wurde mir beschieden, dass derzeit in dieser Sache Verhandlungen geführt würden und dass ein Brief zugunsten meines Projekts von der russischen Botschaft als völlig deplatziert empfunden würde. Ich fragte die Dame im Außenministerium: »Kann ich in meiner Geschichte erwähnen, dass sie zu besorgt sind, um sich bei den Russen dafür einzusetzen?« – »Besser nicht«, lautete die Antwort.

Dann wurde ich einer erfolgreichen Geschäftsfrau vorgestellt, die in Russland stark engagiert ist und die, siehe da, über die richtigen Verbindungen verfügte. Sie nahm sich freundlicherweise meiner Sache an, und ihr gelang es endlich, mit dem russischen Botschafter über mein Projekt zu sprechen. Obwohl er ein Treffen nicht rundweg ablehnte, blieb weiterhin unklar, ob ich tatsächlich jemanden von ihrer Seite würde treffen können. Schließlich gelang es einer gebürtigen Russin (wieder eine Frau, zu einem Viertel armenischer Abstammung, die, wie der Zufall so spielt, als internationale Kuratorin in Bulgarien arbeitet), den armenischen Botschafter zu einer Intervention beim russischen Botschafter zu bewegen, woraufhin am 24. Januar 2007 ein Treffen mit Herrn P. und Herrn V. von der russischen Botschaft im Botschaftsgebäude stattfand.

Herr P. und Herr V. waren beide sehr freundlich und versprachen, mir die Kopie einer Fernsehsendung zu besorgen, die 2006 im russischen Fernsehen ausgestrahlt worden sei und die sich mit dem »Die-Bulgaren-und-unsere-russischen-Waffen-Thema« befasst habe. Die beiden Herren versprachen weiter, nach Möglichkeit ein Treffen mit einem Vertreter der russischen »R…t« – einer zum internationalen Verkauf von Waffen autorisierten Organisation – zu arrangieren, der hoffentlich gegen ein Gespräch über mein Projekt nichts einzuwenden haben werde.

Während ich noch immer voller Hoffnung auf dieses Gespräch wartete, las ich vor einigen Tagen in der Zeitung, dass die Verhandlungen sich offenbar zum Guten wandten und man sich fast schon auf neue Vertragsbedingungen geeinigt habe, die beiden Parteien zum Vorteil gereichten.

Ich weiß nicht, welche Argumente die beiden Seiten vorgebracht haben, um alle Hürden zu überwinden. Ich wage zu vermuten, es dürften ernsthaftere gewesen sein als: »Haben die Russen je das Nutzungsrecht am kyrillischen Alphabet erworben, das sie seit Jahrhunderten verwenden und das, wie jeder weiß, im 9. Jahrhundert von den bulgarischen Brüdern Kyrill und Method erfunden wurde, oder die Erlaubnis zum Genuss des Lactobacillus bulgaricus, jenes winzigen Bakteriums, das den besten Joghurt hervorbringt?« Und so empfinde ich, nach all den Jahren des Feilschens um Eigentumsrechte, eine gewisse persönliche Befriedigung darüber, dass zumindest im Sturmgewehrbereich des internationalen Waffenhandels nun endlich ein wenig Friede einkehren wird.

Nedko Solakov, Februar 2007

—

Zur Arbeit **Sexual Harassment**, Seite 92–93

Vor einiger Zeit bat ich fünf der besten bulgarischen Kunstkuratoren und -kritiker, zunächst ganz ruhig zu werden und sich dann jemanden (oder etwas) vorzustellen, das mit dem historischen Weimar in Verbindung zu bringen ist. Und sobald sie das Bild einmal vor dem inneren Auge haben, sollten sie versuchen, es zu verführen...

S. H. #1 – Jaroslava Boubnova, 10'56"

Ganz allgemein dachte sie an Schiller, weil er romantischer war als Goethe (und auch jünger starb). Während sie sich beim Abspielen des Videos betrachtete, machte sie ein paar Bemerkungen:

– »Wenn ich diesen Blick immer hätte, würde ich es in der Welt (Kunst) weit bringen.«

– »Es gibt Männer, deren Assoziationen (sexueller Natur, würden wir vermuten) zu direkt sind – es ist sehr einfach, mit denen umzugehen.«

– »Oh, nein ...«

– »Meine Studenten sagten mir, dass ich ihnen bei den Vorlesungen nicht in die Augen schaue.«

S. H. #2 – Boris Danailov, 5'30"

Boris Danailov war von einigen Aktdarstellungen von Lucas Cranach inspiriert. Wir hatten einen kleinen Streit: Ich sagte, dass die Akte für meinen Geschmack nicht sexy genug seien, er aber sagte, sie seien perfekt – sie sähen ein wenig pervers aus.

Eine seiner Bemerkungen war: »Was für ein scheinheiliger Typ ich doch bin!«

S. H. #3 – Maria Vassileva, 2'57"

Wir einigten uns, dass Goethe das Thema sein würde, obwohl die Verbindung zum Dichterfürsten doch eher ungewöhnlich war: Maria Vassileva schien stark emotional involviert, als sie sich an eine äußerst köstliche Kirschtorte (mit Schlagsahne) erinnerte, die sie in einem Café aß, nachdem sie das (etwas verstaubte) Goethe-Haus im Jahr 1983 (oder so) während einer Studienreise in die DDR besuchte hatte, welche von der Akademie der Bildenden Künste in Sofia, wo sie damals Kunstgeschichte studierte, organisiert worden war.

»Sie war ganz, ganz köstlich...«, sagte sie.

S. H. #4 – Philip Zidarov, 5'9"
Zidarovs Anwort war kurz:
»Goethes Lotte in Weimar!«

S. H. #5 – Ilina Koralova, 7'34"
Sie dachte an Franz Liszt, das allerdings auf eine seltsame Art. Ein paar Monate vorher hatte sie im bulgarischen Fernsehen einen Film über das Leben Frédéric Chopins in Paris gesehen (Hugh Grant spielte Chopin). Georges Sand und Franz Liszt waren auch dabei. Sie dachte also im Endeffekt an Julian Sands – den Schauspieler, der Liszt gespielt hatte, und auch den Chirurgen in **Boxing Helena.**

—

Zur Arbeit **Fear,** Seite 142–145

Ich habe Flugangst. Ich fürchte mich wirklich. Und zurzeit muss ich ständig irgendwo hinfliegen.

Vor dem Abflug nehme ich eine Tablette. Manchmal, wenn es ein Langstreckenflug ist, sogar zwei. Natürlich reicht das nicht, um meine Angst auszuschalten. Während ich an Bord bin, bete ich ständig als eine Art persönliches Mantra meine eigenen Worte herunter. Das genügt aber auch nicht. Meistens, fast die gesamte Zeit über, balle ich die Fäuste und halte dabei die Daumen hoch, das bringt Glück. Ich berühre so auch das Flugzeug. Das bringt Glück.

Als man mich einlud, für die Keramik-Biennale in Albisola eine Keramikskulptur zu entwerfen, war ich nicht sicher, ob ich zusagen sollte. Als ich dann eines Tages auf dem Weg zur nächsten Ausstellung in der Luft war, mit fest und schmerzhaft geballten Fäusten, wurde mir klar, was in mir vielleicht doch ein Interesse an der Arbeit mit einem so offenkundig klassischen Material wie Ton erwecken könnte.

Ich fragte bei den Veranstaltern nach, und sie schickten mir ein paar Kugeln feinsten Ton aus Albisola.

Zwischen dem 3. Juli und dem 15. September 2002 hielt ich bei allen meinen Flügen zu den verschiedensten Zielen kleine Tonkugeln in der Hand. Es war sehr leicht, aus diesen Kugeln Kunstwerke zu machen. Ich nutzte lediglich meine natürliche (und erworbene) Flugangst und knetete die ganze Zeit hindurch den Ton in den Fäusten. Manche der Kugeln drei Stunden lang, manche nur eine. Das komplexe Material fing die nervösen Zuckungen meiner ängstlichen Hände ein, die durch all das Rumpeln ausgelöst wurden, durch weinende Kleinkinder und Augenblicke des relativ ruhigen Fluges (die für mich schlimmsten Zeiten, weil ich erwarte – Um Himmels Willen, nein! –, dass jeden Augenblick etwas passieren könnte). Ich beendete die Serie **Fear,** als ich eine Strecke noch einmal fliegen sollte, von Sofia nach München. Inzwischen ließ ich die ersten drei Skulpturenpaare der Serie Fear während eines Besuchs in Albisola zum Brennen bei einem professionellen Keramiker. Die übrigen sieben Paare blieben in meinem Atelier in Sofia, wo sie einige Monate trocknen sollten.

Ich brauche wohl nicht hinzuzufügen, dass ich auch noch andere Ängste habe. Eine manifestierte sich in der Sorge, dass die Skulpturen aus rohem Ton beschädigt werden könnten, wenn ich sie mit einem Botendienst nach Italien senden würde. Also beschloss ich, sie in Bulgarien zu brennen und sie später als widerstandsfähigere Terrakottastücke sicher zu versenden. Mein Wissen über das Brennen von Keramik ist allerdings ziemlich vage. Nachdem ich mich nach einem verlässlichen Brennofen umgesehen hatte, beschloss ich schließlich, den eher unprofessionellen Ofen zu verwenden, in dem mein Vater seine eigenen, wunderschönen kleinen abstrakten Plastiken brennt. Er freute sich, mir helfen zu können. Obwohl er keine Erfahrung mit dieser Art von Ton hatte, schlug er vor, so vorzugehen, wie er das normalerweise tat, und die Figuren zunächst bei niedriger Temperatur im Backofen meiner Mutter zu backen, bis die Feuchtigkeit verdampft war, und sie anschließend im richtigen Brennofen zu brennen, der relativ schnell hohe Temperaturen erreicht. Nein, sagte ich, meine **Fear**-Skulpturen sind trocken genug, sie trocknen ja schon sieben Monate. Vielleicht sollte ich noch erwähnen, dass ich trotz meiner Vorsichtigkeit und meiner Zweifel über alles und jedes manchmal auch wirklich dumme Dinge tue. Mein Vater war nicht überzeugt, aber ich setzte mich als der berühmtere Künstler durch.

Die Naturgesetze machten sich natürlich bemerkbar. Nach zwanzig Minuten Brenndauer kam mein Vater ausgesprochen beunruhigt ins Wohnzimmer und sagte, aus dem Brennofen in seinem Atelier kämen dröhnende Geräusche. Wir schalteten den Ofen ab, und als wir die Tür öffneten, bot sich uns ein vernichtendes Bild: Alle Skulpturen aus der Serie **Fear,** die Zeugnisse meiner Panik in 10 000 Meter Höhe, waren in Stücke zerbrochen, einige größer, einige kleiner. Eine andere Form der Angst machte sich breit. Meine Eltern (die beide an schweren Herzkrankheiten leiden) waren extrem besorgt. Ich musste etwas erfinden, um ihnen zu zeigen, dass ich mit der Situation umgehen konnte. Mir fiel das bekannte bulgarische Sprichwort »Alles Schlechte kann auch eine gute Seite haben« ein, und ich überzeugte sie, dass meine Skulpturen nun viel besser aussahen und das Konzept damit viel profunder war. Glücklicherweise war die zweite Gruppe von Skulpturen, die als nächste in den Ofen kommen sollte, unversehrt, und mein Vater brannte sie (zusammen mit den Bruchstücken der ersten Gruppe) auf seine Weise – alles funktionierte natürlich bestens.

Was Sie nun sehen, lieber Besucher, ist eine Kombination zerbrochener und unversehrter Skulpturen aus der Serie Fear. All die winzigen Fragmente, die Sie sehen, gehören wirklich zu dieser oder jener speziellen Arbeit. Ich verbrachte viele Stunden damit, ihre Formen zu rekonstruieren. Wegen meiner Dummheit wurde meine ursprüngliche Idee zunichtegemacht, obwohl der gesamte gebrannte Ton hier, egal in wie vielen Stücken er jetzt zu sehen ist, mit mir in diesen zehn Flugzeugen war, und ich glaube, jedes dieser Stücke trägt Teile meiner Angst auf diesen zehn Flügen in sich.

Ich bin auch abergläubisch. Der alles überschattende Gedanke in meinem Gehirn lautet jetzt: Wenn diese so sorgfältig hergestellten kleinen **Fear**-Skulpturen teilweise zerbrochen sind, wie sieht es dann mit mir und zukünftigen Flügen aus, die ich nehmen soll? Was soll ich jetzt, da ich noch auf dem Boden bin, halten und drücken, um die neue Angst zu überwinden, die von diesen zerbrochenen Skulpturen ausgeht? Sollte ich jetzt überhaupt noch fliegen?

Nedko Solakov, Mai 2003

—

Captions / Bildunterschriften

24–25 **Reattribution,** 2008
Installation view: **Shifting Identities,** Kunsthaus Zürich, 2008; Courtesy of the artist and Kunsthaus Zürich; Photo: Nedko Solakov

26–27 **A (not so) White Cube,** 2001–present
Installation view: **Chat,** solo exhibition, IASPIS Gallery, Stockholm, 2001; Courtesy of the artist and IASPIS Gallery, Stockholm; Photo: Nedko Solakov

28 top / oben **A (not so) White Cube,** 2001–present
Installation view: **Mess,** solo exhibition, de Appel, Amsterdam, 2002; Courtesy of the artist and de Appel, Amsterdam; Photo: Nedko Solakov

28 bottom / unten **A (not so) White Cube,** 2001–present
Installation view: **P.S.1 Special Projects Programme,** P.S.1 Contemporary Art Center, New York, 2001; Courtesy of the artist and P.S.1, New York; Photo: Eileen Costa

29 top / oben **Toilettes** (detail), 2006
Handwritten texts on various surfaces in the toilets of Les Abattoirs Museum; Installation view **Broken Lines/Printemps de septembre,** Toulouse, 2006; Photo: Nedko Solakov

29 bottom / unten **Bad** (detail), 2006
Installation view: **Homework,** Gagosian Gallery Berlin (as part of the 4th Berlin Biennale), Berlin, 2006; Photo: Nedko Solakov

30–33 **A Pass-Controlled Story,** 2008
Installation view: **Shifting Identities,** Kunsthaus Zürich, 2008; Courtesy of the artist and Kunsthaus Zürich; Photo: Nedko Solakov

30–31 and 33 **A Pass-Controlled Story,** 2008
Installation views: Airport Zurich; Photos: Nedko Solakov

34–35 **The Yellow Blob Story** from **The Absent-Minded Man** project, 1997–present
Installation view: **Export–Import,** Sofia City Art Gallery, Sofia, 2003; Courtesy of the artist and the collections of MUMOK Museum Moderner Kunst Stiftung Ludwig Wien, Vienna; MARTa Herford, Herford; Photo: Angel Tzvetanov

36–43 **A Life (Black & White),** 1998–present
Courtesy of the artist, Arndt & Partner Berlin / Zurich, and of the collections of Peter Kogler, Vienna; Susan and Lewis Manilow, Chicago; Hauser & Wirth, St. Gallen; Museum für Moderne Kunst, Frankfurt am Main; Tate Modern, London

36 top / oben, 37 top / oben, 37 bottom / unten
A Life (Black & White), 1998–present
Installation views: **Das Museum, die Sammlung, der Direktor und seine Liebschaften,** Museum für Moderne Kunst, Frankfurt am Main, 2003; Photos: Nedko Solakov

36 bottom / unten **A Life (Black & White),** 1998–present
Installation view: **Das Lebendige Museum,** Museum für Moderne Kunst, Frankfurt am Main, 2003; Photo: Nedko Solakov

39 **A Life (Black & White),** 1998–present
Installation view: **Plateau of Humankind,** 49th Biennale di Venezia, Venice, 2001; Photo: Andrea Stappert

41 **A Life (Black & White),** 1998–present
Installation view: **Das Museum, die Sammlung, der Direktor und seine Liebschaften,** Museum für Moderne Kunst, Frankfurt am Main, 2003; Photo: Nedko Solakov

42–43 top / oben **A Life (Black & White),** 1998–present
Installation view: **Plateau of Humankind,** 49th Biennale di Venezia, Venice, 2001; Photo: Giorgio Colombo

42–43 bottom / unten **A Life (Black & White),** 1998–present
Installation views: **Revolutions—Forms That Turn,** 16th Biennale of Sydney, Sydney; Installation view: Art Gallery of New South Wales, Sydney; Courtesy of the artist, Arndt & Partner Berlin / Zurich, and 16th Biennale of Sydney; Photos: Jenni Carter

60–63 **On the Wing,** 1999–present
Part of the exhibition **Storymakers,** 1999, Casino Luxembourg; Courtesy of the artist, Casino Luxembourg, and Arndt & Partner Berlin / Zurich; Photos: Nedko Solakov

For the **On the Wing** Lambda print edition of 6 and 2 AP; 12 panels; 40 x 60 cm each; overall dimensions approx. 130 x 250 cm; Courtesy of the artist and Arndt & Partner Berlin / Zurich

64–67 **Good News, Bad News,** 1998–present
Installation views: **Stories 1,** solo exhibition, Centre for Contemporary Art, Ujazdowski Castle, Warsaw, 2000; Photos: Mariusz Michalski

68–75 **Top Secret,** 1989–90
Installation views: **Documenta 12,** Kassel, 2007, Collection Van Abbemuseum, Eindhoven; Courtesy of the artist and Arndt & Partner, Berlin / Zurich; Photo: Werner Maschmann, Kassel (pp. 69 and 75); Anatoly Michaylov and Konstantin Shestakov (pp. 71 and 73)

76–83 **Discussion (Property),** 2007
Installation views: **Think with the Senses: Feel with the Mind. Art in the Present Tense,** Biennale di Venezia, Venice, 2007; Courtesy of Arndt & Partner Berlin / Zurich and Galleria Continua, San Gimignano / Beijing; Photos: Ela Bialkowska

92–93 **Sexual Harassment,** 1997
Film stills; Camera: Angel Tzvetanov; digitally remastered by Kalin Serapionov, 2002

94–95 **Help Yourself (Russian Roulette),** 1998
Photo: Angel Tzvetanov; Courtesy of the artist

96–97 **The Real Estate Broker,** 2007
Courtesy of Private Collection, the Netherlands; Photo: Arndt & Partner Berlin / Zurich

98–99 **An Anus Story,** 2005
Courtesy of Nunzia & Vittorio Gaddi, Italy; Photo: Bernd Borchardt, Berlin

100 **A Chubby Story,** 2007
Private Collection, Great Britain; Photo: Bernd Borchardt, Berlin

101 **A Middle-Aged Story,** 2006
From the Collection of Aaron M. Levine of Washington, D.C.; Photo: Bernd Borchardt, Berlin

102–3 **Good and Evil,** 2005
Courtesy of Private Collection, Israel; Photo: Bernd Borchardt, Berlin

104–5 **A Story with a Moral,** 2005
Courtesy of Collection Cathy and Paolo Vedovi, Miami; Photo: Arndt & Partner Berlin / Zurich

106–7 **The Story of the Man Who Came into Life from a Womb with Wings,** 2008
Courtesy of Private Collection, the Netherlands; Photo: Bernd Borchardt, Berlin

108–9 **The Big Picture Story,** 2005
Courtesy of Collection Manja Gideon, Geneva; Photo: Bernd Borchardt, Berlin

110–11 **A Cracked Story,** 2008
Courtesy of Private Collection, France; Photo: David Willems, New York

112–13 **The Wave,** 2007
Courtesy of Private Collection, the Netherlands; Photo: Bernd Borchardt, Berlin

113–15 **The World Beyond Story,** 2006
Courtesy of Arndt & Partner Berlin / Zurich; Photo: Bernd Borchardt, Berlin

132–39 **Fears,** 2006-07
Series of 99 drawings; Installation view: **Documenta 12,** Kassel, 2007; Courtesy of Arndt & Partner Berlin / Zurich and Galleria Continua, San Gimignano / Beijing / E. Righi Collection, Italy; Photos: Werner Maschmann, Kassel (p. 132 top); Bernd Borchardt, Berlin (pp. 132 bottom and 133-39)

140–41 **Some of My Capabilities,** 1995
Digitally remastered by Kalin Serapionov, 2002; Courtesy of the artist and Arndt & Partner Berlin / Zurich

142–45 **Fear,** 2002-03
Courtesy of the artist; Photos: Angel Tzvetanov

146 **...and they lived happily ever after,** 1999
Installation view: **Faiseures d'histoires,** Casino Luxembourg. Forum d'art contemporain, 1999; Courtesy of the artist and Arndt & Partner Berlin / Zurich; Photo: Nedko Solakov

147–53 **...and they lived happily ever after,** 1999
Courtesy of the artist and Arndt & Partner Berlin / Zurich; Photos: Angel Tzvetanov

154–59 **I Love Them,** 2007
Installation views: **Wrong Material,** Galleria Continua, San Gimignano, 2007; Courtesy Galleria Continua, San Gimignano / Beijing; Photos: Ela Bialkowska

160–95 **Some Nice Things to Enjoy While You Are Not Making a Living,** 2007–08
Courtesy of the artist

162 **The Sleeping Child,** 2008
Film still; edited by Kalin Serapionov

163 **A Combo-Icon, 2008**
Photo: Nedko Solakov

164–65 **A Depository,** 2008
Photos: Dimitar Solakov

166–69 **A Sunrise**, 2008
Photo: Angel Tzvetanov

170–71 **A Sunset,** 2008
Photo: Angel Tzvetanov

172–73 **Confidentiality Guaranteed,** 2006–08
Film stills; edited by Kalin Serapionov

174–75 **The Artist's Struggle,** 2008
Executed by Violeta Tanova; Photos: Angel Tzvetanov

176–79 **The Boxes,** 2008
Photos: Dimitar Solakov

180–81 **The Sofa,** 2008
Photos: Dimitar Solakov and Angel Tzvetanov

182–85 **Raising the Price of an Art Work,** 2008
Photos: Nedko Solakov

186–89 **Afterlife Options,** 2008
Photos: Angel Tzvetanov

190–91 **What to Do With Your…?,** 2008

192–93 **The Bankrupt Businessman,** 2008
Film stills

194–95 **Halishte,** 2008
Photo: Dimitar Solakov

Nedko Solakov

1957 Born in Cherven Briag, Bulgaria / Studies at National Academy of Arts, Sofia **1981** Graduation in Mural Painting, Prof. Mito Ganovski **1985–86** Studies at Nationaal Hoger Instituut voor Schone Kunsten, Antwerp **1992** Works in Zurich with a grant from Artest Foundation **1993** Works in Austria with a grant from KulturKontakt, Vienna **1994–95** Works in Künstlerhaus Bethanien, Berlin, with a grant from the Philip Morris Foundation **Since 1995** (Founding) member of the Institute of Contemporary Art, Sofia **2001** Works in Stockholm with a grant from IASPIS—International Artists Studio Program in Sweden **2002** Works in Japan with a grant from CCA—Center for Contemporary Art, Kitakyushu **2007** Received an "Honorable Mention to an Artist Exhibited in the Central International Exhibition," 52nd Biennale di Venezia, Venice

Lives and works in Sofia
www.nedkosolakov.net

Solo Exhibitions (Selection) (C) = catalogue

2009 Emotions, Mathildenhöhe Darmstadt (C); Kunstmuseum St.Gallen (C)

2008 Emotions, Kunstmuseum Bonn, Bonn (C)
A Turnover for Many and a Bit of Luck for One, The Street, Whitechapel Art Gallery, London (C)

2007 Walls & Floor (without the Ceiling), BA-CA Kunstforum, Vienna (with Dan Perjovschi) (C)
A Group Show, Galleria Massimo Minini, Brescia
Wrong Material, Galleria Continua, San Gimignano
A Life (Black & White), Norwich Gallery, Norwich School of Art & Design, Norwich (C)
New Noah's Ark, Stupidity & The Wave, Galerie Arndt & Partner, Berlin

2006 Earlier Works, Galerie Arndt & Partner, Zurich; Kunsthalle Mannheim, Mannheim (C)
Confidentiality Guaranteed, with Sint-Lukasgalerij at Art Brussels, Brussels
Back to Back, Lombard-Freid Projects, New York (with Dan Perjovschi)

2005 Twelve Semipaintings Done in a Very Fast Way, Galerie Georges-Philippe & Nathalie Vallois, Paris
Leftovers: A Selection of My Unsold Pieces from the Private Galleries I Work with, Kunsthaus Zürich, Zurich (C)
Dead-Lock Stories, Galleria Continua, San Gimignano
Garbage People, Tanya Rumpff Gallery, Haarlem

2004 A 12 1/3 (and even more) Year Survey, O.K Centrum für Gegenwartskunst, Linz (C)
Drawings, Magazzino d'Arte Moderna, Rome (with Massimo Bartolini)
Rivals, Centre d'Art Santa Mònica, Barcelona
A 12 1/3 (and even more) Year Survey, Rooseum Center for Contemporary Art, Malmö (C)
A High Level Public Art Project with a Catalogue, Malmö Konsthall, Malmö (C)

2003 A 12 1/3 (and even more) Year Survey, Casino Luxembourg. Forum d'art contemporain, Luxembourg (C)
Advertisement, Sint-Lukasgalerij, Brussels (C)
Alien Auras, The Israel Museum, Jerusalem (C)
Negotiations, Dvir Gallery, Tel Aviv
Seaweeds, Base, Florence (with Slava Nakovska)
Romantic Landscapes with Missing Parts, Espacio Uno, Museo Nacional Centro de Arte Reina Sofía, Madrid (C)
Mirrors, Galerie Georges-Philippe & Nathalie Vallois, Paris

2002 **A High Level Show with a Catalogue,** Center for Contemporary Art, Kitakyushu, Japan (C)
Mess, Stichting de Appel, Amsterdam (C)
Nature People, Museu do Chiado, Lisbon (C)
Studies for Romantic Landscapes with Missing Parts, Galerie Arndt & Partner, Berlin
Romantic Landscapes with Missing Parts, Neuer Berliner Kunstverein, Berlin; Ulmer Museum, Ulm (C)
20.10.2001, Galerie Erna Hecey, Luxembourg

2001 **Chat,** Royal Swedish Academy of Arts; IASPIS Gallery, Stockholm (C)
Vitiligo People, Galleria Laura Pecci, Milan
Marginalia, Módulo–centro Difusor de Arte, Lisbon
A (not so) White Cube, P.S.1 Special Projects Program, P.S.1 Contemporary Art Center, New York
Anywhere, Tanya Rumpff Gallery, Haarlem

2000 **Stories 1,** Centre for Contemporary Art, Ujazdowski Castle, Warsaw (C)
Squared Baroque—Baroqued Square, Ikonen-Museum / Portikus, Frankfurt am Main (C)

1999 **....... #2,** Galerija Dante Marino Cettina, Umag
Announcement, as the official participation of Bulgaria, 48th Biennale di Venezia, Venice (C)
......., ATA Center for Contemporary Art, Sofia (C)

1998 **A Christmas Show,** Galerie arsFutura, Zurich
Silly, Galerie Arndt & Partner, Berlin
Sea Show, TED Gallery, Varna (with Slava Nakovska)
A Quiz, De Vleeshal, Middelburg
Thirteen (maybe), Musée nationale d'histoire et d'art, Luxembourg (C)

1997 **Yellow,** Galerija Anonimus, Ljubljana
The Paranoid Man, Galerie Georges-Philippe & Nathalie Vallois, Paris
The Absent-Minded Man, Fonds régional d'art contemporain de Languedoc-Roussillon, Montpellier
Wars, Galerie Erna Hecey, Luxembourg
Somewhere (under the tree), Deitch Projects, New York
By the Way, Art Connexion, Lille (C)

1996 **Semipoor-Semirich,** The Swiss Ambassador's residence, Sofia
Desires, Galerie Arndt & Partner, Berlin (C)
Doodles, National Museum of Fine Arts' mirrors, Sofia

1995 **To Touch the Antiquity,** Ata-Ray Gallery, Sofia
Mr. Curator, please..., Studio I, Künstlerhaus Bethanien, Berlin (C)

1994 **The Superstitious Man,** Center for Curatorial Studies and Art in Contemporary Culture, Bard College, Annandale-on-Hudson
Documentation, Ata-Ray Gallery, Sofia
The Collector of Art, Ludwig Múzeum, Budapest (C)
The Superstitious Man, Museum of Contemporary Art, Skopje (C)
Notes, National Palace of Culture's toilets, Sofia
Bulgarian-American Souvenirs, American Center, Sofia

1993 **Their Mythological Highnesses,** Ata-Ray Gallery, Sofia
Another World, Ata-Ray Gallery, Sofia
Les aventures (et les visions) de Francois de La Bergeron en terre Bulgare, Institut Français, Sofia
4 (maybe 5) Room Installations, Elemag 2D Gallery, Sofia
Sculpture & Drawings, Lessedra Gallery, Sofia (with Mityo Solakov)
Good Luck, Medizinhistorisches Institut und Museum der Universität Zürich, Zurich

1992 **Just Imagine,** BINZ 39/Artest, Zurich
Neue Arche Noah, ifa-Galerie, Berlin (C)
Nine Objects, National Museum of History, Sofia
7 Paintings, 13 Reliquaries, 1 Installation (New Noah's Ark), National Palace of Culture, Sofia

1990 **Objects,** AIA Gallery, Bourgas

1988 **Autumn Exhibitions,** Plovdiv (C)
Nedko Solakov, Shipka 6 Gallery, Sofia

1987 **Nedko Solakov,** Bahnwärterhaus, Esslingen am Neckar

1985 **Nedko Solakov,** The City Square Gallery, Varna

1983 **Autumn Exhibitions,** Plovdiv

1982 **Nedko Solakov,** Rakovski 108 Gallery, Sofia

Group Exhibitions (Selection)

2008 **Prospect.1 New Orleans,** New Orleans (C) / **Shifting Identities: [Swiss] Art Now,** Kunsthaus Zürich and various other venues, Zurich (C) / **Revolutions: Forms that Turn,** 16th Biennale of Sydney, Sydney (C) / **God & Goods,** Villa Manin, Centro d'Arte Contemporanea, Codroipo (C) / **Ad Absurdum: Energien des Absurden von der klassischen Moderne zur Gegenwart,** MARTa, Herford (C) / **Laughing in a Foreign Language,** Hayward Gallery, London (C) **2007** **Cool Days,** Bonniers Konsthall, Stockholm (C) / **The Word in Art,** MaRT—Museo di Arte Moderna e Contemporanea di Trento e Rovereto, Rovereto (C) / **Constellations—Artissima,** Turin (C) / **Time Present Time Past,** Istanbul Modern Sanat Müzesi, Istanbul (C) / Documenta 12, Kassel (C) / 52nd Biennale di Venezia, Venice (C) / **Footnotes on Geopolitics, Market and Amnesia,** 2nd Moscow Biennale of Contemporary Art, Moscow (C) **2006** **Forms of Classification,** Cisneros Fontanals Art Foundation, Miami (C) / **Unhomely,** 2nd Fundación Bienal Internacional de Arte Contemporáneo de Sevilla, Seville (C) / **Broken Lines,** various venues, Toulouse (C) / **Why Children?,** Periferic 7/ Focusing Iasi: Biennial for Contemporary Art, Iasi (C) / **Homework,** Gagosian Gallery Berlin (4th Berlin Biennale), Berlin / **Peace Tower Project** with Rirkrit Tiravanija and Mark di Suvero, Whitney Biennial, New York (C) / **Dark Places,** Santa Monica Museum of Art, Santa Monica (C) **2005** **EindhovenIstanbul,** Stedelijk Van Abbemuseum, Eindhoven (C) / **Temporary Import: DAAD, Bethanien et al.,** Art Forum Berlin, Berlin (C) / **Sweetest Taboos,** 3rd Tirana Biennale, Tirana (C) / **Istanbul,** 9th International Istanbul Biennial, Istanbul (C) / **Drawing from the Modern, 1975-2005,** The Museum of Modern Art, New York (C) / **Ensemble!,** Museum van Hedendaagse Kunst Antwerpen, Antwerp / **Belongings,** 7th Sharjah Biennial, Sharjah, United Arab Emirates (C) / **What's new, Pussycat?,** Museum für Moderne Kunst, Frankfurt am Main (C) / **Utopia Station,** World Social Forum, Porto Alegre, Brazil **2004** **Nuit Blanche,** various locations, Paris (C) / 1st Łódź Biennale (C) / **Love it or Leave it,** 5th Cetinje Biennale of Visual Arts, Cetinje and Dubrovnik (C) **2003** **Utopia Station,** 50th Biennale di Venezia, Venice (C) / **Durchzug—Draft,** Kunsthalle Zürich, Zurich (C) **2002** **Reconstructions,** 4th Cetinje Biennale of Visual Arts, Cetinje (C) / **De Gustibus,** Palazzo delle Papesse, Centro d'Arte Contemporanea, Siena (C) / **Pause,** 4th Gwangju Biennale, Gwangju (C) / Basics, Kunsthalle Bern, Bern (C) **2001** **Marking the Territory,** Irish Museum of Modern Art, Dublin (C) / **Loop: Alles auf Anfang,** Kunsthalle der Hypo-Kulturstiftung, Munich; P.S.1 Contemporary Art Center, New York (C) / **Plateau of Humankind,** 49th Biennale di Venezia, Venice (C) / **Locus/Focus,** Sonsbeek 9, Arn-hem (C) **2000** **The Last Drawing of the Century (A Window onto Venus),** Center for Contemporary Art, Rome; 6th Bienal de La Habana, Havana (C) / **Partage d'exotismes,** 5th Biennale d'art contemporain de Lyon, Lyon (C) / **L'autre moitié de l'Europe,** Jeu de Paume, Paris (CD-ROM catalogue) **1999** **Zeitwenden: Looking forward into the next millennium,** Kunstmuseum Bonn, Bonn (C) **1998** 7th Triennale der Kleinplastik, Südwest LB Landesbank, Stuttgart (C) **1997** **Unmapping the Earth,** 2nd Gwangju Biennale, Gwangju (C) **1996** **The Scream. Borealis 8,** Arken Museum for Moderne Kunst, Copenhagen (C) / **Manifesta I,** Natuurmuseum, Rotterdam (C) **1995** **Orientation,** 4th International Istanbul Biennial, Istanbul (C) / **Club Berlin,** Kunst-Werke Berlin e.V., 46th Biennale di Venezia, Venice **1994** 22nd Bienal International de São Paulo, São Paulo (C) **1993** **Aperto '93,** 45th Biennale di Venezia, Venice (C) **1992** 3rd International Istanbul Biennial, Istanbul (C) **1990** **Expressions,** Third Eye Centre (now The Centre for Contemporary Arts), Glasgow (C)

Public Collections (Selection)

Bibliotèque nationale de Luxembourg, Luxembourg
Caldic Collectie B.V., Rotterdam
Castello di Ama, Ama
De Vleeshal, Middelburg
Ellipse Foundation Contemporary Art Collection, Lisbon
Fonds national d'art contemporain, Paris
Fonds régional d'art contemporain de Bourgogne, Dijon
Fonds régional d'art contemporain de Bretagne, Chateaugiron
Fonds régional d'art contemporain de Languedoc-Roussillon, Montpellier
Herning Kunstmuseum, Herning
Joslyn Art Museum, Omaha
Kunsthaus Zürich, Zurich
Ludwig Múzeum, Budapest
MARTa Herford, Herford
Moderna galerija, Ljubljana
Musée d'Art Contemporain de Lyon, Lyon
Musée d'Art Moderne Grand-Duc Jean, Luxembourg
Museum Frieder Burda, Baden-Baden
Museum für Moderne Kunst, Frankfurt am Main
Museum Moderner Kunst Stiftung Ludwig Wien, Vienna
National Gallery of Fine Arts, Sofia
Sammlung EVN, Vienna
Sammlung Hauser & Wirth, St. Gallen
Stedelijk Museum voor Actuele Kunst / S.M.A.K., Ghent
Stedelijk Van Abbemuseum, Eindhoven
Suermondt-Ludwig-Museum, Aachen
Szépművészeti Múzeum, Budapest
Tate Modern, London
Teylers Museum, Haarlem
The City Art Gallery, Sofia
The Dakis Joannou Collection, Athens
The Ella Fontanals-Cisneros Collection, Miami
The Museum of Contemporary Art, Skopje
The Museum of Modern Art, New York
Thyssen-Bornemisza Art Contemporary, Vienna
Ulmer Museum, Ulm
Villa Merkel, Esslingen am Neckar

Index of Works / Werkregister

This book is published in conjunction with the exhibition **Emotions** /
Diese Publikation erscheint anlässlich der Ausstellung **Emotions**

Kunstmuseum Bonn
September 20 – November 16, 2008
20. September – 16. November 2008

Kunstmuseum St.Gallen
February 28 – May 10, 2009
28. Februar – 10. Mai 2009

Mathildenhöhe Darmstadt
July 12 – October 4, 2009
12. Juli – 4. Oktober 2009

KUNST
MUSEUM
BONN

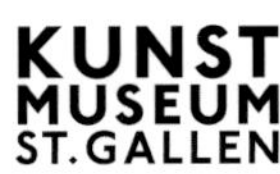

MATHILDENHÖHE
DARMSTADT

With the generous support of / Mit großzügiger Unterstützung von

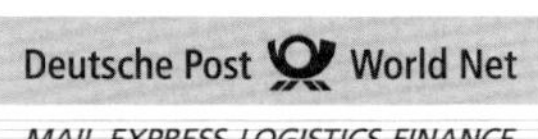

Wissenschaftsstadt
Darmstadt

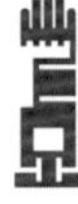

Kunstmuseum Bonn
Friedrich-Ebert-Allee 2, D-53113 Bonn, www.kunstmuseum.bonn.de

Concept and Organization / Konzeption und Organisation: Stephan Berg
Director / Direktor: Stephan Berg
Assistant Director / Stellvertretender Direktor: Christoph Schreier
Press and Public Relations / Öffentlichkeitsarbeit: Ute Herborg-Oberhäuser
Administration / Ausstellungssekretariat: Iris Lölsberg
Registrar / Registrar: Barbara Weber
Workshop Directors / Leitung der Werkstätten: Reiner Behrenbeck, Martin Wolter
Technical Assistance / Ausstellungstechnik: Josef Breuer, Eberhard Wagner
Art Conservation / Restauratorische Betreuung: Antje Janssen, Nicole Stiebel
Museum Education / Museumspädagogik: Sabine Leßmann

—

Kunstmuseum St.Gallen
Museumstrasse 32, CH-9000 St.Gallen, www.kunstmuseumsg.ch

Concept and Organization / Konzeption und Organisation: Konrad Bitterli
Director / Direktor: Roland Wäspe
Curator / Kurator: Konrad Bitterli
Research Assistance / Wissenschaftliche Mitarbeiter: Nadia Veronese, Matthias Wohlgemuth
Art Procurement / Kunstvermittlung: Stefanie Kasper
Press and Public Relations / Öffentlichkeitsarbeit: Ingrid Adamer
Administration / Ausstellungssekretariat: Christine Kalthoff-Ploner, Ingrid Meier, Samuel Reller
Technical Assistance / Ausstellungstechnik: Urs Burger and Crew / und Team

—

Institut Mathildenhöhe Darmstadt
Olbrichweg 13, D-64287 Darmstadt, www.mathildenhoehe.eu

Concept and Organization / Konzeption und Organisation: Ralf Beil
Director / Direktor: Ralf Beil
Exhibition Assistance / Ausstellungsassistenz: Katja Molis, Katharina Siegmann
Press and Public Relations / Öffentlichkeitsarbeit: Axel Braun, Lina Ophoven-Armey
Secretarial Assistance / Sekretariat: Angelika Nitsch, Lina Ophoven-Armey
Technical Assistance / Ausstellungstechnik: Jürgen Preusch, Uwe Brückner, Christian Häussler, Hartmut Kani, Karl-Heinz Köth
Art Conservation / Restauratorische Betreuung: Gitta Hamm
Administration / Administration: Ulli Emig, Michael Heine

Copyediting / Verlagslektorat: Geoffrey Garrison, Birte Kreft, Clemens von Lucius
Translations / Übersetzungen: Robin Cackett, Thomas Frahm, Elisabeth Frank-Großebner, Judith Hayward, Nikolay Kanchev, Allison Plath-Moseley
Graphic design / Grafische Gestaltung: Annett Frey, www.freysign.de
Production / Herstellung: Angelika Hartmann
Typeface / Schrift: Helvetica, FoundryOldStyle
Reproductions / Reproduktionen: Repromayer, Reutlingen-Betzingen
Paper / Papier: LuxoSamtoffset, 150 g/m^2
Binding / Buchbinderei: Conzella Verlagsbuchbinderei, Urban Meister GmbH, Aschheim-Dornach
Printing / Druck: Dr. Cantz'sche Druckerei, Ostfildern

Erschienen im / Published by:
Hatje Cantz Verlag
Zeppelinstrasse 32
73760 Ostfildern
Deutschland / Germany
Tel. +49 711 4405-200
Fax +49 711 4405-220
www.hatjecantz.com

A special collector's edition is available. Please contact Hatje Cantz for more information. / Es erscheint eine Collector's Edition. Nähere Informationen erhalten Sie beim Verlag.

Hatje Cantz books are available internationally at selected bookstores. For more information about our distribution partners please visit our homepage at www.hatjecantz.com

ISBN 978-3-7757-2211-7

Printed in Germany

Cover illustrations / Umschlagabbildungen:
Front / Vorne: Mirror #3 (detail), 2001–03
Gilded wood, mirror, permanent ink, handwritten text; from a series of 7 mirrors; 88 x 52 x 10 cm; Courtesy of the artist and Arndt & Partner Berlin / Zurich; Photo: Bernd Borchardt, Berlin

Back / Hinten: Mirrors, 2001–03
Gilded wood, mirrors, permanent ink, handwritten text; series of 7 mirrors; Installation view: Mirrors, solo exhibition Galerie Georges-Philippe & Nathalie Vallois, Paris, 2003; Photo: Studio Tutti